The Search for the Perfect Language

B

THE MAKING OF EUROPE
Series Editor: Jacques Le Goff

The Making of Europe series is the result of a unique collaboration between five European publishers – Beck in Germany, Blackwell in Great Britain and the United States, Critica in Spain, Laterza in Italy and le Seuil in France. Each book will be published in all five languages. The scope of the series is broad, encompassing the history of ideas, as well as of societies, nations and states, to produce informative, readable, and provocative treatments of central themes in the history of the European peoples and their cultures.

The Search for the Perfect Language

Umberto Eco

Translated by
James Fentress

BLACKWELL
Oxford UK & Cambridge USA

Copyright © Umberto Eco 1995

English translation copyright © Blackwell Publishers Ltd, 1995

First published in 1995 by Blackwell Publishers and by four other publishers: © 1994
Beck, Munich (German); © 1994 Critica, Barcelona (Spanish); © 1994
Editions du Seuil, Paris (French); © 1993 Laterza, Rome and Bari (Italian).

Blackwell Publishers Ltd
108 Cowley Road
Oxford OX4 1JF
UK

Blackwell Publishers Inc.
238 Main Street
Cambridge, Massachusetts 02142
USA

British Library Cataloguing in Publication Data
A CIP catalogue record for this book is available from the British Library.

Library of Congress Cataloging-in-Publication Data
Eco, Umberto.
  [Ricerca della lingua perfetta nella cultura europea. English]
  The search for the perfect language / Umberto Eco; translated by James Fentress.
    p. cm. – (The making of Europe)
  Includes bibliographical references and index.
  ISBN 0–631–17465–6
  1. Language and languages. 2. Language, Universal. 3. Language and culture –
  Europe. I. Title. II. Series.
  P106.E2813 1994
  401′.3–dc20   94–29141
                                                                CIP

Typeset in Sabon 12pt
by Pure Tech Corporation, Pondicherry, India.
Printed in Great Britain by T. J. Press Ltd, Padstow, Cornwall

This book is printed on acid-free paper

Contents

Series Editor's Preface

Europe is in the making. This is both a great challenge and one that can be met only by taking the past into account – a Europe without history would be orphaned and unhappy. Yesterday conditions today; today's actions will be felt tomorrow. The memory of the past should not paralyse the present: when based on understanding it can help us to forge new friendships, and guide us towards progress.

Europe is bordered by the Atlantic, Asia and Africa, its history and geography inextricably entwined, and its past comprehensible only within the context of the world at large. The territory retains the name given it by the ancient Greeks, and the roots of its heritage may be traced far into prehistory. It is on this foundation – rich and creative, united yet diverse – that Europe's future will be built.

The Making of Europe is the joint initiative of five publishers of different languages and nationalities: Beck in Munich; Blackwell in Oxford; Critica in Barcelona; Laterza in Rome; and le Seuil in Paris. Its aim is to describe the evolution of Europe, presenting the triumphs but not concealing the difficulties. In their efforts to achieve accord and unity the nations of Europe have faced discord, division and conflict. It is no purpose of this series to conceal these problems: those committed to the European enterprise will not succeed if their view of the future is unencumbered by an understanding of the past.

The title of the series is thus an active one: the time is yet to come when a synthetic history of Europe will be possible. The books we shall publish will be the work of leading historians, by no means all European. They will address crucial aspects of

European history in every field – political, economic, social, religious and cultural. They will draw on that long historiographical tradition which stretches back to Herodotus, as well as on those conceptions and ideas which have transformed historical enquiry in the recent decades of the twentieth century. They will write readably for a wide public.

Our aim is to consider the key questions confronting those involved in Europe's making, and at the same time to satisfy the curiosity of the world at large: in short, who are the Europeans? where have they come from? whither are they bound?

Jacques Le Goff

I would certainly never advise you to pursue the bizarre conceit which has taken hold of you to follow the dream about universal language.

Francesco Soave, *Riflessioni intorno all'istituzione di una lingua universale*, 1774

[Psammetichus] took two children of the common sort, and gave them over to a herdsman to bring up at his folds, strictly charging him to let no one utter a word in their presence. . . . His object herein was to know . . . what word they would first articulate. . . . The herdsman obeyed his orders for two years, and at the end of that time, on his one day opening the door of their room and going in, the children both ran up to him with outstretched arms, and distinctly said 'Becos'. . . . [Psammetichus] learnt that 'becos' was the Phrygian name for bread. In consideration of this circumstance the Egyptians. . . . admitted the greater antiquity of the Phrygians.

Herodotus, *History*, II, I

[Frederick II] wanted to discover which language and idiom children would use, on reaching adolescence, if they had never had the opportunity to speak to anyone. So he gave orders to the wet nurses and to the feeders to give the infants milk, prohibiting their talking to them. He wanted to find out whether the children would speak Hebrew, which was the first language, or else Greek or Latin or Arabic, or indeed if they did not always speak the language of their natural parents. But the experiment came to nothing, because all the babies or infants died.

Salimbene da Parma, *Cronaca*, 1664

If only God would again inspire your Highness, the idea which had the goodness to determine that I be granted 1200 ecus would become the idea of a perpetual revenue, and then I would be as happy as Raymond Lull, and perhaps with more reason. . . . For my invention uses reason in its entirety and is, in addition, a judge of controversies, an interpreter of notions, a balance of probabilities, a compass which will guide us over the ocean of experiences, an inventory of things, a table of thoughts, a microscope for scrutinizing present things, a telescope for predicting distant things, a general calculus, an innocent magic, a non-chimerical cabal, a script which all will read in their own language; and even a language which one will be able to learn in a few weeks, and which will soon be accepted amidst the world. And which will lead the way for the true religion everywhere it goes.

Leibniz, Letter to Duke of Hanover, 1679

Since words are only names for things, it would be more convenient for all men to carry about them such things as were necessary to express the particular business they are to discourse on. . . . many of the most learned and wise adhere to the new scheme of expressing themselves by things; which hath only this inconvenience attending it, that if a man's business be very great, and of various kinds, he must be obliged, in proportion, to carry a greater bundle of things upon his back, unless he can afford one or two strong servants to attend him. . . . Another great advantage, proposed by this invention was, that it would serve as an universal language, to be understood in all civilized nations. . . . And thus ambassadors would be qualified to treat with foreign princes, or ministers of state, to whose tongues they were utter strangers.

Jonathan Swift, *Gulliver's Travels*, III, 5

Introduction

1

The dream of a perfect language did not only obsess European culture. The story of the confusion of tongues, and of the attempt to redeem its loss through the rediscovery or invention of a language common to all humanity, can be found in every culture (cf. Borst 1957–63). Nevertheless, this book will tell only one strand of that story – the European; and, thus, references to pre- or extra-European cultures will be sporadic and marginal.

This book has another limit as well; that is, a quantitative one. As I was on the verge of writing its final version, there reached my desk at least five recent projects, all of which seem to me related to the ancient prototypes I was dealing with. I should emphasize that I will be limiting myself to those prototypes because Borst, whose own study concerns only the historical discussion on the confusion of tongues, has managed to present us with six volumes. Finishing this introduction, I received Demonet's account of the debate on the nature and origin of language between 1480 and 1580, which takes up seven hundred thick and weighty pages. Couturat and Leau analysed 19 models of *a priori* languages, and another 50 mixed or *a posteriori* languages; Monnerot-Dumaine reports on 360 projects for international languages; Knowlson lists 83 projects of universal languages during the seventeenth and eighteenth centuries;

and, though limiting himself to projects in the nineteenth century, Porset provides a list of 173 titles.

Moreover, in the few years I have dedicated to this subject, I have discovered in antiquarian catalogues a large number of works missing from the bibliographies of the preceding books. Some, by obscure authors, were entirely dedicated to the glottogonic problems; others were by authors known for other reasons, who, none the less, dedicated substantial chapters to the theme of the perfect language. This ought to be enough to convince anyone that our list of titles is still far from complete; and, that therefore, to paraphrase a joke by Macedonio Fernandez, the number of things which are not in the bibliographies is so high that it would be impossible to find room for one more missing item.

Hence my decision to proceed by a campaign of deliberated decimation. I have reserved attention for projects which have seemed to me exemplary (whether for their virtues or their defects); as for the rest I defer to works dedicated to specific authors and periods.

2

Beyond this, I have decided to consider only projects concerning true and proper languages. This means that, with a bitter sigh of relief, I have decided to consider only the following:

1   the rediscovery of languages postulated as original or as mystically perfect – such as Hebrew, Egyptian or Chinese;
2   the reconstruction of languages postulated, either fancifully or not, as original or mother tongues, including the laboratory model of Indo-European;
3   languages constructed artificially for one of three ends:
    (a) perfection in terms of either function or structure, such as the *a priori* philosophical languages of the

seventeenth and eighteenth centuries, which were designed to express ideas perfectly and to discover thereby new connections between the diverse aspects of reality;

(b) perfection in terms of universality, such as the *a posteriori* international languages of the nineteenth century;

(c) perfection in terms of practicality, if only presumed, such as the so-called *polygraphies*;

4 more or less magic languages, whether they be discovered or fabricated, whose perfection is extolled on account of either their mystic effability or their initiatic secrecy.

By contrast, I can give no more than bare notice to any of the following:

1 oneiric languages, not expressly invented, such as the languages of the insane, or of trance states, or of mystic revelations (like the Unknown Language of Saint Hildegarde of Bingen), as well as all the cases of glossolalia or xenoglossia (cf. Samarin 1972; Goodman 1972);

2 fictitious languages, either in narrative (from Rabelais to Foigny up to Orwell's 'Newspeak' and Tolkien), or in poetry (like Chlebnikov's transmental speech). In the majority of these cases, we are presented with only short stretches of speech, supposedly representing an actual language, for which, however, there is provided neither a lexicon nor a syntax (cf. Pons 1930, 1931, 1932, 1979; Yaguello 1984).

3 *bricolage* languages, that is languages that are created spontaneously by the encounter of two linguistically distinct cultures. Typical examples are the pidgins arising in areas of colonialism. As cross-national as they may be, they are not universal. They are, rather, partial and imperfect because they have a limited lexicon and an over-simplified syntax; they are used to facilitate

simple activities such as barter, but are unable to express higher types of experience (cf. Waldman 1977);

4   natural tongues or jargons serving as vehicular languages in multilingual zones. An example of such a language of exchange might be Swahili, the lingua franca of large areas of East Africa. Modern English would be another example. French was formerly an example, if one considers that, during the Convention, the Abbé Gregoire revealed that, out of a population of twenty-six million, fifteen million French men and women spoke a language other than that of Paris (Calvet 1981: 110);

5   formal languages whose use is limited to special scientific purposes, such as the languages of chemistry, algebra and logic (these will be considered only as they derive from projects defined by category 3(a) above;

6   the immense and delectable category of the so-called *fous du langage* (see, for example, Blavier 1982; Yaguello 1984). Admittedly, in such cases it is not always easy to distinguish between technical insanity and mild glottomania, and many of my own characters may sometimes show some aspects of lunacy. Still, it is possible to make a distinction. We will not consider belated glottomaniacs. Nevertheless, I have not always been able to keep down my taste for whimsicality, especially when (even though the belatedness was hardly justifiable) these attempts had, anyway, a certain, traceable, historic influence, or, at least, they documented the longevity of a dream.

Similarly, I do not claim here to examine the whole of the researches on a *universal grammar* (except in cases in which they clearly intersect with my topic), because they deserve a separate chapter of the history of linguistics.

Likewise, this is not (except, again, where the subject intersects with that of the perfect language) a book about the secular, or rather, millennial, question of the *origins of language*. There are infinite discussions on the origins of human language which do not consider the possibility or the opportunity of returning back to the language of our origins, either because they assume that it had definitely disappeared, or because they consider it as radically imperfect.

Finally, were it up to me to decide under which heading this book should be filed in a library catalogue (an issue which, for Leibniz, was bound up with the problem of a perfect language), I would pick neither 'linguistics' nor 'semiotics' (even though the book employs semiotics as its instrument, and demands a certain degree of semiotic interest from its reader). I would pick rather 'history of ideas'. This explains why I make no attempt to construct a rigorous semiotic typology for the various types of *a priori* and *a posteriori* languages: this would require a detailed examination of *each* and *every* project, a job for students of what is now called 'general interlinguistics'. This present book aims instead at delineating, with large brushstrokes and selected examples, the principal episodes of the story of a dream that has run now for almost two thousand years.

3

Having established the boundaries of my discourse, I must pay my debts. I am indebted to the studies of Paolo Rossi for first awakening my interest in the subjects of classical mnemonics, *pansophia* and world theatres; to Alessandro Bausani's witty and learned overview on invented languages; to Lia Formigari's book on the linguistic problems of English empiricism; and to many other authors whom, if I do not cite every time that I have drawn on them, I hope, at least, to have cited on crucial points, as well as to have included in the bibliography. My only regret is that George Steiner had already copyrighted the most appropriate title for this book – *After Babel* – nearly twenty years ago. Hats off.

I would also like to thank the BBC interviewer who, on 4 October 1983, asked me what semiotics meant. I replied that he ought to know the answer himself, since semiotics was defined by Locke in 1690, in Great Britain, and since in the same country was published in 1668 the *Essay towards a Real Character* by Bishop Wilkins, the first semiotic approach to an artificial language. Later, as I left the studio, I noticed an antiquarian bookstore, and, out of curiosity, I walked into it. Lying there I saw a copy of Wilkins' *Essay*. It seemed a sign from heaven; so I bought it. That was the beginning of my passion for collecting old books on imaginary, artificial, mad and occult languages, out of which has grown my personal 'Bibliotheca Semiologica Curiosa, Lunatica, Magica et Pneumatica', which has been a mainstay to me in the present endeavour.

In 1987, I was also encouraged to undertake the study of perfect languages by an early work of Roberto Pellerey, and I shall often be referring to his recent volume on perfect languages in the eighteenth century. I have also given two courses of lectures on this topic in the University of Bologna and one at the Collège de France. Many of my students have made contributions about particular themes or authors. Their contributions appeared, as the rules of academic fairness require, before the publication of this book, in the special issue of *VS* (1992), 61–3, 'Le lingue perfette'.

A final word of thanks to the antiquarian booksellers on at least two continents who have brought to my attention rare or unknown texts. Unfortunately – considering the size prescribed for this book – as rich as the most exciting of these *trouvailles* are, they could receive only passing mention, or none at all. I console myself that I have the material for future excursions in erudition.

Besides, the first draft of this research totalled twice the number of pages I am now sending to the printer. I hope that my readers will be grateful for the sacrifice that I have celebrated for their comfort, and that the experts will forgive me the elliptic and panoramic bent of my story.

Umberto Eco
Bologna, Milan, Paris

1

From Adam to Confusio Linguarum

Genesis 2, 10, 11

Our story has an advantage over many others: it can begin at the Beginning.

God spoke before all things, and said, 'Let there be light.' In this way, he created both heaven and earth; for with the utterance of the divine word, 'there was light' (Genesis 1:3–4). Thus Creation itself arose through an act of speech; it is only by giving things their names that he created them and gave them an ontological status: 'And God called the light Day and the darkness He called Night . . . And God called the firmament Heaven' (1:5, 8).

In Genesis 2:16–17, the Lord speaks to man for the first time, putting at his disposal all the goods in the earthly paradise, commanding him, however, not to eat of the fruit of the tree of the knowledge of good and evil. We are not told in what language God spoke to Adam. Tradition has pictured it as a sort of language of interior illumination, in which God, as in other episodes of the Bible, expresses himself by thunderclaps and lightning. If we are to understand it this way, we must think of a language which, although not translatable into any known idiom, is still, through a special grace or dispensation, comprehensible to its hearer.

It is at this point, and only at this point (2:19ff), that 'out of the ground the Lord God formed every beast of the field, and every fowl of the air; and brought them unto Adam to see what he would call them'. The interpretation of this passage is an extremely delicate matter. Clearly we are here in the presence of a motif, common to other religions and mythologies – that of the nomothete, the name-giver, the creator of language. Yet it is not at all clear on what basis Adam actually chose the names he gave to the animals. The version in the Vulgate, the source for European culture's understanding of the passage, does little to resolve this mystery. The Vulgate has Adam calling the various animals '*nominibus suis*', which we can only translate, 'by their own names'. The King James version does not help us any more: 'Whatsoever Adam called every living creature, that was the name thereof.' But Adam might have called the animals 'by their own names' in two senses. Either he gave them the names that, by some extra-linguistic right, were already *due* to them, or he gave them those names we still use on the basis of a convention initiated by Adam. In other words, the names that Adam gave the animals are either the names that each animal intrinsically *ought* to have been given, or simply the names that the nomothete arbitrarily and *ad placitum* decided to give to them.

From this difficulty, we pass to Genesis 2:23. Here Adam sees Eve for the first time; and here, for the first time, the reader hears Adam's actual words. In the King James version, Adam is quoted as saying: 'This is now bone of my bones, and flesh of my flesh: she shall be called Woman . . .' In the Vulgate the name is *virago* (a translation from the Hebrew *ishhà*, the feminine of *ish*, 'man').[1] If we take Adam's use of *virago* together with the fact that, in Genesis 3:20, he calls his wife Eve, meaning 'life', because 'she was the mother of all living', it is evident that we are faced with names that are not arbitrary, but rather – at least etymologically – 'right'.

The linguistic theme is taken up once more, this time in a very explicit fashion, in Genesis 11:1. We are told that after the Flood, 'the whole earth was of one language, and of one speech.' Yet, men in their vanity conceived a desire to rival the Lord, and thus to erect a tower that would reach up to the heavens. To punish their pride and to put a stop to the construction of their tower, the Lord thought: 'Go to, let us go down, and there confound their language, that they may not understand one another's speech . . . . Therefore is the name of it called Babel; because the Lord did there confound the language of all the earth: and from thence did the Lord scatter them abroad upon the face of all the earth' (Genesis 11:7, 9). In the opinion of various Arab authors (cf. Borst 1957–63: I, II, 9), the confusion was due to the trauma induced by the sight, terrifying no doubt, of the collapse of the tower. This really changes nothing: the biblical story, as well as the partially divergent accounts of other mythologies, simply serves to establish the fact that different languages exist in the world.

Told in this way, however, the story is still incomplete. We have left out Genesis 10. Here, speaking of the diffusion of the sons of Noah after the Flood, the text states of the sons of Japheth that, 'By these [sons] were the isles of the Gentiles divided in their lands; every one after his tongue, after their families, in their nations' (10:5). This idea is repeated in similar words for the sons of Ham (10:20) and of Shem (10:31). How are we meant to interpret this evident plurality of languages prior to Babel? The account presented in Genesis 11 is dramatic, able to inspire visual representations, as is shown by the further iconographic tradition. The account in Genesis 10 is, by contrast, less theatrical. It is obvious that tradition focused on the story in which the existence of a plurality of tongues was understood as the tragic consequence of the confusion after Babel and the result of a divine malediction. Where it was not neglected entirely, Genesis 10 was reduced to a sort of footnote, a provincial episode recounting the diffusion of tribal dialects, not the multiplication of tongues.

Thus Genesis 11 seems to possess a clear and unequivocal meaning: first there was one language, and then there were – depending on which tradition we follow – seventy or seventy-two. It is this story that served as the point of departure for any number of dreams to 'restore' the language of Adam. Genesis 10, however, has continued to lurk in the background with all its explosive potential still intact. If the languages were already differentiated after Noah, why not before? It is a chink in the armour of the myth of Babel. If languages were differentiated not as a punishment but simply as a result of a natural process, why must the confusion of tongues constitute a curse at all?

Every so often in the course of our story, someone will oppose Genesis 10 to Genesis 11. Depending on the period and the theologico-philosophical context, the results will be more or less devastating.

Before and After Europe

Stories accounting for the multiplicity of tongues appear in divers mythologies and theogonies (Borst 1957–63: I, 1). None the less, it is one thing to know why many languages exist; it is quite another to decide that this multiplicity is a wound that must be healed by the quest for a perfect language. Before one decides to seek a perfect language, one needs, at the very least, to be persuaded that one's own is not so.

Keeping, as we decided, strictly to Europe – the classical Greeks knew of peoples speaking languages other than theirs: they called these peoples *barbaroi*, beings who mumble in an incomprehensible speech. The Stoics, with their more articulated notion of semiotics, knew perfectly well that the ideas to which certain sounds in Greek corresponded were also present in the minds of barbarians. However, not knowing Greek, barbarians had no notion of the connection between the Greek sound and the particular idea. Linguistically and culturally speaking, they were unworthy of any attention.

For the Greek philosophers, Greek was the language of reason. Aristotle's list of categories is squarely based on the categories of Greek grammar. This did not explicitly entail a claim that the Greek language was primary: it was simply a case of the identification of thought with its natural vehicle. *Logos* was thought, and *Logos* was speech. About the speech of barbarians little was known; hence, little was known about what it would be like to think in the language of barbarians. Although the Greeks were willing to admit that the Egyptians, for example, possessed a rich and venerable store of wisdom, they only knew this because someone had explained it to them in Greek.

As Greek civilization expanded, the status of Greek as a language evolved as well. At first, there existed almost as many varieties of Greek as there were Greek texts (Meillet 1930: 4). In the period following the conquests of Alexander the Great, however, there arose and spread a common Greek – the *koiné*. This was the language of Polybius, Strabo, Plutarch and Aristotle; it was the language taught in the schools of grammar. Gradually it became the official language of the entire area of the Mediterranean bounded by Alexander's conquests. Spoken by patricians and intellectuals, Greek still survived here under Roman domination as well, as the language of commerce and trade, of diplomacy, and of scientific and philosophical debate. It was finally the language in which the first Christian texts were transmitted (the Gospels and the Septuagint translation of the Bible in the third century BC), and the language of the early church Fathers.

A civilization with an international language does not need to worry about the multiplicity of tongues. Nevertheless such a civilization can worry about the 'rightness' of its own. In the *Cratylus*, Plato asks the same question that a reader of the Genesis story might: did the nomothete chose the sounds with which to name objects according to the objects' nature (*physis*)? This is the thesis of Cratylus, while Ermogene maintains that they were assigned by law or human convention (*nomos*). Socrates moves among these theses with apparent ambiguity. Finally, having subjected both to ironical comment, inventing etymologies that neither he (nor Plato) is eager to accept, Socrates brings forward his own hypothesis: knowledge is founded not on our relation to the names of things, but on our relation to the things themselves – or, better, to the ideas of those things. Later, even by these cultures that ignored Cratylus, every discussion on the nature of a perfect language has revolved around the three possibilities first set out in this dialogue. None the less, the *Cratylus* was not itself a project for a perfect language: Plato discusses the preconditions for semantic adequacy within a given language without posing the problem of a perfect one.

While the Greek *koiné* continued to dominate the Mediterranean basin, Latin was becoming the language of the empire, and thus the universal language for all parts of Europe reached by the Roman legions. Later it became the language of the Roman church. Once again, a civilization with a common language was not troubled by the plurality of tongues. Learned men might still discourse in Greek, but, for the rest of the world, speaking with barbarians was, once again, the job of a few translators, and this only until these same barbarians began to speak their Latin.

Despite this, by the second century AD, there had begun to grow the suspicion that Latin and Greek might not be the only languages which expressed harmoniously the totality of experience. Slowly spreading across the Greco-Roman world, obscure revelations appeared; some were attributed to Persian magi, others to an Egyptian divinity called Thoth-Hermes, to Chaldean oracles, and even to the very Pythagorean and Orphic traditions which, though born on Greek soil, had long been smothered under the weight of the great rationalist philosophy.

By now, the classical rationalism, elaborated and re-elaborated over centuries, had begun to show signs of age. With this, traditional religion entered a period of crisis as well. The imperial pagan religion had become a purely formal affair, no more than a simple expression of loyalty. Each people had been allowed to keep its own gods. These were accommodated to the Latin pantheon, no one bothering over contradictions, synonyms or homonyms. The term characterizing this levelling toleration for any type of religion (and for any type of philosophy or knowledge as well) is *syncretism*.

An unintended result of this syncretism, however, was that a diffused sort of religiosity began to grow in the souls of the most sensitive. It was manifested by a belief in the universal World Soul; a soul which subsisted in stars and in earthly objects alike. Our own, individual, souls were but small particles of the great World Soul. Since the reason of philosophers proved unable to supply truths about important matters such as these, men and women sought revelations beyond reason, through visions, and through communications with the godhead itself.

It was in this climate that Pythagoreanism was reborn. From its beginnings, Pythagoreans had regarded themselves as the keepers of a mystic form of knowledge, and practised initiatory rites. Their understanding of the laws of music and mathematics was presented as the fruit of revelation obtained from the Egyptians. By the time of Pythagoreanism's second appearance, however, Egyptian civilization had been eradicated by the Greek and Latin conquerors. Egypt itself had now become an enigma, no more than an incomprehensible hieroglyph. Yet there is nothing more fascinating than secret wisdom: one is sure that it exists, but one does not know what it is. In the imagination, therefore, it shines as something unutterably profound.

That such a wisdom could exist while still remaining unknown, however, could only be accounted for by the fact that the language in which this wisdom was expressed had remained unknown as well. This was the reasoning of Diogenes Laertius, who wrote in his *Lives of the Philosophers* in the third century AD: 'There are those who assert that philosophy started among the Barbarians: there were, they claim, Magi among the Persians, the Chaldeans, the Babylonians, the Assyrians, the Gymnosophists of India, the Druids among the Celts and Galatians' (I). The classical Greeks had identified the barbarians as those who could not even articulate their speech. It now seemed that these very mumblings were of a sacred language, filled with the promise of tacit revelations (Festugière 1944–54: I).

I have given a summary of the cultural atmosphere at this time because, albeit in a delayed fashion, it was destined to have a deep influence on our story. Although no one at the time proposed the reconstruction of a perfect language, the need for one was, by now, vaguely felt. We shall see that the suggestions, first planted during these years, flowered more than twelve centuries later in humanistic and Renaissance culture (and beyond); this will constitute a central thread in the story I am about to tell.

In the meantime, Christianity had become a state religion, expressed in the Greek of the patristic East and in the Latin still spoken in the West. After St Jerome translated the Old Testament in the fourth century, the need to know Hebrew as a sacred language grew weaker. This happened to Greek as well. A typical example of this cultural lack is given by St Augustine, a man of vast culture, and the most important exponent of Christian thought at the end of the empire. The Christian revelation is founded on an Old Testament written in Hebrew and a New Testament written, for the most part, in Greek. St Augustine, however, knew no Hebrew; and his knowledge of Greek was, to say the least, patchy (cf. Marrou 1958). This amounts to a somewhat paradoxical situation: the man who set himself the task of interpreting scripture in order to discover the true meaning of the divine word could read it only in a Latin translation. The notion that he ought to consult the Hebrew original never really seems to have entered Augustine's mind. He did not entirely trust the Jews, nurturing a suspicion that, in their versions, they might have erased all references to the coming of Christ. The only critical procedure he would allow was that of comparing translations in order to find the most likely version. In this way, St Augustine, though the father of hermeneutics, was certainly not destined to become the father of philology.

There is one sense in which St Augustine did have a clear idea of a perfect language, common to all people. But this was not a language of words; it was, rather, a language made out of things themselves. He viewed the world, as it was later to be put, as a vast book written with God's own finger. Those who knew how to read this book were able to understand the allegories hidden in the scriptures, where, beneath references to simple earthly things (plants, stones, animals), symbolic meanings lay. This Language of the World, instituted by its creator, could not be read, however, without a key; it was the need to provide such a key that provoked a rapid outflowing of bestiaries, lapidaries, encyclopedias and *imagines mundi* throughout the Middle Ages. This represents a tradition that will resurface in our own story as well: European culture will sometimes seize upon hieroglyphs and other esoteric ideograms, believing that truth can only be expressed in emblems or symbols. Still, St Augustine's symbolic interests were not combined with the longing to recover a lost tongue that someone might, or ought to, speak once again.

For Augustine, as for nearly all the early Fathers, Hebrew certainly was the primordial language. It was the language spoken before Babel. After the confusion, it still remained the tongue of the elected people. Nevertheless, Augustine gave no sign of wanting to recover its use. He was at home in Latin, by now the language of the church and of theology. Several centuries later, Isidore of Seville found it easy to assume that, in any case, there were three sacred languages – Hebrew, Greek and Latin – because these were the three languages that appeared written above the cross (*Etymologiarum*, ix, 1). With this conclusion, the task of determining the language in which the Lord said 'Fiat lux' became more arduous.

If anything, the Fathers were concerned about another linguistic puzzle: the Bible clearly states that God brought before Adam all the beasts of the field and all the fowl of the air. What about the fish? Did Adam name the fish? Maybe it seemed inconvenient dragging them all up from the briny deep to parade them in the garden of Eden. We may think this a slight matter; yet the question, whose last trace is to be found in Massey's *Origins and Progress of Letters* published in 1763 (cf. White 1917: II, 196), was never satisfactorily resolved, despite Augustine's helpful suggestion that the fish were named one at a time, as they were discovered (*De Genesi ad litteram libri duodecim,* XII, 20).

Between the fall of the Roman Empire and the early Middle Ages, when Europe had still to emerge, premonitions of its linguistic future lurked unrecorded. New languages came slowly into being. It has been calculated that, towards the end of the fifth century, people no longer spoke Latin, but Gallo-Romanic, Italico-Romanic or Hispano-Romanic. While intellectuals continued to write Latin, bastardizing it ever further, they heard around them local dialects in which survivals of languages spoken before Roman civilization crossed with new roots arriving with the barbarian invaders.

It is in the seventh century, before any known document written in Romance or Germanic languages, that the first allusion to our theme appears. It is contained in an attempt, on the part of Irish grammarians, to defend spoken Gaelic over learned Latin. In a work entitled *Auracepit na n-Éces* ('the precepts of the poets'), the Irish grammarians refer to the structural material of the tower of Babel as follows: 'Others affirm that in the tower there were only nine materials, and that these were clay and water, wool and blood, wood and lime, pitch, linen, and bitumen. . . . These represent noun, pronoun, verb, adverb, participle, conjunction, preposition, interjection.' Ignoring the anomaly of the nine parts of the tower and only eight parts of speech, we are meant to understand that the structure of language and the construction of the tower are analogous. This is part of an argument that the Gaelic language constituted the first and only instance of a language that overcame the confusion of tongues. It was the first, programmed language, constructed after the confusion of tongues, and created by the seventy-two wise men of the school of Fenius. The canonic account in the *Precepts*

shows the action of the founding of this language . . . as a 'cut and paste' operation on other languages that the 72 disciples undertook after the dispersion. . . . It was then that the rules of this language were constructed. All that was best in each language, all there was that was grand or beautiful, was cut out and retained in Irish. . . . Wherever there was something that had no name in any other language, a name for it was made up in Irish. (Poli 1989: 187–9)

This first-born and, consequently, supernatural language retained traces of its original isomorphism with the created world. As long as the proper order of its elements was respected, this ensured a sort of iconic bond between grammatical items and referents, or states of things in the real world.

Why is it, however, that a document asserting the rights and qualities of one language in contrast to others appears at this particular moment? A quick look at the iconographic history increases our curiosity. There are no known representations of the Tower of Babel before the Cotton Bible (fifth or sixth century). It next appears in a manuscript perhaps from the end of the tenth century, and then on a relief from the cathedral of Salerno from the eleventh century. After this, however, there is a flood of towers (Minkowski 1983). It is a flood, moreover, that has its counterpart in a vast deluge of theoretical speculation originating in precisely this period as well. It seems, therefore, that it was only at this point that the story of the confusion of tongues came to be perceived not merely as an example of how divine justice humbled human pride, but as an account of a historical (or metahistorical) event. It was now the story of how a real wound had been inflicted on humanity, a wound that might, in some way, be healed once more.

This age, characterized as 'dark', seemed to witness a reoccurrence of the catastrophe of Babel: hairy barbarians, peasants, artisans, these first Europeans, unlettered and unversed in official culture, spoke a multitude of vulgar tongues of which official culture was apparently unaware. It was the age that saw the birth of the languages which we speak today, whose documentary traces – in the Serments de Strasbourg (842) or the Carta Capuana (960) – inevitably appear only later.

Facing such texts as *Sao ko kelle terre, per kelle fini ke ki contene, trenta anni le possette parte Sancti Benedicti*, or *Pro Deo amur et pro Christian poblo et nostro commun salvament*, the European culture becomes aware of the *confusio linguarum*.

Yet before this confusion there was no European culture, and, hence, no Europe. What is Europe anyway? It is a continent, barely distinguishable from Asia, existing, before people had invented a name for it, from the time that the unstoppable power of continental drift tore it off from the original Pangea. In the sense we normally mean it, however, Europe was an entity that had to wait for the fall of the Roman Empire and the birth of the Romano-Germanic kingdoms before it could be born. Perhaps even this was not enough, nor even the attempt at unification under the Carolingians. How are we going to establish the date when the history of Europe begins? The dates of great political events and battles will not do; the dates of linguistic events must serve in their stead. In front of the massive unity of the Roman Empire (which took in parts of Africa and Asia), Europe first appears as a Babel of new languages. Only afterwards was it a mosaic of nations.

Europe was thus born from its vulgar tongues. European critical culture begins with the reaction, often alarmed, to the eruption of these tongues. Europe was forced at the very moment of its birth to confront the drama of linguistic fragmentation, and European culture arose as a reflection on the destiny of a multilingual civilization. Its prospects seemed troubled; a remedy for linguistic confusion needed to be sought. Some looked backwards, trying to rediscover the language spoken by Adam. Others looked ahead, aiming to fabricate a rational language possessing the perfections of the lost speech of Eden.

Side-effects

The story of the search for the perfect language is the story of a dream and of a series of failures. Yet that is not to say that a story of failures must itself be a failure. Though our story be nothing but the tale of the obstinate pursuit of an impossible dream, it is still of some interest to know how this dream originated, as well as uncovering the hopes that sustained the pursuers throughout their secular course.

Put in this light, our story represents a chapter in the history of European culture. It is a chapter, moreover, with a particular interest today when the peoples of Europe – as they discuss the whys and wherefores of a possible commercial and political union – not only continue to speak different languages, but speak them in greater number than ten years ago, and even, in certain places, arm against one another for the sake of their ethno-linguistic differences.

We shall see that the dream of a perfect language has always been invoked as a solution to religious or political strife. It has even been invoked as the way to overcome simple difficulties in commercial exchange. The history of the reasons why Europe thought that it needed a perfect language can thus tell us a good deal about the cultural history of that continent.

Besides, even if our story is nothing but a series of failures, we shall see that each failure produced its own side-effects. Punctually failing to come to fruition, each of the projects left a train of beneficial consequences in its wake. Each might thus be viewed as a sort of serendipitous *felix culpa*: many of today's theories, as well as many of the practices which we theorize (from taxonomy in the natural sciences to comparative linguistics, from formal languages to artificial intelligence and to the cognitive sciences), were born as side-effects of the search for a perfect language. It is only fair, then, that we acknowledge these pioneers: they have given us a lot, even if it was not what they promised.

Finally, through examining the defects of the perfect languages, conceived in order to eliminate the defects of the natural ones, we shall end up by discovering that these natural languages of ours contain some unexpected virtues. This can finally serve us as consolation for the curse of Babel.

A Semiotic Model for Natural Language

In order to examine the structure of the various natural and artificial languages that we shall be looking at, we need a theoretical model to use as our point of reference. This will be supplied by Hjelmslev (1943).

A natural language (or any other semiotic system) is articulated at two levels or planes. There is an expression-plane, which, in natural languages, consists of a lexicon, a phonology and a syntax. There is also a content-plane, which represents the array of concepts we can express. Each of these two levels can be subdivided into form and substance, and each arises through organizing a still un-shaped continuum. Schematically:

	Continuum

CONTENT	Substance

	Form
	Form

EXPRESSION	Substance

	Continuum

For natural languages, the *expression-form* is represented

by the phonological system, by the lexical repertoire and by the rules of syntax. Realizing through concrete utterances the possibilities provided by the expression-form, we produce *expression-substances*, like the words that we utter or the text that you are now reading. In elaborating its expression-form, a language selects, out of the continuum of sounds that it is theoretically possible for the human voice to make, a particular subset of phonemes, and excludes other sounds which therefore do not belong to that language.

In order for the sounds of speech to become meaningful, the words formed from them must have meanings associated with them; they must, in other words, possess a content. The content-continuum represents everything we can talk or think about: it is the universe, or reality (physical or mental), to which our language refers. Each language, however, organizes the way in which we talk or think about reality in its own particular way, through a *content-form*. Examples of the way in which the form of content organizes our world might be our arrangement of colours in series from light to dark, or from red to violet; the way we use notions such as genus, species and family to organize the animal kingdom; the way we use semantically opposed ideas, such as high v. low or love v. hate, as systematically organized pairs.

By *content-substance* we mean the sense that we give to the utterances produced as instances of the expression-substance.

The mode of organizing content varies from language to language. Different cultures may divide the world of colour according to some criterion other than spectral wavelengths, and consequently recognize and name colours that our culture does not acknowledge. The mode of organizing content may even vary within a language. A scientist interested in colour might need to master a rigorous system which categorized thousands of different spectral phenomena, while the person on the street might only be able to name a few dozen. Normal speakers recognize only a few types of 'bug', while thousands of insects exist for the entomologist. The ways of organizing content are virtually unlimited: an animistic society might apply a term which we would translate as *life* to various aspects of the mineral kingdom.

Since language expresses the modes which organize the way we categorize and classify reality, natural languages must be considered as *holistic* systems. They organize the totality of our vision of the world. It has sometimes been suggested (Whorf 1956; Quine 1960, for example) that there are experiences, recognized by other cultures and capable of being expressed in their languages, which are neither recognized by our own, nor even capable of being expressed in our languages. Although this is a rather extreme view, we will continually be finding ourselves faced with it as we examine the criticisms levelled at the various projects for a perfect language.

In order to be able to convey meaning, a natural language must establish a connection between elements (or units) of the expression-form and elements (or units) of the content-form. Let us consider for a moment the word *dogs*. The lexeme *dog* is a unit of expression-form the content of which is (let us say) 'canine mammal'. The morpheme *s* is another unit of the expression-form that, in that position, means 'more than one'. I said 'in that position', because the same *s* as a sound in the word *sorrow* does not acquire the same content; it is not a morpheme and does not bear any specific meaning. In fact, natural language works by a *double articulation*. The units of first articulation (like words, or lexemes and morphemes arranged into syntagms) are meaningful; the units of second articulation (the phonemes of a natural language) are devoid of meaning. The sound *d* of *dog* (and, in this case, even the letter *d* of the written word) does not represent a part of a dog or of the definition of a dog. In English one can combine the sounds of *dog* to produce a radically different word like *god*.

Moreover, in Hjelmslev's terms the two planes of a natural language (form and content) are *not conformal*. This means that the expression-form and the expression-content are structured according to different criteria: the relationship between the two planes is arbitrary, and variations of form do not automatically imply a point-to-point variation of the corresponding content. If, instead of *dog*, we utter *log*, we do not mean a different kind of dog, or of animal, but something radically different.

However, this feature of natural languages is not necessarily a feature of other semiotic systems, which can be *conformal*. Think of an analogue clock: here the movement of the hands corresponds to the movement of the earth around the sun, but the slightest movement (and every new position) of the hands corresponds to a movement of the earth: the two planes are point-to-point conformal.

The above notions are not irrelevant to our inquiry because, as we shall see, many perfect languages (namely, the so-called 'philosophical' ones) aspired to such a conformal status. They considered both double articulation and the non-conformal relationship as a source of potential ambiguity and tried to assign a precise content to every sound (or to every written character representing a sound).

Furthermore, natural languages do not live on syntax and semantics alone. They also have a *pragmatic* aspect, which concerns rules of usage in different contexts, situations or circumstances; one can also use language for rhetorical purposes, so that words can acquire multiple senses – as happens with metaphors. We shall see that some projects tried to eliminate these pragmatic and rhetorical aspects of a language – while others tried to make them possible.

Finally – and this explains the exclusions I listed in the introduction – many authors advocate a *principle of effability*, according to which a natural language can express anything that can be thought. A natural language is supposedly capable of rendering the totality of our experience –mental or physical – and, consequently, able to express all our sensations, perceptions, abstractions up to the question of why is there Something instead of Nothing. It is true that no purely verbal language ever entirely achieves total effability: think of having to describe, in words alone, the smell of rosemary. We are always required to supplement language with ostensions, expressive gestures and so-called 'tonemic' features. Nevertheless, of all semiotic systems, nothing rivals language in its effability. This is why almost all projects for a perfect language start with natural, verbal languages as their model.

2

The Kabbalistic Pansemioticism

Our story opened with a reference to an eastern text, the Bible. By the time of the last church Fathers, however, knowledge of the language in which this text was composed had been lost. Thus, we were able to begin our story by reading the Bible directly in the Latin of the Vulgate. The Christian West would begin to come to terms with Hebrew only from the Renaissance onwards. However, in the same centuries in which Hebrew was forgotten by Christian scholars, in the Jewish milieu of Provence and Spain there flowered a current of Hebrew mysticism destined to have a profound influence on Europe's search for the perfect language: kabbala, a mystical current that regarded creation itself as a linguistic phenomenon.

The Reading of the Torah

The kabbala (from *qabbalah*, which might be rendered as 'tradition') was a technique of interpretation grafted onto the practice of commenting on the Torah, that is, on the books of the Pentateuch, together with the practice of rabbinical commentary known as the Talmud. In this way, the kabbala appears pre-eminently as a technique of reading and interpreting the sacred text. Yet the actual Torah rolls upon which the kabbalist scholar laboured served him merely as a point of departure: underneath the letters in which the Torah was written, the kabbalist sought to descry the shape of the eternal Torah, created by God before all worlds, and consigned to his angels.

According to some, the primordial Torah was inscribed in black flames upon white fire. At the moment of its creation, it appeared as a series of letters not yet joined up in the form of words. For this reason, in the Torah rolls there appear neither vowels, nor punctuation, nor accents; for the original Torah was nothing but a disordered heap of letters. Furthermore, had it not been for Adam's sin, these letters might have been joined differently to form another story. For the kabbalist, God will abolish the present ordering of these letters, or else will teach us how to read them according to a new disposition, only after the coming of the Messiah.

One school of the kabbalistic tradition, characterized in recent studies as the theosophical kabbala, endeavoured to find beneath the letters of the sacred text references to the ten Sefirot, or the ten hypostases of the divinity. The theosophy of the Sefirot might be compared to the various theories of cosmic chains appearing in the Hermetic, Gnostic and Neo-Platonic traditions; the ten Sefirot were hypostases in the sense of representing either increasing grades of emanation, and, therefore, ten intermediate steps between God and the world, or ten internal aspects of the divinity itself. In either case, in so far as they represented various ways in which the infinite expands itself, actually or potentially, into the finite universe, they also constituted a series of channels or steps through which the soul passes on its journey of return to God.

The kabbalist uses the Torah as a symbolic instrument; beneath the letters of the Torah, beneath the events to which, to the uninstructed, its words seem to allude, there is a text which reveals a mystic and metaphysical reality. To use this instrument to uncover this reality, however, the text needs to be read not only literally but also in three other senses: allegorical-philosophical, hermeneutic and mystic. This is reminiscent of the four ways of reading scripture in Christian exegetical tradition. Beyond this point, however, all analogies between the kabbala and Christian exegesis break down, and kabbalism proceeds by its own, radically individual, route.

In Christian tradition, the four levels are excavated through a labour of interpretation which brings surplus meaning to the surface. Yet it is a labour performed without altering the *expression-plane*, that is, the surface of the text. The commentator tries in many ways to correct scribal errors, so as to re-establish the only and original version according to the alleged intention of the original author. For some kabbalistic currents, by contrast, to read means to anatomize, as it were, the very *expression-substance*, by three fundamental techniques: *notariqon*, *gematria* and *temurah*.

Notariqon was the technique of using acrostics to cipher and decipher a hidden message. The initial (or final) letters of a series of words generate new words. Such a technique was already a familiar artifice in poetry during the late antique and Middle Ages, when it was used for magic purposes under the name of *ars notoria*. Kabbalists typically used acrostics to discover mystic relations. Mosé de Leon, for example, took the initial letters of the four senses of scripture (*Peshat, Remez, Derash* and *Sod*) and formed out of them *PRDS*. Since Hebrew is not vocalized, it was possible to read this as *Pardes* or Paradise. The initial letters of Moses's question in Deuteronomy 30:12, 'Who shall go up for us to heaven?', as they appear in the Torah form *MYLH*, or 'circumcision', while the final letters give *YHWH*, Jahveh. The answer is therefore: 'the circumcised will go up to God.' Abulafia discovered that the final letters of *MVH* ('brain') and *LB* ('heart') recall the initial letters of two Sefirot, *Hokmah* (wisdom) and *Binah* (intelligence).

Gematria was based on the fact that, in Hebrew, numbers are indicated by letters; this means that each Hebrew word can be given a numerical value, calculated by summing the numbers represented by its letters. This allows mystic relations to be established between words having different meanings though identical numerical values. It is these relations that the kabbalist seeks to discover and elucidate. The serpent of Moses, for example, is a prefiguration of the Messiah because the value of both words is 358. Adding up the letters in *YHWH*, we get 72, and kabbalistic tradition constantly searched for the seventy-two names of God.

Temurah is the art of anagrams. In a language in which vowels must be interpolated, anagrams are more exciting than in other idioms. Mosé Cordovero wondered why there appeared in Deuteronomy a prohibition against wearing garments of mixed wool and linen. He found the answer when he discovered that the letters of that passage could be recombined to produce another text which warned Adam not to take off his original garment of light and put on the skin of the serpent, which symbolized demonic power.

Abraham Abulafia (thirteenth century) systematically combined the letter Alef with each of the four letters of the tetragrammaton *YHWH*; then he vocalized each of the resulting units by every possible permutation of five vowels, thus obtaining four tables with fifty entries each. Eleazar ben Yudah of Worms went on to vocalize every unit using twice each of the five vowels, and the total number of combinations increased geometrically (cf. Idel 1988b: 22–3).

Cosmic Permutability and the Kabbala of Names

The kabbalist could rely on the unlimited resources of *temurah* because anagrams were more than just a tool of interpretation: they were the very method whereby God created the world. This doctrine had already been made explicit in the *Sefer Yezirah*, or *Book of Creation*, a little tract written some time between the second and the sixth centuries. According to it, the 'stones' out of which God created the world were the thirty-two ways of wisdom. These were formed by the twenty-two letters of the Hebrew alphabet and the ten Sefirot.

Twenty-two foundation letters: He ordained them, He hewed them, He combined them, He weighed them, He interchanged them. And He created with them the whole creation and everything to be created in the future. (II, 2)

Twenty-two foundation letters: He fixed them on a wheel like a wall with 231 gates and He turns the wheel forward and backward. (II, 4)

How did He combine, weigh, and interchange them? Aleph with all and all with Aleph; Beth with all and all with Beth; and so each in turn. There are 231 gates. And all creation and all language come from one name. (II, 5)

How did He combine them? Two stones build two houses, three stones build six houses, four stones build twenty-four houses, five stones build a hundred and twenty houses, six stones build seven hundred and twenty houses, seven stones build five thousand and forty houses. Begin from here and think of what the mouth is unable to say and the ear unable to hear. (IV, 16)
(*The Book of Creation*, Irving Friedman, ed., New York: Weiser, 1977)

Indeed, not only the mouth and ear, but even a modern computer, might find it difficult to keep up with what happens as the number of stones (or letters) increases. What the *Book of Creation* is describing is the factorial calculus. We shall see more of this later, in the chapter on Lull's art of permutation.

The kabbala shows how a mind-boggling number of combinations can be produced from a finite alphabet. The kabbalist who raised this art to its highest pitch was Abulafia, with his kabbala of the names (cf. Idel 1988a, 1988b, 1988c, 1989).

The kabbala of the names, or the ecstatic kabbala, was based on the practice of the recitation of the divine names hidden in the Torah, by combining the letters of the Hebrew alphabet. The theosophical kabbala, though indulging in numerology, acrostics and anagrams, had retained a basic respect for the sacred text itself. Not so the ecstatic kabbala: in a process of free linguistic creativity, it altered, disarticulated, decomposed and recomposed the textual surface to reach the single letters that served as its linguistic raw material. For the theosophical kabbala, between God and the interpreter, there still remained a text; for the ecstatic kabbalist, the interpreter stood between the text and God.

What justified this process of textual dissolution was that, for Abulafia, each letter, each atomic element, already had a meaning of its own, independent of the meaning of the syntagms in which it occurred. Each letter was already a divine name: 'Since, in the letters of the Name, each letter is already a Name itself, know that Yod is a name, and YH is a name' (*Perush Havdalah de-Rabbi 'Akivà*).

This practice of reading by permutation tended to produce ecstatic effects:

And begin by combining this name, namely, YHWH, at the beginning alone, and examining all its combinations and move it, turn it about like a wheel, returning around, front and back, like a scroll, and do not let it rest, but when you see its matter strengthened because of the great motion, because of the fear of confusion of your imagination, and rolling about of your thoughts, and when you let it rest, return to it and ask [it] until there shall come to your hand a word of wisdom from it, do not abandon it. Afterwards go on to the second one from it, *Adonay*, and ask of it its foundation [*yesodo*] and it will reveal to you its secret [*sodo*]. And then you will apprehend its matter in the truth of its language. Then join and combine the two of them [YHWH and *Adonay*] and study them and ask them, and they will reveal to you the secrets of wisdom . . .

Afterwards combine Elohim, and it will also grant you wisdom, and then combine the four of them, and find the miracles of the Perfect One [i.e. God], which are miracles of wisdom. (*Hayyê ha-Nefes*, in Idel 1988c: 21)

If we add that the recitation of the names was accompanied by special techniques of breathing, we begin to see how from recitation the adept might pass into ecstasy, and from ecstasy to the acquisition of magic powers; for the letters that the mystic combined were the same sounds with which God created the world. This latter aspect came especially into prominence during the fifteenth century. For Yohanan Alemanno, friend and inspirer of Pico della Mirandola, 'the symbolic cargo of language was transformed into a kind of quasi-mathematical command. Kabbalistic symbolism thus turned into – or perhaps returned to – a magical language of incantation' (Idel 1988b: 204–5).

For the ecstatic kabbala, language was a self-contained universe in which the structure of language represented the structure of reality itself. Already in the writings of Philo of Alexandria there had been an attempt to compare the intimate essence of the Torah with the *Logos* as the world of ideas. Such Platonic conceptions had even penetrated into the Haggadic and Midrashic literature in which the Torah was conceived as providing the scheme according to which God had created the world. The eternal Torah was identified with wisdom and, in many passages, with the world of forms or universe of archetypes. In the thirteenth century, taking up a decidedly Averroist line, Abulafia equated the Torah with the active intellect, 'the form of all the forms of separate intellects' (*Sefer Mafteakh ha-Tokhahot*).

In contrast, therefore, with the main philosophical tradition (from Aristotle to the Stoics and to the Middle Ages, as well as to Arab and Judaic philosophers), language, in the kabbala, did not represent the world merely by referring to it. It did not, that is, stand to the world in the relation of signifier to signified or sign to its referent. If God created the world by uttering sounds or by combining written letters, it must follow that these semiotic elements were not representations of pre-existing things, but the very forms by which the elements of the universe are moulded. The significance of this argument in our own story must be plain: the language of creation was perfect not because it merely happened to reflect the structure of the universe in some exemplary fashion; it created the universe. Consequently it stands to the universe as the cast stands to the object cast from it.

The Mother Tongue

Despite this, Abulafia did not think that this matrix of all languages (which coincides with the eternal, but not with the written, Torah) corresponded yet to Hebrew. Here Abulafia made a distinction between the twenty-two letters as a linguistic matrix, and Hebrew as the mother tongue of humanity. The twenty-two Hebrew letters represented the ideal sounds which had presided over the creation of the seventy existing languages. The fact that other languages had more vowels depended on the variations in pronouncing the twenty-two letters. In modern terminology, the new foreign sounds would be called *allophones* of the fundamental Hebrew phonemes.

Other kabbalists had observed that the Christians lacked the letter *Kheth*, while the Arabs lacked *Peh*. In the Renaissance, Yohanan Alemanno argued that the origins of these phonetic deviations in non-Hebrew languages were the noises of beasts; some were like the grunting of pigs, others were like the croaking of frogs, still others were like the sound of a crane. The assimilation of bestial sounds showed that these were the languages of peoples who had abandoned the right path and true conduct of their lives. In this sense, another result of the confusion of Babel was the multiplication of letters. Alemanno was aware that there were also other peoples who considered their languages as superior to all others. He cited Galen, who claimed that Greek was the most pleasing of all languages and the one that most conformed to the laws of reason. Not daring to contradict him, he attributed this fact to affinities he saw as existing between Greek, Hebrew, Arabic and Assyrian.

For Abulafia, the twenty-two Hebrew letters represented the entire gamut of sounds naturally produced by the human vocal organs. It was the different ways of combin-

ing these letters that had given rise to the different languages. The word *zeruf* (combination) and the word *lashon*
(language) had the same numerical value (386): it followed
that the rules of combination provided the explanation to
the formation of each separate language. Abulafia admitted
that the decision to represent these sounds according to
certain graphic signs was a matter of convention; it was,
however, a convention established between God and the
prophets. Being aware that there existed other theories
which claimed that the sounds which expressed ideas or
things were conventional (he could have encountered such
an Aristotelian and Stoic notion in Jewish authors like
Maimonides), Abulafia, nevertheless, invoked a rather
modern distinction between conventionality and arbitrariness. Hebrew was a conventional but not an arbitrary
language. Abulafia rejected the claim, maintained, among
others, by certain Christian authors, that, left entirely to
itself, a child would automatically begin to speak Hebrew:
the child would be unaware of the convention. Yet Hebrew
remained the sacred mother tongue because the names
given by Adam, though conventional, were *in accordance
with nature*. In this sense, Hebrew was the *proto-language*.
Its existence was a precondition for all the rest, 'For if such
a language did not precede it, there couldn't have been
mutual agreement to call a given object by a different name
from what it was previously called, for how would the
second person understand the second name if he doesn't
know the original name, in order to be able to agree to the
changes' (*Sefer or ha-Sekhel*; cf. Idel 1989: 14).

Abulafia lamented that his people in the course of their
exile had forgotten their original language. He looked on
the kabbalist as a labourer working to rediscover the original matrix of all the seventy languages of the world. Still,
he knew that it would not be until the coming of the
Messiah that all the secrets of the kabbala would be definitively revealed. Only then, at the end of time, would all
linguistic differences cease, and languages be reabsorbed
back into the original sacred tongue.

3

The Perfect Language of Dante

The first occasion on which the world of medieval Christianity had to confront a systematic project for a perfect language was the *De vulgari eloquentia* (hereafter DVE) of Dante Alighieri, written presumably between 1303 and 1305.

Dante's text opens with an observation which, obvious though it may be, is still fundamental for us: there is a multitude of vulgar tongues, all of them are natural languages, and all are opposed to Latin – which is a universal but artificial grammar.

Before the blasphemy of Babel, humanity had known but one language, a perfect language, a language spoken by Adam with God and by his posterity. The plurality of tongues arose as the consequence of the *confusio linguarum*. Revealing a knowledge of comparative linguistics exceptional for his time, Dante sought to demonstrate how this fragmentation had actually taken place. The division of the languages born from the confusion, he argued, had proceeded in three stages. First, he showed how languages split up into the various zones of the world; then, using the vernacular word for *yes* as his measuring rod, he showed how languages (within what we today call the Romance area) had further split into the *oc*, *oil* and *sì* groups. Finally, within this last subdivision, Dante showed how particular languages were even further fragmented into a welter of local dialects, some of which might, as in Bologna, even vary from one part of a city to another. All these divisions had occurred, Dante observed, because the human being is – by custom, by habit, by language, and according to differences in time and space – a changeable animal.

If the aim of his project was to discover one language more decorous and illustrious than the others, Dante had to take each of the various vernaculars in turn and subject it to a severe critical analysis. Examining the work of the best Italian poets, and assuming that each in his own way had always gone beyond his local dialect, Dante thought to create a vernacular (*volgare*) that might be more *illustre* (illustrious, in the sense of 'shining with light'), *cardinale* (useful as guiding rule or *cardine*), *regale* (worthy of being spoken in the royal palace of the national king – if the Italians were ever to obtain one), and *curiale* (worthy to be a language of government, of courts of law, and of wisdom). Such a vernacular belonged to every city in Italy, yet to none. It existed only as an ideal form, approached by the best poets, and it was according to this ideal form that all the vulgar dialects needed to be judged.

The second, and uncompleted, part of DVE sketches out the rules of composition for the one and only vernacular to which the term *illustrious* might truly apply – the poetic language of which Dante considered himself to be the founder. Opposing this language to all other languages of the confusion, Dante proclaimed it as the one which had restored that primordial affinity between words and objects which had been the hallmark of the language of Adam.

Latin and the Vernacular

An apology for the vernacular, DVE is written in Latin. As a poet, Dante wrote in Italian; as a philosopher and as a political scientist (as we would say today) who advocated the restoration of a universal monarchy, Dante stuck to the language of theology and law.

DVE defines a vernacular as the speech that an infant learns as it first begins to articulate, imitating the sounds made to it by its nurse, before knowing any rule. The same was not true of that *locutio secundaria* called *grammar* by Romans. Grammar meant a rule-governed language, one, moreover, that could be mastered only after long study to acquire the *habitus*. Considering that in the vocabulary of the Schoolmen *habitus* was a virtue, a capacity to do some specific thing, a present-day reader might take Dante merely to be distinguishing between the instinctive ability to express oneself in language (performance) and grammatical competence. It is clear, however, that by grammar Dante meant scholastic Latin, the only language whose rules were taught in school during this period (cf. also Viscardi 1942: 31ff). In this sense Latin was an *artificial* idiom; it was, moreover, an idiom which was 'perpetual and incorruptible', having been ossified into the international language of church and university through a system of rules by grammarians from Servius (between the fourth and fifth centuries) to Priscian (between the fifth and sixth) when Latin had ceased to be the living language of the Romans.

Having made this distinction between a primary and a secondary language clear, Dante went on to proclaim in no uncertain terms that, of the two, it was the first, the vernacular, that was the more noble. He gave various reasons for this opinion: vernaculars were the first languages of humanity; 'though divided by different words and accents' (I, i, 4) the whole world continues to use them; finally, vernaculars are natural, and not artificial.

This choice led Dante, however, into a double predicament.

First, although assuming that the most noble language must be natural, the fact that natural languages were split into a multiplicity of dialects suggested that they were not natural but conventional.

Second, a vulgar tongue is the language spoken by everyone (by *vulgus*, or common people). But in DVE Dante insists on the variety of the languages of the world.

How can he reconcile the idea that languages are many with the idea that the vernacular was *the* natural language for the whole human race? To say that learning a natural language without the aid of rules is common to the whole human race does not amount to saying that we all speak the *same one*.

A way to escape such a double predicament would be to interpret Dante's argument as if he wanted to say that our ability to learn different natural languages (according to the place of our birth or to the first linguistic training we receive) depends on our native *faculty for languages*. This is certainly an innate faculty which manifests itself in different linguistic forms and substances, that is, in our ability to speak different natural languages (see also Marigo 1938: comment 9, n. 23; Dragonetti 1961: 23).

Such a reading would be legitimated by various of Dante's assertions concerning our faculty to learn a mother tongue; this faculty is natural, it exists in all peoples despite their differences in word and accent, and is not associated with any specific language. It is a general faculty, possessed by humanity as a species, for 'only man is able to speak' (I, ii, 1). The ability to speak is thus a specific trait of human beings; one that is possessed by neither angels, nor beasts, nor demons. Speaking means an ability to externalize our particular thoughts; angels, by contrast, have an 'ineffable intellectual capacity': they either understand the thoughts of others, or they can read them in the divine mind. Animals lack individual feelings, possessing only 'specific' passions. Consequently each knows its own feelings and may recognize feelings when displayed by animals of the same species, having no need to understand the feelings of other species. Each demon immediately recognizes the depths of perfidy of another. (By the way, in the *Divine Comedy* Dante will decide to make his demons talk; they will still sometimes use a speech not quite human: the celebrated diabolical expression of *Inferno*, vii, 1, 'Pape Satan, pape Satan aleppe', is curiously reminiscent of another expression: 'Raphèl maí amècche zabì almi', *Inferno* xxxi, 67 – the

fatal words, spoken by Nimrod, which set off the catastrophe of Babel; even the devils thus speak the languages
of the confusion; cf. Hollander 1980.)

In contrast to these beings, however, humans are guided
by reason. In individuals, this takes the forms of discernment and judgement. Yet human beings also need some
further faculty which might allow them to externalize the
contents of this intellect in outward signs. Dante defines the
faculty for language as the disposition for humans to associate rational signifiers with signifieds perceived by the
senses, thus accepting the Aristotelian doctrine that the
relation between outward signs and both the corresponding
passions of the soul, and the things that they signify, is
conventional and *ad placitum*.

Dante made it very clear that while the linguistic faculty
is a permanent and immutable trait of the human species,
natural languages are historically subject to variation, and
are capable of developing over the course of time, enriching
themselves independently of the will of any single speaker.
Dante was no less aware that a natural language may be
enriched through the creativity of single individuals as well,
for the illustrious vernacular that he intended to shape was
to be the product of just such an individual creative effort.
Yet it seems that between the faculty of language and the
natural languages which are the ultimate result, Dante
wished to posit a further, intermediate stage. We can see
this better by looking at Dante's treatment of the story of
Adam.

Language and Linguistic Behaviour

In referring to his conception of the vernacular, in the
opening chapter of his treatise Dante uses terms such
as *vulgaris eloquentia*, *locutio vulgarium gentium* and
vulgaris locutio, while reserving the term *locutio secundaria* for grammar. We can probably take *eloquentia* as generically 'ability to speak fluently'. Nevertheless, the text

contains a series of distinctions, and these are probably not casual. In certain instances, Dante speaks of *locutio*, in others of *ydioma*, of *lingua* or of *loquela*. He uses the term *ydioma* whenever he refers to the Hebrew language (I, iv, 1; I, vi, 1; I, vi, 7) and when he expresses his notion of the branching off of the various languages of the world – the Romance languages in particular. In vi, 6–7, in speaking of the confusion after Babel, Dante uses the term *loquela*. In this same context, however, he uses *ydioma* for the languages of the confusion as well as for the Hebrew language which remained intact. He can speak of the *loquela* of the Genovese and of the Tuscans while, at the same time, using *lingua* both for Hebrew and for the Italian vernacular dialects. It thus seems that the terms *ydioma*, *lingua* and *loquela* are all to be understood as meaning a tongue or a given language in the modern, Saussurian sense of *langue*.

Often *locutio* is used in this sense too. When he wishes to say that, after the destruction of Babel, the workers on the tower began to speak imperfect languages, he writes: 'tanto rudius nunc barbariusque locuntur.' A few lines later, referring to the Hebrew language in its original state, he uses the phrase 'antiquissima locutione' (I, vi, 6–8).

Nevertheless, although *ydioma*, *lingua* and *loquela* are 'marked' forms (used only where *langue* in the Saussurian sense is meant), the term *locutio* seems to have another, more elastic sense. It is used whenever the context seems to suggest either the activity of speaking, or the functioning of the linguistic faculty. Dante often uses *locutio* to mean the act of speaking: for example, he says of animal sounds that they cannot be construed as *locutio*, meaning by this that they do not qualify as proper linguistic activity (I, ii, 6–7). Dante also uses *locutio* every time that Adam addresses God.

These distinctions are clearest in the passage (I, iv, 1) where Dante asks himself 'to what man was the faculty of speech [*locutio*] first given, and what he said at the beginning [*quod primus locutus fuerit*], and to whom, and where, and when, and in what language [*sub quo ydiomate*] were the first acts of linguistic behaviour [*primiloquium*] emitted?' I think I am justified here in giving *primiloquium* this sense of 'first linguistic behaviour' on the analogy of Dante's use of the terms *tristiloquium* and *turpiloquium* to characterize the evil way of speaking of the Romans and the Florentines.

The First Gift to Adam

In the pages which follow, Dante affirms that, in Genesis, it is written that the first to speak was Eve ('mulierem invenitur ante omnes fuisse locutam') when she talked with the serpent. It seemed to him 'troublesome not to imagine that an act so noble for the human race did not come from the lips of a man but rather from those of a woman'. If anything, of course, we know that it was God that first spoke in Genesis: he spoke to create the world. After that, when God made Adam give names to the animals, Adam presumably emitted sounds as well, though, curiously, the whole episode of the naming of things in Genesis 2:19 is ignored by Dante. Finally, Adam speaks to show his satisfaction at the appearance of Eve. Mengaldo (1979: 42) has suggested that, since, for Dante, speaking means to externalize the thoughts of our mind, speaking implies spoken dialogue. Thus, since the encounter of Eve and the serpent is the first instance of dialogue, it is, therefore, for Dante, the first *instance of linguistic behaviour*. This is an argument that accords well with Dante's choice here of the word *locutio*, whose ambiguous status we have just discussed. We are thus led to imagine that, for Dante, Adam's satisfaction with the creation of Eve would have been expressed in his heart, and that, in naming the animals, rather than speaking (in the usual sense of the word), Adam was laying down the rules of language, and thus performing a metalinguistic act.

In whatever case, Dante mentions Eve only to remark that it seemed to him more reasonable to suppose that Adam had really spoken first. While the first sound that humans let forth is the wail of pain at their birth, Dante thought that the first sound emitted by Adam could only have been an exclamation of joy which, at the same time, was an act of homage towards his creator. The first word that Adam uttered must therefore have been the name of God, *El* (attested in patristic tradition as the first Hebrew name of God). The argument here implies that Adam spoke to God before he named the animals, and that, consequently, God had already provided Adam with some sort of linguistic faculty before he had even constructed a language.

When Adam spoke to God, it was in response. Consequently, God must have spoken first. To speak, however, the Lord did not necessarily have to use a language. Dante is here appealing to the traditional reading of Psalm 148, in which the verses where 'Fire, and hail; snow, and vapour; stormy wind' all 'praise the name of the Lord', thus 'fulfilling his word', are taken to mean that God expresses himself naturally through creation. Dante, however, construes this passage in a very singular way, suggesting that God was able to move the air in such a way that it resonated to form true words. Why did Dante find it necessary to propose such a cumbersome and seemingly gratuitous reading? The answer seems to be that, as the first member of the only species that uses speech, Adam could only conceive ideas through hearing linguistic sounds. Moreover, as Dante also makes clear (I, v, 2), God wanted Adam to speak so that he might use the gift to glorify God's name.

Dante must then ask in what idiom Adam spoke. He criticizes those (the Florentines in particular) who always believe their native language to be the best. There are a great many native languages, Dante comments, and many of these are better than the Italian vernaculars. He then (I, vi, 4) affirms that, along with the first soul, God created a *certam formam locutionis*. Mengaldo wishes to translate this as 'a determined form of language' (Mengaldo 1979: 55). Such a translation, however, would not explain why Dante, shortly thereafter, states that 'It was therefore the

Hebrew language [*ydioma*] that the lips of the first speaker forged [*fabricarunt*]' (I, vi, 7).

It is true that Dante specifies that he is speaking here of a form 'in regard to the expressions which indicate things, as well as to the construction of these expressions and their grammatical endings', allowing the inference that, by *forma locutionis*, he wishes to refer to a lexicon and a morphology and, consequently, to a determined language. Nevertheless, translating *forma locutionis* as 'language' would render the next passage difficult to understand:

qua quidem forma omnis lingua loquentium uteretur, nisi culpa presumptionis humanae dissipata fuisset, ut inferius ostenderentur. Hac forma locutionis locutus est Adam: hac forma locutionis locuti sunt homines posteri ejus usque ad edificationem turris Babel, quae 'turris confusionis' interpretatur: hanc formam locutionis hereditati sunt filii Heber, qui ab eo sunt dicti Hebrei. Hiis solis post confusionem remansit, ut Redemptor noster, qui ex illis oritus erat secundum humanitatem, non lingua confusionis sed gratie frueretur. Fuit ergo hebraicum ydioma illud quod primi locuentis labia fabricarunt. (I, vi, 5)

On the one hand, if Dante wished to use *forma locutionis* here to refer to a given tongue, why, in observing that Jesus spoke Hebrew, does he once use *lingua* and once *ydioma* (and in recounting the story of the confusion – I, vii – he uses the term *loquela*) while *forma locutionis* is only used apropos of the divine gift? On the other hand, if we understand *forma locutionis* as a faculty of language innate in all humans, it is difficult to explain why the sinners of Babel are said to have lost it, since DVE repeatedly acknowledges the existence of languages born after Babel.

In the light of this, let me try to give the translation of the passage:

and it is precisely this *form* that all speakers would make use of in their *language* had it not been dismembered through the fault of human presumption, as I shall demonstrate below. By this *linguistic form* Adam spoke: by this *linguistic form* spoke all his descendants until the construction of the Tower of Babel – which is interpreted as the 'tower of confusion': this was the *linguistic form* that the sons of Eber, called Hebrews after him, inherited. It remained to them alone after the confusion, so that our Saviour, who because of the human side of his nature had to be born of them, could use a *language* not of confusion but of grace. It was thus the Hebrew *tongue* that was constructed by the first being *endowed with speech*.

In this way, the *forma locutionis* was neither the Hebrew language nor the general faculty of language, but a particular gift from God to Adam that was lost after Babel. It is the lost gift that Dante sought to recover through his theory of an illustrious vernacular.

Dante and Universal Grammar

One solution to the problem has been proposed by Maria Corti (1981: 46ff). It is, by now, generally accepted that we cannot regard Dante as simply an orthodox follower of the thought of St Thomas Aquinas. According to circumstances, Dante used a variety of philosophical and theological sources; it is furthermore well established that he was influenced by various strands of the so-called radical Aristotelianism whose major representative was Siger of Brabant. Another important figure in radical Aristotelianism was Boethius of Dacia, who, like Siger, suffered the condemnation of the Bishop of Paris in 1277. Boethius was a member of a group of grammarians called Modistae, and the author of a treatise, *De modis significandi*, which – according to Corti – influenced Dante, because Bologna was the focal point from which, either through a stay in the city, or through Florentine or Bolognese friends, such influences reached Dante.

The Modist grammarians asserted the existence of linguistic universals – that is, of rules underlying the formation of any natural language. This may help clarify precisely what Dante meant by *forma locutionis*. In his *De modis*, Boethius of Dacia observed that it was possible to extract from all existing languages the rules of a universal grammar, distinct from either Greek or Latin grammar (*Quaestio* 6). The 'speculative grammar' of the Modistae asserted a relation of *specular* correspondence between language, thought and the nature of things. For them, it was a given that the *modi intelligendi* and, consequently, the *modi significandi* reflected the *modi essendi* of things themselves.

What God gave Adam, therefore, was neither just the faculty of language nor yet a natural language; what he gave was, in fact, a set of principles for a universal grammar. These principles acted as the formal cause of language: 'the general structuring principle of language, as regards either the lexicon, or the morphological and syntactical components of the language that Adam would gradually forge by living and giving names' (Corti 1981: 47).

Maria Corti's thesis has been vehemently contested (cf., in particular, Pagani 1982; Maierù 1983). It has been objected that there is no clear proof that Dante even knew the work of Boethius of Dacia, that many of the analogies that Maria Corti tries to establish between Dante's text and Boethius cannot be sustained, and that, finally, many of the linguistic notions that one finds in Dante were already circulating in the works of philosophers even before the thirteenth century. Now, even if the first two objections are conceded, there still remains the third. That there were widespread discussions of the subject of universal grammar in medieval culture is something that no one, and certainly not Corti's critics, wishes to place in doubt. As Maierù puts it, it was not necessary to read Boethius to know that grammar has one and the same substance in all languages, even if there are variations on the surface, for this assertion is already found in Roger Bacon. Yet this, if anything, constitutes proof that it was possible that Dante could have been thinking about universal grammar when he wrote DVE. If this is so, he could have conceived of the *forma locutionis* given by God as a sort of innate mechanism, in the same terms as Chomsky's generative grammar, which, interestingly enough, was inspired by the rationalist ideals of Descartes and sixteenth-century grammarians who, in their turn, had rediscovered the ideas of the medieval Modistae.

Yet if this is all there is to it, what is the point of the story of Babel? It seems most likely that Dante believed that, at Babel, there had disappeared the perfect *forma locutionis* whose principles permitted the creation of languages capable of reflecting the true essence of things; languages, in other words, in which the *modi essendi* of things were identical with the *modi significandi*. The Hebrew of Eden was the perfect and unrepeatable example of such a language. What was left after Babel? All that remained were shattered, imperfect *formae locutionis*, imperfect as the various vulgar Italian dialects whose defects and whose incapacity to express grand and profound thoughts Dante pitilessly analysed.

The Illustrious Vernacular

Now we can begin to understand the nature of the *illustre* vernacular that Dante hunts like a perfumed panther (I, xvi, 1). We catch glimpses of it, evanescent, in the works of the poets that Dante considers the most important; but the language still remains unformed and unregulated, its grammatical principles unarticulated. Confronted with the existing vernaculars, natural but not universal languages, and with a grammar that was universal but artificial, Dante sought to establish his dream of the restoration of the natural and universal *forma locutionis* of Eden. Yet unlike those in the Renaissance who wished to restore the Hebrew language itself to its original magic and divinatory power, Dante's goal was to reinstate these original conditions in a modern invention: an illustrious vernacular, of which his own poetry would constitute the most notable achievement, was, to Dante, the only way in which a modern poet might heal the wound of Babel. The entire second part of DVE is therefore to be understood not as a mere treatise of style, but as an effort to fix the conditions, rules, *forma locutionis* of the only conceivable perfect language – the Italian of the poetry of Dante (Corti 1981: 70). The illustrious vernacular would take from the perfect language its *necessity* (as opposed to conventionality) because, just as the perfect *forma locutionis* permitted Adam to speak with God, so the illustrious vernacular would permit the poet to make his words adequate to express what he wished, and what could not be expressed otherwise.

Out of this bold conception for the restoration of a perfect language, and of his own role within it, comes a celebration of the quasi-biological force displayed by language's capacity to change and renew itself over time instead of a lament over the multiplicity of tongues. The assertion of language's creativity, after all, stands at the base of Dante's own project to create a perfect, modern, natural language, without recourse to a dead language as a model. For someone of Dante's temperament, a conviction that the Hebrew of Adam was the one truly perfect language could only have resulted in the learning of Hebrew and in the composition of his poem in that idiom. That Dante did not decide to learn Hebrew shows that he was convinced that the vernacular he intended to invent would correspond to the principles of the universal, God-given form better even than the Hebrew spoken by Adam himself. Thus Dante puts forth his own candidacy as a new (and more perfect) Adam.

Dante and Abulafia

If we turn from DVE to *Paradise*, xxvi (several years having passed in the meantime), we find that Dante has changed his mind. In the earlier work, Dante unambiguously states that it was from the *forma locutionis* given by God that the perfect language of Hebrew was born, and that it was in

this perfect language that Adam addressed God, calling him
El. In *Paradise*, xxvi, 124–38, however, Adam says:

> La lingua ch'io parlai fu tutta spenta
> innanzi che all'ovra incomsummabile
> fosse la gente di Nembròt attenta:
> ché nullo effetto mai razïonabile,
> per lo piacer uman che rinovella
> seguendo il cielo, sempre fu durabile.
> Opera naturale è ch'uom favella,
> ma, così o così, natura lascia,
> poi fare a voi, secondo che v'abbella.
> Pria ch'i' scendessi all'infernale ambascia
> *I* s'appellava in terra il sommo bene,
> onde vien letizia che mi fascia;
> e *EL* si chiamò poi: e ciò convene,
> ché l'uso dei mortali è come fronda
> in ramo, che sen va e altra vene.

The language that I spoke was entirely extinguished before the
uncompletable work [the tower of Babel] of the people of Nem-
brot was even conceived: because no product of the human
reason, from the human taste for always having something new,
following the influence of the stars, is ever stable. It is natural
that man speaks; but whether this way or that, nature lets you
yourselves do as it pleases you. Before I descended into the pains
of Hell, on earth the Highest Good was called *I* – from whence
comes the light of joy that enfolds me; the name then became *EL*:
and this change was proper, because the customs of mortals are
like the leaves on a branch, one goes and another comes.

Born of humanity's natural disposition towards speech,
languages may split, grow and change through human
intervention. According to Adam, the Hebrew spoken before the building of the tower, when God was named *El*,
was not the same as the Hebrew spoken in the earthly
paradise, when Adam called him *I*.

Dante seems here to oscillate between Genesis 10 and
Genesis 11. He must always have known these two texts;
what could have induced him to modify his earlier views?
An intriguing clue is the strange idea that God had once

been called *I*, a term that not one of Dante's legion of commentators has ever been able to explain satisfactorily.

Returning for a moment to the last chapter, we remember that for Abulafia, the atomic elements of any text – the letters – had individual meanings of their own. Thus, in the divine name YHWH, the letter *Yod* was itself a divine name. Dante would have transliterated *Yod* as *I*, and this gives one possible source for his change of opinion. If this is so, it would not be the only idea that Dante seems to have had in common with Abulafia.

We saw in the last chapter that for Abulafia the Torah had to be equated with the active intellect, and the scheme from which God created the world was the same as the gift which he gave to Adam – a linguistic matrix, not yet Hebrew, yet capable of generating all other languages. There were Averroist influences on Abulafia that led him to believe in a single active intellect common to the entire human species. There were demonstrable and undoubted Averroist sympathies in Dante too, especially in his version of the Avicennist and Augustinian concept of the active intellect (equated with divine wisdom) which offers the forms to possible intellect (cf., in particular, Nardi 1942: v). Nor were the Modistae and the others who supported the idea of universal grammar exempt from Averroist influence. Thus there existed a common philosophical ground which, even without positing direct links, would have inclined both Dante and Abulafia to regard the gift of language as the bestowal of a *forma locutionis*, defined as a generative linguistic matrix with affinities to the active intellect.

There are further parallels as well. For Abulafia, Hebrew was the historic proto-language. It was a proto-language, however, that, during their exile, the chosen people had forgotten. By the time of the confusion of Babel, therefore, the language of Adam was, as Dante puts it, 'tutta spenta' (entirely extinguished). Idel (1989: 17) cites an unedited manuscript by a disciple of Abulafia which says:

Anyone who believes in the creation of the world, if he believes that languages are conventional he must also believe that they are of two types: the first is Divine, i.e., agreement between God and Adam, and the second is natural, i.e., based upon agreement between Adam, Eve and their children. The second is derived from the first, and the first was known only to Adam and was not passed on to any of his offspring except for Seth, [. . .] And so, the traditions reached Noah. And the confusion of the tongues during the generation of the dispersion [at the tower of Babel] occurred only to the second type of language, i.e., to natural language.

If we remember that, in such a context, the term 'tradition' can refer to the kabbala itself, it seems evident that the above passage alludes, once again, to a linguistic wisdom, a *forma locutionis*, regarded as a set of rules for constructing the differing languages. If, in its original form, this wisdom was not a language, but rather a universal matrix for all languages, we can not only explain the mutation of Hebrew between Eden and Babel, but also understand the hope that this original wisdom might somehow be recuperated and (in different ways, obviously, for Abulafia and Dante) even be made to bloom again.

Yet could Dante have known the theories of Abulafia?

Abulafia visited Italy on several occasions: he was in Rome in 1260; he remained on the peninsula until 1271, when he returned to Barcelona; he returned to Rome in 1280 with the project of converting the pope. He journeyed afterwards to Sicily, where we lose trace of him somewhere near the end of the 1290s. His ideas incontestably exercised an influence on contemporary Italian Jewish thought. We have a record of a debate in 1290 between Hillel of Verona (who had probably met Abulafia twenty years earlier) and Zerakhya of Barcelona, who arrived in Italy at the beginning of the 1270s (cf. Genot-Bismuth 1988: II).

Hillel, who had contacts in the world of Bologna intellectuals, had written to Zerakhya to ask him the question first posed by Herodotus: in what language would a child speak if it were brought up with no linguistic stimuli? Hillel maintained that such a child would naturally speak Hebrew, because Hebrew was humanity's original natural language. Hillel either did not know, or else disregarded, the fact that Abulafia was of a different opinion. Not so with Zerakhya. He sarcastically remarked that Hillel had been taken in by the siren song of the 'uncircumcised' of Bologna. The first sounds emitted by a child without linguistic education, he asserted, would resemble the barking of dogs. It was madness to maintain that the sacred language could be naturally bestowed on human beings.

Humanity possessed a linguistic potential, but it was a potential that could be activated only through the education of the vocal organs. This, however, required instruction. At this point, Zerakhya brought forward a proof that we shall find in a number of post-Renaissance Christian authors (for example, in the *In Biblia polyglotta prolegomena* by Walton in 1673, or the *De sacra philosophia* of 1652 by Vallesio): had there been the primordial gift of an original sacred language, then all human beings, regardless of their native tongue, would have the innate ability to speak it.

The existence of such a debate is enough to show, without needing to invent a meeting between Dante and Abulafia, that Abulafia's ideas were subject to discussion in Italy, especially in the Bolognese intellectual circles which influenced Dante, and from which, according to Maria Corti, he absorbed his notion of the *forma locutionis*. Nor does the Bologna debate constitute the only point of encounter between Dante and Jewish thought.

Genot-Bismuth has given us a vivid picture of the close of the thirteenth century in which we will later find a Yehuda Romano giving a series of lectures on the *Divine Comedy* for his co-religionists, a Lionello di Ser Daniele who did likewise using a *Divine Comedy* transliterated into Hebrew script, not to mention the surprising personage of Immanuel da Roma, who, in his own poetic compositions, seemed to launch an attack on Dante's ideals almost aspiring to produce a sort of counter-*Comedy* in Hebrew.

Naturally this only establishes the influence of Dante on Italian Jewish culture, not the other way around. Yet Genot-Bismuth is able to show opposing influences as well, even to the point of suggesting that Dante's theory of the four senses of scripture, found in his *Epistula*, XIII (cf. Eco 1985), had a Jewish origin. Such a hypothesis may be too bold: there were any number of Christian sources from which Dante might have drawn this doctrine. What seems less daring, and, in fact, entirely plausible, is the suggestion that, in Bologna, Dante would have heard echoes of the debate between Hillel and Zerakhya. One could say that in DVE he appears still close to the position of the former (or of his Christian inspirers, as Zerakhya reproaches him), while in *Paradise* he turns towards the positions of the latter, that is, the position of Abulafia (even though, when writing DVE, he already had the opportunity to know both theses).

However, it is not necessary to document direct links (even though Genot-Bismuth finds the presence of Jewish influences in certain passages of the *De regimine principium* of Giles of Rome), but rather to demonstrate the existence of an intellectual climate in which ideas could circulate and within which a formal and informal debate between the church and the synagogue might ensue (cf. Calimani 1987: viii). We should remember that, before the Renaissance, a Christian thinker would scarcely wish to admit publicly that he drew on Hebrew doctrine. Like heretics, the Jewish community belonged to a category of outcasts that – as Le Goff shrewdly observes – the Middle Ages officially despised but at the same time admired; regarding them with an admixture of attraction and fear, keeping them at a distance, but making sure that the distance was fixed near enough so they would always remain close at hand. 'What was termed charity in their regard more resembled the game that cats play with mice' (Le Goff 1964: 373).

Before the kabbala was rehabilitated by humanist culture, Christianity knew little of it. It was often simply regarded as a branch of the black arts. Even so, as Gorni has pointed out (1990: vii), in the *Divine Comedy*, Dante seems to share a great deal of knowledge about magic and divinatory practices (astrology, chiromancy, physiognomy, geomancy, pyromancy, hydromancy and, not least, the black arts of magic themselves). In one way or another, Dante seems to have been informed about an excluded and underground culture in which, at least according to vulgar opinion, the kabbala somehow belonged.

In this way, it becomes ever more plausible that, even if it does not derive directly from the theories of the Modistae, Dante's *forma locutionis* is not a language but the universal matrix for all language.

4

The Ars Magna of Raymond Lull

A near contemporary of Dante, Ramón Llull (Latinized as Lullus and Anglicized as Lull – and sometimes as Lully) was a Catalan, born in Majorca, who lived probably between 1232 (or 1235) and 1316. Majorca during this period was a crossroads, an island where Christian, Jewish and Arab cultures all met; each was to play a role in Lull's development. Most of his 280 known works were written initially in Arabic or Catalan (cf. Ottaviano 1930). Lull led a care-free early life which ended when he suffered a mystic crisis. As a result, he entered the order of Tertian friars.

It was among the Franciscans that all of the earlier strands converged in his *Ars magna*, which Lull conceived as a system for a perfect language with which to convert the infidels. The language was to be a universal; it was to be articulated at the level of expression in a universal mathematics of combination; its level of content was to consist of a network of universal ideas, held by all peoples, which Lull himself would devise.

St Francis had already sought to convert the sultan of Babylonia, and the dream of establishing universal concordance between differing races was becoming a recurrent theme in Franciscan thought. Another of Lull's contemporaries, the Franciscan Roger Bacon, foresaw that contact with the infidels (not merely Arabs, but also Tartars) would require study of foreign languages. The problem for him, however, was not that of inventing a new, perfect language, but of learning the languages that the infidels already spoke in order to convert them, or, failing that, at least to enrich western Christian culture with a wisdom that the infidels had wrongfully appropriated ('tamquam ab iniustis possessoribus'). The aims and methods of Lull and Bacon were different; yet both were inspired by ideals of universality and of a new universal crusade based on peaceful dialogue rather than on arms. In this utopia the question of language played a crucial role (cf. Alessio 1957). According to legend, Lull was to die martyred at the hands of the Saracens, to whom he had appeared, armed with his art, believing it to be an infallible means of persuasion.

Lull was the first European philosopher to write doctrinal works in the vulgar tongue. Some are even in popular verses, so as to reach readers who knew neither Latin nor Arabic: 'per tal che hom puscha mostrar / logicar e philosophar / a cels que nin saben lati / ni arabichi' (*Compendium*, 6–9). His art was universal not merely in that it was designed to serve all peoples, but also in that it used letters and figures in a way (allegedly) comprehensible even to illiterates of any language.

The Elements of the *Ars Combinatoria*

Given a number of different elements n, the number of arrangements that can be made from them, in any order whatever, is expressed by their factorial $n!$, calculated as $1*2*3. \ldots *n$. This is the method for calculating the possible anagrams of a word of n letters, already encountered as the art of *temurah* in the kabbala. The *Sefer Yezirah* informed us that the factorial of 5 was 120. As n increases, the number of possible arrangements rises exponentially: the possible arrangements for 36 elements, for example, are 371,993,326,789,901,217,467,999,448,150, 835,200,000,000.

If the strings admit repetitions, then those figures grow

upwards. For example, the 21 letters of the Italian alphabet can give rise to more than 51 billion billion 21-letter-long sequences (each different from the rest); when, however, it is admitted that some letters are repeated, but the sequences are shorter than the number of elements to be arranged, then the general formula for n elements taken t at a time with repetitions is n^t and the number of strings obtainable for the letters of the Italian alphabet would amount to 5 billion billion billion.

Let us suppose a different problem. There are four people, A, B, C and D. We want to arrange these four as couples on board an aircraft in which the seats are in rows that are two across; the order is relevant because I want to know who will sit at the window and who at the aisle. We are thus facing a problem of *permutation*, that is, of arranging n elements, taken t at a time, taking the order into account. The formula for finding all the possible permutations is $n!/(n-t)!$ In our example the persons can be disposed this way:

$$AB \ AC \ AD \ BA \ CA \ DA \ BC \ BD \ CD \ CB \ DB \ DC$$

Suppose, however, that the four letters represented four soldiers, and the problem is to calculate how many two-man patrols could be formed from them. In this case the order is irrelevant (AB or BA are always the same patrol). This is a problem of *combination*, and we solve it with the following formula: $n!/t!(n-t)!$ In this case the possible combinations would be:

$$AB \quad AC \quad AD \quad BC \quad BD \quad CD$$

Such calculuses are employed in the solution of many technical problems, but they can serve as discovery procedures, that is, procedures for inventing a variety of possible 'scenarios'. In semiotic terms, we are in front of an *expression-system* (represented both by the symbols and by the syntactic rules establishing how n elements can be arranged *t* at a time – and where *t* can coincide with *n*), so that the arrangement of the expression-items can automatically reveal possible *content-systems*.

In order to let this logic of combination or permutation work to its fullest extent, however, there should be no restrictions limiting the number of possible content-systems (or worlds) we can conceive of. As soon as we maintain that certain universes are not possible in respect of what is given in our own past experience, or that they do not correspond to what we hold to be the laws of reason, we are, at this point, invoking external criteria not only to discriminate the results of the *ars combinatoria*, but also to introduce restrictions within the art itself.

We saw, for example, that, for four people, there were six possible combinations of pairs. If we specify that the pairing is of a matrimonial nature, and if A and B are men while C and D are women, then the possible combinations become four. If A and C are brother and sister, and we take into account the prohibition against incest, we have only three possible groupings. Yet matters such as sex, consanguinity, taboos and interdictions have nothing to do with the art itself: they are introduced from outside in order to control and limit the possibilities of the system.

The Alphabet and the Four Figures[1]

The *ars combinatoria* of Lull employs an alphabet of nine letters – B to K, leaving out J – and four figures (see figure 4.1). In a *tabula generalis* that appears in several of his works, Lull set out a table of six groups of nine entities, one for each of the nine letters. The first group are the nine absolute principles, or divine dignities, which communicate their natures to each other and spread through creation. After this, there are nine relative principles, nine types of question, nine subjects, nine virtues and nine vices. Lull specifies (and this is an obvious reference to Aristotle's list of categories) that the nine dignities are subjects of

TABULA GENERALIS

	PRINCIPIA ABSOLUTA	PRINCIPIA RELATIVA	QUESTIONES	SUBJECTA	VIRTUTES	VITIA
B	Bonitas	Differentia	Utrum?	Deus	Iustitia	Avaritia
C	Magnitudo	Concordantia	Quid?	Angelus	Prudentia	Gula
D	Aeternitas	Contrarietas	De quo?	Coelum	Fortitudo	Luxuria
E	Potestas	Principium	Quare?	Homo	Temperantia	Superbia
F	Sapientia	Medium	Quantum	Imaginatio	Fides	Acidia
G	Voluntas	Finis	Quale?	Sensitiva	Spes	Invidia
H	Virtus	Majoritas	Quando?	Vegetativa	Charitas	Ira
I	Veritas	Aequalitas	Ubi?	Elementativa	Patientia	Mendacium
K	Gloria	Minoritas	Quomodo? Cum quo?	Instrumentativa	Pietas	Inconstantia

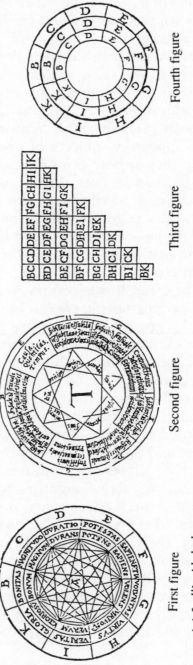

First figure Second figure Third figure Fourth figure

Figure 4.1 Lull's Alphabet

predication, while the other five series are predicates. We shall see that subject and predicate are sometimes allowed to exchange their roles, while in other cases variations of order are not considered as pertinent.

First figure. This traces all the possible combinations between the dignities, thus allowing predications such as 'Goodness [*bonitas*] is great', 'Greatness [*magnitudo*] is glorious', etc. Since the dignities are treated as nouns when they appear as subjects of predications, and as adjectives when they appear as a predicate, the lines connecting them can be read in both directions. The line connecting *magnitudo* and *bonitas* can, for example, be read as both 'Greatness is good' and 'Goodness is great.' This explains why 36 lines produce 72 combinations.

The first figure is designed to allow regular syllogisms to be inferred. To demonstrate, for example, that goodness can be great, it is necessary to argue that 'all that is magnified by greatness is great – but goodness is what is magnified by greatness – therefore goodness is great.' The first table excludes self-predications, like BB or CC, because, for Lull, there is no possibility of a middle term in an expression of the type 'Goodness is good' (in Aristotelian logic, 'all As are B – C is an A – therefore, C is a B' is a valid syllogism because, following certain rules, the middle term A is so disposed as to act as the, as it were, bond between B and C).

Second figure. This serves to connect the relative principles with triples of definitions. They are the relations connecting the divine dignities with the cosmos. Since it is intended merely as a visual mnemonic that helps to fix in the mind the various relations between different types of entity, there is no method of combination associated with the second figure. For example, difference, concordance and opposition (*contrarietas*) can each be considered in reference to (1) two sensible entities, such as a plant and a stone, (2) a sensible and an intellectual entity, like body and soul, and (3) two intellectual entities, like the soul and an angel.

Third figure. Here Lull displayed all possible letter pairings. The figure contains 36 pairs inserted in what Lull calls the 36 *chambers*. The figure makes it seem that he intended to exclude inversions. Yet, in reality, the figure does contemplate inversions in order, and thus the number of chambers is virtually 72 since each letter is permitted to function as either subject or predicate ('Goodness is great' also gives 'Greatness is good': *Ars magna*, VI, 2). Having established the combinations, Lull proceeds to what he calls the 'evacuation of the chambers'. Taking, for example, chamber BC, we read it first according to the first figure, obtaining goodness and greatness (*bonitas* and *magnitudo*); then according to the second figure, obtaining difference and concordance (*differentia* and *concordantia*: *Ars magna*, II, 3). From these two pairs we derive 12 propositions: 'Goodness is great', 'Difference is great', 'Goodness is different', 'Difference is good', 'Goodness is concordant', 'Difference is concordant', 'Greatness is good', 'Concordance is good', 'Greatness is different', 'Concordance is different', 'Greatness is concordant', and 'Concordance is great.'

Going back to the *tabula generalis* in figure 4.1, we find that, under the next heading, *Questiones*, B and C are *utrum* (whether) and *quid* (what). By combining these 2 questions with the 12 propositions we have just constructed, we obtain 24 questions, like 'Whether goodness is great?', or 'What is a great goodness?' (see *Ars magna*, VI, 1). In this way, the third figure generates 432 propositions and 864 questions – at least in theory. In reality, there are 10 additional rules to be considered (given in *Ars magna*, iv). For the chamber BC, for example, there are the rules B and C. These rules depend on the theological definition of the terms, and on certain argumentative constraints which have nothing to do with the rules of combination.

Fourth figure. This is the most famous of the figures, and the one destined to have the greatest influence on subsequent tradition. In this figure, triples generated by the nine elements are considered. In contrast to the preceding figures, which are simply static diagrams, the fourth figure is *mobile*. It is a mechanism formed by three concentric

The Ars Magna of Raymond Lull

circles, of decreasing size, inserted into each other, and held together usually by a knotted cord. If we recall that in the *Sefer Yezirah* the combination of the letters was visually represented by a wheel or a spinning disc, it seems probable that Lull, a native of Majorca, has been influenced here by the kabbalistic tradition that flourished in his time in the Iberian peninsula.

Taken in groups of 3, 9 elements generate 84 combinations – BCD, BCE, CDE, etc. If, in his *Ars breu* and elsewhere, Lull sometimes speaks of 252 (84*3) combinations, it is because to each triple can be assigned three questions, one for each of the letters of the triple (see also the Jesuit Athanasius Kircher, *Ars magna sciendi*, p. 14). Each triple further generates a column of 20 combinations (giving a table of 20 rows by 84 columns) because Lull transforms the triples into quadruples by inserting the letter T. In this way, he obtains combinations like BCDT, BCTB, BTBC, etc. (see examples in figure 4.2).

The letter T, however, plays no role in the art; it is rather a mnemonic artifice. It signifies that the letters that precede it are to be read as dignities from the first figure, while those that follow it are to be read as relative principles as defined in the second figure. Thus, to give an example, the

```
b dk t   beft   begt   beht   befr   bekt   b fgt   bfhd   b ift   b fkt   bght   b git
bd tb    betb   betb   betb   betb   betb   bftb    bftb   bftb    bftb    bgtb   bgtb
bdtd     bete   bete   bete   bete   bete   b ft f  bft,f  bft f   bft f   bgtg   bgtg
bdtk     betf   betg   beth   beti   betk   bftg    bfth   bfti    bftk    bgth   bgti
bktb     bftb   bgtb   bhtb   bitb   bktb   bgtb    bhth   bitb    bktb    bhtb   b itg
bktd     bfte   bgte   bhte   bi te  bkte   bgtf    bhtf   biif    bktf    bhtg   bitg
bktk     bft f  bgtg   bhth   biti   bktk   bgtg    bhth   biti    bkuk    bhth   biti
brbd     brbe   brbe   brbe   brbe   brbe   brbf    brbf   brbf    brbf    brbg   brbg
brbk     brbf   brtg   brbh   brbi   brbk   brbg    brbh   brbi    brbk    brbh   brbi
brdk     bref   bertg  breh   brei   brek   brfg    brfh   brfi    brfk    brgh   brgi
dktb     eftb   egtb   ehtb   eitb   ektb   fgtb    fhtb   fitb    fktb    ghtb   g itb
dktd     efte   egte   ehte   eite   ekte   fgtf    fhtf   fitf    tktf    ghtg   gitg
dktk     eftf   egtg   ehth   eiti   ektk   fgtg    fhth   fiti    fktk    ghth   giti
dtbd     etbe   etbe   etbe   etbe   etbe   ftbf    ftbf   ftbf    ftbf    gtbg   gtbg
dtbk     etbf   etbg   etbh   etbi   etbk   ftbg    ftbh   ftbi    ftbk    gtbh   gtbi
dtdk     etef   eteg   eteh   etei   etek   ftfg    ftfh   ftfi    ftfk    gtgh   gtgi
krbd     frtbe  gtbe   htbe   itbe   ktbe   gtbf    htbf   itbf    ktbf    htbg   itbg
krbk     frbf   grbg   htbh   itbi   ktbk   gtbg    htbh   itbi    ktbk    htbh   itbi
krdk     frtef  grteg  htch   itci   ktck   gtfg    htfh   itfi    ktfk    htgh   itgi
tbdk     fbef   tbeg   tbch   tbei   tbek   tbfg    tbfh   tbfi    tbgk    tbgh   ibgi
```

Figure 4.2 A page of combinations from the Strasbourg edition, 1598

quadruple BCTC must be read: B (= goodness) + C (= greatness) and therefore (switching to the second figure) C (= concordance).

Looking at the *tabula generalis*, we further notice that combinations with an initial B take the question *utrum*, those with an initial C take *quid*, etc. This produces from BCTC the following reading: 'Whether goodness is great inasmuch as it contains in itself concordant things.'

This produces a series of quadruples which seem, at first sight, embarrassing: the series contains repetitions. Had repetitions been permissible, there would have been 729 triples instead of 84. The best solution to the mystery of these repetitions is that of Platzeck (1953–4: 141). He points out that, since, depending on whether it precedes or follows the T, a letter can signify either a dignity or a relation, each letter has, in effect, two values. Thus – given the sequence BCTB – it should be read as BCb. The letters in upper case would be read as dignities, and the one in lower case as a relation. It follows that, in his 84 columns, Lull was not really listing the combinations for three letters but for six. Six different elements taken three at a time give 20 permutations, exactly as many as appear in each column.

The 84 columns of 20 quadruples each yield 1,680 permutations. This is a figure obtained by excluding inversions of order.

At this point, however, a new question arises. Given that all these 1,680 quadruples can express a propositional content, do they all stand for 1,680 valid arguments as well? Not at all, for not every sequence generated by the art is syllogistically valid. Kircher, in his *Ars magna sciendi*, suggests that one must deal with the resulting sequences as if they were anagrams: one starts by forming a complete list of all the possible arrangements of the letters of a particular word, then discards those that do not correspond to other existing words. The letters of the Latin word ROMA, for example, can be combined in 24 different orders: certain sequences form acceptable Latin words, such as AMOR,

MORA, ARMO, RAMO; others, however, such as AOMR, OAMR, MRAO, are nonsense, and are, as it were, thrown away.

Lull's own practice seems to suppose such a criterion. He says, for example, in his *Ars magna, secunda pars principalis*, that in employing the first figure, it is always possible to reverse subject and predicate ('Goodness is great'/'Greatness is good'). It would not, however, be possible to reverse *goodness* and *angel*, for while *angel* participates in *goodness*, *goodness* does not participate in *angel*, since there are beings other than angels which are good. In other words, *angel* entails *goodness* but not vice versa. Lull also adds that the combination 'Greed is good' is inherently unacceptable as well. Whoever wishes to cultivate the art, Lull says, must be able to know what is convertible and what is not.

It follows that Lull's art is not only limited by formal requirements (since it can generate a discovery only if one finds a middle term for the syllogism); it is even more severely limited because the inferences are regulated not by formal rules but rather by the ontological possibility that something can be truly predicated of something else. The formal rules of the syllogism would allow such arguments as 'Greed is different from goodness – God is greedy – Therefore God is different from goodness.' Yet Lull would discard both the premises and the conclusion as false. The art equally allows the formulation of the premise 'Every law is enduring', but Lull rejects this as well because 'when an injury strikes a subject, justice and law are corrupted' (*Ars brevis, quae est de inventione mediorum iuris*, 4.3a). Given a proposition, Lull accepts or rejects its logical conversion, without regard to its formal correctness (cf. Johnston 1987: 229).

Nor is this all. The quadruples derived from the fourth figure appear in the columns more than once. In *Ars magna* the quadruple BCTB, for example, figures seven times in each of the first seven columns. In V, 1, it is interpreted as 'Whether there exists some goodness so great that it is different', while in XI, 1, applying the rule of logical obversion, it is read as 'Whether goodness can be great without being different' – obviously eliciting a positive response in the first case and a negative one in the second. Yet these reappearances of the same argumentative scheme, to be endowed with different semantic contents, do not bother Lull. On the contrary, he assumes that the same question can be solved either by any of the quadruples from a particular column that generates it, or from any of the other columns!

Such a feature, which Lull takes as one of the virtues of his art, represents in fact its second severe limitation. The 1,680 quadruples do not generate fresh questions, nor do they furnish new proofs. They generate instead standard answers to an already established set of questions. In principle, the art only furnishes 1,680 different ways of answering a single question whose answer is already known. It cannot, in consequence, really be considered a logical instrument at all. It is, in reality, a sort of dialectical thesaurus, a mnemonic aid for finding out an array of standard arguments able to demonstrate an already known truth. As a consequence, any of the 1,680 quadruples, if judiciously interpreted, can yield up the correct answer to the question for which it is adapted.

See, for instance, the question 'Whether the world is eternal' ('Utrum mundus sit aeternus'). Lull already knew the answer: negative, because anyone who thought the world eternal would fall into the Averroist error. Note, however, that the question cannot be generated directly by the art itself; for there is no letter corresponding to *world*. The question is thus external to the art. In the art, however, there does appear a term for *eternity*, that is, D; this provides a starting point. In the second figure, D is tied to the relative principle *contrarietas* or opposition, as manifested in the opposition of the sensible to the sensible, of the intellectual to the sensible, and of the intellectual to the intellectual. The same second figure also shows that D forms a triangle with B and C. The question also began with *utrum*, which appears at B under the heading *Questiones* in the *tabula generalis*. This constitutes a hint that the solution needs to be sought in the column in which appear B, C and D.

Lull says that 'the solution to such a question must be found in the first column of the table'; however, he immediately adds that, naturally, 'it could be found in other columns as well, as they are all bound to each other.' At this point, everything depends on definitions, rules, and a certain rhetorical legerdemain in interpreting the letters. Working from the chamber BCDT (and assuming as a premise that goodness is so great as to be eternal), Lull deduces that if the world were eternal, it would also be eternally good, and, consequently, there would be no evil. 'But', he remarks, 'evil does exist in the world as we know by experience. Consequently we must conclude that the world is not eternal.' This negative conclusion, however, is not derived from the logical form of the quadruple (which has, in effect, no real logical form at all), but is merely based on an observation drawn from experience. The art may have been conceived as the instrument to use universal reason to show the Averroist Muslims the error of their ways; but it is clear that unless they already shared with Lull the 'rational' conviction that the world cannot be eternal, they are not going to be persuaded by the art.

The *Arbor Scientarium*

The Lullian art was destined to seduce later generations who imagined that they had found in it a mechanism to explore the numberless possible connections between dignities and principles, principles and questions, questions and virtues or vices. Why not even construct a blasphemous combination stating that goodness implies an evil God, or eternity a different envy? Such a free and uncontrolled working of combinations and permutations would be able to produce any theology whatsoever. Yet the principles of faith, and the belief in a well-ordered cosmos, demanded that such forms of combinatorial incontinence be kept repressed.

Lull's logic is a logic of first, rather than second, intentions; that is, it is a logic of our immediate apprehension of things rather than of our conceptions of them. Lull repeats in various places that if metaphysics considers things as they exist outside our minds, and if logic treats them in their mental being, the art can treat them from both points of view. Consequently, the art could lead to more secure conclusions than logic alone, 'and for this reason the artist of this art can learn more in a month than a logician can in a year' (*Ars magna*, X, 101). What this audacious claim reveals, however, is that, contrary to what some later supposed, Lull's art is not really a formal method.

The art must reflect the natural movement of reality; it is therefore based on a notion of truth that is neither defined in the terms of the art itself, nor derived from it logically. It must be a conception that simply reflects things as they actually are. Lull was a realist, believing in the existence of universals outside the mind. Not only did he accept the real existence of genera and species, he believed in the objective existence of accidental forms as well. Thus Lull could manipulate not only genera and species, but also virtues, vices and every other sort of *differentia* as well; at the same time, however, all those substances and accidents could not be freely combined because their connections were determined by a rigid hierarchy of beings (cf. Rossi 1960: 68).

In his *Dissertatio de arte combinatoria* of 1666, Leibniz wondered why Lull had limited himself to a restricted number of elements. In many of his works, Lull had, in truth, also proposed systems based on 10, 16, 12 or 20 elements, finally settling on 9. But the real question ought to be not why Lull fixed upon this or that number, but why the number of elements should be fixed at all. In respect of Lull's own intentions, however, the question is beside the point; Lull never considered his to be an art where the combination of the elements of expression was free rather than precisely bound in content. Had it not been so, the art would not have appeared to Lull as a perfect language, capable of illustrating a divine reality which he assumed from the outset as self-evident and revealed. The art was the instrument to convert the infidels, and Lull had devoted years to the study of the doctrines of the Jews and Arabs. In his *Compendium artis demonstrativae* ('*De fine hujus libri*') Lull was quite explicit: he had borrowed his terms from the Arabs. Lull was searching for a set of elementary and primary notions that Christians held in common with the infidels. This explains, incidentally, why the number of absolute principles is reduced to nine (the tenth principle, the missing letter A, being excluded from the system, as it represented perfection or divine unity). One is tempted to see in Lull's series the ten Sefirot of the kabbala, but Plazteck observes (1953–4: 583) that a similar list of dignities is to be found in the Koran. Yates (1960) identified the thought of John Scot Erigene as a direct source, but Lull might have discovered analogous lists in various other medieval Neo-Platonic texts – the commentaries of pseudo-Dionysius, the Augustinian tradition, or the medieval doctrine of the transcendental properties of being (cf. Eco 1956). The elements of the art are nine (plus one) because Lull thought that the transcendental entities recognized by every monotheistic theology were ten.

Lull took these elementary principles and inserted them into a system which was already closed and defined, a system, in fact, which was rigidly hierarchical – the system of the Tree of Science. To put this in other terms, according to the rules of Aristotelian logic, the syllogism 'all flowers are vegetables, X is a flower, therefore X is a vegetable' is valid as a piece of formal reasoning independent of the actual nature of X. For Lull, it mattered very much whether X was a rose or a horse. If X were a horse, the argument must be rejected, since it is not true that a horse is a vegetable. The example is perhaps a bit crude; nevertheless, it captures very well the idea of the great chain of being (cf.

Lovejoy 1936) upon which Lull based his *Arbor scientiae* (1296).

Between the first and last versions of his art, Lull's thought underwent a long process of evolution (described by Carreras y Artau and Carreras y Artau 1939: I, 394), in order to render his art able to deal not only with theology and metaphysics, but also with cosmology, law, medicine, astronomy, geometry and psychology. Increasingly, the art became a means of treating the entire range of knowledge, drawing suggestions from the numerous medieval encyclopedias, and anticipating the encyclopedic dreams of the Renaissance and the baroque. All this knowledge, however, needed to be ordered hierarchically. Because they were determinations of the first cause, the dignities could be defined circularly, in reference to themselves; beyond the dignities, however, began the ladder of being. The art was designed to permit a process of reasoning at every step.

The roots of the Tree of Science were the nine dignities and the nine relations. From here, the tree then spread out into sixteen branches, each of which had its own, separate tree. Each one of the sixteen trees, to which there was dedicated a particular representation, was divided into seven parts – roots, trunk, major branches, lesser branches, leaves, fruits and flowers. Eight of the trees clearly corresponded to eight of the subjects of the *tabula generalis*: these are the *Arbor elementalis*, which represents the *elementata*, that is, objects of the sublunary world, stones, trees and animals composed of the four elements; the *Arbor vegetalis*; the *Arbor sensualis*; the *Arbor imaginalis*, which represents images that replicate in the mind whatever is represented on the other trees; the *Arbor humanalis et moralis* (memory, intellect and will, but also the various sciences and arts); the *Arbor coelestialis* (astronomy and astrology); the *Arbor angelicalis*; and the *Arbor divinalis*, which includes the divine dignities. To this list are added another eight: the *Arbor mortalis* (virtues and vices); the *Arbor eviternalis* (life after death); the *Arbor maternalis* (Mariology); the *Arbor Chistianalis* (Christology); the

Arbor imperialis (government); the *Arbor apostolicalis* (church); the *Arbor exemplificalis* (the contents of knowledge); and the *Arbor quaestionalis*, which contains four thousand questions on the various arts.

To understand the structure of these trees, it is enough to look at only one – the *Arbor elementalis*. Its roots are the nine dignities and nine relations. Its trunk represents the conjoining of these principles, out of which emerges the confused body of primordial chaos which occupies space. In this are the species of things and their dispositions. The principal branches represent the four elements (earth, air, fire and water) which stretch out into the four masses which are made from them (the seas and the lands). The leaves are the accidents. The flowers are the instruments, such as hands, feet and eyes. The fruits represent individual things, such as stone, gold, apple, bird.

Calling this a 'forest' of trees would be an improper metaphor: the trees overlay one another to rise hierarchically like the peaked roof of a pagoda. The trees at the lower levels participate in those higher up. The vegetable tree, for example, participates in the tree of elements; the sensual tree participates in the first two; the tree of imagination is built up out of the first three, and it forms the base from which the next tree, the human one, will arise (Llinares 1963: 211–12).

The system of trees reflects the organization of reality itself; it represents the great chain of being the way that it is, and must metaphysically be. This is why the hierarchy constitutes a system of 'true' knowledge. The priority of metaphysical truth over logical validity in Lull's system also explains why he laid out his art the way he did: he wished his system to produce, for any possible argument, a middle term that would render that argument amenable to syllogistic treatment; having structured the system for this end, however, he proceeded to discard a number of well-formed syllogisms which, though logically valid, did not support the arguments he regarded as metaphysically true. For Lull, the significance of the middle term of the syllogism was thus not that of scholastic logic. Its middle term served to bind the elements of the chain of being: it was a substantial, not a formal, link.

If the art is a perfect language, it is so only to the extent to which it can speak of a metaphysical reality, of a structure of being which exists independently of it. The art was not a mechanism designed to chart unknown universes. In the Catalan version of his *Logica Algazelis*, Lull writes, 'De la logica parlam tot breu – car a parlar avem Deu' ('About logic we will be brief, for it is to talk about God').

Much has been written about the analogy between Lull's art and the kabbala. What distinguishes kabbalistic thought from Lull's is that, in the kabbala, the combination of the letters of the Torah had created the universe rather than merely reflected it. The reality that the kabbalistic mystic sought behind these letters had not yet been revealed; it could be discovered only through whispering the syllables as the letters whirled. Lull's *ars combinatoria*, by contrast, was a rhetorical instrument; it was designed to demonstrate what was already known, and lock it for ever in the steely cage of the system of trees.

Despite all this, the art might still qualify as a perfect language if those elementary principles, common to all humanity, that it purported to expound really were universal and common to all peoples. As it was, despite his effort to assimilate ideas from non-Christian and non-European religions, Lull's desperate endeavour failed through its unconscious ethnocentrism. The content-plane, the universe which his art expounded, was the product of the western Christian tradition. It could not change even though Lull translated it into Arabic or Hebrew. The legend of Lull's own agony and death is but the emblem of that failure.

The *Concordia Universalis* of Nicholas of Cusa

The seductive potentiality of Lull's appeal to the principle of universal concord is revealed by the resumption of his project, two centuries later, by Nicholas of Cusa. Nicholas is famous as the figure who revived Plato during the years between the crisis of scholasticism and the beginning of the Renaissance. Nicholas also propounded the idea of an infinitely open universe, whose centre was everywhere and whose circumference nowhere. As an infinite being, God transcended all limits and overcame every opposition. As the diameter of a circle increased, its curvature diminished; so at its limit its circumference became a straight line of infinite length. Likewise, in God all opposites coincide. If the universe had a centre, it would be limited by another universe. But in the universe, God is both centre and circumference. Thus the earth could not be the centre of the universe. This was the starting point for a vision of the plurality of worlds, of a reality founded on mathematical principles, which can be submitted to continuous investigation, where the world, if not infinite in a strict sense, was at least capable of assuming an infinite number of guises. The thought of Nicholas is rich in cosmological metaphors (or models) founded upon the image of the circle and the wheel (*De docta ignorantia*, II, 11), in which the names of the divine attributes (explicitly borrowed from Lull) form a circle where each supports and confirms the others (I, 21).

The influence of Lull is even more explicitly revealed when Nicholas notes that the names by which the Greeks, Latins, Germans, Turks and Saracens designate the divinity are either all in fundamental accord, or derive from the Hebrew tetragrammaton (see the sermon *Dies sanctificatus*).

The ideas of Lull had spread to the Veneto towards the close of the fourteenth century. Nicholas probably came into contact with them in Padua. Their diffusion was, in part, a reaction against a scholastic Aristotelianism now in crisis; yet the diffusion also reflected the feverish cultural atmosphere generated by closer contacts with the East. Just as Catalonia and Majorca had been frontier territories in contact with the Muslim and Jewish worlds at the time of Lull, so the Venetian Republic had opened itself to the

world of Byzantium and of the Arab countries two centuries later. The emerging currents of Venetian humanism
were inspired by a new curiosity and respect for other
cultures (cf. Lohr 1988).

It was thus appropriate that in this atmosphere there
should have re-emerged the thought of a figure whose
preaching, whose theological speculations, and whose research on universal language were all conceived with the
aim of building an intellectual and religious bridge between
the European West and the East. Lull believed that true
authority could not be based on a rigid unity, but rather on
the tension between various centres. It was the laws of
Moses, the revelations of Christ and the preaching of Mo-
hammed that, taken together, might produce a unified
result. Lull's doctrine acted as a mystical and philosophical
stimulus and seemed an imaginative and poetic alternative
to the encyclopedia of Aristotelian scholasticism, but it
provided a political inspiration as well. The works of a
writer who had dared to put his doctrine into the vernacular proved congenial to humanists who, on the one hand,
had begun to celebrate the dignity of their own native
tongues, but, on the other hand, wondered how it was
possible to establish a rational discussion which broke the
boundaries of national traditions, a philosophy which
could reanimate the body of encyclopedic scholasticism by
injecting the leaven of exotic new doctrines, expressed in
languages still entirely unknown.

In his *De pace fidei*, Nicholas opened a polemical dialogue with the Muslims. He asked himself Lull's question:
how might the truth of Christian revelation be demonstrated to followers of the two other monotheistic religions? Perhaps, Nicholas mused, it was a mistake to
translate the persons of the Trinity as 'Father', 'Son' and
'Holy Ghost'. Perhaps they should have been given more
philosophical names (better understandable by other cultures). In his ecumenical fervour, Nicholas even went so far
as to propose to the Jews and the Muslims that, if they
would accept the Gospels, he would see that all Christians

received circumcision. It was a proposal, as he confessed at the end, whose practical realization might present certain difficulties (*De pace fidei*, XVI, 60).

Nicholas retained from Lull the spirit of universal peace as well as his metaphysical vision. Yet before the thrilling potential of Nicholas's own vision of an infinity of worlds could be translated into a new and different version of the art of combination, new ideas would have to fertilize the humanist and Renaissance world. The rediscovery of the art of combination would have to wait for the rediscovery of Hebrew, for Christian kabbalism, for the spread of Hermeticism, and for a new and positive reassessment of magic.

5

The Monogenetic Hypothesis and the Mother Tongues

In its most ancient versions, the search for a perfect language took the form of the monogenetic hypothesis which assumed that all languages descended from a unique mother tongue. Before I tell the story of this hypothesis, however, we should note that most of the attempts suffered from a continuous confusion between different theoretical options.

1 The distinction between a *perfect language* and a *universal language* was not sufficiently understood. It is one thing to search for a language capable of mirroring the true nature of objects; it is quite another to search for the language which everyone might, or ought to, speak. There is nothing that rules out that a language which is perfect might be accessible only to a few, while a language that is universal might be also imperfect.

2 The distinction between the Platonic opposition of *nature* and *convention* was not kept separate from the general problem of the *origin of language* (cf. Formigari 1970). It is possible to imagine a language that expresses the nature of things, but which, none the less, is not original, but arises through invention. It is also possible to discuss whether language originated as an imitation of nature (the 'mimological' hypothesis, Genette 1976) or as the result of a convention, without necessarily

posing the question of whether the former is better than the latter. As a consequence, claims to linguistic superiority on etymological grounds (more direct filiation with an ancient language) are often confused with those on mimological grounds – while the presence of onomatopoetic words in a language can be seen as a sign of perfection, not as the proof of the direct descent of that language from a primordial one.

3 Despite the fact that the distinction was already clear in Aristotle, many authors failed to distinguish between a sound and the alphabetical sign that represented it.

4 As Genette (1976) has often reminded us, before the advent of comparative linguistics in the nineteenth century, most research on languages concentrated on semantics, assembling *nomenclature* families of supposedly related words (often, as we shall see, making up etymologies to match), but neglecting both phonology and grammar.

5 Finally, there was not a clear-cut distinction between *primordial language* and *universal grammar*. It is possible to search for a set of grammatical principles common to all languages without wishing to return to a more primitive tongue.

The Return to Hebrew

From Origen to Augustine, almost all of the church Fathers assumed, as a matter of incontrovertible fact, that, before the confusion, humanity's primordial language was Hebrew. The most notable dissenting voice was Gregory of Nyssa (*Contra Eunomium*). God, he thought, could not have spoken Hebrew; were we to imagine, he said ironically, a schoolmaster God drilling our forefathers in the Hebrew alphabet (cf. Borst 1957–63: I, 2, and II/1, 3.1)? Despite this, the image of Hebrew as the divine language survived through the Middle Ages (cf. De Lubac 1959: II, 3.3).

By the sixteenth and seventeenth centuries, however, it no

longer seemed enough simply to maintain that Hebrew was the proto-language (little being known thereof): it was deemed necessary to promote its study, and, if possible, its diffusion. By now we are in a climate very different from that of St Augustine: not only do the interpreters wish to go back to the text in its original version, but they do it with the conviction that the original and holy language of scripture was the only one capable of expressing its sacred truth. What has happened in the meantime is, of course, the Reformation. Protestants refused to accept the claim of the Catholic church to be the sole mediator and interpreter, placing itself, with its canonic Latin translations, between the believer and the Holy Writ. Out of this refusal to accept the church's traditional interpretation of scripture arose the stimulus to study the languages in which the sacred texts had first been formulated. The contemporary debate over this was varied and complex. The most comprehensive treatment is contained perhaps in Brian Walton's *In biblia polyglotta prolegomena* (1673: especially 1–3). However, the story of this debate during the Renaissance is so complex (see Demonet 1992) that we shall limit ourselves to a gallery of exemplary portraits.

Postel's Universalistic Utopia

A special place in the story of the renewal of Hebrew studies belongs to the French utopian thinker and *érudit*, Guillaume Postel (1510–81). Councillor to the kings of France, close to the major religious, political and scientific personalities of his epoch, Postel returned from a series of diplomatic missions to the Orient, voyages which enabled him to study Arabic and Hebrew as well as to learn of the wisdom of the kabbala, a changed and marked man. Already renowned as a Greek philologist, around 1539, Postel was appointed to the post of 'mathematicorum et peregrinarum linguarum regius interpretes' in that Collège des Trois Langues which eventually became the Collège de France.

In his *De originibus seu de Hebraicae linguae et gentis antiquitate* (1538), Postel argued that Hebrew came directly from the sons of Noah, and that, from it, Arabic, Chaldean, Hindi and, indirectly, Greek had all descended as well. In *Linguarum duodecim characteribus differentium alphabetum, introductio* (1538), by studying twelve different alphabets he proved the common derivation of every language. From here, he went on to advance the project of a return to Hebrew as the instrument for the peaceable fusion of the peoples of differing races.

To support his argument that Hebrew was the proto-language, Postel developed the criterion of divine economy. As there was but one human race, one world and one God, there could be but one language; this was a 'sacred language, divinely inspired into the first man' (*De Foenicum litteris*, 1550). God had educated Adam by breathing into him the capacity to call things by their appropriate names (*De originibus, seu, de varia et potissimum orbi Latino ad hanc diem incognita aut inconsyderata historia*, 1553).

Although Postel does not seem to have thought either of an innate faculty for languages or of a universal grammar, as Dante had done, there still appears in many of his writings the notion of an Averroist active intellect as the repository of the forms common to all humanity, in which the roots of our linguistic faculty must be sought (*Les très merveilleuses victoires des femmes du nouveau monde* together with *La doctrine du siècle doré*, both from 1553).

Postel's linguistic studies were connected to his particular vision of a religious utopia: he foresaw the reign of universal peace. In his *De orbis terrae concordia* (1544: I) he clearly states that his studies in language would help to lay the foundations upon which a universal concord could be created. He envisioned the creation of a linguistic commonwealth that would serve as living proof to those of other faiths that not only was the message of Christianity true, but equally it verified their own religious beliefs: there are some principles of a natural religion, or sets of innate ideas held by all peoples (*De orbis*, III).

Here was the spirit that had inspired Lull and Nicholas of Cusa. Yet Postel was convinced that universal peace could only be realized under the protection of the king of France: among the world's rulers the king of France alone held a legitimate claim to the title of king of the world. He was the direct descendant of Noah, through Gomer, son of Japheth, founder of the Gallic and Celtic races (cf. particularly *Les raisons de la monarchie*, c.1551). Postel (*Trésor des propheties de l'univers*, 1556) supported this contention with a traditional etymology (see, for example, Jean Lemaire de -Belges, *Illustration de Gaule et singularitez de Troye*, 1512–13, fol. 64r): in Hebrew, the term *gallus* meant 'he who overcame the waves'; thus the Gauls were the people who had survived the waters of the Flood (cf. Stephens 1989: 4).

Postel first attempted to convert Francis I to his cause. The king, however, judged him a fanatic, and he lost favour at court. He went to Rome, hoping to win over to his utopian schemes Ignatius of Loyola, whose reformist ideals seemed kindred to his own. It did not take Ignatius long, however, to realize that Postel's ambitions were not identical to those of the Jesuits. Accepting Postel's project might have placed their vow of obedience to the pope at risk. Besides, Ignatius was a Spaniard, and the idea of turning the king of France into the king of the world would hardly have appealed to him. Although Postel continued long afterwards to look upon the Jesuits as the divine instrument for the creation of universal peace, he himself was forced to leave the company after a mere year and a half.

After various peregrinations, Postel found himself in Venice, where, in 1547, he was appointed chaplain of the Hospital of Sts John and Paul (called the Ospedaletto), and censor of books published in the Hebrew language in that city. While in the Ospedaletto, he was appointed confessor to its founder, the fifty-year-old Johanna, or Mother Zuana, a woman who had dedicated her life to helping the poor. Gradually, the conviction grew on Postel that in meeting Johanna, he had come into contact with a great prophetic spirit. He conceived for her a mystic passion in which he saw her as the mother of the world, destined to redeem humanity from its original sin.

After rereading the kabbalist text, the *Zohar*, Postel identified Johanna as Shekinah as well as with the angelical pope whose coming had been foretold in the prophecies of Joachim a Fiore. Finally, he identified her as the second Messiah. According to Postel, the feminine component of humanity, guilty of the sin of Eve, had not been saved by Christ. The salvation of the daughters of Eve would only occur with the coming of a second Messiah (on Postel's 'feminism' cf. Sottile 1984).

The question whether Johanna was truly a mystic with extraordinary capacities or whether these were just qualities that Postel projected into her is hardly an important issue for us. What is important rather is that there was now established an intense spiritual communion: Johanna, the kabbala, universal peace, the last age foretold by Joachim, were all thrown into a single crucible; what emerged was Johanna in the role formerly held by Ignatius Loyola in Postel's utopian schemes. What is more, 'Johanna's "immaculate conception" produces her "little son", Postel, the new Elias' (Kuntz 1981: 91).

Rumours of singular goings on at the Ospedaletto soon spread, however, and, in 1549, Postel was forced to leave Venice. He resumed his wanderings in the Orient, returning to Venice the following year only to learn of the death of Johanna. According to tradition, on hearing the news he fell into a state of prostration mixed with ecstasy in which he claimed to be able to stare into the sun for an hour. He felt the spirit of Johanna gradually invading his body (Kuntz 1981: 104). He began to proclaim his belief in metempsychosis.

Postel next returned to Paris where, with great public acclaim, he resumed his teaching. Yet soon he was announcing the advent of the era of Restitution, a golden century under the sign of Johanna. Once again, he found himself at the centre of a philosophical and religious turmoil. When the king forced him to abandon teaching, he set off on a new journey through various cities, ending up again in Venice, arriving just in time to prevent his books from being placed on the Index. He was questioned by the Inquisition, which tried to induce him to recant. In 1555, in recognition of his services to science and politics, he was declared 'non malus sed amens', not guilty but insane. His life was spared, but he was imprisoned, first in Ravenna and afterwards in Rome.

At the request of the French religious authorities, Postel was later transferred to Paris, in 1564. He retired to the monastery of Saint-Martin-des-Champs where he lived until his death in 1587. During this period, he wrote a repudiation of his heretical doctrines concerning Mother Johanna.

Apart from this final capitulation, Postel seems to have been a relentless defender of ideas which, for this period, were quite unconventional. His particular vision of utopia must be regarded within the cultural context of his time. Demonet (1992: 337ff) underlines that his idea of the 'restitution' of Hebrew as the language of universal concord also required that infidels recognize their error and accept the Christian revelation. None the less, as Kuntz notes (1981: 49), Postel was neither an orthodox Catholic nor an orthodox Protestant; his moderate and pacifist positions infuriated, in fact, extremists of both persuasions. Some of his doctrines were certainly theologically ambiguous: he claimed that Christianity was the only religion that verified the message of Judaism, but – at the same time – that to be a good Christian it was not necessary to belong to a sect (Catholic church included), but rather to feel the presence of the divine within. It followed that a true Christian could, and even should, observe Jewish law, and that the Muslims could be considered half-Christians. More than once, Postel condemned the persecution of the Jews. He spoke of the *Jewishness* of all men, talking of Christian-Jews instead of Jewish Christians (Kuntz 1981: 130). He claimed that the true tradition of Christianity was Judaism with its name changed, and lamented that Christianity had lost its Judaic roots. Such positions could only be seen as extremely provocative by a church still clinging to the pre-Renaissance doctrine that Christianity represented both the correction and the cancellation of Judaism. In order to affirm, as Postel did in his *De orbis*, the existence of a harmony between the faiths, it was necessary to exercise a tolerance on a number of theological issues. Postel's doctrine has thus been described as a universalistic theism (Radetti 1936).

The Etymological Furor

Postel's was a clear and unambiguous demand for the restoration of Hebrew as the universal language. Few, however, made this demand in so radical a fashion. For others, it was usually enough to demonstrate that Hebrew was superior because it was the first language from which all others had derived.

One example is the *Mithridates* of Conrad Gessner. Published in 1555, the *Mithridates* is a book that draws parallels between fifty-five different languages. Having dwelt briefly on the happy condition of some legendary beings with two tongues, one for human speech and the other to speak the language of the birds, Gessner immediately passed to the claim that 'all existing languages had retained words of a Hebrew origin, though in a corrupt state' (1610 edn: 3). Other authors – in order to demonstrate such a parenthood – started a mad etymological chase.

This etymological furor was not a new condition. Between the sixth and seventh centuries, by a fanciful account of the seventy-two existing languages, Isidore of Seville (*Etymologiarum*) elaborated a series of etymologies that has made him the laughing stock of scholars ever since: our *corpus* (body) comes from *corruptus perit* as our body goes to corruption; *homo* (man) derives from the *humus* or mud from which he is born; *iumenta* (mare) comes from *iuvat* because horses help men; *agnus* is a lamb because it recognizes (*agnoscit*) its own mother . . . These are examples of hyper-Cratylian mimological hypothesis, and we shall see that they were taken up by the supporters of Hebrew.

In 1613 Claude Duret published his monumental *Thrésor de l'histoire des langues de cet univers*. Using the Christian kabbala as his starting point, Duret set forth a vast panorama that swept from the origins of language, to an examination of all known tongues, including those of the New World, to a final chapter on the language of animals. Duret started from the premise that Hebrew was the universal language of the human race; it thus appeared to him as self-evident that each animal name in Hebrew should include an encapsulated 'natural history' of that animal. Thus we are told that, in Hebrew,

the Eagle is called *Nescher*, a word formed by the combination of *Schor* and *Isachar*, the first meaning to look and the second to be straight because, above all others, the eagle is a bird of firm sight whose gaze is always directed towards the sun [. . .] The Lion has three names, that is *Aryeh*, *Labi*, and *Layisch*. The first name comes from another which means tear or lacerate; the second is related to the word *leb* which means heart, and *laab*, which means to live in solitude. The third name usually means a great and furious lion, and bears an analogy with the verb *yosh*, which means trample [. . .] because this animal tramples and damages its prey. (p. 40)

Hebrew had managed to retain this proximity to the world of things because it never permitted itself to be polluted by other languages (ch. x). This presumption of Hebrew's natural affinity to the world of things is also demonstrated by its magic potential. Duret recalled that Eusebius and St Jerome had ridiculed the Greeks because they had exalted their own language but were unable to find any mystic significance of their alphabet. Only ask a Hebrew child the significance of the letter *Alef*, and he will respond 'discipline', and so on for all the other letters and for all their combinations (p. 194).

Duret is an example of *retrospective* etymologizing,

aiming at showing how the mother tongue was harmoniously related to the nature of things. Other authors engaged in *prospective* etymologizing, projecting Hebrew words forwards to show how they transmuted themselves into the words of all other languages. In 1606, Estienne Guichard wrote his *L'harmonie étymologique des langues*, where he showed that all existing languages might be derived from Hebrew roots. He started from the premise that Hebrew was the simplest language because in it 'all words are simple, and their substance consists of but three radicals.' Manipulating these radicals through inversion, anagrams and permutations in the best kabbalistic tradition, Guichard provided his etymologies.

In Hebrew, the verb *batar* means to divide. How can we prove that Latin *dividere* comes from *batar*? Simple: by inversion, *batar* produces *tarab*; *tarab* then becomes the Latin *tribus* and, from there, turns into *distribuo* and *dividere* (p. 147). *Zacen* means old. Rearranging the radicals, we get *zanec* from which derives Latin *senex*. A further rearrangement and we have *cazen*, from which derives the Oscan word *casnar*, which is the root of the Latin *canus*, elder (p. 247). By this method we might equally prove that the English *head* comes from the late Latin *testa*, since the anagram of *testa* gives *eatts*.

The thousand or so pages of Guichard are really little more than an extensive raiding expedition in which languages, dead and living, are pillaged for their treasures. More or less by chance, Guichard sometimes manages to hit upon a real etymological connection; but there is little scientific method in his madness. Still, the early attempts by authors such as Duret and Guichard to prove the monogenetic hypothesis did lead to a conception of Hebrew as less 'magical', and this eventually helped clear the way for a more modern conception of comparative linguistics (cf. Simone 1990: 328–9).

During the sixteenth and seventeenth centuries, fantasy and science remained inextricably entangled. In 1667, Mercurius van Helmont published an *Alphabeti veri naturalis*

Hebraici brevissima delineatio, which proposed to examine methods for the teaching to speak of deaf-mutes. This was the sort of project which, during the Enlightenment in the following century, might have been the occasion for valuable reflections upon the nature of language. For van Helmont, however, science was subordinated to his own monogenetic fantasies. He started with the presumption that there must be a primitive language, easy to learn, even for those who had never learned to speak a language at all, and that it could not be but Hebrew. Then van Helmont proceeded to demonstrate that the sounds of Hebrew were the ones most easily reproduced by the human vocal organs. Then, with the assistance of thirty-three wood-cuts, he showed how, in making the sounds of Hebrew, the movements of tongue, palate, uvula and glottis reproduced the shapes of the corresponding Hebrew letters. The result was a radical version of the mimological theory: not only did the Hebrew sounds reflect the inherent nature of things themselves, but the very mud from which the human vocal organs were formed had been especially sculpted to emit a perfect language that God pressed on Adam in not only its spoken but evidently its written form as well (see figure 5.1).

In *Turris Babel* of 1679, Kircher presented a synthesis of the various positions which we have been reviewing. After an examination of the history of the world from the Creation to the Flood, and, from there, to the confusion of Babel, Kircher traced its subsequent historical and anthropological development through an analysis of various languages.

Kircher never questioned Hebrew's priority as the *lingua sancta*; this had been explicitly revealed in the Bible. He held it as self-evident that Adam, knowing the nature of each and every beast, had named them accordingly, adding that 'sometimes conjoining, sometimes separating, sometimes permutating the letters of the divers names, he recombined them according to the nature and properties of the various animals' (III, 1, 8). Since this idea is based on a

Figure 5.1

citation from the kabbalist writings of the Rabbi R. Becchai, we can infer that Kircher was thinking of Adam defining the properties of the various animals by permutating the letters of their names. To be precise, first the names themselves mimic some property of the animals to which they refer: *lion*, for example, is written *ARYH* in Hebrew; and Kircher takes the letters *AHY* as miming the heavy sound of a lion panting. After naming the lion 'ARYH', Adam rearranged these letters according to the kabbalist technique of *temurah*. Nor did he limit himself to anagrams: by interpolating letters, he constructed entire sentences in which every word contained one or more of the letters of the Hebrew word. Thus Kircher was able to generate a sentence which showed that the lion was *monstrans*, that is, able to strike terror by his sole glance; that he was luminous as if a light were shining from his face, which, among other things, resembled a mirror . . . We see here Kircher playing with etymological techniques already suggested in Plato's *Cratylus* (which he, in fact, cites, p. 145) to twist names to express a more or less traditional lore about people and animals.

At this point, Kircher took the story up to the present. He told how, after the confusion, five dialects arose out of Hebrew: Chaldean, Samaritan (the ancestor of Phoenician), Syriac, Arabic and Ethiopic. From these five he deduced, by various etymological means, the birth of various other languages (explaining the successive stages by which the alphabet developed along the way) until he reached the European languages of his own time. As the story approaches the present, the argument becomes more plausible: linguistic change is seen as caused by the separation and mixture of peoples. These, in turn, are caused by the rise and fall of empires, migrations due to war and pestilence, colonialization and climatic variation. He is also able to identify the process of creolization which can occur when two languages are put into contact with one another. Out of the multiplication of languages, moreover, are born the various idolatrous religions, and the multiplication of the names of the gods (III, I, 2).

Conventionalism, Epicureanism and Polygenesis

By now, however, time was running out for the theories of Kircher, Guichard and Duret. Already in the Renaissance, Hebrew's status as the original and sacred language had begun to be questioned. By the seventeenth century, a new and complex set of arguments had evolved. We might, emblematically, place these arguments under the sign of Genesis 10. In these, attention moved away from the problem of the primordial language to that of *matrices linguae*, or mother tongues – this was an expression first coined by Giuseppe Giusto Scaligero (*Diatribe de europaeorum linguis*, 1599). Scaligero individuated eleven language families, seven major and four minor. Within each family, all languages were related; between the language families, however, kinship was impossible to trace.

The Bible, it was noted, had given no explicit information about the character of the primordial language. There were many who could thus maintain that the division of tongues had originated not at the foot of the shattered tower, but well before. The notion of *confusio* could be interpreted as a natural process. Scholars set about trying to understand this process by uncovering the grammatical structures common to all languages: 'it was no longer a question of "reduction", but of a classification aimed at revealing a common system latent within all languages, while still respecting their individual differences' (Demonet 1992: 341, and II, 5, *passim*).

In his *Histoire critique du Vieux Testament* (1678), Richard Simon, considered one of the founders of modern biblical criticism, discarded the hypothesis of the divine origin of Hebrew, citing the ironic remarks of Gregory of Nyssa. Language, he wrote, was a human invention; since human reason differs in different peoples, so languages must differ as well. God willed that different peoples speak different languages in order that 'each might explain themselves in their own way.'

Meric Casaubon (*De quattor linguis commentatio*, 1650) accepted the idea of Grotius that – in so far as it had ever existed – the primordial language had long since disappeared. Even if the words spoken by Adam had been inspired directly by God, humanity had since developed its languages autonomously. The Hebrew of the Bible was just one of the languages that arose after the Flood.

Leibniz also insisted that the historic language of Adam was irredeemably lost, and that, despite our best efforts, 'nobis ignota est.' In so far as it had ever existed, it had either totally disappeared, or else survived only as relics (undated fragment in Gensini 1990: 197).

In this climate, the myth of a language that followed the

contours of the world came to be rearticulated in the light of the principle of the arbitrariness of the sign. This was a principle that, in any case, philosophical thought had never entirely abandoned, as it formed part of the Aristotelian legacy. In precisely this period, Spinoza, from a fundamentally nominalist point of view, asked how a general term such as *man* could possibly express man's true nature, when different individuals formed their ideas in different ways:

for example, those who are accustomed to contemplate with admiration the height of men will, on hearing the name *man*, think of an animal with an erect posture; those, instead, who are in the habit of contemplating some other feature, will form another of the common images of man – man as a laughing animal, as a biped, as featherless, as rational. Thus every individual will form images of universals according to the dispositions of their own bodies. (*Ethica*, 1677: proposition XL, scolion I)

Implicitly challenging the idea that Hebrew was the language whose words corresponded to the nature of things, Locke considered that words used by human beings were signs of their ideas, 'not by any natural connexion, that there is between particular articulated Sounds and certain *Ideas*, for then there would be but one Language amongst all Men; but by voluntary Imposition' (*An Essay concerning Human Understanding*, 1690: III, 2, 1). As soon as ideas lost their quality as innate, Platonic entities, becoming nominal ideas instead, language itself lost its aura of sacrality, turning into a mere instrument for interaction – a human construct.

In *Leviathan* (1651: I, 4, 'Of Speech'), Hobbes admitted that the first author of speech could only have been God himself, and that he had taught Adam what to name the animals. Yet, immediately thereafter, Hobbes abandons the scriptural account to picture Adam as striking out on his own. Hobbes argued that Adam continued freely to add new names 'as the experience and use of the creatures should give him occasion'. In other words, Hobbes left

Adam to confront his own experiences and his own needs; and it was from these needs (necessity being, as we know, the mother of all invention) that the languages after Babel were born.

During these same years, thinkers also returned to reflect upon an older suggestion made by Epicurus, who, in a letter to Herodotus, gave his opinion that the names of things were not originally due to convention; human beings themselves had rather created them from their own natures. Those of differing tribes, 'under the impulse of special feelings and special presentations of sense', uttered 'special cries'. The air thus emitted was moulded by their different feelings or sense perceptions (letter to Herodotus, in Diogenes Laertius, *Lives of the Philosophers*, X, 75–6).

Epicurus went on to add that, to eliminate confusion and for reasons of economy, the various peoples *subsequently* came to an agreement over what name they should give things. He had no fixed opinion on whether this agreement had been made from instinct or 'by rational thought' (cf. Formigari 1970: 17–28; Gensini 1991: 92; Manetti 1987: 176–7). That was the first part of Epicurus' thesis, which emphasized the natural rather than conventional origin of languages; however, this idea was taken up by Lucretius: nature prompted human beings to emit the sounds of language; necessity gave birth to the names of things.

Therefore to suppose that someone then distributed names among things, and from him that men learnt their first words, is folly. For why should he have been able to mark all things with titles and to utter the various sounds of the tongue, and at the same time others not be thought able to have done it? . . . Therefore if it is the various sensations that they feel which drive animals to emit differing sounds, even though they remain mute, how much more just is it to say that sensations induce mortals to indicate different things with different sounds. (*De rerum natura*, W.H.D. Rouse, tr., London: Heinemann, 1975: V, 1041–90)

This was a new view, one which we may call the materialist-biological theory of the origin of language. Language arose out of a natural inclination to transform sensations into ideas, which, for the sake of civil convenience, were then translated into sounds. If it were true, as Epicurus had suggested, that this process of transformation might vary in different races, climates and places, it was hardly too much to imagine that, in divers times and ways, the different races had originated different families of languages. This was the intuition behind the theory that evolved in the eighteenth century: each language had its own *genius*.

Epicurus' thesis could not help but seem seductive in the 'libertine' milieu of seventeenth-century France, in an atmosphere of scepticism ranging from sarcastic agnosticism to confessed atheism. In 1655 there appeared the *Systema theologicum ex prae-Adamitarum hypothesi*, written by a Calvinist named Isaac de La Peyrère. Starting from an extremely original reading of the fifth chapter of St Paul's Epistle to the Romans, La Peyrère argued for the *polygenesis* of races and peoples. Reports of missionaries and explorers had represented non-European civilizations, such as the Chinese, as so ancient that their histories were incommensurable with biblical chronology, especially in regard to their accounts of the origin of the world. La Peyrère inferred from this that there existed a pre-Adamite human race, untouched by original sin. He concluded that the stories both of the original sin and of the Flood concerned only Adam and his descendants in the land of the Hebrews (cf. Zoli 1991: 70). This was a hypothesis that had already appeared in Islamic culture. Drawing on the Koran (2:31), al-Maqdisi, in the tenth century, had alluded to the existence of different races prior to Adam (cf. Borst 1957–63: I, II, 9).

Quite apart from the obvious theological implications of such an assumption (and the works of La Peyrère were condemned to be burnt), it was clear that, by now, Hebrew civilization – along with its holy language – was falling from its throne. If one accepted that species had developed differentially in differing conditions, and that their linguistic capacity reflected their degree of evolution and of adaptation to environment, it was easy to accept the polygenetic hypothesis.

A particular brand of polygeneticism – certainly not of libertine inspiration – can be ascribed to Giambattista Vico. Vico was a thinker who naturally proceeded against the grain of his times. Instead of searching for actual chronological origins, he set out to delineate an ideal and eternal history. Paradoxically, by jumping outside the bounds of history, Vico was to become one of the founders of modern historicism. What Vico wished to tell was not, or – depending on how one wishes to take the chronological table at the beginning of his *Scienza nuova seconda* (1744) – not only, a historical course, but rather the ever recurring conditions in which languages are born and develop in every time and in every place. Vico described an ideal line of descent which traced the development of language from the language of the gods to that of heroes and, finally, to that of human beings. The first language had to be *hieroglyphic* ('sacred or divine'), the second *symbolic* ('by heroic signs and devices'), and the third *epistolary* ('for men at a distance to communicate to each other the current needs of their lives', para. 432).

According to Vico, language, at its ideal point of origin, was directly motivated by, and metaphorically congruent with, the human experience of nature. Only at a later state did language become organized in a more conventional form. Vico affirms, however, that 'as gods, heroes, and men began at the same time (for they were, after all, men who imagined the gods and who believed their own heroic nature to be a mixture of the divine and human natures), so these three languages began at the same time' (446). Thus, circumventing the seventeenth-century question of whether or not a natural linguistic stage was succeeded by a conventional one, Vico directly addressed the question of why there existed as many different languages as there were different peoples. He responded by asserting 'this great truth . . . that, as the peoples have certainly by the diversity of climates acquired different natures, from which have sprung as many different customs, so from their different natures and customs as many different languages have arisen' (445).

As to the story of the primacy of Hebrew, Vico disposes of it in a series of observations tending to prove that, if anything, the Hebrews had derived their alphabet from the Greeks and not vice versa. Nor was Vico susceptible to the Hermetic fantasies of the Renaissance, according to which all wisdom came from the Egyptians. From his description there emerges instead a complex network of cultural and commercial trafficking, in which the Phoenicians – prompted by mercantile necessity – exported their characters to both the Egyptians and the Greeks, while, at the same time, spreading throughout the Mediterranean basin the set of hieroglyphic characters that they had borrowed from the Chaldeans and had adapted to fit their need for a numerical system to keep track of their stocks of merchandise (441–3).

The Pre-Hebraic Language

Alongside these philosophical discussions, other inspired glottogonists (for whom the defeat of the Hebraic hypothesis was a consummated fact) were breaking new theoretical ground. The explorers and missionaries of the sixteenth and seventeenth centuries had discovered civilizations, older than the Hebrews, which had their own cultural and linguistic traditions. In 1699, John Webb (*An Historical Essay endeavouring the Probability that the Language of the Empire of China is the Primitive Language*) advanced the idea that, after the Flood, Noah had landed his Ark and had gone to live in China. Consequently, it was the Chinese language which held primacy. Furthermore, since the Chinese had not participated in the construction of the Tower of Babel, their language had remained immune from the effects of the *confusio*; Chinese had survived intact for centuries, protected from foreign invasion. Chinese thus conserved the original linguistic patrimony.

Ours is a story that proceeds through many strange anachronisms. Near the end of the eighteenth century, just at the moment when, quite unconnected with any form of the monogenetic hypothesis, a comparative methodology was about to emerge, there appeared the most gigantic attempt to date to rediscover the primitive language. In 1765, Charles de Brosses wrote a *Traité de la formation méchanique des langues*. The treatise propounded a theory of language that was both naturalistic (the articulation of terms reflects the nature of things – sweet sounds designate sweet objects) and materialistic (language is reduced to physical operations, supernatural entities are seen as the result of linguistic play: cf. Droixhe 1978). As part of this theory, however, de Brosses could not resist indulging in a series of speculations about the nature of the primitive language, 'organic, physical, and necessary, that not one of the world's peoples either knows or practises in its simplicity, but which, none the less, was spoken by all men, and constitutes the basis of language in every land' ('Discours préliminaire', xiv–xv).

The linguist must analyse the mechanisms of different languages, discovering which of those features arise through natural necessity. From this he may, moving through a chain of natural inferences, work his way back from each of the known languages to the original, unknown matrix. It is only a matter of locating a small set of primitive roots that might yield a universal nomenclature for all languages, European and oriental.

Radically Cratylian and mimologist as it was (cf. Genette 1976: 85–118), the comparative approach of de Brosses took the vowels to constitute the raw material in a continuum of sound upon which the consonants acted to sculpt out the intonations and the caesurae. Their effect, often more visible to the eye than to the ear (remember the persistent failure to distinguish between sounds and letters), is to render consonantal identity the key criterion of comparative analysis.

Like Vico, de Brosses considered that the invention of articulated sounds had proceeded in step with the invention of writing. Fano (1962: 231; English tr., p. 147) sums up his theory very well:

De Brosses imagines this process as follows: like the good school teacher who takes chalk in hand to make his lesson clearer from a didactic viewpoint, the cave man intermingled his discourses with little explicative figures. If, for example, he wanted to say 'a raven flew away and rested on the top of a tree', he would first imitate the croaking of the bird, then he would express the flight with a 'frrr! frrr!' and eventually take a piece of coal and draw a tree with a raven on top.

Another Herculean effort in the cause of the mimological hypothesis was that of Antoine Court de Gébelin, who, between 1773 and 1782, published nine quarto volumes, totalling over five thousand pages, giving to this opus – multiple, creaking, though not utterly devoid of interest – the title *Le monde primitif analysé et comparé avec le monde moderne* (cf. Genette 1976: 119–48).

Court de Gébelin knew the results of previous comparativist research. He also knew that the human linguistic faculty was exercised through a specific phonatory apparatus; and he was acquainted with its anatomy and physiology. He followed, moreover, the doctrines of the Physiocrats, and when he sought to explain the origin of language, he did so through a re-reading of ancient myths, interpreting them as allegories describing the relation of man the farmer to the land (vol. I). Writing, too, was susceptible to this sort of explanation. Although it was born before the separation of peoples, writing could be interpreted as having evolved in the time of the agrarian states, which needed to develop an instrument that would keep track of landed property and foster commerce and law (vol. III, p. xi) . . . Yet there still shines Court de Gébelin's dream of uncovering the original language of the primitive world, the language which served as the origin and basis of a universal grammar through which all existing languages might be explained.

In the preliminary discourse to volume III, dedicated to the natural history of speech or the origins of language, Court de Gébelin affirmed that words were not born by chance: 'each word has its own rationale deriving from Nature' (p. ix). He developed a strongly mimological theory of language accompanied by an ideographic theory of writing, according to which the alphabet itself is nothing but the primitive hieroglyphic script reduced to a small set of radical characters or 'keys' (III, xii).

As a faculty based upon a determined anatomical structure, language might certainly be considered as God's gift, but the elaboration of a primitive tongue was a human endeavour. It followed that when God spoke first to human beings, he had to use a language that they could understand, because it was a product of their own (III, 69).

To uncover this primitive language, Court de Gébelin undertook an impressive etymological analysis of Greek, Latin and French. Nor did he neglect coats of arms, coins, games, the voyages of the Phoenicians around the world, American Indian languages, medallions, and civil and religious history as manifested in calendars and almanacs. As a basis for this original language he set out to reconstruct a universal grammar, founded on necessary principles, valid in all times and in all places, so that the moment that one of these principles was discovered lying immanent in any one language it could be projected into all the others.

Court de Gébelin seems, in the end, to have wanted too much. He wanted a *universal grammar*; he wanted the *mother tongue*; he wanted the *biological and social origins of language*. He ended up, as Yaguello observes (1984: 19), by muddling them all together in a confused mass. To top it all off, he fell victim in the end to the siren call of the Celto-nationalist hypothesis which I shall be describing in the next section. Celtic (being similar to oriental languages from which it originated) was the tongue of Europe's first inhabitants. From Celtic had derived Greek, Latin, Etruscan, Thracian, German, the Cantabrian of the ancient Spaniards, and the Runic of the Norsemen (vol. V).

The Nationalistic Hypotheses

Another alternative was to accept that Hebrew had been the original perfect language, but to argue that, after the *confusio*, the crown of perfection had been bestowed upon other languages. The first text which countenances this sort of 'nationalistic' reconstruction of linguistic history is the *Commentatio super opera diversorum auctorum de antiquitatibus loquentium* of 1498 by Giovanni Nanni, or Annius, which tells how, before it was colonized by the Greeks, Etruria had been settled by Noah and his descendants. Nanni is here reflecting on the contradiction between Genesis 11, the story of Babel, and Genesis 10. In 10:5, the sons of Japheth settle the 'isles of the Gentiles . . . *every one after his tongue*'.

The notion of a lineage ascending from modern Tuscan through Etruscan to the Aramaic of Noah was elaborated in Florence by Giovann Battista Gelli (*Dell'origine di Firenze*, 1542–4) and by Piero Francesco Giambullari (*Il Gello*, 1564). Their thesis, fundamentally anti-humanist, accepted the idea that the multiplication of tongues had preceded Babel (citing what Dante had had to say in *Paradise*, xxvi).

This thesis was passionately received by Guillaume Postel, who, we have seen, had already argued that Celtic had descended from Noah. In *De Etruriae regionis* (1551) Postel embraced the position of Gelli and Giambullari concerning the relationship of the Etruscan to Noah, qualifying it, however, by the claim that the Hebrew of Adam had remained – at least in its hieratic form – uncontaminated throughout the centuries.

More moderate were the claims of Spanish Renaissance authors. The Castilian tongue too might claim descent from one of Japheth's many sons – in this case Tubal. Yet it was still only one of the seventy-two languages formed after Babel. This moderation was more apparent than real, however, for, in Spain, the term 'language of Babel' became an emblem of antiquity and nobility (for Italian and Spanish debates, cf. Tavoni 1990).

It was one thing to argue that one's own national language could claim nobility on account of its derivation from an original language – whether that of Adam or that of Noah – but quite a different matter to argue that, for this reason, one's language ought to be considered as the one and only perfect language, on a par with the language of Adam. Only the Irish grammarians cited in the first chapter and Dante had had, so far, the audacity to arrive at such a daring conclusion (and even Dante – who had aspired to create a perfect language from his own vernacular – made sarcastic remarks on those who consider their native language as the most ancient and perfect: cf. DVE, I, vi). By the seventeenth century, however, linguistic nationalism had begun to bud; this prompted a plethora of such curious claims.

Goropius Becanus (Jan van Gorp) in his *Origines Antwerpianae* of 1569 agreed with all claims made about the divine inspiration of the original language, and about its motivated and non-arbitrary relation between words and things. According to him there was only a single living language in which this motivated concordance existed to an exemplary degree; that language was Dutch, particularly the dialect of Antwerp. The ancestors of the burghers of Antwerp were the Cimbri, the direct descendants of the sons of Japheth. These had not been present under the Tower of Babel, and, consequently, they had been spared the *confusio linguarum*. Thus they had preserved the language of Adam in all its perfection. Such an assertion, Becanus claimed, could be proved by etymological demonstrations. He produced a string of arguments whose level of etymological wishful thinking matched those of Isidore and Guichard; they later became known as 'becanisms' or 'goropisms'. Becanus further claimed that his thesis was also proved by the facts that Dutch had the highest number of monosyllabic words, possessed a richness of sounds superior to all other languages, and favoured in the highest degree the formation of compound words.

Becanus' thesis was later supported by Abraham Mylius (*Lingua belgica*, 1612) as well as by Adrian Schrickius (*Adversariorum Libri III*, 1620), who wished to demonstrate 'that Hebrew was divine and firstborn' and 'that Teutonic came immediately afterwards'. 'Teutonic' here meant the Dutch spoken in Antwerp, which, at the time, was its best-known dialect. In both cases, the demonstration was supported by etymological proofs little better than those of Becanus.

Despite its improbability, the so-called 'Flemish thesis' proved remarkably long-lasting. It survived even into the nineteenth century. It did so, however, less on its scientific merits than because it was part of a larger nationalist polemic. In his *La province de Liège . . . Le flamand langue primordiale, mère de toutes les langues* of 1868, the baron de Ryckholt proclaimed that 'Flemish is the only language spoken in the cradle of humanity' and that 'it alone is a language, while all the rest, dead or living, are but mere dialects or debased forms more or less disguised' (cf. Droixhe 1990; for linguistic *follies de grandeur* in general, Poliakov 1990).

With such a persistent and ebullient Flemish claim, it can hardly be surprising that there should be a Swedish candidacy as well. In 1671, Georg Stiernhielm wrote his *De linguarum origine praefatio*. In 1688, his fellow countryman, Andreas Kempe, wrote *Die Sprachen des Paradises*; this included a scene in which God and Adam conversed with one another, God speaking in Swedish while Adam spoke in Danish; while they were talking, however, Eve was busy being seduced by a French-speaking serpent (cf. Borst 1957–63: III, 1, 1338; Olender 1989, 1993). We are, by now, close to parody; yet we should not overlook the fact that these claims were made precisely in Sweden's period as a major power on the European chessboard. Olaus Rudbeck, in his *Atlantica sive Mannheim vera Japheti posterorum sedes ac patria* of 1675, demonstrated that Sweden was the home of Japheth and his line, and that from this racial and linguistic stock all the Gothic idioms were born. Rudbeck identified Sweden, in fact, as the mythical Atlantis, describing it as the ideal land, the land of the Hesperides, from which civilization had spread to the entire world.

This was an argument that Isidore himself had already used. In his *Etymologiarum*, IX, ii, 26–7, he had suggested that the progenitor of the Goths was another of Japheth's sons – Magog. Vico was later to comment acidly on all such claims (*Scienza nuova seconda*, 1744: II, 2.4, 430):

Having now to enter upon a discussion of this matter, we shall give a brief sample of the opinions that have been held respecting it – opinions so uncertain, inept, frivolous, pretentious or ridiculous, and so numerous, that we need not relate them. By way of sample then: because in the returned barbarian times Scandinavia by the conceit of the nations was called *vagina gentium* and was believed to be the mother of all other nations of the world, therefore by the conceit of the scholars Johannes and Olaus Magnus were of the opinion that their Goths had preserved them from the beginning of the world the letters divinely inspired by Adam. This dream was laughed at by all the scholars, but this did not keep Johannes van Gorp from following suit and going one better by claiming his own Dutch language, which is not much different from Saxon, has come down from the Earthly Paradise and is the mother of all other languages. [. . .] And yet this conceit swelled to bursting point in the *Atlantica* of Olaus Rudbeck, who will have it that the Greek letters came from the runes; that the Phoenician letters, to which Cadmus gave the order and values to those of the Hebrew, were inverted runes; and that the Greeks finally straightened them here and rounded them there by rule and compass. And because the inventor is called Merkurssman among the Scandinavians, he will have it that the Mercury who invented letters for the Egyptians was a Goth.

Already by the fourteenth century, the idea of a German linguistic primacy was shaking the German-speaking world. The idea later appeared in Luther, for whom German was the language closest to God. In 1533 Konrad Pelicanus (*Commentaria bibliorum*) set out the analogies between German and Hebrew, without, however, coming to a final judgement over which of the two was truly the *Ursprache* (cf. Borst 1957–63: III/1, 2). In the baroque period, Georg Philipp Harsdörffer (*Frauenzimmer Gesprächspiele*, 1641, Niemayer Tubingen, ed., 1968: 335ff) claimed that the German language:

speaks in the languages of nature, quite perceptibly expressing all its sounds. [. . .] It thunders with the heavens, flashes lightning with the quick moving clouds, radiates with the hail, whispers with the winds, foams with the waves, creaks with the locks, sounds with the air, explodes with the cannons; it roars like the lion, lows like the oxen, snarls like the bear, bells like the stag, bleats like the sheep, grunts like the pig, barks like the dog, whinnies like the horse, hisses like the snake, meows like the cat, honks like the goose, quacks like the duck, buzzes like the bumble bee, clucks like the hen, strikes its beak like the stork, caws like the crow, coos like the swallow, chirps like the sparrow. [. . .] On all those occasions in which nature gives things their own sound, nature speaks in our own German tongue. For this, many have wished to assert that the first man, Adam, would not have been able to name the birds and all the other beasts of the fields in anything but our words, since he expressed, in a manner conforming to their nature, each and every innate property and inherent sound; and thus it is not surprising that the roots of the larger part of our words coincide with the sacred language.

German had remained in a state of perfection because Germany had never been subjected to the yoke of a foreign ruler. Lands that had been subjected had inevitably adapted their customs and language to fit those of the victor. This was also the opinion of Kircher. French, for example, was a mix of Celtic, Greek and Latin. The German language, by contrast, was richer in terms than Hebrew, more docile than Greek, mightier than Latin, more magnificent in its pronunciation than Spanish, more gracious than French, and more correct than Italian.

Ideas similar to these were expressed by Schottel (*Teutsche Sprachkunst*, 1641), who celebrated the German language as the one which, in its purity, remained closest to the language of Adam (adding to this the idea that language was the expression of the native genius of a people). Others even claimed that Hebrew had derived from German. They repeated the claim that their language had descended from Japheth, who, in this rendition, had supposedly settled in Germany. The name of the exact locality changed, of course, to fit the needs of different authors; yet Japheth's grandson, Ascenas, was said to have lived in the principality of Anhalt even before the *confusio*. There he was the progenitor of both Arminius and Charlemagne.

In order to understand these claims, one must take into account the fact that, during the sixteenth and seventeenth centuries, Protestant Germany rallied to the defence of the language of Luther's Bible. It was in this period that claims to the linguistic primacy of German arose, and many of these assumptions 'should be seen within the context of Germany's political fragmentation after the Thirty Years War. Since the German language was one of the main forces capable of uniting the nation, its value had to be emphasized and the language itself had to be liberated from foreign influences' (Faust 1981: 366).

Leibniz ironized on these and other theories. In a letter of 7 April 1699 (cited in Gensini 1991: 113) he ridiculed those who wished to draw out everything from their own language – Becanus, Rudbeck, a certain Ostroski who considered Hungarian as the mother tongue, an abbé François and Pretorius, who did respectively the same for Breton and Polish. Leibniz concluded that if one day the Turks and Tartars became as learned as the Europeans, they would have no difficulty finding ways to promote their own idioms to the rank of mother tongue for all humanity.

Despite these pleasantries, Leibniz was not entirely immune himself to nationalist temptations. In his *Nouveaux essais* (III, 2) he made a good-natured jibe at Goropius Becanus, coining the verb *goropiser* for the making of bad etymologies. Still, he conceded, Becanus might not always have been entirely wrong, especially when he recognized in the Cimbrian, and, consequently, in Germanic, a language that was more primitive than Hebrew. Leibniz, in fact, was a supporter of the Celto-Scythian hypothesis, first advanced in the Renaissance (cf. Borst 1957–63: III/1, iv, 2; Droixhe 1978). In the course of over ten years of collecting linguistic materials and subjecting them to minute comparisons, Leibniz had become convinced that at the root of the entire Japhetic stock there lay a Celtic language that was common to both the Gauls and the Germans, and that 'we may conjecture that this [common stock] derives from the time of the common origin of all these peoples, said to be among the Scythians, who, coming from the Black Sea, crossed the Danube and the Vistula, and of whom one part may have gone to Greece, while the other filled Germany and Gaul' (*Nouveaux essais*, III, 2). Not only this: Leibniz even discovered analogies between the Celto-Scythian languages and those which we would today call the Semitic languages, due, he conjectured, to successive migrations. He held that 'there was nothing that argues either against or for the idea of a single, common origin of all nations, and, in consequence, of one language that is radical and primitive.' He admitted that Arabic and Hebrew seemed closer than others, their numerous alterations notwithstanding. He concluded, however, that 'it seems that Teutonic has best preserved its natural and Adamitic aspect (to speak like Jacques Böhm [*sic*])'. Having examined various types of German onomatopoeia, he finally concluded that the Germanic language seemed most primitive.

In presenting this scheme in which a Scythian language group progressively diffused throughout the Mediterranean world, and in distinguishing this group from the other group of southern or Aramaic languages, Leibniz designed a linguistic atlas. Most of the conjectures in Leibniz's own particular scheme were, in the end, erroneous; nevertheless, in the light of comparative linguistic work which would come afterwards, he had some brilliant intuitions (cf. Gensini 1990: 41).

In the British context, the Celtic hypothesis had naturally quite a different meaning; it meant, for one thing, an opposition to the theory of a Germanic origin. In the eighteenth century the thesis of Celtic primacy was supported by Rowland Jones, who argued 'no other language, not even English, shows itself to be so close to the first universal language, and to its natural precision and correspondence between words and things, in the form and in the way in which we have presented it as universal language.' The English language is

the mother of all the western dialects and the Greek, elder sister of all orientals, and in its concrete form, the living language of the Atlantics and of the aborigines of Italy, Gaul and Britain, which furnished the Romans with much of their vocables . . . The Celtic dialects and knowledge derived their origin from the circles of Trismegistus, Hermes, Mercury or Gomer . . . [and] the English language happens more peculiarly to retain its derivation from that purest fountain of languages. ('Remarks on the Circles of Gomer', *The Circles of Gomer*, 1771: II, 31–2)

Etymological proofs follow.

Such nationalistic hypotheses are comprehensible in the seventeenth and eighteenth centuries, when the larger European states began to take form, posing the problem of which of them was to be supreme on the continent. In this period, spirited claims to originality and superiority arise no longer from the visionary quest for universal peace, but – whether their authors realized this or not – from concrete reasons of state.

In whatever case, and whatever their nationalistic motivations, as a result of what Hegel calls the astuteness of reason, the furious search for etymologies, which was supposed to prove the common descent of every living language, eventually ended by creating the conditions in which serious work in comparative linguistics might become more profitable. As this work expanded, the phantom of an original mother tongue receded more and more into the background, remaining, at most, a mere regulative hypothesis. To compensate for the loss, there arose a new and pressing need to establish a typology of fundamental linguistic stocks. Thus, in this radically altered perspective, the search for the original mother tongue transformed itself into a general search for the origins of a given language. The need to document the existence of the primeval language had resulted in theoretical advances such as the identification and delimitation of important linguistic families (Semitic and Germanic), the elaboration of a model of linguistic descent with the inheritance of common linguistic traits, and, finally, the emergence of an embryonic comparative method typified in some synoptic dictionaries (Simone 1990: 331).

The Indo-European Hypothesis

Between the eighteenth and the nineteenth centuries a new perspective opened. The battle for Hebrew had been definitively lost. It now seemed clear that, even had it existed, linguistic change and corruption would have rendered the primitive language irrecuperable. What was needed instead was a typology in which information about known languages might be codified, family connections established, and relations of descent traced. We are here at the beginning of a story which has nothing to do with our own.

In 1786, in the *Journal of the Asiatick Society* of Bombay, Sir William Jones announced that

The Sanscrit language, whatever be its antiquity, is of a wonderful structure; more perfect than Greek, more copious than Latin, and more exquisitely refined than either, yet bearing to both of them a stronger affinity, both in the root of verbs and in the forms of grammar [. . .] No philosopher could examine them all three, without believing them to have sprung from some common source, which, perhaps, no longer exists. ('On the Hindus', *The Works of Sir William Jones*, III, London 1807, 34–5)

Jones advanced the hypothesis that Celtic, Gothic and even

ancient Persian were all related to Sanskrit. Note that he spoke not only of similar verbal roots, but also of similar grammatical structures. We have left behind the study of lexical analogies, and are beginning a research on syntactic similarities and phonetic affinities.

Already in 1653, John Wallis (*Grammatica linguae anglicanae*) had posed the problem of how one might establish the relation between a series of French words – *guerre, garant, gard, gardien, garderobe, guise* – and the English series – *war, warrant, ward, warden, wardrobe, wise* – by proving the existence of a constant shift from *g* to *w*. Later in the nineteenth century, German scholars, such as Friedrich and Wilhelm von Schlegel and Franz Bopp, deepened the understanding of the relation between Sanskrit, Greek, Latin, Persian and German. They discovered a set of correspondences in the conjugation of the verb *to be* in all these languages. Gradually they came to the conclusion that not only was Sanskrit the original language of the group, its *Ursprache*, but that there must have existed, for this entire family, an even more primitive proto-language from which they all, Sanskrit included, had derived. This was the birth of the Indo-European hypothesis.

Through the work of Jakob Grimm (*Deutsche Grammatik*, 1818) these insights became organized in a scientific fashion. Research was based on the study of sound shifts (*Lautverschiebungen*) which traced how from the Sanskrit *p* were generated *pous–podos* in Greek, *pes–pedes* in Latin, *fotus* in Gothic, and *foot* in English.

What had changed between the utopian dream of an Adamic language and the new perspective? Three things. Above all, scholars had elaborated a set of scientific criteria. In the second place, the original language no longer seemed like an archaeological artefact that, one day, might actually be dug up. Indo-European was an ideal point of scholarly reference only. Finally, Indo-European made no claim to being the original language of all humanity; it merely represented the linguistic root for just one family – the Aryan.

But are we really able to say that with the birth of the modern science of linguistics the ghost of Hebrew as the holy language had finally been laid to rest? Unfortunately not. The ghost simply reconstituted itself into a different, and wholly disturbing, Other.

As Olender (1989, 1993) has described it, during the nineteenth century, one myth died only to be replaced by another. With the demise of the myth of linguistic primacy, there arose the myth of the primacy of a culture – or of a race. When the image of the Hebrew language and civilization was torn down, the myth of the Aryan races rose up to take its place.

The reality of Indo-European was only virtual; yet it was still intrusive. Placed face to face with such a reality, Hebrew receded to the level of metahistory. It became a symbol. At the symbolic level, Hebrew ranged from the linguistic pluralism of Herder, who celebrated it as a language that was fundamentally poetic (thus opposing an intuitive to a rationalistic culture), to the ambiguous apology of Renan, who – by contrasting Hebrew as the tongue of monotheism and of the desert to Indo-European languages (with their polytheistic vocation) – ends up with oppositions which, without our sense of hindsight, might even seem comic: the Semitic languages are incapable of thinking in terms of multiplicity, are unwilling to countenance abstraction; for this reason the Semitic culture would remain closed to scientific thinking and devoid of a sense of humour.

Unfortunately, this is not just a story of the gullibility of scientists. We know only too well that the Aryan myth had political consequences that were profoundly tragic. I have no wish to saddle the honest students of Indo-European with blame for the extermination camps, especially as – at the level of linguistic science – they were right. It is rather that, throughout this book, we have been sensitive to side-effects. And it is hard not to think of these side-effects when we read in Olender the following passage from the great linguist, Adolphe Pictet, singing this hymn to Aryan culture:

In an epoch prior to that of any historical witnesses, an epoch lost in the night of time, a race, destined by providence to one day rule the entire world, slowly grew in its primitive birthplace, a prelude to its brilliant future. Privileged over all others by the beauty of their blood, by their gifts of intelligence, in the bosom of a great and severe nature that would not easily yield up its treasures, this race was summoned from the very beginning to conquer. [. . .] A language in which each of their impressions came to be spontaneously reflected, their tender feelings, their ingenuous admiration, but also their impulse to find a superior world; a language which was filled with images and intuitive ideas, which bore the seeds of all the future richness of a magnificent poetic expansion and of the most profound thought (I, 7–8) [. . .] Is it not perhaps curious to see the Aryas of Europe, after a separation of four or five thousand years, close the circle once again, reach their unknown brothers in India, dominate them, bring to them the elements of a superior civilization, and then to find ancient evidence of a common origin? (*Les origines indo-européennes ou les Aryas primitifs*, 1859–63: III, 537, cited in Olender 1989: 130–9)

At the end of a thousand-year long ideal voyage to the East in search of roots, Europe had at last found some ideal reasons to turn that virtual voyage into a real one – for the purposes not of intellectual discovery, however, but of conquest. It was the ideal of the 'white man's burden'. With that, there was no longer any need to discover a perfect language to convert old or new brothers. It was enough to convince them to speak an Indo-European language, in the name of a common origin.

Philosophers against Monogeneticism

Although in the eighteenth century a de Brosses or a Court de Gébelin might still persist in his glottogonic strivings, by the time of the Enlightenment, philosophers had already laid the basis for the definitive liquidation of the myth of the mother tongue and of the notion of a linguistic paradise existing before Babel. Rousseau, in his *Essai sur l'origine des langues* (published posthumously in 1781, but certainly written several decades earlier), used arguments already present in Vico to turn the tables on the older myths. The very negative characteristics that philosophers had once attributed to the languages after Babel, Rousseau now discovered in the primitive language itself.

Primitive language spoke by metaphors. This meant that, in a primitive language, words did not, and could not, express the essence of the objects that they named. Reacting in front of an unknown object only instinctively, primitive people were slaves to their passions. Primitive human beings would, metaphorically and erroneously, call beings slightly bigger or stronger than them *giants* (ch. 3). Such a primitive language was less articulated, closer to song, than a properly verbal language. It was replete with synonyms to express a single entity in its differing aspects and relations. Furnished with few abstract terms, its grammar was irregular and full of anomalies. It was a language that represented without reasoning (ch. 4).

Furthermore, the very dispersion of peoples after the Flood made research into this original language a vain undertaking (ch. 9). Du Bos, in his *Reflexions critiques sur la poésie et sur la peinture* (edn: 1764: I, 35) preferred to speak of the language of the age of huts, rather than of the language of origins. But even this language was not only lost for ever: it was radically imperfect. History has begun to assert its rights. A return was impossible, and, in any event, would not have meant a return to a knowledge that was still full and whole.

Concerning the question of the genesis of language, the eighteenth century was divided into two camps; one maintaining a rationalist hypothesis, the other an empirico-sensationalist one. Many Enlightenment thinkers remained under the influence of Descartes, whose philosophical principles were expressed in semiotic terms by the *Grammaire* (1660) and the *Logique* (1662) of Port Royal. Authors such as Beauzée and Du Marsais (both collaborators in the

Encyclopédie) postulated a thoroughgoing isomorphism between language, thought and reality. Much of the discussion about the rationalization of grammar moved in this direction as well. Under the heading 'Grammar', for example, Beauzée wrote that 'the word is nothing but a sort of painting [*tableau*] of which the thought is the original.' Language's proper function was to provide a faithful copy of the original thought. Thus, it seemed to follow that 'there must be a set of fundamental principles, common to all languages, whose indestructible truth is prior to all those arbitrary and haphazard conditions which have given birth to the various idioms which divide the human race.'

During this same period, however, there flowered another current, which Rosiello (1967) has termed 'Enlightenment linguistics'. This was based on Lockean empiricism as it had been developed into the sensationalism of Condillac. In contradistinction to the Cartesian doctrine of innate ideas, Locke had described the human mind as a blank slate, devoid of figures, which drew its ideas directly from the senses. It is through our senses that we have access to the outside world, and through reflection that we know the workings of our minds. From these two activities derive all simple ideas, which intelligence later takes up, manipulating them and compounding them into the infinite variety of complex ideas.

In his *Essai sur l'origine des connaissances humaines* (1746), Condillac took Locke's empiricism and reduced it to a radical sensationalism. According to Condillac, it was not only perception that derived from the senses, but all the working of our minds – memory, awareness, comparison and, consequently, judgement. If a statue could be made possessing an internal organization identical to our own, Condillac argued, that statue would gradually, through its primary sensations of pain and pleasure, derive a collection of abstract notions identical to our own. In this genesis of ideas, signs play a fundamental role: they express at first our primary feelings, by cries and gestures – a *language of action*. Afterwards this purely emotional language evolves to function as the mode in which we fix our thoughts – a *language of institution*.

The notion of a language of action had already been expressed by William Warburton (*The Divine Legation of Moses*, 1737–41). It was an idea that was to become an important tenet of sensationalist philosophy, as it provided a link that helped explain how human beings had passed from simple, immediate responses to more complex forms of cultural behaviour, in the course of an irreversible historical development. At the very end of the century, the Idéologues began to fill this picture in, elaborating a vision of the early course of human history that was, at once, materialist, historicist and sensitive to social factors. They began to investigate every form of expression: various types of pictographic sign, gestures in the pantomime or in the language of deaf-mutes, orators and actors, algebraic characters, the jargons and passwords of secret societies (for it was in this period that masonic confraternities were founded and spread).

In works such as the *Eléments d'idéologie* by Antoine-Louis-Claude Destutt De Tracy (1801–15, 4 vols) and, even more, *Des signes* by Joseph-Marie de Degérando (1800: I, 5) a great historic panorama began to emerge. At the first stage, human beings sought to make their intentions known to each other through simple actions; at the next stage they passed gradually to a language of nature, that is, an imitative language in which they could represent, by a sort of pantomime, a real action. This would be a language still subject to misunderstandings, for there would be nothing to guarantee that both parties in a conversation would associate the mimed sign with the same idea, and that, consequently, the receiver would draw the intended conclusions about the purposes and circumstances for which the pantomime had been enacted. Where the purpose was to refer to an object that was actually present, all that was necessary was a sign we might call *indexical* – a cry or glance in the direction of the object, a pointing of a finger. Indexical signs would no longer do, however, where the intention was to refer to an object not present, either because the object was physically located at some other place or time, or because the 'object' was, in fact, an interior state. Where the absent object was physical and material, a mimed imitation might still be able to denote it – trying to imitate not substances but actions. To refer to non-physical, interior states, however, it was necessary to develop a more figurative language, a language of metaphor, synecdoche and metonymy. Two weights hefted by the hands might, for example, suggest making a judgement between two parties; a flame might symbolize an ardent passion, and so on. Up to this point, we are still in a *language of analogies*, expressed in gestures, cries and primitive onomatopoeia, or by a symbolic or pictographic form of writing. Slowly, however, these *signs of analogy* become *signs of habitude*; they are codified, more or less arbitrarily, up to the birth of a language in the strict sense of the term. Thus, the semiotic machinery constructed by humanity is determined by environmental and historical factors.

This elaboration by the Idéologues implied a cogent and devastating critique of any idea of a perfect original language. It is a critique, moreover, that brought an argument initiated over two centuries earlier to a close. This was the argument that had begun with the rediscovery of the hypothesis of Epicurus, and with the first reflections of Montaigne and Locke on the variety of cultures and the differences in beliefs among the variety of exotic peoples that the accounts of the explorers of their times were revealing.

Thus, under the entry 'Language' in the *Encyclopédie*, Jaucourt could say that since languages were all reflections of the 'genius' of the various peoples, it is impossible to conceive of a universal tongue. Since customs and ideas were determined by climate, upbringing and government, it was not possible to impose the same customs, or the same ideas of vice and virtue, on all nations.

In this formulation, the notion of 'genius' was employed as a means of explaining how each language contains its own particular vision of the world. Yet such a notion also implies that languages were mutually incommensurable. This was an idea that already appears in Condillac (*Essai sur l'origine des connaissances humaines*, II, I, 5). It also appeared in Herder (*Fragmente über die neuere deutsche Literatur*, 1766–7), and was developed by Humboldt (*Fragmente über die Verschiedenheit des menschlichen Sprachbaues und ihren Einfluss auf die geistige Entwicklung des Menschengeschlects*, 1836), for whom every language possesses its own *innere Sprachform*, an inner form expressing the vision of the world of the people who speak it.

When one assumes that there is an organic relation and a reciprocal influence between language and thought, it is clear that such an interaction does not only work within a given language at a given historical time: it affects the very historical development of every language and of every culture (cf. De Mauro 1965: 47–63).

A Dream that Refused to Die

Even faced with the results of the research of comparative linguistics, however, monogenetic theories refuse to give up the ghost. The bibliography of belated monogeneticism is immense. In it, there is to be found the lunatic, the crank, the misfit, the bizarre mystic, as well as a number of students of unimpeachable rigour.

In 1850, for example, the Enlightenment notion of a language of action received a radically monogenetic reading in the *Dactylologie et langage primitif restitués d'après les monuments* by J. Barrois. Assuming that the first language of humanity was a language of action and that this language was exclusively gestural, Barrois sought to prove that even the passages of the Bible which referred to God addressing Adam referred not to speaking in a verbal sense, but instead to a non-verbal, mimed language. 'The designation of the divers animals which Adam made was achieved by means of a special miming which recalled their form, instinct, habit, and qualities, and, finally, their essential properties' (p. 31). The first time that an unambiguous reference to verbal speech appears in the Bible is when God speaks to Noah; before this, all references seem vague. For Barrois, this was evidence showing that only slowly, in the immediately antediluvian age, did a phonetic form of language become common. The *confusio linguarum* arose out of discord between gestural and spoken language. The primitive vocal language was born closely accompanied by gestures which served to underline its most important words – just as occurs today in the speech of negroes and Syrian merchants (p. 36).

A dactylological language (expressed by the movement of the fingers and deriving from the primitive language of action) was born later, as a form of short-hand support for the phonetic language, when this latter emerged as the dominant form. Barrois examines iconographic documents of all ages, demonstrating that the dactylological language remained unaltered through various civilizations.

As for the everlasting idea of an original Hebrew, we might cite the figure of Fabre d'Olivet, whose *La langue hébraïque restituée*, written in 1815, is still a source of inspiration for belated kabbalists today. He told of a primitive language that no people had ever spoken, of which Hebrew (the Egyptian dialect of Moses) was but the most illustrious offspring. This insight leads him on to the search for a mother tongue in which Hebrew is carefully combed and then subjected to fantastic reinterpretations. D'Olivet was convinced that, in this language, every phoneme, every single sound, must have its own special meaning. We will not follow d'Olivet as he re-explores this old terrain; it is enough to say that he presents a string of nonsensical etymologies which, though in the spirit of Duret, Guichard and Kircher, are, if anything, even less convincing.

We might, however, provide just one example to show how traces of an original Hebrew mimology can be discovered in a modern language as well. D'Olivet constructed an etymology for the French term *emplacement*. *Place* derives from the Latin *platea* and from the German *Platz*. In both these words, the sound AT signifies protection, while the sound L means extension. LAT means, therefore, a 'protected extension'. MENT, in its turn, derives from the Latin *mens* and the English *mind*. In this syllable, E is the sign of absolute life, and N stands for reflexive existence. Together, as ENS, they mean 'bodily spirit'. M refers to existence at a given point. Therefore, the meaning of *emplacement* is 'la manière dont une extension fixe et determinée peut être conçue et se presente aux yeux'. As one critic has put it, Fabre d'Olivet has demonstrated that *emplacement* means 'emplacement' (cf. Cellier 1953: 140; Pallotti 1992).

And yet. No less a figure than Benjamin Lee Whorf took Fabre d'Olivet as the starting point for a series of reflections on the curious subject of 'oligosynthesis'. He was wondering about the possible applications of a science capable of 'restoring a possible common language of the human race or [of] perfecting an ideal natural tongue constructed of the original psychological significance of sounds, perhaps a future common speech, into which all our varied languages may be assimilated, or, putting it differently, to whose terms they may be reduced' (Whorf 1956: 12; see also 74–6). This is neither the first nor the last of the paradoxes in our story: we associate Whorf with one of the least monogenetic of all the various glottogonic hypotheses; it was Whorf who developed the idea that each language was a 'holistic' universe, expressing the world in a way that could never be wholly translated into any other language.

Again apropos of the crusty old myth of Hebrew as the original language, we can follow it in the entertaining compilation given in White (1917: II, 189–208). Between the first and the ninth editions of the *Encyclopaedia Britannica* (1771 and 1885), a period of over one hundred years, the article dedicated to 'Philology' passed from a partial acceptance of the monogenetic hypothesis to manifestations of an increasingly modern outlook in scientific linguistics. Yet the shift took place only gradually – a series of timid steps. The notion that Hebrew was the sacred original language still needed to be treated with respect; throughout this period, theological fundamentalists continued to level fire at the theories of philologists and comparative linguists. Still in 1804, the Manchester Philological Society pointedly excluded from membership anyone who denied divine revelations by speaking of Sanskrit or Indo-European.

The monogeneticist counterattacks were many and varied. At the end of the eighteenth century, the mystic and theosophist Louis-Claude de Saint-Martin dedicated much of the second volume of his *De l'esprit des choses* (1798–9) to primitive languages, mother tongues and hieroglyphics. His conclusions were taken up by Catholic legitimists such as De Maistre (*Soirées de Saint Petersburg*, ii), De Bonald (*Recherches philosophiques*, iii, 2) and Lamennais (*Essai sur l'indifférence en matière de religion*). These were authors less interested in asserting the linguistic primacy of Hebrew as such than in contesting the polygenetic and materialist or, worse, the Lockean conventionalist account of the origin of language. Even today, the aim of 'reactionary' thought is not to defend the contention that Adam spoke to God in Hebrew, but rather to defend the status of language itself as the vehicle of revelation. This can only be maintained so long as it is also admitted that language can directly express, without the mediation of any sort of social contract or adaptations due to material necessity, the relation between human beings and the sacred.

Our own century has witnessed counterattacks from an apparently opposite quarter as well. In 1956, the Georgian linguist Nicolaij Marr elaborated a particular version of polygenesis. Marr is usually remembered as the inventor of a theory that language depended upon class division, which was later confuted by Stalin in his *Marxism and Linguistics* (1953). Marr developed his later position out of an attack on comparative linguistics, described as an outgrowth of bourgeois ideology – and against which he supported a radical polygenetic view. Ironically, however, Marr's polygeneticism (based upon a rigid notion of class struggle) in the end inspired him – again – with the utopia of a perfect language, born of a hybrid of all tongues when humanity will no more be divided by class or nationality (cf. Yaguello 1984: 7, with a full anthology of extracts).

New Prospects for the Monogenetic Hypothesis

Doubting the possibility of obtaining scientific agreement upon an argument whose evidence had been lost in the mists of time, about which nothing but conjectures might be offered, the Société de Linguistique of Paris in 1866 decided that it would no longer accept scientific communications on the subject of either universal languages or origins of language. In our century that millenary debate took the form of research on the *universals of language*, now based on the comparative analysis of existing languages. Such a study has nothing to do with more or less fantastic historic reconstructions and does not subscribe to the utopian idea of a perfect language (cf. Greenberg 1963; Steiner 1975: I, 3). However, comparatively recent times have witnessed a renewal of the search for the origins of language (cf., for example, Fano 1962; Hewes 1975, 1979).

Even the search for the mother tongue has been revived in this century by Vitalij Ševorškin (1989), who has re-proposed the *Nostratic* hypothesis, originally advanced in Soviet scientific circles in the 1960s, and associated with the names of Vladislav Il'ič-Svitych and Aron Dolgoposkiji. According to this hypothesis, there was a proto-Indo-European, one of the six branches of a larger linguistic family deriving from *Nostratics* – which in its turn derives from a proto-*Nostratics*, spoken approximately ten thousand years ago. The supporters of this theory have compiled a dictionary of several hundred terms of this language. But the proto-*Nostratics* itself would derive from a more ancient mother tongue, spoken perhaps fifty thousand years ago in Africa, spreading from there throughout the entire globe (cf. Wright 1991).

According to the so-called 'Eve's hypothesis', one can thus imagine a human couple, born in Africa, who later emigrated to the Near East, and whose descendants spread throughout Eurasia, and possibly America and Australia as well (Ivanov 1992: 2). To reconstruct an original language for which we lack any written evidence, we must proceed like

molecular biologists in their quest to understand the evolution of life. The biochemist identifies molecular elements that perform similar functions in widely divergent species, to infer the characteristics of the primordial cell from which they are presumed to have descended. So does the linguist seek correspondences in grammar, syntax, vocabulary, and vocalization among known languages in order to reconstruct their immediate forebears and ultimately the original tongue. (Gamkrelidze and Ivanov 1990: 110)

Cavalli-Sforza's work on genetics (cf., for example, 1988, 1991) tends to show that linguistic affinities reflect genetic affinities. This supports the hypothesis of a single origin of all languages, reflecting the common evolutionary origin of all human groups. Just as humanity evolved only once on the face of the earth, and later diffused across the whole planet, so language. Biological monogenesis and linguistic monogenesis thus go hand in hand and may be inferentially reconstructed on the basis of mutually comparable data.

In a different conceptual framework, the assumption that both the genetic and the immunological codes can, in some sense, be analysed semiotically seems to constitute the new scientific attempt to find a language which could be defined as the primitive one *par excellence* (though not in historical but rather in biological terms). This language would nest in the roots of evolution itself, of phylogenesis as of onto-genesis, stretching back to before the dawn of humanity (cf. Prodi 1977).

6

Kabbalism and Lullism in Modern Culture

Hebrew was not the only beneficiary of the passion for archaic wisdom that gripped scholars from the end of the Middle Ages onwards. The dawn of the modern era also saw a revival of interest in Greek thought and in the Greeks' fascination with Egypt and its mysterious hieroglyphic script (see ch. 7). Greek texts were rediscovered and enthusiastically assigned an antiquity that they did not, in fact, possess. They included the *Orphic Hymns*, attributed to Orpheus, but, in fact, written probably between the second and third centuries AD; the *Chaldean Oracles*, also written in the second century, but attributed to Zoroaster; and, above all, the *Corpus Hermeticum*. This was a compilation acquired in 1460 for Cosimo de' Medici in Florence, and immediately rushed to Marsilio Ficino so that he might translate it.

This last compilation, as was later shown, was the least archaic of all. In 1614, by using stylistic evidence and by comparing the innumerable contradictions among the documents, Isaac Casaubon, in his *De rebus sacris et ecclesiasticis*, showed that it was a collection of texts by different authors, all writing in late Hellenistic times under the influences of Egyptian spirituality. None of this was apparent in 1460, however. Ficino took the texts to be archaic, directly written by the mythical Hermes or Mercurius Trismegistus. Ficino was struck to discover that his account of the creation of the universe resembled that of

Genesis, yet – he said – we should not be amazed, because Mercurius could be none other than Moses himself (*Theologica platonica*, 8, 1). This enormous historical error, as Yates says, was destined to have surprising results (1964: 18–19).

The Hermetic tradition provided a magico-astrological account of the cosmos. Celestial bodies exercise their power and influence over earthly things, and by knowing the planetary laws one can not only predict these influences, but also manipulate them. There exists a relation of sympathy between the universal macrocosm and the human microcosm, a latticework of forces which it is possible to harness through astral magic.

Astral magic was practised through words and other signs, because there is a language by which human beings can command the stars. Such miracles can be performed through 'talismans', that is, images which might guarantee safe recovery, health or physical prowess. In his *De vita coelitus comparanda*, Ficino provided a wealth of details concerning how such talismans were to be worn; how certain plants linked by sympathy to certain stars were to be consumed; how magical ceremonies were to be celebrated with the proper perfumes, garments and songs.

Talismanic magic works because the bond which unites the occult virtues of earthly things and the celestial bodies which instilled them is expressed by *signatures*, that is, formal aspects of material things that recall certain features (properties or powers) of the corresponding heavenly bodies. God himself has rendered the sympathies between macrocosm and microcosm perceptible by stamping a mark, a sort of seal, onto each object of this world (cf. Thorndike 1923–58; Foucault 1966; Couliano 1984; Bianchi 1987).

In a text that can stand as the foundation for such a doctrine of signatures, Paracelsus declared that:

The *ars signata* teaches the way in which the true and genuine names must be assigned to all things, the same names that Adam, the Protoplastus, knew in the complete and perfect way [. . .] which show, at the same time, the virtue, the power, and the property of this or that thing. [. . .] This is the *signator* who signs the horns of the stag with branches so that his age may be known: the stag having as many years as his horns have branches. [. . .] This is the *signator* who covers the tongue of a sick sow with excrescences, so that her impurity may be known; if the tongue is impure so the whole body is impure. This is the *signator* who tints the clouds with divers colours, whereby it is possible to forecast the changes of the heavens. (*De natura rerum*, I, 10, 'De signatura rerum')

Even the Middle Ages were aware that 'habent corpora omnia ad invisibilia bona simulitudinem' (Richard of Saint Victor, *Benjamin Major*, *PL*, 196, 90): all bodies possess qualities which give them similarities with invisible goods. In consequence, every creature of the universe was an image, a mirror reflecting our terrestrial and supernatural destinies. Nevertheless, it did not occur to the Middle Ages that these images might speak in a perfect language. They required interpretation, explication and comment; they needed to be enclosed in a rational didactic framework where they could be elucidated, deciphered, in order to make clear the mystical affinities between a symbol and its content. For Renaissance Platonism, by contrast, the relation between the images and the ideas to which they referred was considered so intuitively direct that the very distinction between a symbol and its meaning disappeared (see Gombrich 1972: 'Icones Symbolicae', v).

Magic Names and Kabbalistic Hebrew

The date 1492 is an important one for Europe: it marks not only the discovery of America, but also the fall of Granada, through which Spain (and thus all Europe) severed its last link with Islamic culture. As a consequence of Granada, moreover, their Christian majesties expelled the Jews from Spain, setting them off on a journey that carried them across the face of Europe. Among them there were the kabbalists, who spread their influence across the whole continent.

The kabbala of the names suggested that the same sympathetic links holding between sublunar objects and celestial bodies also apply to names. According to Agrippa, Adam took both the properties of things and the influence of the stars into account when he devised his names; thus 'these names contain within them all the remarkable powers of the things that they indicate' (*De occulta philosophia*, I, 70). In this respect, Hebrew writing must be considered as particularly sacred; it exhibits perfect correspondence between letters, things and numbers (I, 74).

Giovanni Pico della Mirandola attended the Platonic academy of Marsilio Ficino where he had, in the spirit of the times, begun his study of the languages of ancient wisdom whose knowledge had gone into eclipse during the Middle Ages; Greek, Hebrew, Arabic and Chaldean. Pico rejected astrology as a means of divination (*Disputatio adversos astrologos divinatores*), but accepted astral magic as a legitimate technique for avoiding control by the stars, replacing it with the illuminated will of the magus. If it were true that the universe was constructed from letters and numbers, it would follow that whoever knew the mathematical rules behind this construction might act directly on the universe. According to Garin (1937: 162), such a will to penetrate the secrets of nature in order to dominate it presaged the ideal of Galileo.

In 1486 Pico made the acquaintance of the singular figure of a converted Jew, Flavius Mithridates, with whom he began a period of intense collaboration (for Mithridates see Secret 1964: 25ff). Although Pico could boast a certain familiarity with Hebrew, he needed the help of the translations that Mithridates prepared for him to plumb the depths of the texts he wished to study. Among Pico's sources we find many of the works of Abulafia (Wirszubski 1989). Mithridates' translations certainly helped Pico; at the same time, however, they misled him – misleading all succeeding Christian kabbalists in his wake. In order for a reader to use properly the kabbalist techniques of *notariqon*, *gematria* and *temurah*, it is obvious that the texts must remain in Hebrew: as soon as they are translated, most of the kabbalist wordplays become unintelligible or, at least, lose their flavour. In the translations he provided for Pico, Mithridates did often insert original Hebrew terms into his text; yet Pico (in part because typesetters of this period lacked Hebrew characters) often translated them into Latin, so augmenting the ambiguity and the obscurity of the text itself. Beyond this, Mithridates, in common with many of the first Christian kabbalists, also had the vice of interpolating into the Hebrew texts references supposedly demonstrating that the original author had recognized the divinity of Christ. As a consequence, Pico was able to claim: 'In any controversy between us and the Jews we can confute their arguments on the basis of the kabbalistic books.'

In the course of his celebrated nine hundred *Conclusiones philosophicae, cabalisticae et theologicae*, among which are included twenty-six *Conclusiones magicae* (1486), Pico demonstrated that the tetragrammaton, the sacred name of God, Yahweh, turned into the name of Jesus with the simple insertion of the letter *sin*. This proof was used by all successive Christian kabbalists. In this way, Hebrew, a language susceptible to all the combinatory manipulations of the kabbalist tradition, was raised, once again, to the rank of a perfect language.

For example, in the last chapter of the *Heptaplus* (1489) Pico, taking off with an interpretation of the first word of Genesis (*Bereshit*, 'In the beginning'), launches himself on a series of death-defying permutational and anagrammatical leaps. To understand the logic of Pico's reading, notice that in the following quotation the Hebrew characters have been substituted with the current name of the letters, Pico's transliterations have been respected, and he is working upon the Hebrew form of the word: *Bet, Resh, Alef, Shin, Yod, Tau.*

I say something marvellous, unparalleled, incredible . . . If we take the third letter and unite it with the first, we get [Alef Bet] *ab*. If we take the first, double it, and unite it with the second, we get [Bet Bet Resh] *bebar*. If we read all except the first, we get [Resh Alef Shin Yod Tau] *resith*. If we unite the fourth with the first and the last, we get [Shin Bet Tau] *sciabat*. If we place the first three in the order in which they appear, we get [Bet Resh Alef] *bara*. If we leave the first and take the next three, we get [Resh Alef Shin] *rosc*. If we leave the first two and take the two that follow, we get [Alef Shin] *es*. If, leaving the first three, we unite the fourth with the last, we get [Shin Tau] *seth*. Once again, if we unite the second with the first, we get [Resh Bet] *rab*. If we put after the third, the fifth and the fourth, we get [Alef Yod Shin] *hisc*. If we unite the first two letters with the last two, we get [Bet Resh Yod Tau] *berith*. If we unite the last to the first, we obtain the twelfth and last letter, which is [Tau Bet] *thob*, turning the *thau* into the letter *theth*, an extremely common procedure in Hebrew . . .

Ab means the father; *bebar* in the son and through the son (in fact, the *beth* put before means both things); *resith* indicates the beginning; *sciabath* means rest and end; *bara* means he created; *rosc* is head; *es* is fire; *seth* is fundament; *rab* means of the great; *hisc* of the man; *berith* with a pact; *tob* with goodness. Thus taking the phrase all together and in order, it becomes: 'The father in the son and for the son, beginning and end, that is, rest, created the head, the fire, and the fundament of the great man with a good pact.'

When Pico (in his 'Magic Conclusion' 22) declared that 'Nulla nomina ut significativa, et in quantum nomina sunt, singula et per se sumpta, in Magico opere virtutem habere possunt, nisi sint Hebraica, vel inde proxima derivata' ('No name, in so far as it has a meaning, and in so far as it is a name, singular and self-sufficient, can have a virtue in Magic, unless that name be in Hebrew or directly derived from it'), he meant to say that, on the basis of the supposed correspondence between the language of Adam and the structure of the world, words in Hebrew appeared as forces, as sounds which, as soon as they are unleashed, are able to influence the course of events.

The idea that Hebrew was a language endowed with a mystical 'force' had already appeared in both the ecstatic kabbala (described in ch. 2) and the *Zohar*, where (in 75 b, *Noah*) it is declared not only that the original Hebrew was the language that expressed the desires of the heart in prayer, but also that it was the only language understood by the celestial powers. By confusing the tongues after the disaster of Babel, God had hindered the rebellious tower-builders from ever pressing their will upon heaven again. Immediately afterwards, the text goes on to observe that, after the confusion, human power was weakened, because only the words uttered in the sacred tongue reinforce the power of heaven. The *Zohar* was thus describing a language that not only 'said' but 'did', a language whose utterances set supernatural forces in motion.

To use this sacred tongue as an acting force, rather than as a means of communication, it was not even necessary to understand it. Some, of course, had studied Hebrew grammar in order to discover the revelations therein; for others, however, Hebrew was all the more sacred and efficacious for remaining incomprehensible. The less it was penetrable, the brighter its aura of 'mana' shone, and the more its dictates escaped human intelligences, the more they became clear and ineluctable to supernatural agents.

Such a language no longer even had to be the original Hebrew. All it needed to do was to seem like it. And thus, during the Renaissance, the world of both black and white magic became populated with a vast array of more or less Semitic-sounding names, such as the clutch of angels' names which Pico released into a Renaissance culture already abundantly muddled by the vagaries of both Latin transliteration and the innocence of the printers – Hasmalim, Aralis, Thesphsraim . . .

In that part of his *De occulta philosophia* dedicated to ceremonial magic, Agrippa also paid particular attention to the pronunciation of names, both divine and diabolic, on the principle that 'although all the devils or intelligences speak the languages of the countries over which they preside, they speak only Hebrew whenever they deal with someone who knows their mother tongue' (III, 23). The spirits can be bent to our wills only if we take care to pronounce their natural names properly: 'These names [. . .] even though their sound and meaning are unknown, have, in the performance of magic [. . .] a greater power than meaningful names, when one, left dumbfounded by their enigma [. . .] firmly believing to be under divine influence, pronounces them with reverence, even if one does not understand them, to the glory of the divinity' (*De occulta philosophia*, III, 26).

The same could also be said of magical seals. Like Paracelsus, Agrippa made an abundant use of alphabets with pseudo-Hebraic characters. By a process of graphic abstraction, mysterious configurations were wrought from the original Hebrew letters and became the basis for talismans, pentacles and amulets bearing Hebrew sayings or versicles from the Bible. These were then put on to propitiate the benign or to terrorize the evil spirits.

John Dee – not only magus and astrologer to Queen Elizabeth I, but profound *érudit* and sharp politician as well – summoned angels of dubious celestial provenance by invoking names like Zizop, Zchis, Esiasch, Od and Iaod, provoking the admiring comment, 'He seemeth to read as Hebrew is read' (cf. *A True and Faithful Relation* of 1659).

There exists, however, a curious passage in the Arabic Hermetic treatise, known in the Middle Ages through a Latin translation, called the *Picatrix* (III, I, 2: cf. Pingree 1986), in which the Hebrew and Chaldean idioms are associated with the saturnine spirit, and, hence with melancholy. Saturn, on the one hand, was the sign of the knowledge of deep and secret things and of eloquence. On the other, however, it carried a set of negative connotations inherited from Judaic law, and was associated with black cloths, obscure streams, deep wells and lonely spots, as well as with metals like lead, iron and all that is black and fetid, with thick-leafed plants and, among the animals, with 'camelos nigros, porcos, simias, ursos, canes et gattos [*sic*]' ('black camels, pigs, monkeys, bears, dogs and cats'). This is a very interesting passage; if the saturnine spirit, much in vogue during the Renaissance, was associated with sacred languages, it was also associated with things, places and animals whose common property was their aura of black magic.

Thus, in a period in which Europe was becoming receptive to new sciences that would eventually alter the known face of the universe, royal palaces and the elegant villas in the Tuscan hills around Florence were humming with the faint burr of Semitic-sounding incantations – often on the lips of the scientists themselves – manifesting the fervid determination to win a mastery of both the natural and the supernatural worlds.

Naturally, things could not long remain in such a simple state. Enthusiasm for kabbalist mysticism fostered the emergence of a Hebrew hermeneutics that could hardly fail to influence the subsequent development of Semitic philology. From the *De verbo mirifico* and the *De arte kabbalistica* by Reuchlin, to the *De harmonia mundi* of Francesco Giorgi or the *Opus de arcanis catholicae veritatis* by Galatinus, all the way to the monumental *Kabbala denudata* by Knorr von Rosenroth (passing through the works of Jesuit authors whose fervour at the thought of new discoveries allowed them to overcome their scruples at handling such suspect material), there crystallized traditions for reading Hebrew texts. This is a story filled with exciting exegetical adventures, numerological fabulizing, mixtures of Pythagoreanism, Neo-Platonism and kabbalism. Little of it has any bearing on the search for a perfect language. Yet the perfect language was already there: it was the Hebrew of the kabbalists, a language that revealed by concealing, obscuring and allegorizing.

To return to the linguistic model outlined in our first chapter, the kabbalists were fascinated by an *expression-substance* – the Hebrew texts – of which they sought to retrieve the *expression-form* (the grammar), always remaining rather confused apropos of the corresponding *content-form*. In reality, their search aimed at rediscovering, by combining new expression-substances, a *content-continuum* as yet unknown, formless, though seemingly dense with possibility. Although the Christian kabbalists continually discovered new methods of segmenting an infinite continuum of content, its nature continued to elude them. In principle, expression and content ought to be *conformal*, but the expression-form appeared as the iconic image of something shrouded in mystery, thus leaving the process of interpretation totally adrift (cf. Eco 1990).

Kabbalism and Lullism in the Steganographies

A peculiar mixture of kabbalism and neo-Lullism arose in the search for secret writings – steganographies. The progenitor of this search, which was to engender innumerable contributions between humanism and the baroque, was the prolific Abbot Johannes Trithemius (1462–1516). Trithemius made no references to Lull in his works, relying instead on kabbalistic tradition, advising his followers, for instance, that before attempting to decipher a passage in secret writing they should invoke the names of angels such as Pamersiel, Padiel, Camuel and Aseltel.

On a first reading, these seem no more than mnemonic aids that can help either in deciphering or in ciphering messages in which, for example, only the initial letters of words, or only the initial letters of even-numbered words (and so on according to different sets of rules), are to be considered. Thus Trithemius elaborated texts such as 'Camuel Busarchia, menaton enatiel, meran sayr abasremon'. Trithemius, however, played his game of kabbala and steganography with a great deal of ambiguity. His *Poligraphia* seems simply a manual for encipherment, but with his posthumous *Steganographia* (1606 edition) the matter had become more complex. Many have observed (cf. Walker 1958: 86–90, or Clulee 1988: 137) that if, in the first two books of this last work, we can interpret Trithemius' kabbalist references in purely metaphorical terms, in the third book there are clear descriptions of magic rituals. Angels, evoked through images modelled in wax, are subjected to requests and invocations, or the adept must write his own name on his forehead with ink mixed with the juice of a rose, etc.

In reality, true steganography would develop as a technique of composing messages in cipher for political or military ends. It is hardly by chance that this was a technique that emerged during the period of conflict between emerging national states and flourished under the absolutist monarchies. Still, even in this period, a dash of kabbalism gave the technique an increased spice.

It is possible that Trithemius' use of concentric circles rotating freely within each other owed nothing to Lull: Trithemius employed this device not, as in Lull, to make discoveries, but simply to generate (or decipher) cryptograms. Every circle contains the letters of the alphabet; if one rotates the inner wheel so as to make the inner A correspond, let us say, to the outer C, the inner B will be enciphered as D, the inner C as E and so on (see also our ch. 9). It seems probable that Trithemius was conversant enough with the kabbala to know certain techniques of *temurah*, by which words or phrases might be rewritten, substituting for the original letters the letters of the alphabet in reverse (Z for A, Y for B, X for C, etc.). This technique was called the 'atbash sequence'; it permitted, for example, the tetragrammaton YHWH to be rewritten as MSPS. Pico cited this example in one of his *Conclusiones* (cf. Wirzubski 1989: 43). But although Trithemius did not cite him, Lull was cited by successive steganographers. The *Traité des chiffres* by Vigenère (1587) not only made specific references to Lullian themes, but also connected them as well to the factorial calculations first mentioned in the *Sefer Yezirah*. However, Vigenère simply follows in the footsteps of Trithemius, and, afterwards, of Giambattista Della Porta (with his 1563 edition of *De furtivis literarum notis*, amplified in subsequent editions): he constructed tables containing 400 pairs generated by 20 letters; these he combined in triples to produce what he was pleased to call a 'mer d'infini chiffrements à guise d'un autre Archipel tout parsemé d'isles ... un embrouillement plus malaisé à s'en depestrer de tous les labrinthes de Crete ou d'Egypte' (pp. 193–4), a sea of infinite cryptograms like a new Archipelago all scattered with isles, an imbroglio harder to escape from than all the labyrinths of Crete and Egypt. The fact that these tables were accompanied by lists of mysterious alphabets, some invented, some drawn from Middle Eastern scripts, and all presented with an air of secrecy, helped keep alive the occult legend of Lull the kabbalist.

There is another reason why steganography was propelling a Lullism that went far beyond Lull himself. The steganographers had little interest in the content (or the truths) expressed by their combinations. Steganography was not a technique designed to discover truth: it was a device by which elements of a given expression-substance (letters, numbers or symbols of any type) might be correlated randomly (in increasingly differing ways so as to render their decipherment more arduous) with the elements of another expression-substance. It was, in short, merely a technique in which one symbol replaced another. This encouraged formalism: steganographers sought ever more complex combinatory stratagems, but all that mattered was engendering new expressions through an increasingly mind-boggling number of purely syntactic operations. The letters were dealt with as unbound variables.

By 1624, in his *Cryptometrices et cryptographie libri IX*, Gustavus Selenus was designing a wheel of 25 concentric volvelles, each of them presenting 24 pairs of letters. After this, he displays a series of tables that record around 30,000 triples. From here, the combinatory possibilities become astronomical.

Lullian Kabbalism

We have now reached a point where we must collect what seem the various *membra disiecta* of the traditions we have been examining and see how they combined to produce a Lullian revival.

We can begin with Pico della Mirandola: he cited Lull in his *Apologia* of 1487. Pico, of course, would have been aware that there existed analogies between the permutational techniques of Lull and the *temurah* (which he called 'revolutio alphabetaria'). He was acute enough, however, to realize that they were two different things. In the 'Quaestio Sexta' of the *Apologia*, where Pico proved that no science demonstrates the divinity of Christ better than magic and the kabbala, he distinguished two doctrines which might be termed kabbalist only in a figurative (*transumptive*) sense: one was the supreme natural magic; the other was the *hokmat ha-zeruf* of Abulafia that Pico termed an 'ars combinandi', adding that 'apud nostros dicitur ars Raymundi licet forte diverso modo procedat' ('it is commonly designated as the art of Raymond, although it proceeds by a different method').

Despite Pico's scruples, a confusion between Lull and the kabbala was, by now, inevitable. It is from this time that the pathetic attempts of the Christian kabbalists to give Lull a kabbalistic reading begin. In the 1598 edition of Lull's works there appeared, under Lull's name, a short text entitled *De auditu kabbalistico*: this was nothing other than Lull's *Ars brevis* into which had been inserted a number of kabbalistic references. It was supposedly first published in Venice in 1518 as an *opusculum Raimundicum*. Thorndike (1923–58: v, 325) has discovered the text, however, in manuscript form, in the Vatican Library, with a different title and with an attribution to Petrus de Maynardis. The manuscript is undated, but, according to Thorndike, its calligraphy dates it to the fifteenth century. The most likely supposition is that it is a composition from the end of that century in which the suggestions first made by Pico were taken up and mechanically applied (Scholem et al. 1979: 40–1).

In the following century, the eccentric though sharp-witted Tommaso Garzoni di Bagnacavallo saw through the imposture. In his *Piazza universale di tutte le arti* (1589: 253), he wrote:

The science of Raymond, known to very few, might be described with the term, very improper in itself, of Cabbala. About this, there is a notion common to all scholars, indeed, to the whole world, that in the Cabbala can be found teachings concerning everything. [. . .] and for this reason one finds in print a little booklet ascribed to him [Lull] (though on this matter people beyond the Alps write many lies) bearing the title *De Auditu Cabalistico*. This is nothing but a brief summary of the *Arte Magna* as abbreviated, doubtlessly by Lull himself, into the *Arte Breve*.

Still, the association persisted. Among various examples, we might cite Pierre Morestel, who published an *Artis kabbalisticae, sive sapientiae divniae academia* in 1621, no more than a modest compilation from the *De auditu*. Except for the title, and the initial identification of the *Ars* of Lull with the kabbala, there was nothing kabbalistic in it. Yet Morestel still thought it appropriate to include the preposterous etymology for the word kabbala taken from *De auditu*: 'cum sit nomen compositum ex duabus dictionibus, videlicet abba et ala. Abba enim arabice idem quod pater latine, et ala arabice idem est quod Deus meus' ('as this name is composed of two terms, that is *abba* and *ala*. *Abba* is an Arabic word meaning Latin *pater*; *ala* is also Arabic, and means *Deus meus*'). For this reason, kabbala means 'Jesus Christ'.

The cliché of Lull the kabbalist reappears with only minimum variation throughout the writings of the Christian kabbalists. Gabriel Naudé, in his *Apologie pour tous les grands hommes qui ont esté accuséz de magie* (1625), energetically rebutted the charge that the poor Catalan mystic engaged in the black arts. None the less, French (1972: 49) has observed that by the late Renaissance, the letters from B to K, used by Lull, had become associated with Hebrew letters, which for the kabbalists were names of angels or of divine attributes.

Numerology, magic geometry, music, astrology and Lull-ism were all thrown together in a series of pseudo-Lullian alchemistic works that now began to intrude onto the scene. Besides, it was a simple matter to inscribe kabbalistic terms onto circular seals, which the magical and alchemical tradition had made popular.

It was Agrippa who first envisioned the possibility of taking from the kabbala and from Lull the technique of combination in order to go beyond the medieval image of a finite cosmos and construct the image of an open and expanding cosmos, or of different possible worlds. In his *In artem brevis R. Lulli* (appearing in the *editio princeps* of the writings of Lull published in Strasbourg in 1598), Agrippa assembled what seems, at first sight, a reasonably faithful and representative anthology from the *Ars magna*. On closer inspection, however, one sees that the number of combinations deriving from Lull's fourth figure has in-creased enormously because Agrippa has allowed repeti-tions. Agrippa was more interested in the ability of the art to supply him with a large number of combinations than in its dialectic and demonstrative properties. Consequently, he proposed to allow the sequences permitted by his art to proliferate indiscriminately to include subjects, predicates, rules and relations. Subjects were multiplied by distributing them, each according to its own species, properties and accidents, by allowing them free play with terms that are similar or opposite, and by referring each to its respective causes, actions, passions and relations.

All that is necessary is to place whatever idea one intends to consider in the centre of the circle, as Lull did with the letter A, and calculate its possible concatenations with all other ideas. Add to this that, for Agrippa, it was per-missible to add many other figures containing terms extra-neous to Lull's original scheme, mixing them up with Lull's original terms: the possibilities for combination become almost limitless (Carreras y Artau and Carreras y Artau 1939: 220–1).

Valerio de Valeriis seems to want the same in his *Aureum*

opus (1589), when he says that the *Ars* 'teaches further and further how to multiply concepts, arguments, or any other complex unto infinity, *tam pro parte vera quam falsa*, mixing up roots with roots, roots with forms, trees with trees, the rules with all these other things, and very many other things as well' ('De totius operis divisione').

Authors such as these still seem to oscillate, unable to decide whether the *Ars* constitutes a logic of discovery or a rhetoric which, albeit of ample range, still serves merely to organize a knowledge that it has not itself generated. This is evident in the *Clavis universalis artis lullianae* by Alsted (1609). Alsted is an author, important in the story of the dream of a universal encyclopedia, who even inspired the work of Comenius, but who still – though he lingered to point out the kabbalist elements in Lull's work – wished to bend the art of combination into a tightly articulated system of knowledge, a tangle of suggestions that are, at once, Aristotelian, Ramist and Lullian (cf. Carreras y Artau and Carreras y Artau 1939: II, 239–49; Tega 1984: I, 1).

Before the wheels of Lull could begin to turn and grind out perfect languages, it was first necessary to feel the thrill of an infinity of worlds, and (as we shall see) of all of the languages, even those that had yet to be invented.

Bruno: *Ars Combinatoria* and Infinite Worlds

Giordano Bruno's cosmological vision presented a world without ends, whose circumference, as Nicholas of Cusa had already argued, was nowhere to be found, and whose centre was everywhere, at whatever point the observer chose to contemplate the universe in its infinity and substantial unity. The panpsychism of Bruno had a Neo-Platonic foundation: there was but a single divine breath, one principle of motion pervading the whole of the infinite universe, determining it in its infinite variety of forms. The master idea of an infinite number of worlds was compounded with the notion that every earthly object can also serve as the Platonic shade of other ideal aspects of the universe. Thus every object exists not only in itself, but as a possible sign, deferral, image, emblem, hieroglyph of something else. This worked also by contrast: an image can lead us back to the unity of the infinite even through its opposite. As Bruno wrote in his *Eroici furori*, 'To contemplate divine things we need to open our eyes by using figures, similitudes, or any of the other images that the Peripatetics knew under the name of phantasms' (*Dialoghi italiani*, Florence: Sansoni, 1958: 1158).

Where they did not emerge directly from his own inflamed imagination, Bruno chose images found in the Hermetic repertoire. These served as storehouses of revelations because of a naturally symbolic relationship that held between them and reality. Their function was no longer, as in previous arts of memory, that of merely helping to order information for ease of recall, or this was, at least, by now a minor aspect: their function was rather that of helping to understand. Bruno's images permitted the mind to discover the essence of things and their relations to each other.

The power of revelation stored inside these images was founded on their origin in far-off Egypt. Our distant progenitors worshipped cats and crocodiles because 'a simple divinity found in all things, a fecund nature, a mother watching over the universe, expressed in many different ways and forms, shines through different subjects and takes different names' (*Lo spaccio della bestia trionfante, Dialoghi italiani*, 780–2).

But these images possess more than the simple capacity to reawaken our dormant imagination: they possess an authentic power to effect magical operations on their own, and functioned, in other words, in exactly the same way as the talismans of Ficino. It is possible, of course, to take many of Bruno's magical claims in a metaphorical sense, as if he was merely describing, according to the sensibility of his age, intellectual operations. It is also possible to infer that these images had the power to pull Bruno, after prolonged concentration, into a state of mystic ecstasy (cf. Yates

1964: 296). Still, it is difficult to ignore the fact that some of Bruno's strongest claims about the theurgic potential of seals appeared in a text that bore the significant title of *De Magia*:

nor even are all writings of the same utility as these characters which, by their very configuration, seem to indicate things themselves. For example, there are signs that are mutually inclined to one another, that regard each other and embrace one another; these constrain us to love. Then there are the opposite signs, signs which repel each other so violently that we are induced to hatred and to separation, becoming so hardened, incomplete, and broken as to produce in us ruin. There are knots which bind, and there are separated characters which release. [. . .] These signs do not have a fixed and determined form. Anyone who, obeying his own furor, or the dictates of his soul, naturally creates his own images, be these of things desired or things to hold in contempt, cannot help but represent these images to himself and to his spirit as if the imagined things were really present. Thus he experiences his own images with a power that he would not feel were he to represent these things to himself in the form of words, either in elegant oration, or in writing. Such were the well-defined letters of the ancient Egyptians, which they called hieroglyphs or sacred characters [. . .] by which they were able to enter into colloquies with the gods and to accomplish remarkable feats with them. [. . .] And so, just as, where there lacks a common tongue, men of one race are unable to have colloquies with those of another, but must resort instead to gestures, so relations of any sort between ourselves and certain powers would be impossible were we to lack the medium of definite signs, seals, figures, characters, gestures, and other ceremonies. (*Opera latine conscripta*, Naples–Florence, 1879–1891, vol. III: 39–45)

Concerning the specific iconological material that Bruno employs, we find figures deriving directly from the Hermetic tradition, such as the Thirty-six Decans of the Zodiac, others drawn from mythology, necromantic diagrams that recall Agrippa or John Dee, Lullian suggestions, animals, plants and allegorical figures deriving from the repertoire of emblems and devices. This is a repertoire with an extraordinary importance in the history of iconology, where the ways in which a certain seal, for example, refers back to a specific idea are largely governed by rhetorical criteria: phonetic similarities (a horse, *equus*, can correspond to an honest, *aequus*, man); the concrete for the abstract (a Roman soldier for Rome); antecedent for the consequent; accident for subject (or vice versa); and so on. Sometimes the analogy is based upon the similarity of the initial syllable (*asinus* for *asyllum*); and certainly Bruno did not know that this procedure, as we shall see in chapter 7, was followed by the Egyptians themselves when using their hieroglyphs. At other times the relations might be based on kabbalistic techniques such as anagrams or paronomasias (like *palatio* standing for *Latio*: cf. Vasoli 1958: 285–6).

Thus this language claimed to be so perfect as to furnish the keys to express relations between things, not only of this world, but of any of the other infinite worlds in their mutual concordance and opposition. Nevertheless, in its semiotic structure, it was little more than an immense lexicon, conveying vague meanings, with a very simplified syntax. It was a language that could be deciphered only by short-circuiting it, and whose decipherment was the privilege only of the exegete able to dominate all its connections, thanks to the furor of Bruno's truly heroic style.

In any case, even if his techniques were not so different from those of other authors of arts of memory, Bruno (like Lull, Nicholas of Cusa and Postel, and like the reformist mystics of the seventeenth century – at whose dawn he was to be burnt at the stake) was inspired by a grand utopian vision. His flaming hieroglyphical rhetoric aimed at producing, through an enlargement of human knowledge, a reform, a renovation, maybe a revolution in the consciousness, customs, and even the political order of Europe. Of this ideal, Bruno was the agent and propagandist, in his wandering from court to European court.

Here, however, our interest in Bruno is limited to seeing how he developed Lullian techniques. Certainly, his own metaphysics of infinite worlds pushed him to emphasize the formal and architectonic aspects of Lull's endeavour. One of his mnemonic treatises, *De lampade combinatoria lulliana ad infinita propositiones et media inveniendi* (1586), opens by mentioning the limitless number of propositions that the *Ars* is capable of generating, and then says: 'The properties of the terms themselves are of scant importance; it is only important that they show an order, a texture, an architecture' (I, ix).

In the *De umbris idearum* (1582) Bruno described a set of movable, concentric wheels subdivided into 150 sectors. Each wheel contained 30 letters, made up of the 23 letters of the Latin alphabet, plus 7 letters from the Greek and Hebrew alphabets to which no letter corresponded in Latin (while, for instance, A could also stand for *Alpha* and *Alef*). To each of the single letters there corresponded a specific image, representing for each respective wheel a different series of figures, activities, situations, etc. When the wheels were rotated against each other in the manner of a combination lock, sequences of letters were produced which served to generate complex images. We can see this in Bruno's own example (*De umbris*, 163):

	Wheel 1 *(homines)*	Wheel 2 (actiones)	*Wheel 3* *(insignia)*
A	Lycas	in convivium	cathenatus
B	Deucalion	in lapydes	vittatus
C	Apollo (etc.)	in Pythonem	baltheatus

In what Bruno called the 'Prima Praxis', the second wheel was rotated so as to obtain a combination such as CA ('Apollo in a banquet'). Turning the third wheel, he might obtain CAA ('Apollo enchained in a banquet'). We shall see in a moment why Bruno did not think it necessary to add fourth and fifth wheels as he would do for the 'Secunda Praxis', where they would represent, respectively, *adstantia* and *circumstantias*.

In his 'Secunda Praxis', by adding the 5 vowels to each of the 30 letters of his alphabet, Bruno describes 5 concentric wheels, each having 150 alphabetical pairs, like AA, AE, AI, AO, AU, BA, BE, BO, and so on through the entire alphabet. These 150 pairs are repeated on each of the 5 wheels. As in the 'Prima Praxis', the significance changes with every wheel. On the first wheel, the initial letter signifies a human agent, on the second, an action, on the third, an insignia, on the fourth, a bystander, on the fifth, a set of circumstances.

By moving the wheels it is possible to obtain images such as 'a woman riding on a bull, combing her hair while holding a mirror in her left hand, accompanied by an adolescent carrying a green bird in his hand' (*De umbris*, 212, 10). Bruno speaks of images 'ad omnes formationes possibile, adaptabiles' (*De umbris*, 80), that is, susceptible of every possible permutation. In truth, it is almost impossible to write the number of sequences that can be generated by permutating 150 elements 5 at a time, especially as inversions are allowed (*De umbris*, 223). This distinguishes the art of Bruno, which positively thirsts after infinity, from the art of Lull.

In his critical edition of *De umbris* (1991), Sturlese gives an interpretation of the use of the wheels that differs sharply from the 'magical' interpretation given by Yates (1972). For Yates, the wheels generated syllables by which one memorizes images to be used for magical purposes. Sturlese inverts this: for her, it is the images that serve to recall the syllables. Thus, for Sturlese, the purpose of the entire mnemonical apparatus was the memorization of an infinite multitude of words through the use of a fixed, and relatively limited, number of images.

If this is true, then it is easy to see that Bruno's system can no longer be treated as an art where alphabetic combinations lead to images (as if it were a scenario-generating machine); rather it is a system that leads from combined images to syllables. Such a system not only aids memorization but, equally, permits the generation of an almost unlimited number of words – be they long and complex like *incrassatus* or *permagnus*, or difficult like many Greek, Hebrew, Chaldean, Persian or Arabic terms (*De umbris*, 169), or rare like scientific names of grass, trees, minerals, seeds or animal genera (*De umbris*, 152). The system is thus designed to generate languages – at least at the level of nomenclature.

Which interpretation is correct? Does Bruno concatenate the sequence CROCITUS to evoke the image of Pilumnus advancing rapidly on the back of a donkey with a bandage on his arm and a parrot on his head, or has he assembled these images so as to memorize CROCITUS?

In the 'Prima Praxis' (*De umbris*, 168–72) Bruno tells us that it is not indispensable to work with all five wheels because, in most known languages, it is rare to find words containing syllables with four or five letters. Furthermore, where such syllables do occur (for instance, in words like *trans-actum* or *stu-prans*), it is usually easy to devise some artifice that will obviate the necessity of using the fourth and fifth wheel. We are not interested in the specific short cuts that Bruno used except to say that they cut out several billion possibilities. It is the very existence of such short cuts that seems significant. If the syllabic sequences were expressing complex images, there should be no limit for the length of the syllables. On the contrary, if the images were expressing syllables, there would be an interest in limiting the length of the words, following the criteria of economy already present in most natural languages (even though there is no formal limit, since Leibniz will later remark that there exists in Greek a thirty-one-letter word).

Besides, if the basic criterion of every art of memory is to recall the unfamiliar through the more familiar, it seems more reasonable that Bruno considered the 'Egyptian' traditional images as more familiar than the words of exotic languages. In this respect, there are some passages in *De umbris* that are revealing: 'Lycas in convivium cathenatus presentabat tibi AAA. . . . Medusa, cum insigni Plutonis presentabit AMO' ('Lycaon enchained in a banquet presents to you AAA . . . Medusa with the sign of Pluto

presents AMO'). Since all these names are in the nominative case, it is evident that they present the letters to the user
of the system and not the other way around. This also
follows from a number of passages in the *Cantus circaeus*
where Bruno uses perceivable images to represent mathematical or abstract concepts that might not otherwise be
imaginable or memorizable (cf. Vasoli 1958: 284ff).

That Bruno bequeathed all this to the Lullian posterity
can be seen from further developments of Lullism.

Infinite Songs and Locutions

Between Lull and Bruno might be placed the game invented
by H. P. Hardsdörffer in his *Matematische und philosoph-
ische Erquickstunden* (1651: 516–19). He devises 5 wheels
containing 264 units (prefixes, suffixes, letters and syllables). This apparatus can generate 97,209,600 German
words, including many that were still non-existent but
available for creative and poetic use (cf. Faust 1981: 367).
If this can be done for German, why not invent a device
capable of generating all possible languages?

The problem of the art of combination was reconsidered
in the commentary *In spheram Ioannis de sacro bosco* by
Clavius in 1607. In his discussion of the four primary
qualities (hot, cold, dry and wet), Clavius asked how many
pairs they might form. Mathematically, we know, the
answer is six. But some combinations (like 'hot and cold',
'dry and wet') are impossible, and must be discarded,
leaving only the four acceptable combinations: 'cold
and dry' (earth), 'hot and dry' (fire), 'hot and wet' (air),
'cold and wet' (water). We seem to be back with the problem of Lull: a conventional cosmology limits the combinations.

Clavius, however, seemed to wish to go beyond these
limits. He asked how many *dictiones*, or terms, might be
produced using the 23 letters of the Latin alphabet (*u* being
the same as *v*), combining them 2, 3, 4 at a time, and so on

until 23. He supplied a number of mathematical formulae for the calculations, yet he soon stopped as he began to see the immensity of the number of possible results – especially as repetitions were permissible.

In 1622, Paul Guldin wrote a *Problema arithmeticum de rerum combinationibus* (cf. Fichant 1991: 136–8) in which he calculated the number of possible locutions generated by 23 letters. He took into account neither the question of whether the resulting sequences had a sense, nor even that of whether they were capable of being pronounced at all. The locutions could consist of anything from 2 to 23 letters; he did not allow repetitions. He arrived at a result of more than 70,000 billion billion. To write out all these locutions would require more than a million billion billion letters. To conceive of the enormity of this figure, he asked the reader to imagine writing all these words in huge notebooks: each of these notebooks had 1,000 pages; each of these pages had 100 lines; each of these lines could accommodate 60 characters. One would need 257 million billion of these notebooks. Where would you put them all? Guldin then made a careful volumetric study, imagining shelf space and room for circulation in the libraries that might store a consignment of these dimensions. If you housed the notebooks in large libraries formed by cubes whose sides measured 432 feet, the number of such cubic buildings (hosting 32 million volumes each) would be 8,050,122,350. And where then would you put them all? Even exhausting the total available surface space on planet earth, one would still find room for only 7,575,213,799!

In 1636 Father Marin Mersenne, in his *Harmonie universelle*, asked the same question once again. This time, however, to the *dictiones* he added 'songs', that is, musical sequences. With this, the conception of universal language has begun to appear, for Mersenne realizes that the answer would necessarily have to include all the locutions in all possible languages. He marvelled that our alphabet was capable of supplying 'millions more terms than the earth has grains of sand, yet it is so easy to learn that one hardly needs memory, only a touch of discernment' (letter to Peiresc, c.April 1635; cf. Coumet 1975; Marconi 1992).

In the *Harmonie*, Mersenne proposed to generate only *pronounceable* words in French, Greek, Arabic, Chinese and every other language. Even with this limitation one feels the shudder provoked by a sort of Brunian infinity of possible worlds. The same can be said of the musical sequences that can be generated upon an extension of 3 octaves, comprising 22 notes, without repetitions (shades of future 12-tone compositions!). Mersenne observed that to write down all these songs would require enough reams of paper to fill in the distance between heaven and earth, even if every sheet contained 720 of these 22-note songs and every ream was so compressed as to be less than an inch thick. In fact the number of possible songs amounted to 1,124,000,727,777,607,680,000 (*Harmonie*, 108). By dividing this figure by the 362,880 songs contained in each ream, one would still obtain a 16-digit figure, whilst the number of inches between the centre of the earth and the stars is only 28,826,640,000,000 (a 14-digit figure). Anyone who wished to copy out all these songs, a thousand per day, would have to write for 22,608,896,103 years and 12 days.

Mersenne and Guldin were anticipating Borges' Babel Library *ad abundantiam*. Not only this, Guldin observed that if the numbers are these, who can marvel at the existence of so many different natural languages? The art was now providing an excuse for the *confusio linguarum*. It justifies it, however, by showing that it is impossible to limit the omnipotence of God.

Are there more names than things? How many names, asks Mersenne (*Harmonie*, II, 72), would we need if we were to give more than one to each individual? If Adam really did give names to *everything*, how long would he have had to spend in Eden? In the end, human languages limit themselves to the naming of general ideas and of species; to name an individual thing, an indication with a finger is usually sufficient (p. 74). If this were not so, it might easily 'happen that for every hair on the body of an animal and for each hair on the head of a man we might require a particular name that would distinguish it from all others. Thus a man with 100,000 hairs on his head and 100,000 more on his body would need to know 200,000 separate words to name them all' (pp. 72–3).

In order to name every individual thing in the world one should thus create an artificial language capable of generating the requisite number of locutions. If God were to augment the number of individual things unto infinity, to name them all it would be enough to devise an alphabet with a greater number of letters, and this would provide us with the means to name them all (p. 73).

From these giddy heights there dawns a consciousness of the possibility of the infinite perfectibility of knowledge. Man, the new Adam, possesses the possibility of naming all those things which his ancestor had lacked the time to baptize. Yet such an artificial language would place human beings in competition with God, who has the privilege of knowing all things in their particularity. We shall see that Leibniz was later to sanction the impossibility of such a language. Mersenne had led a battle against the kabbala and occultism only to be seduced in the end. Here he is cranking away at the Lullian wheels, seemingly unaware of the difference between the real omnipotence of God and the potential omnipotence of a human combinatory language. Besides, in his *Quaestiones super Genesim* (cols 49 and 52) he claimed that the presence of the sense of infinity in human beings was itself a proof of the existence of God.

This capacity to conceive of a quasi-infinite series of combinations depends on the fact that Mersenne, Guldin, Clavius and others (see, for example, Comenius, *Linguarum methodus novissima*, 1648: III, 19), unlike Lull, were no longer calculating upon concepts but rather upon simple alphabetic sequences, pure elements of expression with no inherent meaning, controlled by no orthodoxy other than the limits of mathematics itself. Without realizing it, these authors are verging towards the idea of a 'blind thought', a

notion that we shall see Leibniz proposing with a greater
critical awareness.

7

The Perfect Language of Images

Already in Plato, as in Pythagoras before him, there appeared a veneration for the ancient wisdom of the Egyptians. Aristotle was more sceptical, and when he came to recount the history of philosophy in the first book of the *Metaphysics*, he started directly with the Greeks. Influenced by Aristotle, the Christian authors of the Middle Ages showed relatively little curiosity about ancient Egypt. References to this tradition can be found only in marginal alchemical texts like *Picatrix*. Isidore of Seville shortly mentioned the Egyptians as the inventors of geometry and astronomy, and said that the original Hebrew letters became the basis for the Greek alphabet when Isis, queen of the Egyptians, found them and brought them back to her own country (*Etymologiarum*, I, iii, 5).

By contrast, one could put the Renaissance under the standard of what Baltrušaitis (1967) has called the 'search for Isis'. Isis became thus the symbol for an Egypt regarded as the wellspring of original knowledge, and the inventor of a sacred scripture, capable of expressing the unfathomable reality of the divine. The Neo-Platonic revival, in which Ficino played the role of high priest, restored to Egypt its ancient primacy.

In the *Enneads* (V, 8, 5–6) Plotinus wrote:

The wise sages of Egypt [. . .] in order to designate things with wisdom do not use designs of letters, which develop into discourses and propositions, and which represent sounds and words; instead they use designs of images, each of which stands for a distinct thing; and it is these that they sculpt onto their temples. [. . .] Every incised sign is thus, at once, knowledge, wisdom, a real entity captured in one stroke.

Iamblicus, in his *De mysteriis aegyptiorum*, said that the Egyptians, when they invented their symbols, imitating the nature of the universe and the creation of the gods, revealed occult intuitions by symbols.

The translation of the *Corpus Hermeticum* (which Ficino published alongside his translations of Iamblicus and other Neo-Platonic texts) was under the sign of Egypt, because, for Ficino, the ancient Egyptian wisdom came from Hermes Trismegistus.

Horapollo's *Hieroglyphica*

In 1419 Cristoforo de' Buondelmonti acquired from the island of Andros a mysterious manuscript that was soon to excite the curiosity of philosophers such as Ficino: the manuscript was the Greek translation (by a certain Philippos) of the *Horapòllonos Neiloùs ieroglyphikà*. The original author, Horapollo – or Horus Apollus, or Horapollus – was thus qualified as 'Nilotic'. Although it was taken as genuinely archaic throughout the Renaissance, scholars now believe this text to be a late Hellenistic compilation, dating from as late as the fifth century AD. As we shall see, although certain passages indicate that the author did possess exact information about Egyptian hieroglyphs, the text was written at a time when hieroglyphic writing had certainly fallen out of use. At best, the *Hieroglyphica* seems to be based on some texts written a few centuries before.

The original manuscript contained no images. Illustrations appeared only in later editions: for instance, though the first translation into Italian in 1547 is still without illustrations, the 1514 translation into Latin was illustrated by Dürer. The text is divided into short chapters in which it is explained, for example, that the Egyptians represented age by depicting the sun and the moon, or the month by a palm branch. There follows in each case a brief description of the symbolic meaning of each figure, and in many cases its polysemic value: for example, the vulture is said to signify mother, sight, the end of a thing, knowledge of the future, year, sky, mercy, Minerva, Juno, or two drachmas. Sometimes the hieroglyphic sign is a number: pleasure, for example, is denoted by the number 16, because sexual activity begins at the age of sixteen. Since it takes two to have intercourse, however, this is denoted by two 16s.

Humanist philosophical culture was immediately fascinated by this text: hieroglyphs were regarded as the work of the great Hermes Trismegistus himself, and therefore as a source of inexhaustible wisdom.

To understand the impact of Horapollo's text on Europe, it is first necessary to understand what, in reality, these mysterious Egyptian symbols were. Horapollo was describing a writing system whose last example (as far as Egyptologists can trace) is on the Theodosius temple (AD 394). Even if these inscriptions were still similar to those elaborated three thousand years before, the Egyptian language of the fifth century had changed radically. Thus, when Horapollo wrote his text, the key to understanding hieroglyphs had long been lost.

The Egyptian Alphabet

The hieroglyphic script is undoubtedly composed, in part, of iconic signs: some are easily recognizable – vulture, owl, bull, snake, eye, foot, man seated with cup in hand; others are stylized – the hoisted sail, the almond-like shape for a mouth, the serrated line for water. Some other signs, at least to the untrained eye, seem to bear only the remotest resemblance to the things that they are supposed to represent – the little square that stands for a seat, the sign of folded cloth, or the semicircle that represents bread. All these signs are not icons (representing a thing by direct similarity) but rather *ideograms*, which work by a sort of rhetorical substitution. Thus an inflated sail serves to represent the wind; a man seated with a cup means to drink; a cow's ear means to understand; the head of a cynocephalus stands for the god Thoth and for all his various attributes, such as writing and counting.

Not everything, however, can be represented ideographically. One way that the ancient Egyptians had found to circumvent this difficulty was to turn their ideograms into simple *phonograms*. In order to represent a certain sound they put the image of a thing whose name sounded similar. To take an example from Jean François Champollion's first decipherment (*Lettre à Dacier*, 17 September 1822, 11–12), the mouth, in Egyptian *ro*, was chosen to represent the Greek consonant *P* (*rho*). It is ironic to think that while, for Renaissance Hermeticists, sounds had to represent the nature of things, for the Egyptians, things (or their corresponding images) were representing sounds (see, for a similar procedure, my remarks in chapter 6 on Bruno's mnemonics).

By the time interest in Egyptian hieroglyphics had revived in Europe, however, knowledge of the hieroglyphic alphabet had been lost for over a thousand years. The necessary premise for the decipherment of hieroglyphs was a stroke of pure fortune, like the discovery of a bilingual dictionary. In fact, as is well known, decipherment was made possible by the discovery not of a dictionary, but of a trilingual text, the famous Rosetta stone, named after the city of Rashid where it was found by a French soldier in 1799, and, as a result of Napoleon's defeat at the hands of Nelson, soon transferred to London. The stone bore an inscription in hieroglyphic, in demotic (a cursive, administrative script elaborated about 1,000 BC), and in Greek. Working from reproductions, Champollion, in his *Lettre à Dacier*, laid the foundation for the decipherment of hieroglyphs. He compared two cartouches which, from their position in the text, he guessed must refer to the names of

Ptolemy (ΠΤΟΛΟΜΑΙΟΣ) and Cleopatra (ΚΛΟΠΑΤΡΑ). He identified the five letters that both names have in common (Π, Τ, Ο, Λ, Α), and found that the two cartouches had five hieroglyphs in common as well. By supposing that each other instance of the same sign represented the same sound, Champollion could easily infer the phonetic value of the remaining text.

Champollion's decipherment does not, however, explain a series of phenomena which can justify the interpretation of Horapollo. Greek and Roman colonizers had imposed on Egypt their commerce, their technology and their gods. By the time of the spread of Christianity, Egypt had already abandoned many of its ancient traditions. Knowledge of sacred writing was still preserved and practised only by priests living within the sacred enclosures of the ancient temples. These were a dwindling breed: in those last repositories of a lost knowledge, cut off from the rest of the world, they cultivated the monuments of their ancient culture.

Since the sacred writing no longer served any practical use, but only initiatory purposes, these last priests began to introduce complexities into it, playing with the ambiguities inherent in a form of writing that could be differently read either phonetically or ideographically. To write the name of the god Ptah, for example, the P was expressed phonetically and placed at the top of the name with the ideogram for sky (*p[t]*), the H was placed in the middle and represented by the image of the god Heh with his arms raised, and the T was expressed by the ideogram for the earth (*ta*). It was an image that not only expressed *Ptah* phonetically, but also carried the visual suggestion that the god Ptah had originally separated the earth from the sky. The discovery that, by combining different hieroglyphs, evocative visual emblems might be created inspired these last scribes to experiment with increasingly complicated and abstruse combinations. In short, these scribes began to formulate a sort of kabbalistic play, based, however, on images rather than on letters. Around the term represented by a sign (which was given an initial phonetic reading) there formed a halo of visual connotations and secondary senses, a sort of chord of associated meanings which served to amplify the original semantic range of the term. The more the sacred text was enhanced by its exegetes, the more the conviction grew that they expressed buried truths and lost secrets (Sauneron 1957: 123–7).

Thus, to the last priests of a civilization sinking into oblivion, hieroglyphs appeared as a perfect language. Yet their perfection could only be understood by visually reading them; if by chance still pronounced, they would have lost any magic (Sauneron 1982: 55–6).

Now we can understand what Horapollo sought to reveal. He wished to preserve and transmit a semiotic tradition whose key was, by now, entirely lost. He still managed to grasp certain features at either the phonetic or the ideographic level, yet much of his information was confused or scrambled in the course of transmission. Often he gives, as the canonical solution, a reading elaborated only by a certain group of scribes during a certain, limited period. Yoyotte (1955: 87) shows that when Horapollo asserts that Egyptians depicted the father with the ideogram for the scarab beetle, he almost certainly had in mind that, in the Late Period, certain scribes had begun to substitute the scarab for the usual sign for *t* to represent the sound *it* ('father'), since, according to a private cryptography developed during the eighteenth dynasty, a scarab stood for *t* in the name *Atum*.

Horapollo opened his text by saying that the Egyptians represented eternity with the images of the sun and the moon. Contemporary Egyptologists debate whether, in this explanation, he was thinking of two ideograms used in the Late Period which could be read phonetically as, respectively, *r'nb* ('all the days') and *r tr.wi* ('night and day' that is, 'always'); or whether Horapollo was thinking instead of Alexandrine bas-reliefs where the two ideograms, appearing together, already signify 'eternity' (in which case they would not be an Egyptian symbol, but one derived from

Asian, even Hebraic sources). In other places, Horapollo seems to have misunderstood the voices of tradition. He says, for instance, that the sign to indicate a word is depicted by a tongue and a blood-shot eye. There exists a verbal root *mdw* ('to speak') in whose ideogram there appears a club, as well as the word *dd* ('to say') in whose ideogram appears a snake. It is possible that either Horapollo or his source has erroneously taken either the club or the snake or both as representing a tongue. He then says that the course of the sun during the winter solstice is represented by two feet stopped together. In fact, Egyptologists only know a sign representing two legs in motion, which supports the sense 'movement' when accompanying signs meaning 'to stop', 'to cease activity' or 'to interrupt a voyage'. The idea that two stopped feet stand for the course of the sun seems merely to be a whim of Horapollo.

Horapollo says that Egypt is denoted by a burning thurible with a heart over it. Egyptologists have discovered in a royal epithet two signs that indicate a burning heart, but these two signs seem never to have been used to denote Egypt. It does emerge, however, that (for a Father of the church such as Cyril of Alexandria) a brazier surmounted by a heart expressed anger (cf. Van der Walle and Vergote 1943).

This last detail may be an important clue. The second part of *Hieroglyphica* is probably the work of the Greek translator, Philippos. It is in this part that a number of clear references appear to the late Hellenistic tradition of the *Phisiologus* and other bestiaries, herbariums and lapidaries that derive from it. This is a tradition whose roots lie not only in ancient Egypt, but in the ancient traditions throughout Asia, as well as in the Greek and Latin world.

We can look for this in the case of the stork. When the *Hieroglyphica* reaches the stork, it recites:

How [do you represent] he who loves the father.
If they wish to denote he who loves the father, they depict a stork. In fact, this beast, nourished by its parents, never

separates itself from them, but remains with them until their old age, repaying them with piety and deference.

In fact, in the Egyptian alphabet, there is an animal like a stork which, for phonetic reasons, stands for 'son'. Yet in I, 85, Horapollo gives this same gloss for the hoopoe. This is, at least, an indication that the text has been assembled syncretistically from a variety of sources. The hoopoe is also mentioned in the *Phisiologus*, as well as in a number of classical authors, such as Aristophanes and Aristotle, and patristic authors such as St Basil. But let us concentrate for a moment on the stork.

The *Hieroglyphica* was certainly one of the sources for the *Emblemata* of Andrea Alciati in 1531. Thus, it is not surprising to find here a reference to the stork, who, as the text explains, nourishes its offspring by bringing them pleasing gifts, while bearing on its shoulders the worn-out bodies of its parents, offering them food from its own mouth. The image that accompanies this description in the 1531 edition is of a bird which flies bearing another on its back. In subsequent editions, such as the one from 1621, for this is substituted the image of a bird that flies with a worm in its beak for its offspring, waiting open-mouthed in the nest.

Alciati's commentary refers to the passage describing the stork in the *Hieroglyphica*. Yet we have just seen that there is no reference either to the feeding of the young or to the transport of the parents. These features are, however, mentioned in a fourth-century AD text, the *Hexaemeron* of Basil (VIII, 5).

In other words, the information contained in the *Hieroglyphica* was already at the disposal of European culture. A search for traces of the stork from the Renaissance backwards is filled with pleasant surprises. In the *Cambridge Bestiary* (twelfth century), we read that storks nourish their young with exemplary affection, and that 'they incubate the nests so tirelessly that they lose their own feathers. What is more, when they have moulted in this way, they in

turn are looked after by the babies, for a time corresponding in length to the time which they themselves have spent
in bringing up and cherishing their offspring' (*The Bestiary*,
T. H. White, ed. New York: Putnam's Sons, 1960: 117–
18). The accompanying image shows a stork that carries a
frog in its beak, obviously a dainty morsel for its young.

The *Cambridge Bestiary* has taken this idea from Isidore
of Seville, who, in the *Etymologiarum* (XII, vii), says more
or less the same. Who then are Isidore's sources? St Basil we
have already seen; there was St Ambrose as well (*Hexaemeron*, V, 16, 53), and possibly also Celsus (cited in Origen,
Contra Celsum, IV, 98) and Porphyry (*De abstinentia*, III,
23, 1). These, in their turn, used Pliny's *Naturalis historia*
(X, 32) as their source.

Pliny, of course, could have been drawing on an Egyptian
tradition, if Aelian, in the second to third century AD, could
claim (though without citing Pliny by name) that 'Storks
are venerated among the Egyptians because they nourish
and honour their parents when they grow old' (*De animalium natura*, X, 16). But the idea can be traced back even
further. The same notion is to be found in Plutarch (*De
solertia animalium*, 4), Cicero (*De finibus bonorum et mal-
orum*, II, 110), Aristotle (*Historia animalium*, IX, 7, 612b,
35), Plato (*Alcibiades*, 135 E), Aristophanes (*The Birds*,
1355), and finally in Sophocles (*Electra*, 1058). There is
nothing to prevent us from imagining that Sophocles himself was drawing on ancient Egyptian tradition; but, even if
he were, it is evident that the story of the stork has been
part of occidental culture for as long as we care to trace it.
It follows that Horapollo did not reveal anything hot.
Moreover, the origin of this symbol seems to have been
Semitic, given that, in Hebrew, the word for stork means
'the one who has filial piety'.

Read by anyone familiar with medieval and classical
culture, Horapollo's booklet seems to differ very little from
the bestiaries current in the preceding centuries. It merely
adds some information about specifically Egyptian
animals, such as the ibis and the scarab, and neglects to

make certain of the standard moralizing comments or biblical references.

This was clear even to the Renaissance. In his *Hiero-glyphica sive de sacris Aegyptorum aliarumque gentium literis* of 1556, Pierio Valeriano never tired of employing his vast stock of knowledge of classical and Christian sources to note the occasions where the assertions of Horapollo might be confirmed. Yet instead of reading Horapollo in the light of a previous tradition, he revisits this whole tradition in the light of Horapollo.

With a barrage of citations from Latin and Greek authors, Giulio Cesare Capaccio displayed, in his *Delle imprese* of 1592, his perfect mastery of older traditions. Yet fashion now demanded that he interpreted this tradition in a Egyptian key. 'Without hieroglyphic observation', and without having recourse to the *Monas hieroglyphica* of 'quel Giovanni Dee da Londino', it was impossible, he said, to endow these images (coming from centuries of western culture) with their proper recondite meanings.

We are speaking of the 're-reading' of a text (or of a network of texts) which had not been changed during the centuries. So what has changed? We are here witnessing a semiotic incident which, as paradoxical as some of its effects may have been, was, in terms of it own dynamic, quite easy to explain. Horapollo's text (qua text) differs but little from other similar writings, which were previously known. None the less, the humanists read it as a series of unprecedented statements. The reason is simply that the readers of the fifteenth century saw it as coming from a *different* author. The text had not changed, but the 'voice' supposed to utter it was endowed with a different charisma. This changed the way in which the text was received and the way in which it was consequently interpreted.

Thus, as old and familiar as these images were, the moment they appeared as transmitted not by the familiar Christian and pagan sources, but by the ancient Egyptian divinities themselves, they took on a fresh, and radically different, meaning. For the missing scriptural commentaries there were substituted allusions to vague religious mysteries. The success of the book was due to its polysemy. Hieroglyphs were regarded as *initiatory symbols*.

They were *symbols*, that is, expressions that referred to an occult, unknown and ambivalent content. In contradistinction to conjecture, in which we take a visible symptom and infer from it its cause, Kircher defined a symbol as:

a *nota significativa* of mysteries, that is to say, that it is the nature of a symbol to lead our minds, by means of certain similarities, to the understanding of things vastly different from the things that are offered to our external senses, and whose property it is to appear hidden under the veil of an obscure expression. [. . .] Symbols cannot be translated by words, but expressed only by marks, characters, and figures. (*Obeliscus Pamphilius*, II, 5, 114–20).

These symbols were *initiatory*, because the allure of Egyptian culture was given by the promise of a knowledge that was wrapped in an impenetrable and indecipherable enigma so as to protect it from the idle curiosity of the vulgar multitudes. The hieroglyph, Kircher reminds us, was the symbol of a sacred truth (thus, though all hieroglyphs are symbols, it does not follow that all symbols are hieroglyphs) whose force derived from its impenetrability to the eyes of the profane.

Kircher's Egyptology

When Kircher set out to decipher hieroglyphics in the seventeenth century, there was no Rosetta stone to guide him. This helps explain his initial, mistaken, assumption that every hieroglyph was an ideogram. Understandable as it may have been, this was an assumption which doomed his enterprise at the outset. Notwithstanding its eventual failure, however, Kircher is still the father of Egyptology, though in the same way that Ptolemy is the father of astronomy, in spite of the fact that his main hypothesis was wrong. In a vain attempt to demonstrate his hypothesis, Kircher amassed observational material and transcribed documents, turning the attention of the scientific world to the problem of hieroglyphs. Kircher did not base his work on Horapollo's fantastic bestiary; instead, he studied and made copies of the royal hieroglyphic inscriptions. His reconstructions, reproduced in sumptuous tables, have an artistic fascination all of their own. Into these reconstructions Kircher poured elements of his own fantasy, frequently reportraying the stylized hieroglyphs in curvaceous baroque forms. Lacking the opportunity for direct observation, even Champollion used Kircher's reconstructions for his study of the obelisk standing in Rome's Piazza Navona, and although he complained of the lack of precision of many of the reproductions, he was still able to draw from them interesting and exact conclusions.

Already in 1636, in his *Prodromus Coptus sive Aegyptiacus* (to which was added, in 1643, a *Lingua Aegyptiaca restituta*), Kircher had come to understand the relation between the Coptic language and, on the one hand, Egyptian, and, on the other, Greek. It was here that he first broached the possibility that all religions, even those of the Far East, were nothing more than more or less degenerated versions of the original Hermetic mysteries.

There were more than a dozen obelisks scattered about Rome, and restoration work on some of them had taken place from as early as the time of Sixtus V. In 1644, Innocent X was elected pope. His Pamphili family palace was in Piazza Navona, and the pope commissioned Bernini to execute for him the vast fountain of the four rivers, which remains there today. On top of this fountain was to be placed the obelisk of Domitian, whose restoration Kircher was invited to superintend.

As the crowning achievement of this restoration, Kircher published, in 1650, his *Obeliscus Pamphilius*, followed, in 1652–4, by the four volumes of his *Oedipus Aegyptiacus*. This latter was an all-inclusive study of the history, religion, art, politics, grammar, mathematics, mechanics, medicine, alchemy, magic and theology of ancient Egypt, compared with all other eastern cultures, from Chinese ideograms to the Hebrew kabbala to the language of the brahmins of India. The volumes are a typographical *tour de force* that demanded the cutting of new characters for the printing of the numerous exotic, oriental alphabets. It opened with, among other things, a series of dedications to the emperor in Greek, Latin, Italian, Spanish, French, Portuguese, German, Hungarian, Czech, Illirian, Turkish, Hebrew, Syriac, Arabic, Chaldean, Samaritan, Coptic, Ethiopic, Armenian, Persian, Indian and Chinese. Still, the conclusions were the same as those of the earlier book (and would still be the same in the *Obelisci Aegyptiaci nuper inter Isaei Romani rudera effosii interpretatio hieroglyphica* of 1666 and in the *Sphinx mystagoga* of 1676).

At times, Kircher seemed to approach the intuition that certain of the hieroglyphs had a phonetic value. He even constructed a rather fanciful alphabet of 21 hieroglyphs, from whose forms he derives, through progressive abstractions, the letters of the Greek alphabet. Kircher, for example, took the figure of the ibis bending its head until it rests between its two feet as the prototype of the capitalized Greek *alpha*, A. He arrived at this conclusion by reflecting on the fact that the meaning of the hieroglyphic for the ibis was 'Bonus Daemon'; this, in Greek, would have been *Agathos Daimon*. But the hieroglyph had passed into Greek through the mediation of Coptic, thanks to which the first sounds of a given word were progressively identified with the form of the original hieroglyph. At the same time, the legs of the ibis, spread apart and resting on the ground, expressed the sea, or, more precisely, the only form in which the ancient Egyptians were acquainted with the sea – the Nile. The word *delta* has remained unaltered in its passage into Greek, and this is why the Greek letter *delta* (Δ) has retained the form of a triangle.

It was this conviction that, in the end, hieroglyphs all *showed* something about the natural world that prevented

Kircher from ever finding the right track. He thought that only later civilizations established that short-circuit between image and sound, which on the contrary characterized hieroglyphic writing from its early stages. He was unable, finally, to keep the distinction between a sound and the corresponding alphabetic letter; thus his initial intuitions served to explain the generation of later phonetic alphabets, rather than to understand the phonetical nature of hieroglyphs.

Behind these errors, however, lies the fact that, for Kircher, the decipherment of hieroglyphs was conceived as merely the introduction to the much greater task – an explanation of their mystic significance. Kircher never doubted that hieroglyphs had originated with Hermes Trismegistus – even though several decades before, Isaac Casaubon had proved that the entire *Corpus Hermeticum* could not be earlier than the first centuries of the common era. Kircher, whose learning was truly exceptional, must have known about this. Yet he deliberately ignored the argument, preferring rather to exhibit a blind faith in his Hermetic axioms, or at least to continue to indulge his taste for all that was strange or prodigious.

Out of this passion for the occult came those attempts at decipherment which now amuse Egyptologists. On page 557 of his *Obeliscus Pamphylius*, figures 20–4 reproduce the images of a cartouche to which Kircher gives the following reading: 'the originator of all fecundity and vegetation is Osiris whose generative power bears from heaven to his kingdom the Sacred Mophtha.' This same image was deciphered by Champollion (*Lettre à Dacier*, 29), who used Kircher's own reproductions, as 'ΑΟΤΚΡΤΛ (Autocrat or Emperor) sun of the son and sovereign of the crown, ΚΗΣΡΣ ΤΜΗΤΕΝΣ ΣΒΣΤΣ (Caesar Domitian Augustus)'. The difference is, to say the least, notable, especially as regards the mysterious Mophtha, figured as a lion, over which Kircher expended pages and pages of mystic exegesis listing its numerous properties, while for Champollion the lion simply stands for the Greek letter *lambda*.

In the same way, on page 187 of the third volume of the *Oedipus* there is long analysis of a cartouche that appeared on the Lateran obelisk. Kircher reads here a long argument concerning the necessity of attracting the benefits of the divine Osiris and of the Nile by means of sacred ceremonies activating the Chain of Genies, tied to the signs of the zodiac. Egyptologists today read it as simply the name of the pharaoh Apries.

Kircher's Chinese

In an earlier chapter, we saw the suggestion made that Chinese might be the language of Adam. Kircher lived in a period of exciting discoveries in the Orient. The Spanish, Portuguese, English, Dutch, and, later, French conquered the route to the Indies, the Sunda seas, the way to China and to Japan. But even more than by merchants, these pathways were traversed by Jesuits, following in the footsteps of Matteo Ricci who, a century before, had brought European culture to the Chinese, and returned to give Europe a deeper understanding of China. With the publication of the *Historia de las cosas más notables, ritos y costumbres del gran reino de la China* by Juan Gonzales de Mendoza in 1585, there appeared in print in Europe characters in Chinese script. In 1615 there finally appeared Ricci's *De christiana expeditione apud Sinas ab Societate Ieus suscepta*, in which he explained that in Chinese, there existed as many characters as there were words. He insisted as well on the international character of the Chinese script, which, he wrote, was readily understood not only by the Chinese, but also by the Japanese, the Koreans, the Cochin-Chinese and the Formosans. We shall see that this was a discovery that would initiate the search for a *real character* from Bacon onwards. Already in 1627, in France, Jean Douet published a *Proposition présentée au roy, d'une escriture universelle, admirable pour ses effects, très-utile à tous les hommes de la terre*, in which Chinese was offered as a model for an international language.

At the same time, there had begun to appear information about the pictographic writings of Amerindians. Attempts at interpretation had yielded contradictory results; and this was discussed in works such as the *Historia natural y moral de las Indias* by José de Acosta in 1570, and the *Relación de las cosas de Yucatán* by Diego de Landa, written in the sixteenth century, although appearing only in the eighteenth; in 1609 there also appeared the *Comentarios reales que tratan del origine de los Yncas* by Garcilaso de la Vega. An observation often repeated by these early observers was that contact with the indigenous natives was at first carried out by means of gestures. This awoke an interest in gesture's potential as a universal language. The universality of gestures and the universality of images turned out to be related themes (the first treatise on this subject was Giovanni Bonifacio's *L'arte de' cenni* of 1616; on this topic in general, see Knox 1990).

The reports of his Jesuit brothers gave Kircher an incomparable source of ethnographic and linguistic information (see Simone 1990 on 'Jesuit or Vatican linguistics'). In his *Oedipus*, Kircher was especially interested in the diffusion of Chinese. He took up the same arguments, in a more elliptical form, in his *China monumentis quà sacris quà profanis, nec non variis naturae et artis spectaculis, aliarum rerum memorabilis argumentis illustrata* of 1667. This latter work was more in the nature of a treatise in ethnography and cultural anthropology which, with its splendid and sometimes documented illustrations, collected all the reports that arrived from the missionaries of the Company, and described every aspect of Chinese life, culture and nature. Only the sixth and last part of the work was dedicated to the alphabet.

Kircher presumed that the mysteries of hieroglyphic writing had been introduced to the Chinese by Noah's son Ham. In the *Arca Noe* of 1675 (pp. 210ff) he identified Ham with Zoroaster, the inventor of magic. But, unlike

Egyptian hieroglyphs, Chinese characters were not for Kircher a puzzle. Chinese was a writing system still in use, and the key to its understanding had already been revealed. How could such a comprehensible language be sacred and a vehicle for occult mysteries?

Kircher realized that Chinese characters were originally iconic and only later had grown extremely stylized over time, so as to lose their original similarity with things. He reconstructed after his own fancy what he took to be the designs of fish and birds that had formed the starting points for current ideograms. Kircher also realized that these ideograms did not express either letters or syllables, but referred to concepts. He noted that in order to translate our dictionary into their idiom we would need as many different characters as we had words (*Oedipus*, III, 11). This led him to reflect on the amount of memory that was necessary for a Chinese scholar to know and remember all these characters.

Why did the problem of memory arise only here, and not in regard to Egyptian hieroglyphs? The reason was that hieroglyphs discharged their allegorical and metaphorical force immediately, in virtue of what Kircher held to be their inherent power of revelation, since they 'integros conceptos ideales involvebant'. By using the verb *involvere* (to wind or wrap up), however, Kircher meant the exact opposite of what we might, today, suppose when we think of the natural and intuitive similarity between a given image and a thing. Hieroglyphs do not *make clear* but rather *conceal* something.

This is the reason for which Kircher speaks of the inferiority of Amerindian characters (*Oedipus*, III, 13–14). They seemed to Kircher inferior because they were immediately pictographic, as they were representing only individuals and events; thus they looked like mere mnemonic notes unable to bear arcane revelations (*Oedipus*, IV, 28; on the inferiority of Amerindian characters see also Brian Walcott, *In biblia polyglotta prolegomena*, 2.23). Chinese ideography was undoubtedly superior to Amerindian 'pictography because it was capable of expressing abstract concepts. Yet, despite the fact that it also permitted witty combinations (cf. *Oedipus*, III, 13–14), its decipherment remained too univocal. The Egyptians, Kircher argued, saw in the sign of the scarab not a mere scarab, but the sun – and not the material sun that warms the world of our senses, but the sun as archetype of the intelligible world.

We shall see (ch. 10) that in seventeenth-century England, Chinese writing was considered perfect in so far as with ideograms every element on the expression-plane corresponded to a semantic unit on the content-plane. It was precisely these one-to-one correspondences that, for Kircher, deprived Chinese writing of its potential for mystery. A Chinese character was monogamously bound to the concept it represented; that was its limitation: an Egyptian hieroglyph showed its superiority by its ability to summon up entire 'texts', and to express complex chunks of infinitely interpretable content.

Kircher repeated this argument in his *China*. There was nothing hieratic about the Chinese character; there was nothing that veiled it from profane eyes, hiding unfathomable depths of truth; it was a prosaic instrument of everyday communication. Knowledge of Chinese could, of course, be motivated on ethnological grounds, especially as the Jesuits had acquired so many interests in China. Still, Chinese could not qualify for inclusion in the list of holy languages. As to the Amerindian signs, not only were they patently denotative, but they revealed the diabolic nature of a people who had lost the last vestige of archaic wisdom.

As a civilization, Egypt no longer existed, and for the Europeans it was not yet a land for future conquest. Ignored in its geopolitical inconsistency, it became a Hermetical phantom. In this role it could be identified as the spiritual ancestor of the Christian West, the progenitor of the occident's patrimony of mystic wisdom. China, by contrast, was no phantom but a tangible Other. It was concretely there, still a political force of respectable dimensions, still a culture alternative to that of the West. The

Jesuits themselves had revealed the deep roots of Chinese culture. 'The Chinese, moral and virtuous though pagan, when forgetting the truth revealed in the structure of hieroglyphs, converted their ideography into a neutral and abstract instrument of communication, and this led to the belief that their conversion would be easy to achieve' (Pellerey 1992b: 521). The Americas, by contrast, were designated as the land of conquest; here there would be no compromise with idolaters and their low-grade species of writing: the idolaters were to be converted, and every trace of their original culture, irredeemably polluted with diabolic influences, was to be wiped away. 'The demonization of the native American cultures found here a linguistic and theoretical justification' (ibid.: 521).

The Kircherian Ideology

It would be idle to hold Kircher responsible for his inability to understand the nature of hieroglyphic writing, for which in his time nobody had the key. Yet his ideology magnified his errors. 'Nothing can explain the duplicity of the research of Kircher better than the engraving which opens the *Obeliscus Pamphilius*: in this cohabit both the illuminated image of Philomatià to whom Hermes explains every mystery and the disquieting gesture of Harpocrates who turns away the profane, hidden by the shadow of the cartouche' (Rivosecchi 1982: 57).

The hieroglyphic configurations had become a sort of machine for the inducing of hallucinations which then could be interpreted in any possible way. Rivosecchi (1982: 52) suggests that Kircher exploited this very possibility in order to discuss freely a large number of potentially dangerous themes – from astrology to alchemy and magic – disguising his own opinions as those of an immemorial tradition, one in which, moreover, Kircher traced prefigurations of Christianity. In the midst of this hermeneutic bulimia, however, there glimmers the exquisitely baroque temperament of Kircher at play, delighting in his taste for the great theatre of mirrors and lights, for the surprising museographic collection (and one has only to think of that extraordinary *Wunderkammer* which was the museum of the Jesuit Collegio Romano). Only his sensitivity to the incredible and the monstrous can explain the dedication to the Emperor Ferdinand III that opens the third volume of *Oedipus*:

I unfold before your eyes, O Most Sacred Caesar, the polymorphous reign of Morpheus Hieroglyphicus. I tell of a theatre in which an immense variety of monsters are disposed, and not the nude monsters of nature, but adorned by the enigmatic Chimeras of the most ancient of wisdoms so that here I trust sagacious wits will draw out immeasurable treasures for the sciences as well as no small advantage for letters. Here there is the Dog of Bubasti, the Lion Saiticus, the Goat Mendesius, here there is the Crocodile, horrible in the yawning of its jaws, yet from whose uncovered gullet there emerges the occult meanings of divinity, of nature, and of the spirit of Ancient Wisdom espied through the vaporous play of images. Here there are the Dipsodes thirsting for blood, the virulent Asp, the astute Icneumon, the cruel Hippopotami, the monstrous Dragons, the toad of swollen belly, the snail of twisted shell, the hairy caterpillar and the innumerable other spectres which all show the admirably ordered chain which extends itself into the depths of nature's sanctuaries. Here is presented a thousand species of exotic things in many and varied images, transformed by metamorphosis, converted into human figures, and restored once more to themselves again in a dance of the human and the savage intertwined, and all in accordance with the artifices of the divine; and finally, there appears the divinity itself which, to say it with Porphyry, scours the entire universe, ordering it with all things in a monstrous connubium; where now, sublime in its variegated face, it raises its canine cervix to reveal itself as Cinocephalus, now as the wicked Ibis, now as the Sparrow-hawk wrapped in a beaky mask. [. . .] now, delighting in its virgin aspect, under the shell of the Scarab it lies concealed as the sting of the Scorpion [these descriptions carry on for four more pages] in this pantomorphic theatre of nature unfolded before our gaze, under the allegorical veil of occult meanings.

This is the same spirit which informed the medieval taste for encyclopedias and for *libri monstruorum*, a genre which reappears from the Renaissance onwards under the 'scientific' guise of the medical studies of Ambroise Paré, the naturalist works of Ulisse Aldrovandi, the collection of monsters of Fortunio Liceti, the *Physica curiosa* of Gaspar Schott. Here it is combined, with a quality of frenzied dissymmetry that is almost Borrominian, recalling the aesthetic ideals presiding over the construction of the hydraulic grottos and mythological *rocailles* in the gardens of the period.

Beyond this, however, Rivosecchi has put his finger on another facet of the Kircherian ideology. In a universe placed under the sign of an ancient and powerful solar deity, the myth of Osiris had become an allegory of the troubled search for stability in the world still emerging from the aftermath of the Thirty Years War, in which Kircher was directly involved. In this sense, we might read the dedications to Ferdinand III, which stand out at the beginning of each volume of the *Oedipus*, in the same light as the appeals of Postel to the French monarchy to restore harmony a century before, or as the analogous appeals of Bruno, or as Campanella's celebration of a solar monarchy, prelude to the reign of Louis XIV, or as the calls for a golden century which we will discuss in the chapter on the Rosicrucians. Like all the utopian visionaries of his age, the Jesuit Kircher dreamed of the recomposition of a lacerated Europe under a stable monarchy. As a good German, moreover, he repeated the gesture of Dante and turned to the Germanic, Holy Roman emperor. Once again, as in the case of Lull, though in ways so different as to void the analogy, it was the search for a perfect language that became the instrument whereby a new harmony, not only in Europe, but across the entire planet, was to be established. The knowledge of exotic languages aimed not so much at recovering their original perfection, but rather at showing to the Jesuit missionaries 'the method of bearing the doctrine of Christ to those cut off from it by diabolic malice' (preface to *China*, but also *Oedipus*, I, I, 396–8).

In the last of Kircher's works, the *Turris Babel*, the story of the confusion of tongues is once again evoked, this time in an attempt to compose 'a grandiose universal history, embracing all diversities, in a unified project of *assimilation* to Christian doctrine. [. . .] The peoples of all the world, dispersed after the confusion, are to be called back together from the Tower of the Jesuits for a new linguistic and ideological reunification' (Scolari 1983: 6).

In fact, hungry for mystery and fascinated by exotic languages though he was, Kircher felt no real need to discover a perfect language to reunite the world in harmony; his own Latin, spoken with the clear accents of the Counter-Reformation, seemed a vehicle perfectly adequate to transport as much gospel truth as was required in order to bring the various peoples together. Kircher never entertained the thought that any of the languages he considered, not even the sacred languages of hieroglyphics and kabbalistic permutations, should ever again be spoken. He found in the ruins of these antique and venerated languages a garden of private delight; but he never conceived of them as living anew. At most he toyed with the idea of preserving these languages as sacred emblems, accessible only to the elect, and in order to show their fecund impenetrability he needed elephantine commentaries. In every one his books, he showed himself as a baroque scholar in a baroque world; he troubled more over the execution of his tables of illustrations than over the writing (which is often wooden and repetitive). Kircher was, in fact, *incapable of thinking other than in images* (cf. Rivosecchi 1982: 114). Perhaps his most lasting achievement, and certainly his most popular book, was the *Ars magna lucis et umbrae* of 1646. Here he explored the visible in all its nooks and crannies, drawing from his exploration a series of scientifically valid intuitions which even faintly anticipate the invention of the techniques of photography and the cinema.

Later Critics

About a century later, Vico took it for granted that the first language of humanity was in the form of hieroglyphics – that is, of metaphors and animated figures. He saw the pantomime, or acted-out rebus, with which the king of the Scythians replied to Darius the Great as an example of hieroglyphic speech. He had intimated war with just 'five real words': a frog, a mouse, a bird, a ploughshare, and a bow. The frog signified that he was born in Scythia, as frogs were born from the earth each summer; the mouse signified that he 'like a mouse had made his home where he was born, that is, he had established his nation there'; the bird signified 'there the auspices were; that is that he was subject to none but God'; the plough signified that he had made the land his own through cultivation; and finally the bow meant that 'as supreme commander in Scythia he had the duty and the might to defend his country' (*Scienza nuova*, II, ii, 4, 435).

Despite its antiquity and its primacy as the language of the gods, Vico attributed no quality of perfection to this hieroglyphic language. Neither did he regard it as inherently either ambiguous or secret: 'we must here uproot the false opinion held by some of the Egyptians that the hieroglyphs were invented by philosophers to conceal in them their mysteries of lofty esoteric wisdom. For it was by a common natural necessity that all the first nations spoke in hieroglyphs' (ibid.).

This 'speaking in things' was thus human and natural; its purpose was that of mutual comprehension. It was also a poetic form of speaking that could not, by its very nature, ever be disjoined from either the symbolic language of heroes or the epistolary language of commerce. This last form of speech 'must be understood as having sprung up by their [the plebians'] free consent, by this eternal property, that vulgar speech and writing are a right of the people' (p. 439). Thus the language of hieroglyphs, 'almost entirely mute, only very slightly articulate' (p. 446), once reduced to a mere vestibule of heroic language (made up of images, metaphors, similes and comparisons, that 'supplied all the resources of poetic expression', p. 438) lost its sacred halo of esoteric mystery. Hieroglyphs would become for Vico the model of perfection for the artistic use of language, without making any claim, however, to replace the ordinary languages of humanity.

Other eighteenth-century critics were moving in the same direction. Nicola Frèret (*Reflexions sur les principes généraux de l'art d'écrire*, 1718) wrote of hieroglyphic writing as an archaic artifice; Warburton considered it hardly more advanced than the writing systems of the Mexicans (*The Divine Legation of Moses*, 1737–41). We have seen what the eighteenth century had to say on the subject of monogeneticism. In this same period, critics were developing a notion of writing as evolving in stages from a pictographic one (representing things), through hieroglyphs (representing qualities and passions as well) to ideograms, capable of giving an abstract and arbitrary representation of ideas. This, in fact, had been Kircher's distinction, but now the sequence followed a different order and hieroglyphs were no longer considered as the originary language.

In his *Essai sur l'origine des langues* (1781) Rousseau wrote that 'the cruder the writing system, the more ancient the language', letting it be understood that the opposite held as well: the more ancient the language, the cruder the writing. Before words and propositions could be represented in conventional characters, it was necessary that the language itself be completely formed, and that the people be governed by common laws. Alphabetic writing could be invented only by a commercial nation, whose merchants had sailed to distant lands, learning to speak foreign tongues. The invention of the alphabet represented a higher stage because the alphabet did more than represent words, it analysed them as well. It is at this point that there begins to emerge the analogy between money and the alphabet: both serve as a universal medium in the process of exchange

– of goods in the first instance, of ideas in the second (cf. Derrida 1967: 242; Bora 1989: 40).

This nexus of ideas is repeatedly alluded to by Chevalier de Jaucourt in the entries that he wrote for the *Encyclopédie*: 'Writing', 'Symbol', 'Hieroglyph', 'Egyptian writing' and 'Chinese writing'. Jaucourt was conscious that if hieroglyphics were entirely in the form of icons, then the knowledge of their meanings would be limited to a small class of priest. The enigmatic character of such a system (in which Kircher took such pride) would eventually force the invention of more accessible forms such as demotic and hieratic. Jaucourt went further in the attempt to distinguish between different types of hieroglyph. He based his distinctions on rhetoric. Several decades earlier, in fact, in 1730, Du Marsais had published his *Traité des tropes*, which had tried to delimit and codify all the possible values that a term might take in a process of rhetorical elaboration that included analogies. Following this suggestion, Jaucourt abandoned any further attempt at providing Hermetic explanations, basing himself on rhetorical criteria instead: in a 'curiological' hieroglyph, the part stood for the whole; in the 'tropical' hieroglyph one thing could be substituted for another on the grounds of similarity. This limited the scope for interpretative licence; once the mechanics of hieroglyphs could be anchored in rhetoric, the possibility for an infinite proliferation of meanings could be reined in. In the *Encyclopédie* the hieroglyphs are presented as a mystification perpetrated at the hands of the Egyptian priesthood.

The Egyptian vs. the Chinese Way

Although today many are still of the opinion that images provide a means of communication that can overcome language barriers, the explanation of the way in which images can accomplish this by now takes one of two forms: the Egyptian and the Chinese way. The Egyptian way today belongs only to art history. We believe that visual media such as paintings, sequences in films, etc. are 'texts' which convey emotions and feelings that could not be expressed verbally: we cannot represent by mere words Mona Lisa to a blind person. The meanings that such texts can express are multiple, because there is no universal code: the rules of representation (and of recognizability) for an Egyptian mural, an Arab miniature, a painting by Turner or a comic strip are simply not the same in each case.

It is true that some ideograms have been used as characters of a universal code, for instance many road signals; in the same vein we are using more or less universal pictograms (think of the schematic crossed knives and forks which signal a restaurant in an airport, or of the stylized 'ladies' and 'gentlemen' on public lavatory doors). Sometimes visual signs are merely substituting alphabetical letters, as happens with semaphores or flag signals; sometimes a yellow flag meaning 'contagious disease on board' simply stands for a verbal sentence (cf. Prieto 1966). Likewise, the gestural languages of Trappist monks, Indian merchants, gypsies or thieves, as well as the drummed and whistled languages of certain tribes (cf. La Barre 1964), are equally dependent on the model of natural languages. As useful, convenient and ingenious as some of these systems of communication may be, they make no claims to being 'perfect' languages in which philosophers might one day wish to compose a treatise.

Any language of images is based on the alleged fact that images exhibit some properties of the represented things. Yet in any representable thing there will always be a multitude of properties, and there are infinite points of view under which an image can be judged similar to something else. Moreover, 'that a picture looks like nature often means only that it looks the way nature is usually painted' (Goodman 1968: 39).

We can see this by looking at the various versions of a semiotic apparatus (if not a true language) which remained alive for centuries and which flowered in the same period when the western culture was looking for perfect visual languages: the arts of memory (cf. Rossi 1960; Yates 1966).

An art of memory establishes at its expression-plane a system of *loci* (that is, of *places* in the literal sense of the word) which may be imagined as the rooms of a building or palace, or as an urban street or square. This system of *loci* is destined to house a set of images, drawn from the same iconographical field, which will play the role of lexical units. The content-plane is given by a system of *res memoranda*, in other words, of things to be remembered, usually belonging to the same conceptual framework. In this way, an art of memory is a semiotic system.

For instance, in mnemonic systems like those presented by the *Congestorius artificiosae memoriae* by Romberch (1520), the *Dialogo del modo di accrescere e conservare la memoria* by Dolce (1575), or the *Artificiosae memoriae fundamenta* by Paepp (1619), the system of grammatical cases is expressed (and thus recalled) by the different parts of the human body. Not only is this a case of one system expressing another system; it is also a case where the two planes are (in Hjelmslev's sense) conformal. It is not arbitrary that the head stands for nominative, the chest, which can receive blows, stands for accusative, and the hands, which possess and offer, stand for genitive and dative, and so on.

This shows that a mnemonic image, in order to express its content easily, should evoke it by similarity. But no mnemonic system was ever able to find a univocal criterion of resemblance. The criteria are the same as those that linked the *signature* to its *signatum*. If we look back and see (ch. 6) what Paracelsus had to say about the language of Adam, the *Protoplastus*, we see that he represented him as naming one animal on the basis of a morphological similarity (from which a virtue derived), while, in another case, the name derived directly from a virtue not manifested by the form of the object. In other cases, the name that Adam gave reflected neither morphology nor causal relations, but was inferred symptomatically: for instance, the horn of the stag permitted us to infer the age of the animal from the complexity of its branching.

On the subject of signatures, Della Porta said that spotted plants which imitated the spots of animals also shared their virtues (*Phytognomonica*, 1583, III, 6): the bark of a birch tree, for example, imitated the plumage of a starling and is *therefore* good against impetigo, while plants that have snake-like scales protect against reptiles (III, 7). Thus in one case, morphological similarity is a sign for alliance between a plant and an animal, while in the next it is a sign for hostility. Taddeus Hageck (*Metoscopicorum libellus unus*, 1584: 20) praises among the plants that cure lung diseases two types of lichen: however, one bears the form of a healthy lung, while the other bears the stained and shaggy shape of an ulcerated one. The fact that another plant is covered with little holes is enough to suggest that this plant is capable of opening the pores. We are thus witnessing three very distinct principles of relation by similarity: resemblance to a healthy organ, resemblance to a diseased organ, and an analogy between the form of a plant and the therapeutic result that it supposedly produced.

This indifference as to the nature of the connection between signatures and *signatum* holds in the arts of memory as well. In his *Thesaurus artificiosae memoriae* (1579), Cosma Roselli endeavoured to explain how, once a system of *loci* and images had been established, it might actually function to recall the *res memoranda*. He thought it necessary to explain 'quomodo multis modis, aliqua res alteri sit similis' (*Thesaurus*, 107), how, that is, one thing could be similar to another. In the ninth chapter of the second part he tried to construct systematically a set of criteria whereby images might correspond to things:

according to similarity, which, in its turn, can be divided into similarity of substance (such as a man as the microcosmic image of the macrocosm), similarity in quantity (the ten fingers for the Ten Commandments), according to metonymy or antonomasia (Atlas for astronomers or for astronomy, a bear for a wrathful man, a lion for pride, Cicero for rhetoric):

by homonyms: a real dog for the dog constellation;

by irony and opposition: the fatuous for the wise;

by trace: the footprint for the wolf, the mirror in which Titus admired himself for Titus;

by the name differently pronounced: *sanum* for *sane*;

by similarity of name: Arista [awn] for Aristotle;

by genus and species: leopard for animal;

by pagan symbol: the eagle for Jove;

by peoples: Parthians for arrows, Scythians for horses, Phoenicians for the alphabet;

by signs of the zodiac: the sign for the constellation;

by the relation between organ and function;

by common accident: the crow for Ethiopia;

by hieroglyph: the ant for providence.

The *Idea del teatro* by Giulio Camillo (1550) has been interpreted as a project for a perfect mechanism for the generation of rhetorical sentences. Yet Camillo speaks casually of similarity by morphological traits (a centaur for a horse), by action (two serpents in combat for the art of war), by mythological contiguity (Vulcan for the art of fire), by causation (silk worms for couture), by effects (Marsyas with his skin flayed off for butchery), by relation of ruler to ruled (Neptune for navigation), by relation between agent and action (Paris for civil courts), by antonomasia (Prometheus for man the maker), by iconism (Hercules drawing his bow towards the heavens for the sciences regarding celestial matters), by inference (Mercury with a cock for bargaining).

It is plain to see that these are all rhetorical connections, and there is nothing more conventional than a rhetorical figure. Neither the arts of memory nor the doctrine of signatures is dealing, in any degree whatsoever, with a 'natural' language of images. Yet a mere appearance of naturalness has always fascinated those who searched for a perfect language of images.

The study of gesture as the vehicle of interaction with exotic people, united with a belief in a universal language of images, could hardly fail to influence the large number of studies which begin to appear in the seventeenth century on the education of deaf-mutes (cf. Salmon 1972: 68–71). In 1620, Juan Pablo Bonet wrote a *Reducción de las letras y arte para enseñar a hablar los mudos*. Fifteen years later, Mersenne (*Harmonie*, 2) connected this question to that of a universal language. John Bulwer suggested (*Chirologia*, 1644) that only by a gestural language can one escape from the confusion of Babel, because it was the first language of humanity. Dalgarno (see ch. 11) assured his reader that his project would provide an easy means of educating deaf-mutes, and he again took up this argument in his *Didascalocophus* (1680). In 1662, the Royal Society devoted several debates to Wallis's proposals on the same topic.

As the debate carried over into the eighteenth century, an increased social awareness and pedagogical attention began to be shown. We catch the traces of this in a tract written for quite different purposes, Diderot's *Lettre sur l'éducation des sourds et muets* in 1751. In 1776, the Abbé de l'Epée (*Institutions des sourds et muets par la voie des signes méthodiques*) entered into a polemic against the common, dactylological form of deaf-mute speak, which, then as now, was the common method of signing with fingers the letters of the alphabet. De l'Epée was little interested that this language helped deaf-mutes communicate in a dactylological version of the French language; instead he was besotted by the vision of a perfect language. He taught his deaf-mutes to write in French; but he wished, above all, to teach them to communicate in a visual language of his own devising; it was a language not of letters but of concepts – therefore an ideography that, he thought, might one day become universal.

We can take for an example his method of teaching the meaning of 'I believe', thinking that his method might also work between speakers of different languages:

I begin by making the sign of the first person singular, pointing the index finger of my right hand towards my chest. I then put my finger on my forehead, on the concave part in which is supposed to reside my spirit, that is to say, my capacity for thought, and I make the sign for *yes*. I then make the same sign on that part of the body which, usually, is considered as the seat of what is called the heart in its spiritual sense. [. . .] I then make the same sign *yes* on my mouth while moving my lips. [. . .] Finally, I place my hand on my eyes, and, making the sign for *no* show that I do not see. At this point, all I need to do is to make the sign of the present [the Abbé had devised a series of sign gestures in which pointing once or twice in front of or behind the shoulders specified the proper tense] and to write *I believe*. (pp. 80–1)

In the light of what we have been saying, it should appear evident that the visual performances of the good Abbé might be susceptible to a variety of interpretations were he not to take the precaution of employing a supplementary means (like writing out the word) to provide an *anchor* to prevent the fatal polysemy of his images.

It has sometimes been observed that the true limitation of iconograms is that, as well as they signify form or function, they cannot so easily signify actions, verb tenses, adverbs or prepositions. In an article with the title 'Pictures can't say "ain't"', Sol Worth (1975) argued that an image cannot assert the non-existence of what it represents. It is obviously possible to think of a code containing graphic operators signifying 'existence/non-existence' or 'past/future' and 'conditional'. But these signs would still depend (parasitically) on the semantic universe of the verbal language – as would happen (see ch. 10) with the so-called universal characters.

The ability of a visual language to express more than one meaning at once is also, therefore, its limitation. Goodman has noted (1968: 23) that there is a difference between a *man-picture* and *a picture of a man*. The picture of a human being can be devised to represent (1) any member of the human race, (2) an individual person so-and-so, (3) a given person on the verge of doing something, dressed in a certain way, and so on. Naturally the title can help to disambiguate the intention of the artist, but once again images are fatally 'anchored' to words.

There have been any number of proposals for visual alphabets, some quite recent. We might cite Bliss's *Semantography*, Eckhardt's *Safo*, Janson's *Picto* and Ota's *LoCoS*. Yet, as Nöth has observed (1990: 277), these are all cases of pasigraphy (which we shall discuss in a later chapter) rather than true languages. Besides, they are based on natural languages. Many, moreover, are mere lexical codes without any grammatical component. The *Nobel* by Milan Randic consists of 20,000 visual lemmas, which can be combined together: a crown with an arrow pointing at a square with the uppermost side missing means 'abdication' (where the square stands for a basket); two legs signify 'to go', and when this sign is united with the sign for 'with' it means 'to accompany'. We seem to have returned to a sort of simplified hieroglyph which, in any case, will require us to learn a double set of conventions: the first to assign univocal meanings to single signs, the second to assign univocal meanings to sign clusters.

Each of these purely visual systems thus represents (1) a segment of artificial language, (2) endowed with a quasi-international extension, (3) capable of being used in only limited sectors, (4) debarred from creative use lest the images lose their capacity for univocal denotation, (5) without a grammar capable of generating an infinite or unlimited number of 'sentences', (6) unable to express new ideas because every element of expression always corresponds to a predetermined element of content, known in advance.

One could say that there is only a single system which can claim the widest range of diffusion and comprehensibility: the images of cinema and television. One is tempted to say that this is certainly a 'language' understood around the earth. Nevertheless, even such a language displays certain disadvantages: it has difficulties in presenting mathematical abstractions and philosophical arguments; its alleged universal comprehensibility is problematic, at least as far as its editing syntax is concerned; finally, if there is no difficulty involved in receiving cinematic or televised images, it is extremely difficult to produce them. Ease of execution is a notable argument in favour of verbal languages. Anyone who wished to communicate in a strictly visual language would probably have to go about with a camcorder, a portable television set, and a sackful of tapes, resembling Swift's wise men who, having decided that it was necessary to show any object they wanted to designate, were forced to drag enormous sacks behind them.

Images for Aliens

Perhaps the most discomforting document for the future of the language of images is the report drawn up in 1984 by Thomas A. Sebeok (Sebeok 1984). He had been commissioned by the Office of Nuclear Waste Isolation and by a group of other institutions to elaborate answers to a question posed by the US Nuclear Regulatory Commission. The American government had chosen several desert areas in the US for the burial (at the depth of hundreds of metres) of nuclear waste. The problem was not so much that of protecting the area from imprudent intrusions today, but rather that the waste would remain radioactive for another ten thousand years. That is more than enough time for great empires and flourishing civilizations to perish. We have seen how, a few centuries after the last pharaoh had disappeared, knowledge of how to read hieroglyphs had disappeared as well. It is easily conceivable that, ten thousand years hence, something similar will have happened to us. We may have reverted to barbarism. We may even be visited by inhabitants of other planets: how will we warn these alien visitors that they are in a danger zone?

Almost immediately, Sebeok discarded the possibility of any type of verbal communication, of electric signals as needing a constant power supply, of olfactory messages as being of brief duration, and of any sort of ideogram based on convention. Even a pictographic language seemed problematic. Sebeok analysed an image from an ancient primitive culture where one can certainly recognize human figures but it is hard to say what they are doing (dancing, fighting, hunting?).

Another solution would be to establish temporal segments of three generations each (calculating that, in any civilization, language will not alter beyond recognition between grandparents and grandchildren), giving instructions that, at the end of each segment, the message would be reformulated, adapting it to the semiotic conventions prevailing at the moment. But even this solution presupposes precisely the sort of social continuity that the original question had put into doubt. Another solution was to fill up the entire zone with messages in all known languages and semiotic systems, reasoning that it was statistically probable that at least one of these messages would be comprehensible to the future visitors. Even if only part of one of the messages was decipherable, it would still act as a sort of Rosetta stone, allowing the visitors to translate all the rest. Yet even this solution presupposed a form of cultural continuity (however weak it would be).

The only remaining solution was to institute a sort of 'priesthood' of nuclear scientists, anthropologists, linguists and psychologists supposed to perpetuate itself by co-opting new members. This caste would keep alive the knowledge of the danger, creating myths and legends about it. Even though, in the passage of time, these 'priests' would probably lose a precise notion of the peril that they were committed to protect humanity from, there would still survive, even in a future state of barbarism, obscure but efficacious taboos.

It is curious to see that, having been presented with a choice of various types of universal language, the choice finally fell on a 'narrative' solution, thus reproposing what really did happen millennia ago. Egyptian has disappeared, as well as any other perfect and holy primordial language, and what remains of all this is only myths, tales without a code, or whose code has long been lost. Yet they are still capable of keeping us in a state of vigil in our desperate effort at decipherment.

8

Magic Language

In a climate of extraordinary spiritual tension, the seventeenth century awaited change – a general reform of knowledge and morals, a reawakening of religious sensibility. The period was dominated by a belief that a new, golden century was dawning; Postel had already used the term 'golden century' in the title of one of his works. This was, moreover, an expectation shared by Catholics and Protestants alike, though each in different forms. Authors from Campanella to Andreae had drawn up projects for an ideal republic. Not only Postel but other thinkers in different countries had designed schemes for a universal monarchy. The Thirty Years War acted as a catalyst: conflict had flared in one region after another, creating, on the one hand, confessional hatreds and nationalist rivalries, engendering the modern notion of the *raison d'état*, on the other producing a pleiad of mystic spirits dreaming of universal peace (cf. De Mas 1982).

It was in this climate, then, that, in 1614, there appeared an anonymous tract written in German: *Allgemeine und general Reformation der gantzen weiten Welt*. Though this was only discovered later, the first part was largely a re-elaboration of a satire written by Traiano Boccalini and published in 1612–13, called *Ragguagli di Parnaso*. The second part, however, took the form of a manifesto, entitled *Fama fraternitatis R.C.* In this, the mysterious confraternity of the Rosicrucians openly declared its existence, supplying details concerning its own history as well as that of its mythical founder, Christian Rosencreutz. In the following year, 1615, the German manifesto was republished together with a second manifesto, written this time in Latin, with the title *Confessio fraternitatis Roseae crucis. Ad eruditos Europae* (we shall use the first English translation, *The Fame and the Confession of the Fraternity of R.C.*, London, 1652).

The first manifesto proclaimed its wish that there should be 'a Society in Europe [. . .] with which such as be Governors might be brought up, for to learn all that which God hath suffered Man to know' (p. 9). Both the manifestos emphasized the secret character of the confraternity and the fact that their members were not permitted to reveal its true aims and nature. It was a call, addressed to the learned of Europe, beseeching them to make contact with the writers of the manifesto; this made the final appeal of the *Fama* even more ambiguous:

And although at this time we make no mention either of our names, or meetings, yet nevertheless every ones opinion shal assuredly come to our hands, in what language so ever it be, nor any body shal fail, who so gives but his name to speak with some of us, either by word of mouth, or else if there be some lett in writing [. . .] Also our building (although one hundred thousand people had very near seen and beheld the same) shal for ever remain untouched, undestroyed, and hidden to the wicked world. (pp. 31–2)

Immediately, from almost every corner of Europe, responses to the Rosicrucian appeal were written. No one claimed to be a Rosicrucian. Almost no one claimed even to know who the Rosicrucians were. Yet almost everyone tried to claim that his own programme was synonymous with that of the Rosicrucian brotherhood. Some authors professed an extreme humility. In his *Themis aurea* (1618), for example, Michael Maier insisted that though the brotherhood really existed, he was too humble an individual to be admitted as a member. Yet, as Yates observed, this was typical of the behaviour of Rosicrucian authors: not only did they deny being Rosicrucians, they claimed never to have encountered a single member of the confraternity.

Thus when, in 1623, a set of – naturally anonymous – manifestos appeared in Paris, announcing the arrival of the Rosicrucians, a furious polemic ensued in which the common opinion emerged that the Rosicrucians were worshippers of Satan. It was said of Descartes that, in the course of a trip to Germany, he had tried (unsuccessfully of course) to make contact with the brotherhood. On his return to Paris, he even fell under suspicion of being a member. He readily found a logical argument to exculpate himself, however; since it was well known that the Rosicrucians were *invisible*, Descartes showed up (making himself *visible*) in public places and on public occasions (see A. Baillet, *Vie de Monsieur Descartes*, 1693). In 1623, a certain Neuhaus published, first in German and then in French, an *Advertissiment pieux et utile des frères de la Rosee-Croix*, in which he asked whether or not they existed, and, if so, who they were and what was the origin of their name. Neuhaus proved their existence by means of a rather startling argument: 'By the very fact that they change and alter their name and that they mask their age, and that, by their own confession, they come and go without making themselves known, there is no Logician that could deny the necessity that they exist' (p. 5).

It would be tedious to recount here the entire story of books and tracts contradicting each other in an endeavour to reveal the truth about the Rosicrucians (it has sometimes been claimed, for instance, that the same author, using two different pseudonyms, was responsible for two or more tracts pro- and anti-Rosicrucians: see Arnold 1955; Edighoffer 1982). It means that, when conditions are ripe, it takes but one spark – be it an obscure and ambiguous appeal for the spiritual reform of all humanity – to set off unexpected reactions. It almost seemed that everyone had been waiting for the Rosicrucian manifesto to appear as the missing piece in a polemic in which all sides – Catholic and Protestant – were waiting to join. Thus, although the Jesuits were soon in the forefront of the battle against the Rosicrucians, there were not lacking those who insinuated that behind the Rosicrucians was the Society of Jesus itself, seeking to smuggle Catholic dogma into the Protestant world (see *Rosa jesuitica*, 1620).

The most intriguing aspect of the whole story was that the people immediately suspected of being the authors of the manifestos – Johann Valentin Andreae and his circle of friends in Tubingen – spent the rest of their lives either denying their involvement, or minimizing it as nothing more than a literary exercise.

As one might expect, given the spirit of the times, it was impossible to offer to the people of all lands a new philosophy without also offering them a perfect language in which to express it. The manifestos, of course, spoke of this language; yet its perfection was mirrored by its secrecy (*Fama*, 287). According to the *Confessio*, the four founders of the brotherhood had 'created the magic language and writing':

and thenceforth our Trumpet shall publiquely sound with a loud sound, and great noise, when namely the fame (which at this present is shewed by few, and is secretly, as thing to come, declared in Figures and Pictures) shall be free, and publiquely proclaimed, and the whole World be filled withall [. . .] So, the secret hid Writings and Characters are most necessary for all such things which are found out by Men: Although that great Book of Nature stand open to all Men, yet there are but few that can read and understand the same [. . .] The Characters and Letters, as God hath here and there incorporated them in the holy Scripture the Bible, so hath he imprinted them most apparently into the wonderful Creation of Heaven and Earth, yea in all Beasts [. . .] From the which Characters and Letters we have borrowed our Magick writing, and have found out, and made a new Language for our selves, in the which withall is expressed and declared the Nature of all Things; So that it is no wonder that we are not so eloquent in other Languages, the which we know that they are altogether disagreeing to the Language of our forefathers, Adam and Enoch, and were through the Babylonical Confusion wholly hidden. (pp. 43, 47, 48)

Hypotheses

By the term 'Rosicrucian linguistics' Ormsby-Lennon (1988) indicates a current of thought prevalent in Germany and England in the seventeenth century, whose influences could still be traced in the proposals for the invention of scientific languages by Dalgarno and Wilkins. According to Ormsby-Lennon the Rosicrucians derived their notion of magic language from Jacob Böhme's theory of signatures. Böhme, a mystic whose ideas had a great influence on later European culture, was well known in Rosicrucian circles in Germany. From here, through a series of translations that continued into the eighteenth century, his influence passed into English theosophist culture. Webster, in his *Academiarum examen* of 1654, observed that the ideas of Böhme were recognized and adopted by the most enlightened confraternity of the Rosy Cross (pp. 26–7).

Böhme drew, in his turn, on Paracelsus' conviction that every natural element bore a sign that revealed its special occult powers, which in its turn recalls the tradition of physiognomics: powers were 'signed' or marked in the forms and figures of all material things in the same way as the qualities of a man were revealed by the form of his face. Nature had created nothing that failed to manifest its internal qualities through external signs, because the external forms of objects were, so to speak, nothing more than the result of the working of these same internal qualities. Knowing this, humanity was on the way to discovering the essence of essences, that is to say, 'the Language of Nature, in which each thing speaks of its particular properties' (*Signatura rerum*, 1662, I).

In the writings of Böhme, however, the idea of signatures

did not follow the previous magical tradition, but rather evolved as a mystical metaphor expressing the ideal of an unending search for the traces of the divine force which pervades the whole creation. For Böhme, the mystic way started with a contemplation of simple, material objects which, at a certain point, might, as it were, burst into flames in an epiphany which revealed the true nature of the invisible. His own vocation had been decided when, being still a young man, gazing at a tin pot struck by the rays of the sun, he was suddenly vouchsafed a vision that became, like Borges's Alef, a privileged moment in which the light of God present in all things suddenly disclosed itself.

Böhme spoke of the speech of nature, or *Natursprache*, in his *Mysterium Magnum* of 1623; he described it as a 'sensual speech' ('sensualische Sprache') which was both 'natural' and 'essential'. It was the speech of all of creation, the speech which Adam had used to name material things:

During the time when all peoples spoke the same language, everyone naturally understood each other. When they no longer wished to use the sensual speech, however, they lost this proper understanding because they transferred the spirit of sensual speech into a crudely external form. [. . .] Today, while the birds of the air and the beasts of the forests may still, each according to their own qualities, understand each other, not one of us understands the sensual speech any longer. Let man therefore be aware of that from which he has excluded himself and that with which, moreover, one day, he will once again be born again, though no longer here on earth, but in another, spiritual world. Spirits speak only to each other in sensual speech, and have no need for any other form of speech, because this is the Speech of Nature. (*Sämmtliche werke*, Leipzig, 1922: V, 261–2)

In this passage, it is evident that, for Böhme, such a *Natursprache* was no longer simply the language of signatures. When the spirits of the other world hold converse with one another, it is obvious that they use something more than natural signs. It seems that the sensual speech was the same in which Adam named the animals and the same as the language given the apostles at Pentecost, an 'open sensual speech' that comprehended all other languages. Although this gift was lost in the confusion of Babel, it will, one day, return to us when the time is ripe, and we will be ready to converse with God. It seems evident that what Böhme is here describing is the language of glossolalic enthusiasm, or the so-called language of tongues.

Böhme's notion of sensual speech seems very similar to Reuchlin's notion of the language of Adam alluded to in his *De verbo mirifico* (II, 6); this was a language manifested as a 'simplex sermo purus, incorruptus, sanctus, brevis et constans [. . .] in quo Deus cum homine, et homines cum angelis locuti perhibentur coram, *et non per interpretem*, facie ad facie [. . .] sicut solet amicus cum amico' ('a simple and pure speech, uncorrupted, holy, brief, and constant, in which God and men, and men and angels could talk in each other's presence, *not through interpretation*, but face to face, just as is usual between friends'). Or perhaps it was the same as the language of the birds, in which Adam during his sojourn in Eden could converse with (as well as name) every beast of the field, and every fowl of the air. After the Fall, the speech of birds was, once more, revealed to King Solomon, who taught it to the Queen of Sheba. It was a form of speech revealed as well to Apollonius of Tyana (see Ormsby-Lennon 1988: 322–3).

We find a reference to this language of the birds in the chapter entitled 'Histoire des oiseaux' in the *Empires du Soleil* of Cyrano de Bergerac (on Cyrano and language see Erba 1959: 23–5). In this chapter, the traveller meets a marvellous bird whose tail is green, whose stomach is of an enamel blue, and whose purple head is surmounted by a golden crown. The bird addresses the traveller in a 'singing speech' and he, to his amazement, finds that he is able to understand all that the bird has to say. Noting the perplexity on the traveller's face, the bird explains:

Among you humans there have been those able to speak and understand our Language. There was Apollonius of Tyana, Anaximander, and Aesop, and many others whose names I will not mention as you would not recognize them. Just so, there are to be found among the birds those who can speak and understand your own language. Thus, just as you will encounter birds that do not say a word, others that merely twitter, and others still that can speak, so you may even encounter one of the most perfect birds of all – those who can use all idioms.

Was it then the practice of speaking in tongues that the Rosicrucians had in mind in their manifestos to the learned of Europe? Yet, if this is so, how are we to understand the allusions to a 'secret writing . . . expressed symbolically by numbers and designs'? Why did they use the terms 'characters and letters' when, in this period, these were notions associated with the search for the alphabetic characters capable of expressing the nature of things?

Dee's Magic Language

In his *Apologia compendiaria* (1615) Fludd noted that the Rosicrucian brothers practised that type of kabbalistic magic that enabled them to summon angels. This is reminiscent of the steganography of Trithemius. Yet it is no less reminiscent of the necromancy of John Dee, a man whom many authors considered the true inspirer of Rosicrucian spirituality.

In the course of one of the angelic colloquies recorded in *A True and Faithful Relation of what Passed for Many Yeers between Dr. John Dee [. . .] and Some Spirits* (1659: 92), Dee found himself in the presence of the Archangel Gabriel, who wished to reveal to him something about the nature of holy language. When questioned, however, Gabriel simply repeated the information that the Hebrew of Adam, the language in which 'every word signifieth the quiddity of the substance', was also the primal language – a notion which, in the Renaissance, was hardly a revelation. After this, in fact, the text continues, for page after page, to expatiate on the relations between the names of angels, numbers and secrets of the universe – to provide, in short, another example of the pseudo-Hebraic formulae which were the stock in trade of the Renaissance magus.

Yet it is perhaps significant that the 1659 *Relation* was published by Meric Casaubon, who was later accused of partially retrieving and editing Dee's documents with the intention of discrediting him. There is nothing, of course, surprising in the notion that a Renaissance magus invoked spirits; yet, in the case of John Dee, when he gave us an instance of cipher, or mystic language, he used other means.

In 1564, John Dee wrote the work upon which his contemporary fame rested – *Monas hieroglyphica*, where he speaks of a geometrical alphabet with no connection to Hebrew. It should be remembered that Dee, in his extraordinary library, had many of Lull's manuscripts, and that many of his kabbalistic experiments with Hebrew characters in fact recall Lull's use of letters in his art of combination (French 1972: 49ff).

Dee's *Monas* is commonly considered a work of alchemy. Despite this, the network of alchemical references with which the book is filled seems rather intended to fulfil a larger purpose – that of explicating the cosmic implications deriving from Dee's fundamental symbol, the Monad, based upon circles and straight lines, all generated from a single point. In this symbol (see figure 8.1), the main circle represented the sun that revolves around its central point, the

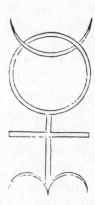

Figure 8.1

earth, and in its upper part was intersected by a semi-circle representing the moon. Both sun and moon were supported on an inverted cross which represented both the ternary principle – two straight lines which intersect plus their point of intersection – and the quaternary principle – the four right angles formed at the intersections of the two lines. The sum of the ternary and quaternary principles constituted a further seven-fold principle, and Dee goes even on to squeeze an eight-fold principle from the diagram. By adding the first four integers together, he also derives a ten-fold principle. By such a manipulatory vertigo Dee then derives the four composite elements (heat and cold, wet and dry) as well as other astrological revelations.

From here, through 24 theorems, Dee makes his image undergo a variety of rotations, decompositions, inversions and permutations, as if it were drawing anagrams from a series of Hebrew letters. Sometimes he considers only the initial aspects of his figure, sometimes the final one, sometimes making numerological analyses, submitting his symbol to the kabbalistic techniques of *notariqon*, *gematria* and *temurah*. As a consequence, the Monas should permit – as happens with every numerological speculation – the revelation of the whole of the cosmic mysteries.

However, the Monad also generates alphabetic letters. Dee was emphatic about this in the letter of dedication with which he introduced his book. Here he asked all 'grammarians' to recognize that his work 'would explain the form of the letters, their position and place in the alphabetical order, and the relations between them, along with their numerological values, and many other things concerning the primary Alphabet of the three languages'. This final reference to 'the three languages' reminds us of Postel (whom Dee met personally) and of the Collège des Trois Langues at which Postel was professor. In fact, Postel, to prove that Hebrew was the primal language in his 1553 *De originibus*, had observed that every 'demonstration of the world' comes from point, line and triangle, and that sounds themselves could be reduced to geometry. In his

De Foenicum literis, he further argued that the invention of the alphabet was almost contemporary with the spread of language (on this point see many later kabbalistic speculations over the origins of language, such as Thomas Bang, *Caelum orientis*, 1657: 10).

What Dee seems to have done is to take the geometrical argument to its logical conclusion. He announced in his dedicatory letter that 'this alphabetic literature contains great mysteries', continuing that 'the first Mystic letters of Hebrews, Greeks, and Romans were formed by God and transmitted to mortals [. . .] so that all the signs used to represent them were produced by points, straight lines, and circumferences of circles arranged by an art most marvellous and wise.' When he writes a eulogy of the geometrical properties of the Hebrew *Yod*, one is tempted to think of the Dantesque *I*; when he attempts to discover a generative matrix from which language could be derived, one thinks of the Lullian *Ars*. Dee celebrates his procedure for generating letters as a 'true Kabbalah [. . .] more divine than grammar itself'.

These points have been recently developed by Clulee (1988: 77–116), who argues that the *Monas* should be seen as presenting a system of writing, governed by strict rules, in which each character is associated with a thing. In this sense, the language of *Monas* is superior to the kabbala, for the kabbala aims at the interpretation of things only as they are said (or written) in language, whereas the *Monas* aims directly at the interpretation of things as they are in themselves. Thanks to its universality, moreover, Dee can claim that his language invents or restores the language of Adam. According to Clulee, Dee's graphic analysis of the alphabet was suggested by the practice of Renaissance artists of designing alphabetical letters using the compass and set-square. Thus Dee could have thought of a unique and simple device for generating both concepts and all the alphabets of the world.

Neither traditional grammarians nor kabbalists were able to explain the form of letters and their position within the

alphabet; they were unable to discover the origins of signs
and characters, and for this reason they were uncapable to
retrieve that universal grammar that stood at the bases of
Hebrew, Greek and Latin. According to Clulee, what Dee
seems to have discovered was an idea of language 'as a
vast, symbolic system through which meanings might be
generated by the manipulation of symbols' (1988: 95).

Such an interpretation seems to be confirmed by an
author absent from all the bibliographies (appearing, to the
best of my knowledge, only in Leibniz's *Epistolica de
historia etymologica dissertatio* of 1717, which discusses
him in some depth). This author is Johannes Petrus Ericus,
who, in 1697, published his *Anthropoglottogonia sive
linguae humanae genesis*, in which he tried to demonstrate
that all languages, Hebrew included, were derived from
Greek. In 1686, however, he had also published a *Principium philologicum in quo vocum, signorum et punctorum
tum et literarum massime ac numerorum origo*. Here he
specifically cited Dee's *Monas Hieroglyphica* to derive from
that matrix the letters of all alphabets (still giving pre-
cedence to Greek) as well as all number systems. Through
a set of extremely complex procedures, Ericus broke down
the first signs of the Zodiac to reconstruct them into Dee's
Monad; he assumed that Adam had named each animal by
a name that reproduced the sounds that each emitted; then
he elaborated a rather credible phonological theory identifying classes of letters such as 'per sibilatione per dentes',
'per tremulatione labrorum', 'per compressione labrorum',
'per contractione palati', 'per respiratione per nares'. Ericus
concluded that Adam used vowels for the names of the
birds of the air, semi-vowels for the names of the beasts of
the fields, and mutes for the fish. This rather elementary
phonetics also enabled Ericus to deduce the seven notes of
the musical scale as well as the seven letters which designate
them – these letters being the basic elements of the Monas.
Finally, he demonstrated how by rotating this figure,
forming, as it were, visual anagrams, the letters of all
other alphabets could be derived.

Thus the magic language of the Rosicrucians (if they existed, and if they were influenced by Dee) could have been a matrix able to generate – at least alphabetically – all languages, and, therefore, all the wisdom of the world. Such a language would have been more than a universal grammar: it would have been a grammar without syntactic structures, or, as Demonet (1992: 404) suggests, a 'grammar without words', a silent communication, close to the language of angels, or similar to Kircher's conception of hieroglyphs. Thus, once again, this perfect language would be based upon a sort of communicative short-circuit, capable of revealing everything, but only if it remained initiatically secret.

Perfection and Secrecy

We might think it is a pity that the search for a language that was as perfect as it was *universal* should lead to such a conception of a tongue reserved for the 'happy few'. But it is perhaps nothing more than our 'democratic' illusion to imagine that perfection must imply universality.

In order to understand the cultural framework of both Kircher's Egyptology and Rosicrucian holy languages, it must be remembered that for the Hermetic tradition truth was not usually regarded as accessible to the many. Indeed, there existed a marked tendency to believe that what is true is unknown and hardly knowable, if not to a restricted elite (cf. Eco 1990).

There is a radical difference between the gnostic and Neo-Platonist ideas of late antiquity (as well as their Renaissance versions – which survived in the Counter-Reformation Catholicism of Kircher) and the Christian message, as it was proclaimed throughout most of the Middle Ages. For medieval Christianity, salvation was promised to the meek and humble in spirit, and did not require any special knowledge: everyone can understand what is required in order to deserve the kingdom of heaven. Medieval teaching reduced the aura of mystery that accompanied the revelation – which was explained by formulae, parables and images that even the uneducated might grasp: truth was considered *effable*, therefore *public*. For Hermetic thought, instead, the cosmic drama could only be understood by an aristocracy of wisdom, able to decipher the hieroglyphs of the universe; the main characteristic of truth was its *ineffability*: it could not be expressed in simple words, was ambiguous by nature, was to be found through the coincidence of opposites, and could be expressed only by initiatic revelations.

Within this tradition, public accessibility was simply not a criterion by which a perfect language was judged. If one does not understand this point, one cannot understand why the cryptographers of this period dedicated their ciphers to grand-dukes deep in military campaigns and political machinations, presenting them as arcane suggestions. Perhaps this is all merely another manifestation of the natural hypocrisy of a century fascinated by dissimulation, a feature that constitutes the continuing charm of baroque civilization.

It remains uncertain if that celebrated book *Breviarium politicorum secundum rubricas Mazarinicas* (1684) really collects Mazarin's political thoughts or is a libel invented to defame him: in whatever case, it certainly reflects the image of a man of politics in the 1600s. It is notable that in the chapter entitled 'Reading and writing' it recommends that, if one needs to write in a public place, it is convenient to place upon a lectern several already written pages as if one intended to copy them out, letting them be visible and concealing under them the paper upon which one is really writing, guarded in such a way that no one who approaches you will be able to read it. Resorting to ciphers is suggested, but in such a way that at first glance the message looks understandable and provides irrelevant information (the canonical reference is to Trithemius). Not only must the message be translated in a secret writing, but this writing must also conceal its own secrecy, because a cipher that blatantly appears as such can arouse suspicion and encourage decipherment.

Thus on the one hand the mystic who writes about perfect and holy languages winks his eye at the politician who will use this language as his secret code; on the other hand the cryptographer sells to the politician a cipher (that is, an instrument of power and dominion) that for him, the Hermetic initiate, is also a key to supernatural truths.

Such a man was Johann Valentin Andreae, whom many have considered (and many still do consider) to be, if not the author, at least the inspirer of the Rosicrucian manifestos. Andreae was a Lutheran mystic and writer of utopian works, like the *Christianopolis* of 1619, similar in spirit to those of Bacon and Campanella. Edighoffer (1982: 175ff) has noted that many of his authentic works, like the *Chemical Weddings*, abound with ciphered expressions, according to the expressed principle that 'Arcana publicata vilescunt' and that one ought not to cast pearls before swine. In the same vein Andreae used ciphered messages in his correspondence with Augustus, Duke of Brunswick. Edighoffer remarks that there is nothing surprising in this: it was a correspondence filled with political observations, one, moreover, that took place during the Thirty Years War, when the difference between political and religious comments was minimal and the risks in both were the same.

In the light of these, as it were, 'private' practices of the Rosicrucians, their public appeals concerning the need to use a secret language to inaugurate a universal reform must seem even more ambiguous. They are so to such an extent as to make credible what not only modern historians but even the supposed authors of the manifestos themselves had always claimed: the manifestos were nothing but a joke, a sophomoric game, an exercise in literary pastiche made up of all the buzz-topics of the day: the search for the language of Adam, the dream of a sensual language, glossolalic illusions, cryptography, kabbala . . . And since everything went into this *pot au feu*, anything could be fished out again. Thus, as will always happen when the spectre of mystery is raised, there were those who read the Rosicrucian manifestos 'paranoically', discovering in them what they wanted to believe anyway, and needed to rediscover continually.

9

Polygraphies

Steganographies were used to cipher messages in order to guarantee secrecy and security. However, even though disregarding many terminological details (or differences) used today by the cryptographers, one must distinguish between the activity of *coding* and *decoding* messages when one knows the key, or code, and *cryptoanalysis*; that is, the art of discovering an unknown key in order to decipher an otherwise incomprehensible message. Both activities were strictly linked from the very beginning of cryptography: if a good steganography could decode a ciphered message, it ought to allow its user to understand an unknown language as well.

When Trithemius wrote his *Polygraphia*, which was published in 1518, before his *Steganographia*, and did not earn the sinister fame of the latter work, he was well aware that, by his system, a person ignorant of Latin might, in a short time, learn to write in that 'secret' language (1518: biiii). Speaking of Trithemius' *Polygraphia*, Mersenne said (*Quaestiones celeberrimae in Genesim*, 1623: 471) that its 'third book contains an art by which even an uneducated man who knows nothing more than his mother tongue can learn to read and write Latin in two hours'. Steganography thus appeared both as an instrument to encipher messages conceived in a known language and as the key to deciphering unknown languages.

In order to cipher a message one must substitute the letters of a plain message (written in a language known by both the sender and the addressee) with other letters prescribed by a key or code (equally known by sender and addressee). To decipher a message encoded according to an unknown key, it is frequently sufficient to detect which letter of the encoded message recurs most frequently, and it is easy to infer that this represents the letter that occurs most frequently in a given known language. Usually the decoder tries various hypotheses, checking upon different languages, and at a certain point finds the right solution.

The decipherment is made, however, more difficult if the encoder uses a new key for every new word of the message. A typical procedure of this kind was the following. Both the encoder and the decoder refer to a table like this:

ABCDEFGHIJKLMNOPQRSTUVWXYZ
BCDEFGHIJKLMNOPQRSTUVWXYZA
CDEFGHIJKLMNOPQRSTUVWXYZAB
DEFGHIJKLMNOPQRSTUVWXYZABC
EFGHIJKLMNOPQRSTUVWXYZABCD
FGHIJKLMNOPQRSTUVWXYZABCDE
GHIJKLMNOPQRSTUVWXYZABCDEF
HIJKLMNOPQRSTUVWXYZABCDEFG
IJKLMNOPQRSTUVWXYZABCDEFGH
(and so on for 26 lines).

Now, let us suppose that the key is the Latin word CEDO. The first word of the message is encoded according to the third line of the table (beginning with C), so that A becomes C, B becomes D and so on. The second word is encoded according to the fifth line (beginning with E), so that A becomes E and so on. The third word is encoded according to the fourth line, the fourth according to the fifteenth one . . . At the fifth word one starts the process all over again. Naturally the decoder (who knows the key) proceeds in the opposite way.

In order to decipher without knowing the key, if the table is that simple and obvious, there is no problem. But even in cases of more complicated tables the decipherer can try with all possible tables (for instance, with alphabets in reverse order, with alternate letters, such as ACEG), and it is usually only a matter of time before even the most complex of codes are broken.

Observing this, Heinrich Hiller, in his *Mysterium artiis steganographicae novissimum* (1682), proposed to teach a method of learning to decipher messages not only in code, but also in Latin, German, Italian and French, simply by observing the incidence of each letter and diphthong in each language. In 1685, John Falconer wrote a *Cryptomenysis patefacta: or the Art of Secret Information Disclosed Without a Key*, where he noted that, once someone has understood the rules of decipherment in a given language, it is possible to do the same with all the others (A7v).

Kircher's Polygraphy

Kircher wrote his *Polygraphia nova et universalis ex combinatoria arte detecta* in 1663, several years after his early works on Egypt and hieroglyphics, but he was concerned with the problem of universal writing from the beginning of the decade, and it seems evident that he was at the same time fascinated by the hieroglyphic mysteries and the polygraphic publicity. It is also significant that in this same volume Kircher designed not only a polygraphy, or international language open to all, but also, in the wake of Trithemius, a steganography, or secret language in which to cipher messages. What (at the end of the previous chapter) seemed to us a contradiction appeared to Kircher rather as a natural connection. He cited, at the outset, an Arab proverb: if you have a secret, hide it or reveal it ('si secretum tibi sit, tege illud, vel revela'). Such a decision was not so obvious, after all, since in his works on Egyptology

Kircher had chosen a 'fifty–fifty solution', saying something by concealing it, alluding without revealing. Finally, the second part of the title of Kircher's work reveals that, in designing his polygraphy, Kircher was also using Lull's art of combination (contrary to the opinion of Knowlson 1975: 107–8).

In the enthusiastic preface that the author addressed to the emperor Ferdinand III, he celebrated polygraphy as 'all languages reduced to one' ('linguarum omnium ad unam reductio'). Using polygraphy, 'anyone, even someone who knows nothing other than his own vernacular, will be able to correspond and exchange letters with anybody else, of whatever their nationality.' Thus Kircher's polygraphy was in reality a *pasigraphy*, that is, a project for a written language, or international alphabet, which was not required to be spoken.

It is easy to confuse Kircher's project with a double pentaglottic dictionary, in A and B versions (both in Latin, Italian, Spanish, French and German). In Kircher's time, English was not considered an important international language, and, in his *Character*, Becher had assumed that French was sufficient, as a vehicular language, for English, Italian, Spanish and Portuguese native speakers. Ideally, Kircher thought (p. 7) that his dictionary should also include Hebrew, Greek, Bohemian, Polish, Lithuanian, Hungarian, Dutch, English and Irish ('linguae doctrinales omnibus communes') – as well as Nubian, Ethiopic, Egyptian, Congolese, Angolan, Chaldean, Arabic, Armenian, Persian, Turkish, Tartar, Chinese, Mexican, Peruvian, Brazilian and Canadian. Kircher did not, it seems, feel himself ready to confront such a gigantic task; perhaps he intuited that the missionary activity, followed eventually by colonialism, would drastically simplify the problem (transforming many exotic languages into mere ethnological remnants): Spanish would substitute for Mexican, French for Canadian, Portuguese for Brazilian, and various pidgins would substitute for all the rest.

Kircher's A and B dictionaries each contain 1,228 items.

The grounds for selection were purely empirical: Kircher chose the words that seemed to him most commonly used.

Dictionary A served to encode messages. It started with a list of common nouns and verbs, in alphabetical order. There followed alphabetic lists of proper nouns (regions, cities, persons), and of adverbs and prepositions. Added to this there was also a list of the conjugations of both the verbs *to be* and *to have*. The whole material was subdivided into 32 tables, marked by Roman numerals, while every item of each table was marked by an Arabic numeral. The dictionary was set out in five columns, one for each of the five languages, and the words in each language were listed in their proper alphabetical order. Consequently, there is no necessary semantic correspondence between the terms recorded on the same line, and only the terms scored with the same Roman and Arabic numerals were to be considered synonymous. We can see this best by giving the first two lines of the dictionary:

Latin	Italian	Spanish	French	German
abalienare I.1	astenere I.4	abstenir I.4	abstenir I.4	abhalten I.4
abdere I.2	abbracciare II.10	abbraçar II.10	abayer XII.35	abschneinden I.5

The Roman numerals refer to tables found in dictionary B; the Arabic numerals refer to the items themselves. Latin acts as the parameter language: for each specific term, the numbers refer to the Latin alphabetic ordering. For example, the code for the French word *abstenir* is I.4, which indicates that the position of its Latin synonym, *abstinere*, is fourth in the Latin column I (obviously, to encode the Latin word *abstinere*, one also writes I.4).

To decode the message, it was necessary to use dictionary B. This too was arranged in 32 tables, each assigned a Roman numeral. But for each column (or language) the words did not follow their alphabetic order (except the Latin one), while the Arabic numbers marking each term were in an increasing arithmetical order. Thus all the terms on the same line were synonymous and each synonym was marked by the same Arabic number.

Again, it is easiest to see how this worked by citing the first two lines of the first table:

abalienare alienare 1		estrañar 1	estranger 1	entfremden 1
1				
abdere 2	nascondere 2	esconder 2	musser 2	verbergen 2

Thus, if one wants to send the Latin word *abdere* (to hide), according to the dictionary A one encodes it as I.2. A German addressee, receiving the message I.2, goes to dictionary B, first table, German column, and looks for the second word, which is exactly *verbergen* (to hide). If the same addressee wants to know how to translate this term in Spanish, one finds in the same line that the synonymous term is *esconder*.

However, Kircher found that a simple lexicon did not suffice; he was forced to invent 44 supplementary signs (*notae*) which indicated the tense, mood and number of verbs, plus 12 more signs which indicated declensions (nominative, genitive, dative, etc., both singular and plural). Thus, to understand the following example, the sign N meant nominative, while a sign like a D indicated the third person singular of the past tense. In this way, the ciphered expression 'XXVII.36N, XXX.21N, II.5N, XXIII.8D, XXVIII.10, XXX.20' can be decoded as 'Petrus noster amicus, venit ad nos' (literally, 'Peter our friend came to us'), and, on the basis of Latin, can be transformed into an equivalent sentence in any of the other four languages.

Kircher proudly claims that, by dictionary A, we can write in any language even though we know only our own, as well as that, with dictionary B, we can understand a text written in an unknown language. The system also works when we receive a non-ciphered text written in a natural foreign language. All we have to do is to look up the reference numbers for each foreign word in dictionary A (where they are listed in alphabetical order), then, with the reference numbers, find the corresponding words in dictionary B, in the column for our own language.

Not only was this process laborious, but the entire project was based on the assumption that all other languages could be directly reduced to the Latin grammar. One can imagine the results of such a method if one thinks of translating literally, word by word, a German sentence into an English one.

Kircher never confronted the problem of why an item-by-item translation should be syntactically correct, or even comprehensible, in the new language. He seemed to rely on the good will and good sense of whoever used his system. Yet even the most willing users might slip up. In August 1663, after reading the *Polygraphia*, Juan Caramuel y Lobkowitz wrote to Kircher to congratulate him on his wonderful invention (Mss. Chigiani f.59 v., Biblioteca Apostolica Vaticana; cf. Casciato et al. 1986: table 5). Appropriately, Caramuel chose to congratulate Kircher in his own polygraphy. Yet his first problem was that Kircher's own first name, Athanasius, did not appear in the list of proper names. Adopting the principle that where a term is missing, an analogous one must be sought, Caramuel addressed his letter to 'Anastasia'. Moreover, there are passages that can be decoded fairly easily, while for others one suspects that the labour of consulting the dictionary to obtain reference numbers for every word proved so tedious that even Caramuel began to nod. Thus we find ourselves in front of a passage which, in Latin, would need to be translated as follows: '*Dominus* + sign of vocative, *Amicus* + sign of vocative, *multum sal* + sign of vocative, *Anastasia, a me* + sign of accusative, *ars* + sign of accusative, *ex illius* + sign of ablative, *discere posse* + sign of second person plural, future active, *non est loqui vel scribere sub lingua* + ablative, *communis* + ablative.' After many heroic efforts, one can try to render it (in a sort of 'Me Tarzan–You Jane' language) as 'O Lord and Friend, O witty Athanasius, to me (?) you could learn from him an art (which) is not speaking and writing under a common language.'

Beck and Becher

In 1657, Cave Beck had published *The Universal Character, by which All the Nations of the World may Understand One Another's Conceptions, Reading out of one Common Writing their Own Mother Tongues*, presenting a project which was not so different from Kircher's. Here is an example from his system:

	Honour	*thy*	*Father*	*and*	*thy*	*Mother*
leb	2314	p	2477	&	pf	2477

The numbers specified nouns and verbs, *p* stood for the personal pronoun, second person, with *pf* as the feminine form (which permits one to use the same term, 2477 = 'parent', in both cases); *leb* indicated imperative plural. Beck tried to turn his pasigraphy into a *pasilaly* as well, that is a system of universal pronunciation. Thus the above sentence was to be pronounced *leb totreónfo pee tofosénsen and pif tofosénsen*. The only difficulty was that, in order to pronounce the sentence, one had to memorize the whole dictionary, remembering the right number for every word.

In 1661, two years before Kircher's *Polygraphia* (but some of Kircher's ideas had circulated in manuscript form since 1660), Joachim Becher published his *Character pro notitia linguarum universali* (sometimes known under its frontispiece title of *Clavis convenientiae linguarum*). Becher's project was not unlike Kircher's; the major difference was that Becher constructed a Latin dictionary that was almost ten times more vast (10,000 items). Yet he did not include synonyms from other languages, expecting the accommodating reader to make them up for him. As in Kircher, nouns, verbs and adjectives composed the main list, with a supplementary list of proper names of people and places making up an appendix.

For each item in Becher's dictionary there is an Arabic number: the city of Zürich, for example, is designated by the number 10283. A second Arabic number refers the user to grammatical tables which supply verbal endings, the endings for the comparative and superlative forms of adjectives, or adverbial endings. A third number refers to case endings. The dedication 'Inventum Eminentissimo Principi' is written 4442. 2770:169:3. 6753:3, that is, '(My) Invention (to the) Eminent + superlative + dative singular, Prince + dative singular'.

Unfortunately Becher was afraid that his system might prove difficult for peoples who did not know the Arabic numbers; he therefore thought up a system of his own for the direct visual representation of numbers. The system is atrociously complicated and almost totally illegible. Some authors have imagined that it is somehow akin to Chinese. This is hardly true. What we have, in fact, is a basic graphical structure where little lines and dots at various points on the figure represent different numbers. Lines and points affixed to the right and centre of the figure refer to lexical items; those on the left of the figure refer to grammatical categories. Figure 9.1 provides only an excerpt of a list that keeps going for four tables.

In the chapter 'Mirabilia graphica' in his *Technica curiosa* (1664), Gaspar Schott tried to improve on Becher's project.

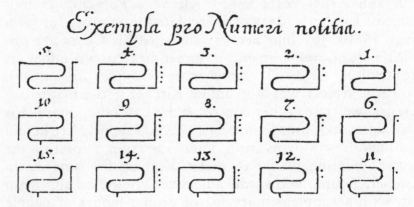

Figure 9.1

He simplified the system for the representation of numbers and added partial lexicons for other languages. Schott proposed using small grids of eight cases each, where the lower horizontal line represents units, the next one up tens, the next hundreds, and the top thousands. Units were represented by dots; fives were represented by strokes. Numbers on the left referred to lexical units, while those on the right to grammatical morphemes. Thus figure 9.2 must be read as 23:1, 15:15, 35:4, and can be translated as 'The horse eats the fodder.'

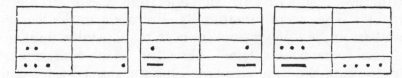

Figure 9.2

Becher's and Schott's systems appear totally impracticable for normal human use, but have been seen as tentative models for future practices of computer translation (cf. Heilmann 1963; De Mauro 1963). In fact, it is sufficient to think of Becher's pseudo-ideograms as instructions for electronic circuits, prescribing to a machine which path to follow through the memory in order to retrieve a given linguistic term, and we have a procedure for a word-for-word translation (with all the obvious inconveniences of such a merely mechanical program).

First Attempts at a Content Organization

Probably in 1660, three years before the publication of the *Polygraphia*, Kircher wrote a manuscript bearing the title *Novum hoc inventum quo omnia mundi idiomata ad unum reducuntur* (Mss. Chigiani I, vi, 225, Biblioteca Apostolica Vaticana; cf. Marrone 1986). Schott says that Kircher kept his system a secret at the express wish of the emperor, who had requested that his polygraphy be reserved for his exclusive use alone.

The *Novum inventum* was still tentative and incomplete; it contained an extremely elementary grammar plus a lexicon of 1,620 words. However, the project looks more interesting than the later one because it provides a list of 54 fundamental categories, each represented by an icon. These icons are reminiscent of those that one might find today in airports and railway stations: some were schematically representative (like a small chalice for drinking); others were strictly geometrical (rectangles, triangles, circles). Some were furthermore superficially derived from Egyptian hieroglyphics. They were functionally equivalent to the Roman numbers in the *Polygraphia* (in both texts, Arabic numbers referred to particular items). Thus, for example, the square representing the four elements plus the numeral 4 meant water as an element; water as something to drink was instead expressed by a chalice (meaning the class of drinkable things) followed by the numeral 3.

There are two interesting features in this project. The first is that Kircher tried to merge a polygraphy with a sort of hieroglyphical lexicon, so that his language could be used (at least in the author's intention) without translating it into a natural language. Seeing a 'square + 4', the readers should immediately understand that the named thing is an element, and seeing 'chalice + 3' they should understand that one is referring to something to drink. The difficulty was due to the fact that, while both Kircher's *Polygraphia* and Becher's *Character* allow a translating operator (be it a human being or a machine) to work independently of any knowledge of the meaning of the linguistic items, the *Novum inventum* requires a non-mechanical and quasi-philosophical knowledge: in order to encode the word *aqua* as 'square + 4', one should previously know that it is the name of an element – information that the term of a natural language does not provide.

Sir Thomas Urquhart, who published two volumes describing a sort of polygraphy (*Ekskubalauron*, 1652, and *Logopandecteision*, 1653), noted that, arbitrary as the order of the alphabet might be, it was still easier to look things up in alphabetical order than in a categorical order.

The second interesting feature of Kircher's initial project is certainly given by the effort to make the fundamental concepts independent of any existing natural language. Its weakness is due to the fact that the list of the 54 categories was notably incongruous: it included divine entities, angelic and heavenly, elements, human beings, animals, vegetables, minerals, the dignities and other abstract concepts deriving from the Lullian *Ars*, things to drink, clothes, weights, numbers, hours, cities, food, family, actions such as seeing or giving, adjectives, adverbs, months of the year. It was perhaps the lack of internal coherency in this system of concepts that induced Kircher to abandon this line of research, and devote himself to the more modest and mechanical method used in the *Polygraphia*.

Kircher's incongruous classification had a precedent. Although he regarded Kircher as the pioneer in the art of polygraphy, in his *Technica curiosa* (as well as in his *Jocoseriorum naturae et artiis sive magiae naturalis centuriae tres*) Gaspar Schott gave an extended description of a 1653 project that was certainly earlier than Kircher's (the *Novum inventum* is dedicated to Pope Alexander VII, who ascended the pontifical throne only in 1655). The project was due to another Jesuit, a Spaniard ('whose name I have forgotten', as Schott says on p. 483), who had presented in Rome (on a single folio) an *Artificium*, or an *Arithmeticus nomenclator, mundi omnes nationes ad linguarum et sermonis unitatem invitans* ('Arithmetical Glossary, inviting all the nations of the world to unity of languages and speech').

Schott says that the anonymous author wrote a pasigraphy because he was a mute. As a matter of fact the subtitle of the *Artificium* also reads *Authore linguae (quod mirere) Hispano quodam, vere, ut dicitur, muto* ('The author of this language – a marvellous thing – being a Spaniard, truly, it is said, dumb'). According to Ceñal (1946) the author was a certain Pedro Bermudo, and the subtitle of the manuscript would represent a word play since, in Castilian, 'Bermudo' must be pronounced almost as *Ver-mudo*.

It is difficult to judge how reliable the accounts of Schott are; when he described Becher's system, he improved it, adding details that he derived from the works of Kircher. Be that as it may, Schott described the *Artificium* as having divided the lexicon of the various languages into 44 fundamental classes, each of which contained between 20 and 30 numbered items. Here too a Roman number referred to the class and an Arabic number referred to the item itself. Schott noted that the system provided for the use of signs other than numbers, but gave his opinion that numbers comprised the most convenient method of reference since anyone from any nation could easily learn their use.

The *Artificium* envisioned a system of designating endings (marking number, tense or case) as complex as that of Becher. An Arabic number followed by an acute accent was the sign of the plural; followed by a grave accent, it became the *nota possessionis*. Numbers with a dot above signified verbs in the present; numbers followed by a dot signified the genitive. In order to distinguish between vocative and dative, it was necessary to count, in one case, five, and, in the other, six, dots trailing after the number. *Crocodile* was written 'XVI.2' (class of animals + crocodile), but should one have occasion to address an assembly of crocodiles ('O Crocodiles!'), it would be necessary to write (and then read) 'XVI.2'. . . . .'. It was almost impossible not to muddle the points behind one word with the points in front of another, or with full stops, or with the various other orthographic conventions that the system established. In short, it was just as impracticable as all of the others. Still, what is interesting about it is the list of 44 classes. It is worth listing them all, giving, in parenthesis, only some examples of the elements each contained.

1. Elements (fire, wind, smoke, ashes, Hell, Purgatory, centre of the earth). 2. Celestial entities (stars, lightning bolts, rainbows . . .).

3. Intellectual entities (God, Jesus, discourse, opinion, suspicion, soul, stratagems, or ghosts). 4. Secular statuses (emperor, barons, plebs). 5. Ecclesiastical states. 6. Artificers (painters, sailors). 7. Instruments. 8. Affections (love, justice, lechery). 9. Religion. 10. Sacramental confession. 11. Tribunal. 12. Army. 13. Medicine (doctor, hunger, enema). 14. Brute animals. 15. Birds. 16. Fish and reptiles. 17. Parts of animals. 18. Furnishings. 19. Foodstuffs. 20. Beverages and liquids (wine, beer, water, butter, wax, and resin). 21. Clothes. 22. Silken fabrics. 23. Wool. 24. Homespun and other spun goods. 25. Nautical and aromas (ship, cinnamon, anchor, chocolate). 26. Metal and coin. 27. Various artifacts. 28. Stone. 29. Jewels. 30. Trees and fruits. 31. Public places. 32. Weights and measures. 33. Numerals. 34. Time. 35–42. Nouns, Adjectives, Verbs, etc. 43. Persons (pronouns and appellations such as Most Eminent Cardinal). 44. Vehicular (hay, road, footpad).

The young Leibniz would criticize the absurdity of arrangements such as this in his *Dissertatio de arte combinatoria*, 1666.

This sort of incongruity will affect as a secret flaw even the projects of a philosophically more sophisticated nature – such as the *a priori* philosophic languages we will look at in the next chapter. This did not escape Jorge Luis Borges. Reading Wilkins, at second hand as he admits (in *Other Inquisitions*, 'The analytical idiom of John Wilkins'), he was instantly struck by the lack of a logical order in the categorical divisions (he discusses explicitly the subdivisions of stones), and this inspired his invention of the Chinese classification which Foucault posed at the head of his *The Order of Things*. In this imaginary Chinese encyclopedia bearing the title *Celestial Emporium of Benevolent Recognition*, 'animals are divided into: (a) belonging to the Emperor, (b) embalmed, (c) tame, (d) sucking pigs, (e) sirens, (f) fabulous, (g) stray dogs, (h) included in the present classification, (i) frenzied, (j) innumerable, (k) drawn with a very fine camelhair brush, (l) *et cetera*, (m) having just broken the water pitcher, (n) that from a long way off look like flies.').

Borges's conclusion was that there is no classification of the universe that is not arbitrary and conjectural. At the end of our panorama of philosophical languages, we shall see that, in the end, even Leibniz was forced to acknowledge this bitter conclusion.

10

A Priori Philosophical Languages

The advent of *a priori* philosophic languages entails a change in paradigm. For the authors we have considered up to now, the search for a perfect language arose from profound tensions of a religious nature; the authors we are about to consider imagined on the contrary a philosophical language which could eliminate the *idola* responsible for clouding the minds of men and for keeping them afar from the progress of science.

Not by chance, most of the agitation for a new and universal language arose from Britain. There is more to this than a reflection of the English expansion during this period; there was a specifically religious aspect as well. Although Latin was still the common language of scholars, to the English mind, it was associated with the Catholic church. Besides, it was also too difficult for English speakers. Charles Hooke complained of 'the frequent Sarcasmes of the Foreiners, who deride to see such a disability in Englishmen (otherwise Scholars good enough) to speak in Latine' (cf. Salmon 1972: 56).

In the endeavour for a common speech the English had commercial reasons (they thought indeed that a universal language would facilitate the exchange of goods at the Frankfurt fair) as well as educational reasons, since English spelling in the seventeenth century was more irregular than it is today (see Salmon 1972: 51–69). This was also a period which witnessed the first experiences in teaching language to deaf-mutes, and Dalgarno conducted a number of experiments in this field. Cave Beck (*The Universal Character*, 1657) wrote that the invention of a universal language would be of advantage to mankind as it would encourage commerce as well as saving the expense of hiring interpreters. It is true that he added that it would serve to propagate the Gospel as well, but it seems evident that for him evangelization was really just another aspect of European expansion in the new lands of conquest. He was obsessed, like other linguistic theorists of the epoch, by the accounts of the gestural languages through which the explorers conducted their first exchanges with the inhabitants of those distant shores. In his account of his exploits in the New World in 1527, Alvaro Nuñez Cabeza de Vaca had complained of the difficulty involved in dealing with native populations which spoke thousands of different dialects, describing how much recourse to the language of gesture had helped the explorers. Beck's work contained a frontispiece which showed a European consigning Beck's project to a Hindu, an African, and to an American Indian who expresses himself with a gesture of his hand.

There was finally the problem of scientific language itself. New discoveries being made in the physical and natural sciences made the problem of finding an adequate nomenclature more urgent, in order to counteract the symbolic and allegorical vagueness of alchemical terms.

Dalgarno confronted this problem in the section entitled 'To the reader' of his 1661 *Ars signorum*: it was necessary to find a language which reduced redundancies, anomalies, equivocations and ambiguities. He specified that such a language could not fail to encourage contact between peoples as well as help to cure philosophy of sophisms and logomachy. What had long been considered one of the sacred writ's greatest strengths – its vagueness and symbolic density – was now viewed as a limitation.

Bacon

As the renovator of scientific inquiry, Francis Bacon was only marginally interested in perfect languages. Yet, marginal though they may have been, his remarks on the subject have a notable philosophic interest. A central theme in Bacon's works was the destruction of *idola*, that is, false ideas arising either from human nature, collective or individual, or from philosophical dogmas handed down by tradition, or else – and this is what interests us the most – from the way we use language itself (*idola fori*). Such linguistic usages have been determined by the needs of common people, so disturbing our way of reasoning (*Novum organum*, I, 43), and the *idola* that common speech imposes are either names for non-existent things, or confused, ill-defined and partial names for existing things (*Novum organum*, I, 60). An example of a confused notion is that of the moist: this may signify a great variety of things; it can mean that which spreads rapidly around another body, that which is devoid of cohesion and consistence, that which is easily moved in whatever direction, that which can be divided and dispersed, that which can easily be reunited and gathered up, that which attaches itself easily to another body and moistens it, that which easily passes into a liquid state and dissolves. To speak scientifically means thus to implement a speech therapy.

The idea of a linguistic therapy was a recurrent theme in Anglo-Saxon philosophy. In the *Leviathan* (1651: IV), Hobbes noted that there are four main uses of speech,

First, to register, what by cogitation, wee find to be the cause of any thing [. . .] Secondly, to shew to others that knowledge which we have attained [. . .] Thirdly, to make known to others our wills, and purposes [. . .] Fourthly, to please and delight our selves, or others, by playing with our words, for pleasure and ornament, innocently. To these uses, there are also foure correspondent Abuses. First, when men register their thoughts wrong,

by the inconstancy of the signification of their words [. . .]
Secondly, when they use words metaphorically [. . .] Thirdly,
when by words they declare that to be their will, which is not.
Fourthly, when they use them to grieve one another.

In the third book of the *Essay concerning Human Understanding*, Locke observed that:

For since Sounds are voluntary and indifferent signs of any Ideas,
a Man may use what Words he pleases, to signify his own Ideas
to himself: and there will be no ir perfection in them, if he
constantly uses the same Word for the same Idea [. . .] The chief
End of Language in Communication being to be understood,
Words serve not well for that end [. . .] when any Word does not
excite in the Hearer, the same Idea which it stands for in the
Mind of the Speaker. (III, IX, 2, 4)

For Bacon, signs might be of two types. Signs *ex congruo*
(we would say iconic, motivated) – like hieroglyphs, gestures or emblems – reproduce in some way the properties of
the things they signify; signs *ad placitum* are arbitrary and
conventional. Yet even a conventional sign can be defined
as a 'real character' when it refers not to a sound, but
directly to a corresponding thing or concept.

Bacon thus speaks of 'Characteres quidam Reales, non
Nominales; qui scilicet nec literas, nec verba, sed res et
notiones exprimunt' (*De Augmentis Scientiarum*, VI, 1). In
this sense, the signs used by the Chinese are real characters;
they represent concepts without, however, bearing any
similarity to the signified objects. We see here that, unlike
Kircher, Bacon was unaware of the vague iconism of
Chinese ideograms; this, however, was a misapprehension
that Bacon shared with a number of other contemporary authors. Even Wilkins commented that, beyond the
difficulties and perplexities that these characters generated, there seemed to be no analogies between their forms
and the forms of the things that they represented (*Essay*,
451). Probably Kircher had the advantage of knowing the
direct reports on Chinese culture of his fellow Jesuits, and
was thus able to form a clearer picture of Chinese ideo-

grams than English scholars forced to rely on indirect accounts.

For Bacon, then, Chinese ideograms were examples of signs which, though arbitrary and conventional, stand directly for a signified notion without the mediation of a verbal language. He remarked that, even though the Chinese and the Japanese spoke different languages and thus called things by different names, both recognized them by the same ideograms, and, therefore, could understand each other by writing.

According to an example by Lodwick, if we propose to denote the sky with a 0, such a real character would be distinct from a vocal character

in that it signifieth not the sound or word 'heaven' but what we call heaven, the Latin coelum etc., so that the carracter being accepted will by the English be read heaven without respect to what the Latin would name the same thing [. . .] A frequent instance hereof we have in the numerical carracters 1.2.3., which signify not the severall sounds by which the severall nations in their severall languages express them but that common notion wherein those severall nations agree as to them. (Ms Sloane 897 f32r; in Salmon 1972: 223)

Bacon did not think that a character supplied the image of the thing or revealed its intrinsic nature; his characters were nothing other than a conventional sign which, however, referred to a clear and precise notion. His problem, then, became that of formulating an alphabet of fundamental notions; his *Abecedarium novum naturae*, composed in 1622, which was to appear as the appendix of the *Historia naturalis et experimentalis*, represented an attempt to make an index of knowledge, and was not connected to any project for a perfect language (see Blasi 1992; Pellerey 1992a). Later attempts were none the less inspired by the fact that Bacon decided to associate Greek letters with every item of his index, so that, for example, α meant 'dense and rare', ε 'volatile and fixed', εεεε 'natural and monstruous', ooooo 'hearing and sound'.

Comenius

The British quest was also influenced by the presence of Comenius (Jan Amos Komensky). In fact Comenius was a member of the Bohemian Brotherhood, a mystic branch of Hussite reformers, and he played a role – albeit a polemical one – in the Rosicrucian story (cf. his *Labyrinth of the World*, 1623, in Czech). Thus he was inspired by religious ideals which were alien to the scientific purposes of the English milieu. On this complex cultural geography see Yates (1972, 1979): one is really facing a web of different projects, at once similar and antithetical, in which the search for a perfect language was but a single aspect (see Rossi 1960; Bonerba 1992; Pellerey 1992a: 41–9).

Comenius' aspirations must be seen in the framework of the tradition of *pansophia*, yet his pansophic aims were influenced by educational preoccupations. In his *Didactica magna* of 1657, he proposed a scheme for reforming teaching methods; for, as he observed, a reform in the education of the young formed the basis upon which any subsequent political, social and religious reform must be built. It was essential that the teacher furnish the learners with a set of images that would stamp themselves indelibly on their imaginations. This meant placing what is visible before the eyes, what is audible before the ears, what is olfactory before the nose, gustatory before the tongue, and tactile before the touch.

In an earlier manual for the teaching of Latin, *Janua linguarum*, written in 1631, Comenius was first of all concerned that the learner should have an immediate visual apprehension of what was being spoken of. Equally he was concerned that the images and notions that the learner was studying in the Latin lexicon be arranged in a certain logical order. Thus lessons progressed from the creation of the world to the elements, to the mineral, vegetable and animal kingdoms, etc. By the time of the *Didactica magna* Comenius had begun to rearrange his notions according to the suggestions of Bacon. In 1658 there appeared the *Orbis sensualium pictus quadrilinguis*, which represented his attempt to present a figured nomenclature which would include the fundamental things of the world together with human actions. So important were the images that Comenius delayed publication until he was able to obtain satisfactory engravings that were not mere ornaments, but bore an iconic relation with the things represented, for which the verbal names appeared as nothing but titles, explanations and complements. The manual was prefaced by an alphabet in which every letter was associated with the image of a particular animal whose voice recalled the sound of the letter – so that the result resembles Harsdörffer's onomatopoetic fantasies concerning the sounds of German. Therefore the image of a crow is commented by 'Die Krähe krächzet, cornix cornicatur, la cornacchia gracchia, la corneille gazoüille,' or, for a snake, 'Die Schlange zischtet, Serpens sibilat, il Serpe fsschia [sic], le Serpent siffle.'

Comenius was a severe critic of the defects of natural languages. In his *Pansophiae Christianae liber III* (1639–40), he advocated a reform that would eliminate the rhetorical and figurative use of words, which he regarded as a source of ambiguity. The meaning of words should be fixed, he demanded, with one name for each thing, thus restoring words to their original meanings. In 1668, in the *Via lucis*, Comenius offered prescriptions for the creation of an artificial universal language. By now, pansophy was more than an educational method; it was a utopian vision in which a world council was supposed to create the perfect state along with its perfect philosophical language, the Panglossia. It is interesting to consider that Comenius had in fact written this work before 1641, when, after wandering through the whole of Europe in the course of the Thirty Years War, he had taken refuge in London. *Via lucis* certainly circulated, in manuscript form, in the English milieu at that time (see, for example, Cram 1989).

Although Comenius was never to construct his new language *in extenso*, he had broached the idea of a universal tongue which had to overcome the political and structural limitations of Latin. The lexicon of the new language would reflect the composition of reality and in it every word should have a definite and univocal meaning, every content should be represented by one and only one expression, and the contents were not supposed to be products of fancy, but should represent only every really existing thing, no more and no less (see Pellerey 1992a: 48).

Thus, on one side we have a utopian thinker, inspired by Rosicrucian ideals, whose goal was to discover a pansophy which aimed at picturing the unmoving and harmonical connection of every element of the creation, so as to lead the human mind to an unceasing quest for God; on the other side, rejecting the possibility of rediscovering the original perfect language, and looking, for educational purposes, for an easy artificial method, Comenius became the forerunner of that search for an *a priori* philosophical language that would later be implemented by English utopian thinkers whose inspiration was more scientific than theological or mystical.

Descartes and Mersenne

More or less at the same period, the problem of a real character was discussed in France, with a more sceptical attitude. In 1629, Father Marin Mersenne sent Descartes news of a project for a *nouvelle langue* invented by a certain des Vallées. We are told by Tallemant des Réau that this des Vallées was a lawyer who had an immense talent for languages and who claimed to have discovered 'a matrix language through which he could understand all others'. Cardinal Richelieu asked him to publish his project, but des Vallées replied he was only willing to divulge such a great secret against the promise of a state pension. 'This the Cardinal denied him, and so the secret ended up buried with des Vallées' (*Les historiettes*, 1657: 2, 'Le Cardinal de Richelieu').

On 20 November 1629, Descartes wrote back to Mersenne giving his thoughts about the story. Learning a language, Descartes noted, involved learning both the meaning of words and a grammar. All that was required to learn new meanings was a good dictionary, but learning a foreign grammar was more difficult. It might be possible, however, to obviate this difficulty by inventing a grammar that was free from the irregularities of natural languages, all of which had been corrupted through usage. The resulting language would be a simplified one and might seem, in comparison to natural languages, the basic one, of which all the other natural languages would then appear as so many complex dialects. It was sufficient to establish a set of primitive names for actions (having synonyms in every language, in the sense in which the French *aimer* has its synonym in the Greek *philein*), and the corresponding substantive might next be derived from such a name by adding to it an affix. From here, a universal writing system might be derived in which each primitive name was assigned a number with which the corresponding terms in natural languages might be recovered.

However, Descartes remarked, there would remain the problem of sounds, since there are ones which are easy and pleasant for speakers of one nation and difficult and unpleasant for those of another. On the one hand, a system of new sounds might also prove difficult to learn; on the other hand, if one named the primitive terms from one's own language, then the new language would not be understood by foreigners, unless it was written down by numbers. But even in this case, learning an entire new numeral lexicon seemed to Descartes a tremendous expense of energy: why not, then, continue with an international language like Latin whose usage was already well established?

At this point, Descartes saw that the real problem lay elsewhere. In order not only to learn but to remember the primitive names, it would be necessary for these to correspond to an order of ideas or thoughts having a logic akin to that of the numbers. We can generate an infinite series of numbers, he noted, without needing to commit the whole set to memory. But this problem coincided with that of discovering the true philosophy capable of defining a system of clear and distinct ideas. If it were possible to enumerate the entire set of simple ideas from which we generate all the complex ones that the human mind can entertain, and if it were possible to assign to each a character – as we do with numbers – we could then articulate them by a sort of mathematics of thought – while the words of natural languages evoke only confused ideas.

Now I believe that such a language is possible and that it is possible to discover the science upon which it must depend, a science through which peasants might judge the truth better than philosophers do today. Yet I do not expect ever to see it in use, for that would presuppose great changes in the present order of things; this world would have to become an earthly paradise, and that is something that only happens in the *Pays des Romans*.

Descartes thus saw the problem in the same light as Bacon did. Yet this was a project that he never confronted. The observations in his letter to Mersenne were no more than commonsensical. It is true that, at the moment he wrote this letter, Descartes had not yet started his own research into clear and distinct ideas, as would happen later with his *Discours de la méthode*; however, even later he never tried to outline a complete system of simple and clear ideas as the grounds on which to build a perfect language. He provided a short list of primitive notions in the *Principia philosophiae* (I, XLVIII), yet these notions were conceived as permanent substances (order, number, time, etc.) and there is no indication that from this list a system of ideas could be derived (see Pellerey 1992a: 25–41; Marconi 1992).

The English Debate on Character and Traits

In 1654 John Webster wrote his *Academiarum examen*, an attack on the academic world, which had allegedly given an insufficient amount of attention to the problem of universal language. Like many of his English contemporaries, Webster was influenced by Comenius' propaganda for a universal language. He foresaw the birth of a 'Hieroglyphical, Emblematical, Symbolical, and Cryptographical learning'. Describing the general utility of algebraic and mathematical signs, he went on to note that 'the numerical notes, which we call figures and cyphers, the Planetary Characters, the marks for minerals, and many other things in Chymistry, though they be alwaies the same and vary not, yet are understood by all nations in Europe, and when they are read, every one pronounces them in their own Countrey's language and dialect' (pp. 24–5).

Webster was not alone; other authors were taking up and elaborating ideas which had first originated with Bacon. Another writer championing universal characters was Gerhard Vossius in *De arte grammatica*, 1635 (1.41). Nevertheless, for the men from whose ranks the Royal Society would later be formed, Webster's demand for research in hieroglyphic and emblematic characters sounded too much like Father Kircher's Egyptian linguistics. In effect, Webster was indeed thinking of a language of nature in opposition to the institutionalized language of men (see Formigari 1970: 37).

Responding to Webster, in another pamphlet, also published in 1654 (*Vindiciae academiarum*, to which Wilkins himself added an introduction), Seth Ward denounced the mystic propensities of his opponent (see Slaughter 1982: 138ff). Ward made no objection to the idea of the real character as such, provided that it was constructed upon the algebraic model invented by Viète in the sixteenth century and elaborated by Descartes, where letters of the alphabet stand for mathematical quantities. It is, however, evident that what Ward thought of was not what Webster had in mind.

Ward argued that only the real character of which he spoke could be termed as 'a naturall Language and would afford that which the *Cabalists* and Rosycrucians have

vainely sought for in the Hebrew' (p. 22). In his introduction Wilkins went even further: Webster, he wrote, was
nothing but a credulous fanatic. Even in his *Essay*, which
we will soon discuss, Wilkins could not resist shooting, in
his introduction, indignant darts in Webster's direction
without naming him directly.

In spite of all this, however, the projects of the religious
mystics did have something in common with those of the
'scientists'. In that century the play of reciprocal influence
was very complex and many have detected relationships
between Lullists or Rosicrucians and the inventors of
philosophical languages (see Ormsby-Lennon 1988;
Knowlson 1975; and, of course, Yates and Rossi). Nevertheless, in contrast to the long tradition of the search for the
lost language of Adam, the position of Ward, with the aid
of Wilkins, was entirely secular. This is worth emphasizing:
there was no longer any question of discovering the lost
language of humanity; the new language was to be a new
and totally artificial language, founded upon philosophic
principles, and capable of realizing, by rational means, that
which the various purported holy languages (always
dreamt of, never really rediscovered) had sought but failed
to find.

In every one of the holy and primordial languages we have
so far considered, at least in the way they were presented,
there was an excess of content, never completely circumscrib-
able, in respect of expression. By contrast, the search was
now for a scientific or philosophical language, in which, by
an unprecedented act of *impositio nominum*, expression and
content would be locked in permanent accord.

Men such as Ward and Wilkins thus aimed at being the
new Adam; it was this that turned their projects into a
direct challenge to the older tradition of mystic speculation.
In the letter to the reader that introduced the *Essay*,
Wilkins writes:

This design would likewise contribute much to the clearing of
some of our modern differences in Religion, by unmasking many

wild errors, that shelter themselves under the disguise of affected phrases; which being Philosophically unfolded, and rendered according to the genuine and natural importance of Words, will appear to be inconsistencies and contradictions. (B1r)

This was nothing less than a declaration of war on tradition, a promise of a different species of therapy that would finally massage out the cramps in language; it is the first manifestation of that sceptical-analytic current of thought, exquisitely British, that, in the twentieth century, would use linguistic analysis as an instrument for the confutation of metaphysics.

Despite the persistence of the Lullian influences, there can be no doubt that, in order to realize their project, British philosophers paid close attention to Aristotle's system of classification. The project of Ward is an example. It was not enough simply to invent real characters for the new language; it was necessary also to develop a criterion that would govern the primitive features that would compose these characters:

All Discourses being resolved in sentences, these into words, words signifying either simple notions or being resolvable into simple notions, it is manifest, that if all the sorts of simple notions be found out, and have Symboles assigned to them, those will be extremely few in respect of the other [. . .] the reason of their composition easily known, and the most compounded ones at once will be comprehended [. . .] so to deliver the nature of things. (*Vindiciae*, 21)

Primitives and Organization of Content

In order to design characters that directly denote notions (if not the things themselves that these notions reflect), two conditions must be fulfilled: (1) the identification of primitive notions; (2) the organization of these primitives into a system which represents the model of the organization of content. It is for this reason that these languages qualify as philosophical and *a priori*. Their formulation required individuating and organizing a sort of philosophical 'grammar of ideas' that was independent from any natural language, and would therefore need to be postulated *a priori*. Only when the content-plane had been organized would it be possible to design the characters that would express the semantic primitives. As Dalgarno was later to put it, the work of the philosopher had to precede that of the linguist.

For the polygraphers, invention was simply the job of assigning numbers to a collection of words from a given natural language. The inventors of philosophic *a priori* languages needed to invent characters that referred to things or notions: this meant that their first step was to draw up a list of notions and things. This was not an easy task. Since the lexicon of any natural language is always finite in number, while the number of things, including physically existing objects, rational entities, accidents of all types, is potentially infinite, in order to outline a list of real characters it is necessary to design an inventory which is not only universal: it must also be in some way limited. It is mandatory to establish which notions are the most universally common, and then to go on by analysing the derivate notions according to a principle of compositionality by primitive features. In this way, the entire set of possible contents that the language is able to express has to be articulated as a set of 'molecular aggregates' that can be reduced to atomic features.

Suppose we had three semantic atoms such as ANIMAL, CANINE and FELINE. Using them, we might analyse the following four expressions:

	ANIMAL	CANINE	FELINE
Dog	+	+	−
Wolf	+	+	−
Tiger	+	−	+
Cat	+	−	+

Yet the features that analyse the content of the above expressions ought to be entities totally extraneous to the object language. The semantic feature CANINE, for example, must not be identifiable with the word *canine*. The semantic features ought to be extra-linguistic and possibly innate entities. At least they should be postulated as such, as when one provides a computer with a dictionary in which every term of a given language can be split into minor features posited by the program. In any case, the initial problem is how to identify these primitive and atomic features and set a limit on their number.

If one means by 'primitive' a simple concept, it is very difficult to decide whether and when one concept is simpler than another. For the normal speaker, the concept of 'man' is simpler – that is, easier to understand – than the one of 'mammal'. By contrast, according to every sort of semantic analysis, 'mammal' is a component of (therefore simpler than) 'man'. It has been remarked that for a common dictionary it is easier to define terms like *infarct* than terms like *to do* (Rey-Debove 1971: 194ff).

We might decide that the primitives depend on our world experience; they would correspond to those that Russell (1940) called 'object-words', whose meanings we learn by ostension, in the same way as a child learns the meaning of the word *red* by finding it associated with different occurrences of the same chromatic experience. By contrast, according to Russell, there are 'dictionary-words' that can be defined through other words, such as *pentagram*. Yet, Russell remarks, for a child who had grown up in a room decorated with motifs in the form of a pentagram, this word would be an object one.

Another alternative would be to regard primitives as innate Platonic ideas. This solution would be philosophically impeccable; yet not even Plato himself was able to establish what and how many these innate ideas were. Either there is an idea for every natural kind (for horses, platypuses, fleas, elms and so on – which means an atomic feature for every element of the furnishing of the world), or there are a few abstract ideas (the One, the Many, the Good and mathematical concepts), but through them it would be difficult to define compositionally a horse or a platypus.

Suppose instead we decided to order the system of primitives by dichotomic disjunctions so that, by virtue of the systematic relations obtaining between the terms, they must remain finite in number. With such a structure we would be able to define by a finite number of atomic primitives a great number of molecular entities. A good example of this alternative is the reciprocally embedded system of hyponyms and hyperonyms used by lexicographers. It is organized hierarchically in the form of a tree of binary disjunctions: to each opposed pair of hyponyms there corresponds a single hyperonym, which, in its turn, is opposed to another hyperonym to form the next level of hyponyms, to which a further hyperonym will correspond, and so on. In the end, regardless of how many terms are embedded in the system, the whole structure must finish at its apex in a single patriarch-hyperonym.

Thus the example of the table on p. 222 above would take the following format:

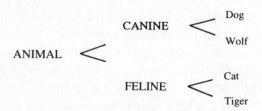

Figure 10.1

According to many contemporary authors, this kind of semantic structure would analyse the content in the format of a dictionary (as opposed to an encyclopedia). In an encyclopedia-like representation one introduces elements of world knowledge (for example that a tiger is a yellow cat with stripes on its fur), and these elements are potentially infinite in number. In a dictionary-like representation the features are, on the contrary, analytic, in the sense that they are the only and necessary conditions for the definition of a given content: a cat is necessarily a feline and an animal and it would be contradictory to assert that a cat is not an animal, since the feature 'animal' is analytically a part of the definition of *cat*. In this sense it would be easy to distinguish analytical from synthetical judgements. 'A tiger is a feline animal' would be analytical, so uniquely depending on our rigorously organized dictionary competence (which is exclusively linguistic), while 'tigers are man-eaters' would depend on our extra-linguistical world knowledge.

Nevertheless, such a dictionary-like structure would not allow us to define the difference between a cat and a tiger, or even between a canine and a feline animal. To do this, it is necessary to insert *differences* into the classification.

Aristotle, in his studies of definition, said that, in order to define the essence of a thing, we should select such attributes which 'although each of them has a wider extension than the subject, all together they have not' (*Posterior Analytics* II, 96a, 35).

Such a structured representation was known in the Middle Ages as Porphyry's Tree (because it was derived from the *Isagoge* of the Neo-Platonic philosopher Porphyry, living in the second–third century AD), and was still taken as a definitional model by the English searchers for a real character. In a Porphyrian Tree each genus is divided by two differences which constitute a pair of opposites. Each genus, with the addition of one of its divisive differences, produces an underlying species, which is so defined by its genus and its constitutive difference.

In figure 10.2, there is an example of how a Porphyrian

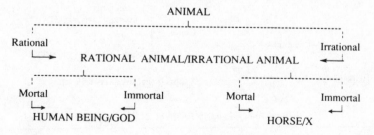

Figure 10.2

Tree establishes the difference between human beings and gods (understood as natural forces) and between human beings and beasts. The terms in upper-case refer to genera and species while those in lower-case refer to differences, that is, to particular accidents which occur only in a given species. We see that the diagram defines a human being as a 'rational and mortal animal', which, in classical terms, is considered a satisfactory definition because there cannot be a rational and mortal animal which is not a human being, and only human beings are so.

Unfortunately this diagram does not tell us anything about the differences between dogs and cats, or horses and wolves, or cats and tigers. In order to obtain new definitions, new differences need to be inserted into the diagram. Besides this, we can see that, although differences occur in one species, in this tree there are differences, such as 'mortal/immortal', which occur in two different species. This makes it difficult to know whether or not the same differences will be reproduced at some further point in the tree when it becomes necessary to specify the difference not just between dogs and cats, but also between violets and roses, diamonds and sapphires, and angels and demons.

Even taxonomy as practised by modern zoology defines through dichotomies. Dogs are distinguished from wolves, and cats from tigers, on the basis of a dichotomy by taxonomic entities known as taxa (figure 10.3).

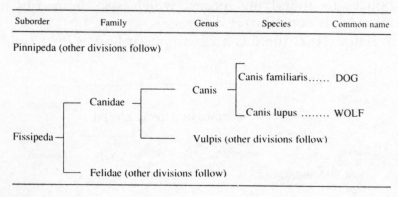

Figure 10.3

Yet modern zoologists are well aware that a system of classification is not the same as a system of definitions. Classification does not capture the essence of the thing itself; it simply embeds things in a system of increasingly inclusive classes, where the lower nodes are linked by entailment to the upper ones: if something is a *Canis familiaris*, it cannot but be, by entailment, a *Canis*, a canid and a fissiped. But *Canidae* or *Fissipeda* are taken as primitives only in the framework of the classification and are not considered as semantic primitives.

Zoologists know that, within their classification, at the node *Canidae* they must presuppose a set of properties common to the whole family, and that at the node *Carnivora* there is a set of properties common to the whole order: in the same vein, 'mammal' is not a semantic primitive but a technical name which stands for (more or less) 'viviparous animal which nourishes its young by the secretion of milk through its mammary glands'.

The name of a substance can be either designative (thus indicating the genus to which that substance belongs) or diagnostic, that is, transparent and self-definitory. In *Species plantarum* by Linnaeus (1753), given the two species, *Arundo calamogrostis* and *Arundo arenaria*, their designative names show that they belong to the same genus and establish their difference; however, their properties are then made clearer by a diagnostic description which specifies that the *Arundo calamogrostis* is 'calycibus unifloris, cumulo ramoso', while the *Arundo arenaria* is 'calycibus unifloris, foliis involutiis, mucronato pungentibus' (see Slaughter 1982: 80).

However, the terms used for this description are no longer pseudo-primitives – like those of the metalanguage of taxas; they are terms of the common natural language used for diagnostic purposes. By contrast, for the authors of *a priori* languages, each expression had to express all the properties of the designated thing. We will see how such a difficulty will affect all the projects discussed in the following chapters.

11

George Dalgarno

It is difficult to make a precise evaluation of George Dalgarno's *Ars signorum*, published in 1661. In contrast to Wilkins' *Essay*, Dalgarno's tables are summary and the text, in its expository sections, is written in a language that is extremely cryptic, sometimes contradictory, and almost always strikingly allusive. The book is filled with printer's errors, especially where Dalgarno provides examples of real characters – not an inconsiderable problem in reading a language where the misprint of one letter changes the whole sense of the character. We might note that the difficulty in printing a text free of errors shows how cumbersome the philosophic languages were, even for their own creators.

Dalgarno was a Scottish schoolmaster who passed most of his life at Oxford, where he taught grammar at a private school. He was in touch with all the contemporary scholars at the university, and in the list of acknowledgements at the beginning of his book he mentions men such as Ward, Lodwick, Boyle and even Wilkins. It is certain that, as he was preparing his *Essay* (published seven years later), Wilkins contacted Dalgarno and showed him his own tables. Dalgarno regarded them as too detailed, and chose to follow what seemed to him an easier path. When Wilkins finally made his project public, however, Dalgarno felt himself to be the victim of plagiarism. The suspicion was unjust: Wilkins had accomplished what Dalgarno had only promised to do. Besides, various other authors had already anticipated many of the elements appearing in the project of Dalgarno. Still, Wilkins resented the insinuation of wrong-doing. In the acknowledgements that prefaced his *Essay*, Wilkins was prodigal with his thanks to inspirers and collaborators alike, but the name of Dalgarno does not appear – except in an oblique reference to 'another person' (b2r).

In any case, it was the project of Wilkins that Oxford took seriously. In 1668 the Royal Society instituted a commission to study the possible applications of the project; its members included Robert Hook, Robert Boyle, Christopher Wren and John Wallis. Although we are not informed of the conclusions they finally reached, subsequent tradition, from Locke to the *Encyclopédie*, invariably treated Wilkins as the author of the most important project. Perhaps the only scholar who considered Dalgarno respectfully was Leibniz, who, in a rough draft for his own encyclopedia, reproduced Dalgarno's list of entities almost literally (see Rossi 1960: 272).

Wilkins, of course, was perfectly at home at the Royal Society. He served as its secretary, and could freely avail himself of the help, advice, patronage and attention of his fellow members. Dalgarno, by contrast, was not even a member of the university.

Dalgarno saw that a universal language needed to comprehend two distinct aspects: first, a content-plane, that is, a classification of all knowledge, and that was a task for a philosopher; second, an expression-level, that is, a grammar that organized the characters so that they can properly denote the content elements – and this was a task for a grammarian. Dalgarno regarded himself as a grammarian rather than a philosopher; hence he merely outlined the principles of classification upon which his language would be based, hoping that others might carry this task to fruition.

As a grammarian, Dalgarno was sensitive to the problem

that his language would need to be spoken and not just written. He was aware of the reserves Descartes had expressed about the difficulty of devising a philosophic language that might be pronounced by speakers of differing tongues; thus he introduced his project with a phonetic analysis which sought to identify those sounds which were most easily compatible with the human organs of speech. The letters from which he later composed his character were not, as they might seem, chosen arbitrarily; he chose instead those which he considered most easy to utter. Even when he came to elaborate the syntagmatic order of his character, he remained concerned with ease of pronunciation. To this end, he made sure that consonants were always followed by vowels, inserting in his character a number of diphthongs whose function is purely euphonious. This concern certainly ensured ease of pronunciation; unfortunately, it also rendered his character increasingly difficult to identify.

After phonetics, Dalgarno passed to the problem of the semantic primitives. He believed that these could all be derived solely in terms of genus, species and difference, arguing that such a system of embedded dichotomies was the easiest to remember (p. 29). For a series of logico-philosophical reasons (explained pp. 30ff), he excluded negative differences from his system, retaining only those which were positive.

The most ambitious feature of Dalgarno's project (and Wilkins' as well) was that his classification was to include not only natural genera and species (comprehending the most precise variations in animals and plants) but also artifacts and accidents – a task never attempted by the Aristotelian tradition (see Shumaker 1982: 149).

In fact, Dalgarno based his system of classification on the rather bold assumption that all individual substances could be reduced to an aggregate of accidents (p. 44). This is an assumption which, as I have tried to show elsewhere (Eco 1984: 2.4.3), arises as an almost mechanical consequence of using Porphyry's Tree as a basis for classification; it is a consequence, moreover, that the entire Aristotelian tradition has desperately tried to ignore. Dalgarno confronted the problem, even though recognizing that the number of accidents was probably infinite. He was also aware that the number of species at the lowest order was unmanageably large – he calculated that they would number between 4,000 and 10,000. This is probably one of the reasons why he rejected the help of Wilkins, who was to persevere until he had classified 2,030 species. Dalgarno feared that such a detailed classification ran the risk of a surgeon who, having dissected his cadavers into minute pieces, could no longer tell which piece belonged to Peter and which to John (p. 33).

In his endeavour to contain the number of primitives, Dalgarno decided to introduce tables in which he took into consideration only fundamental genera (which he numbered at 17), together with the intermediary genera and the species. Yet, in order to gather up all the species in this tripartite division, Dalgarno was forced to introduce into his tables a number of intermediate disjunctions. These even received names in the language: warm-blooded animals, for example, are called *NeiPTeik*; quadrupeds are named *Neik*. Yet in the names only the letters for genera, intermediary genera, and species are taken into account. (Mathematical entities are considered as concrete bodies on the assumption that entities like points and lines are really forms.)

Figure 11.1 presents an extremely simplified, partial reconstruction of the tables, which limits itself to following only two of the subdivisions – animals with uncleft hooves and the principal passions. The 17 fundamental genera are printed in bold capitals, and are marked with 17 capital letters. Intermediate genera and species are represented in lower case. Dalgarno also employs three 'servile' letters: *R* signifies a reversal in meaning (if *pon* means love, *pron* means hate); *V* indicates that the letters that precede it are to be read as numbers; *L* signifies a medium between two extremes.

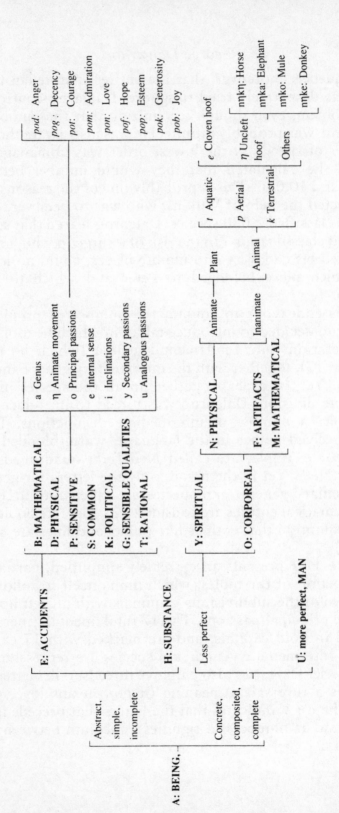

Figure 11.1

See for instance how from concrete, corporeal, physical entities, signified by an *N*, animals are deduced. See also how, in order to reach the subdivision *animal*, Dalgarno introduces an intermediate division (*animate/inanimate*) which is neither a genus nor a species, and is not marked by any letter. The animals are subdivided into three classes – aquatic, aerial and terrestrial. Among the terrestrial animals (*k*) appear those with uncleft hooves [η], or perissodactyls. Thus the character *Nηk* stands for the class of perissodactyls. At this point, however, Dalgarno adds several sub-species – viz. the horse, elephant, mule and donkey.

As far as the accidents (*E*) are concerned, see for instance how the principal passions (*o*) are classified as species of the sensitive (*P*). After this, we are presented with a list that is not dichotomized: admiration takes *pom* as its character, because *P* is the fundamental genus and *o* is the intermediate genus. The *m*, however, is just the 'number' that the species admiration is assigned in the list's order.

It is curious that, for animals, the intermediate genus is given by the third letter in the character and the species by the second vowel, while for the accidents the opposite happens. Dalgarno acknowledges the existence of such an irregularity, without offering any explanation (p. 52). The motive is doubtless euphony; still, there seems to have been nothing to prevent Dalgarno from assigning to the intermediate genera of concrete beings vowels instead of consonants and to the species consonants instead of vowels. In this way, he could have used the same criterion throughout the table.

The problem, however, is more complex than it seems. The expression *Nηk* applied to the perissodactyls is motivated by the divisions; only an arbitrary decision, on the contrary, motivates the decision to specify elephant with the addition of an *a*. But it is not the arbitrariness of the choice itself which creates problems; it is rather that while *k* means 'those terrestrials which are animal because they are animated and therefore physically concrete' (so that the division explains or reflects in some way the nature of the thing itself), the *a* at the end of *Nηka* only means 'that thing which is numbered *a* on the list of perissodactyls and is called elephant'. The same observation applies to the *m* in *pom*. All it really signifies is 'position number *m* on the list of those sensitive accidents which are principal passions, i.e. admiration'. Since the dichotomic division does not reach the lower species, Dalgarno is forced to tack on lists in an alphabetical or almost alphabetical order.

Dalgarno (p. 42) noted, however, that this procedure was simply a mnemonic artifice for those who did not wish to learn the defining name. At the end of the book there is indeed a philosophical lexicon giving the characters for many terms in Latin. In particular, there exists at the end of this list a special section devoted to concrete physical objects. Thus it seems that a philosophical definition of final species is possible; the only difficulty is that, given the purely exemplary nature of the lexicon, Dalgarno has left the naming of a large number of species up to the speaker, who can infer it from the tables.

Sometimes, however, Dalgarno gives taxonomically accurate examples: for instance the name for garlic, *nebghn agbana* (but for Dalgarno it is *nebgηn agbana*) is decoded by Slaughter (1982: 152) as follows: *n = concretum physicum, e = in radice, b = vesca, g = qualitas sensibilis, h = sabor, n = pingue, a = partes annuae, g = folium, b = accidens mathematicum, a = affect, prima, n = longum.* But even in this instance 'the tables only classify and name up to a point; the lexicon provides the rest of the definition but not the classification' (Slaughter 1982: 152).

Dalgarno may not have considered it indispensable to arrive at a classification of complex entities in all their particularities, yet making definitions requires classification. As a result the decision on how to classify complex entities, and, consequently, what name to give them, seems left as it were to the discretion of the user of the language.

Thus, ironically, a system that was intended to provide a

single set of objective and univocal definitions ends up by lending itself to the creative fancies of its users. Here are some of Dalgarno's own suggestions (I have separated the radicals with a slash to make them more decipherable):

horse = *Nηk/pot* = animal with uncleft hoof/courageous [why could we not say the same of the elephant?]

mule = *Nηk/sof/pad* = animal with uncleft hoof/deprived/sex

camel = *nek/braf/pfar* = quadruped with cloven hoof/humped/back

palace = *fan/kan* = house/king

abstemious = *sof/praf/emp* = deprived/drink/adjectival

stammering = *grug/shaf/tin* = illness [the opposite of *gug*, health]/impediment/speaking

gospel = *tib/sηb* = teach/way of being

Dalgarno also admitted that the same object regarded from a different perspective might take different names. The elephant can be called *Nηksyf* (uncleft hoof/superlative) or *Nηkbeisap* (uncleft hoof/mathematical accident/architectural metaphor for the proboscis).

It is not a system that is at all easy to memorize. The difference between *Nηke*, donkey, and *Nηko*, mule, is minimal and easy to muddle. Dalgarno advised the reader to use old mnemonic tricks. The name for table was *fran*; the name for plough was *flan*; Dalgarno suggested associating the first with FRANce and the second with FLANders. In this way the speaker needed to learn both a philosophical language and a mnemonic code.

Dalgarno somewhat compensates the reader for the transcendental difficulties in the lexicon and the rules of composition by providing a grammar and syntax of great simplicity. All that remains of the categories of classical grammar is the noun along with several pronouns (I = *lal*, you = *lêl*, he = *lel* . . .). Adverbs, adjectives, comparatives and even verbal forms are derived by adding suffixes to nouns. Thus from *sim* (good) one can generate *simam* (very good) and *sinab* (better). From *pon* (love) we can get *pone* (lover), *pono* (loved) and *ponomp* (lovable). To translate verbs, Dalgarno thought all that was necessary was the copula: 'we love' becomes 'we' + present tense + copula + 'lovers' (that is, 'we are lovers'; see p. 65). The notion that verbs could all be reduced to the copula plus an adjective already circulated among the Modists in the thirteenth century; it was taken up by Campanella in the *Philosophia rationalis* (1638) and accepted by both Wilkins and Leibniz.

Dalgarno's treatment of syntax was no less radical (see Pellerey 1992c). Although other projects for philosophic languages preserved the Latin model, Dalgarno eliminated the declensions for nouns. All that counted was word order: the subject preceded the verb and the verb preceded the object. The ablative absolute was rendered by temporal particles which stood for terms like *cum*, *post* or *dum*. The genitive was rendered either by an adjectival suffix or by a formula of possession (*shf* = to belong). Shumaker has commented (1982: 155) that forms of the latter type are adopted by pidgin English, in which the phrase 'master's hand' is rendered 'hand-belong-master'.

Simplified to this degree, the language seems syntactically crude. Yet Dalgarno, deeply suspicious of rhetorical embellishments, was convinced that only an essential logical structure gave a language an austere elegance. Besides, grace, elegance and transparent clarity were given full play in the composition of the names, and for this reason, Dalgarno compared his language to the philosophical language *par excellence*, ancient Greek.

One final aspect of Dalgarno's system that he shared with both Wilkins and Lodwick has been underlined by Frank (1979: 65ff). By using particles, prefixed and suffixed to names, to transform nouns into other grammatical categories, changing their meanings thereby, and inserting prepositions, such as *per*, *trans*, *praeter*, *supra*, *in* and *a*, among the mathematical accidents – and thus as equivalent to nouns – Dalgarno tended 'to postulate an all-comprehending semantics which took over all, or almost all of the functions traditionally assigned to grammar'. Dalgarno, in other words, abolished the classical distinction between categorematic terms, or terms that have independent meanings, and syncategorematic terms, or terms which acquire a meaning only within a context. This, in logic, is equivalent to the distinction between logical variables that can be bound to specific meanings and logical connectives. This is a tendency that is contrary to the tenets of modern logic; yet it is consistent with some trends in contemporary semantics.

12

John Wilkins

Already in the *Mercury*, a book principally devoted to secret writing, published in 1641, Wilkins had begun to design a project for universal language. It was not until 1668, however, that he was ready to unveil his *Essay towards a Real Character, and a Philosophical Language* – the most complete project for a universal and artificial philosophical language that the seventeenth century was ever to produce.

Since 'the variety of Letters is an appendix to the Curse of Babel' (p. 13), after a dutiful bow in the direction of the Hebrew language and a sketch of the evolution of languages from Babel onwards (including an examination of the Celto-Scythian hypothesis that we considered in ch. 5), and after an acknowledgement of his precursors and his collaborators in the compilation of classifications and of the final dictionary, Wilkins turned to his major task – the construction of a language founded on real characters 'legible by any Nation in their own Tongue' (p. 13).

Wilkins observed that most earlier projects derived their list of characters from the dictionary of one particular language rather than drawing directly on the nature of things, and from that stock of notions held in common by all humanity. Wilkins' approach required, as a preliminary step, a vast review of all knowledge to establish what these notions held in common by all rational beings really were.

Wilkins never considered that these fundamental notions might be Platonic ideas like Lull's dignities. His list was rather based upon empirical criteria and he sought those notions to which all rational beings might either attest or, reasonably, be expected to attest: thus, if everybody agrees on the idea of a God, everybody would likewise agree on the botanical classification supplied to him by his colleague John Ray.

In reality, the image of the universe that Wilkins proposed was the one designed by the Oxonian culture of his time. Wilkins never seriously wondered whether other cultures might have organized the world after a different fashion, even though his universal language was designed for the whole of humanity.

The Tables and the Grammar

In appearance the classification procedure chosen by Wilkins was akin to the method of the Porphyrian Tree of Aristotelian tradition. Wilkins constructed a table of 40 major genera (see figure 12.1) subdivided into 251 characteristic differences. From these he derived 2,030 species, which appear in pairs. Figure 12.2 provides a simplified example of the procedure: starting from the major genus of Beasts, after having divided them into viviparous and oviparous, and after having subdivided the viviparous ones into whole footed, cloven footed and clawed, Wilkins arrives at the species Dog/Wolf.

I might add parenthetically that Wilkins' tables occupy a full 270 pages of his ponderous folio, and hope that the reader will excuse the summary nature of the examples which follow.

After presenting the tables, which supposedly design the whole knowable universe, Wilkins turned his attention to his natural (or philosophical) grammar in order to establish morphemes and the markers for derived terms, which can permit the generation, from the primitives, of declensions,

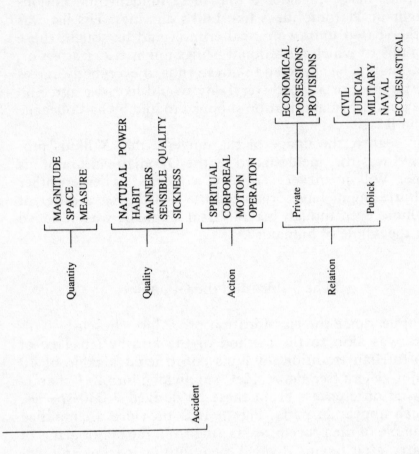

Figure 12.1 Common notions

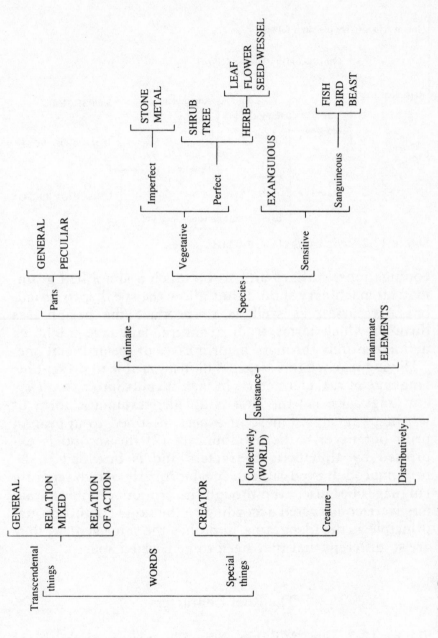

Figure 12.1 Common notions

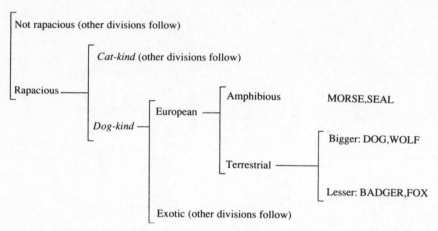

Figure 12.2 Viviparous clawed beasts

conjugations, suffixes and so on. Such a simplified grammatical machinery should thus allow the speaker to articulate discourses, as well as to produce the periphrases through which terms from a natural language might be defined entirely through the primitives of the artificial one.

Having reached this stage, Wilkins was able to present his language of real characters. In fact, it splits into two different languages: (1) the first is an ideogrammatic form of writing, vaguely Chinese in aspect, destined to appear in print but never to be pronounced; (2) the second is expressed by alphabetic characters and is intended to be pronounced. It is possible to speak properly of two separate languages because, even though the pronounceable characters were constructed according to the same compositional principle as the ideograms, and obey the same syntax, they are so different that they need to be learned apart.

The Real Characters

Figure 12.3 gives Wilkins' own illustration of the signs characterizing the 40 major genera as well as the signs used

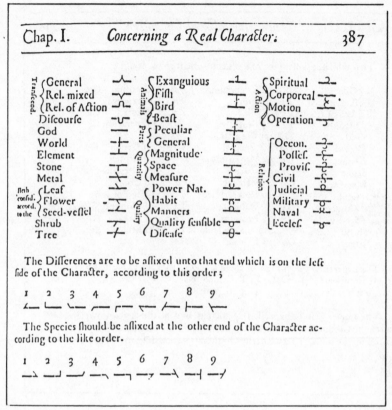

Figure 12.3

to indicate differences and species. The fundamental sign is a simple dash with a modification at its centre to indicate genus. Differences and species are indicated by little hooks and bars attached to the two extremities of the dash: those attached to the left extremity signify differences; those to the right signify species. A different series of signs, extremely difficult to read, is provided to indicate opposition, grammatical forms, copula, adverbs, prepositions, conjunctions, etc., as we have already seen for analogous writing systems. As I have said, the system also specifies the way in which the characters are to be pronounced. In figure 12.4 we see that each of the genera is assigned its own two-letter symbol, while the differences are expressed by

Chap. III.   *Concerning a Real Character.*   415

That which at present seems most convenient to me, is this ;

ꜰʀᴀᴅᴇᴅ.	General	Bα	Exanguious	Ƶα	Spiritual	Cα
	Rel. mixed	Ba	Fish	Za	Corporeal	Ca
	Rel. of Action	Be	Bird	Ze	Motion	Ce
	Discourse	Bi	Beast	Zi	Operation	Ci
	God	Dα	Peculiar	Pα		
	World	Da	General	Pa	Œcon.	Co
	Element	De	Magnitude	Pe	Possess.	Cy
	Stone	Di	Space	Pi	Provis.	Sα
	Metal	Do	Measure	Po	Civil	Sa
Herb consid. accord. to the	Leaf	Gα	Power Nat.	Tα	Judicial	Se
	Flower	Ga	Habit	Ta	Military	Si
	Seed-vessel	Ge	Manners	Te	Naval	So
	Shrub	Gi	Quality sensible	Ti	Ecclef.	Sy
	Tree	Go	Disease	To		

The *Differences* under each of these *Genus's*, may be expressed by these Consonants ⌠ B, D, G, P, T, C, Z, S, N.
in this order ;⌡ 1 2 3 4 5 6 7. 8 9.

The *Species* may be expressed by putting one of the seven Vowels after the Consonant, for the Difference ; to which may be added (to make up the number) two of the Dipthongs, according to this order
⌠α, a, e, i, o, ʊ, y, yi, yʊ.
⌡1 2 3 4 5 6 7 8 9.

Figure 12.4

the consonants B, D, G, P, T, C, Z, S, N and the species by the addition of seven vowels and two diphthongs. Here is one of Wilkins' own examples:

For instance if (De) signifie *Element*, then (Deb) must signifie the first difference; which (according to the Tables) is *Fire*: and (Debα) will denote the first Species, which is *Flame*. (Det) will be the fifth difference under that Genus, which is, *Appearing meteor*; (Detα) the first Species, *viz. Rainbow*; (Deta) the second, *viz. Halo*. (p. 415)

Figure 12.5 gives the first line of the Lord's Prayer in characters.

The first sign indicates the first person plural of the possessive pronoun; the second is the sign of *Econ-*

omic Relations modified by a hook on the left, which indicates the first difference (relations of consanguinity), and another on the right which indicates the second species, *Direct Ascendent.* The first two signs therefore mean 'Our Father' and are pronounced *Hai coba.* As a matter of fact, the phonetic language is clearer also as a form of writing, and our following examples will mainly rely on it.

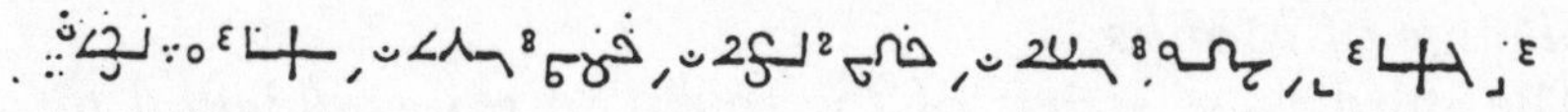

Figure 12.5

The Dictionary: Synonyms, Periphrases, Metaphors

Wilkins' language provides names for 2,030 primitives, that is to say, species. These species include not only natural genera and artifacts, but also relations and actions. From these latter are derived the verbs. As in Dalgarno, Wilkins used the copula + adjective formula for verbs, so 'I love' is, again, 'I am lover.' Besides this, the grammatical particles allow for the expression of tenses and modes for the verbs *to be* and *to have* as well as for pronouns, articles, exclamations, prepositions, conjunctions; the accidental differences express number, case, gender and comparatives.

But 2,030 primitive terms are still far too few to support discourse on a wide enough variety of topics. To increase the range of his language, Wilkins provided at the end of his *Essay* a list of 15,000 English terms not directly represented in his language, indicating the way that these might still be expressed.

The first way was by *synonyms.* For terms not included among the original 2,030, the list seeks to find the semantically closest primitive. To translate *Result,* the list suggests using primitive terms such as *Event, Summe* or *Illation,* without specifying in which context one should use the most appropriate synonym. The list of possible synonyms can sometimes be very complex; for *Corruption*

Wilkins suggests *Evil, Destruction, Spoiling, Infection, Decay* or *Putrefaction*. Some lists are even comic, as in the sequence of synonyms *box–chest of drawers–ark–dresser–coffin–table.*

The second way is *periphrasis.* The final dictionary records the term *Abbie* which has no corresponding primitive. There are primitives, however, for both *Colledge* and *Monk.* Thus, through periphrasis, *Abbie* can be rendered as *Colledge of Monks.*

The third way is that of the so-called *transcendental particles.* Faithful to his conception of a componential semantics based on primitive terms, Wilkins argued that there was no need to provide an additional character for *Calf*, since it is possible to express the same concept through *Cow + Young,* nor a primitive for *Lioness* when there was both a primitive for *Lion* and a marker for the feminine gender. Thus in his grammar, Wilkins provided a system of transcendental particles (which then become a system of special markers for writing and pronunciation) that amplified or changed the meaning of the characters to which they were linked. The 48 particles were articulated into eight classes, though there was little system in the classification. In fact, Wilkins drew from the Latin grammar the idea of different terminations such as 'inceptives' (*lucesco, aquosus, homunculus*), 'segregates' (*gradatim* or *verbatim*), endings indicating place (*vestiarium*) or agent (*arator*). Sometimes these markers were essentially grammatical; as happens with those of gender, but for others Wilkins also took into account rhetorical devices such as metaphor, metonymy and synecdoche. The particles in the class 'metaphorical–like' indicate that the terms to which they are apposited are to be taken in a figurative sense. In this way, the primitive *root* can be modified so as to mean *original,* or *light* to mean *evident.* Other particles seem to indicate relations such as cause and effect, container and thing contained, function and activity. Here are a few examples:

    like + foot = pedestal
    like + dark = mystical

    place + metal = mine
    officer + navy = admiral
    artist + star = astronomer
    voice + lion = roaring

Unfortunately, this incorporation of rhetorical solutions adds an element of imprecision to the entire system, and this weakens the project as a whole. Although Wilkins gave a list of examples showing the correct use of the particles, he was forced to acknowledge that they were just examples. This list remains open, and its further elaboration is left to the inventiveness of the individual speaker (p. 318). Once set the speaker free to invent, and it is hard to avoid the risk of ambiguity.

Still, it is important to observe that – if the presence of a particle can produce ambiguity – its absence proves without any shade of doubt that a given term must be taken literally. This represents an advance over Dalgarno, in whose system there was nothing to indicate when terms should be understood literally or figuratively.

The fact is that Wilkins the author of a philosophical grammar seems to be working against Wilkins the inventor of a philosophic *a priori* language in real characters. Wilkins' attempt to take into account the figurative side of language also is certainly an interesting effort; however, it affects the precision of his language and its original claim to reduce the ambiguities present in ordinary language. Note that, in order to render his language as univocal as possible, Wilkins had even decided to eliminate from the tables names of mythological (therefore non-existent) beings such as Sirens, Griffins, Harpies and Phoenixes, which could be at most written in natural language as proper names of individuals (for an analogy with Russell's preoccupations, see Frank 1979: 160).

Wilkins also admitted that his language was unsuited to capturing the minutiae of food and drink, like different types of grape, jam, coffee, tea and chocolate. The problem could naturally be solved, he claimed, through periphrasis;

yet it is easy to foresee that to do so the language would have been overloaded with a lot of new, awkward syntagms, as happens today with papal encyclicals, where video-cassettes become *sonorarum visualiumque taeniarum cistellulae*, and advertising men turn into *laudativis nuntiis vulgatores*. Besides, in Latin it would have been possible to avoid such monstrosities by coining new words such as *videocapsulae* or *publicitarii* (see Bettini 1992), while Wilkins' language seems to have closed the door to neologisms. The only way to escape this difficulty would be to assume that the list of primitives was *open*.

An Open Classification?

In reality, Wilkins' classification ought to be regarded as an open one. Following a suggestion of Comenius' (in the *Via lucis*), Wilkins argued that the task of constructing an adequate classification could only be undertaken by a group of scientists working over a considerable period of time, and to this end he solicited the collaboration of the Royal Society. The *Essay* was thus considered no more than a first draft, subject to extensive revision. Wilkins never claimed that the system, as he presented it, was *finished*.

Looking back at figures 12.3 and 12.4, it is evident that there are only nine signs or letters to indicate either differences or species. Does this mean that each genus may have no more than nine species? It seems that the number nine had no ontological significance for Wilkins, and that he chose it simply because he thought nine was the maximum number of entities that might easily be remembered. He realized that the actual number of species for each genus could not be limited. In fact, certain of the genera in the tables only have six species, but there are ten species for the *Umbelliferous* and seventeen for the *Verticillates Non Fruticose*.

To accommodate genera with over nine species Wilkins invented a number of graphic artifices. For simplicity's sake, let us say that, in the spoken language, to specify a second group of nine species an *l* is added after the first consonant of the name, and that to specify a third group an *r* is added. Therefore if *Gɑpe* is normally *Tulip* (third species of the fourth difference of the genus *Herbs* according to their leaves), then *Glɑpe* will be *Ramsom*, because the addition of the *l* means that the final *e* no longer indicates the third species in the genus but the twelfth.

Yet it is precisely at this point that we come across a curious error. In the example we just gave, we had to correct Wilkins' text (p. 415). The text uses the normal English terms *Tulip* and *Ramsom*, but designates them in characters by *Gɑde* and *Glɑde* rather than *Gɑpe* and *Glɑpe* (as it should be). If one checks carefully on the tables, one discovers that *Gɑde* denotes *Barley*, not *Tulip*. Wilkins' mistake can be easily explained: regardless of whatever botanical affinities the plants might possess, in common English, the words *Tulip* and *Barley* are phonetically dissimilar, and thus unlikely ever to be confused with each other. In a philosophical language, however, members of the same species are easy to muddle either phonetically or graphically. Without constant double-checking against the tables, it is difficult to avoid misprints and misunderstandings. The problem is that *in a characteristic language, for every unit of an expression one is obliged to find a corresponding content-unit*. A characteristic language is thus not founded – as happens with natural languages – on the principle of double articulation, by virtue of which meaningless sounds, or phonemes, are combined to produce meaningful syntagms. This means that in a language of 'real' characters any alteration of a character (or of the corresponding sound) entails a change of sense.

This is a disadvantage that arises from what was intended as the great strength of the system, that is, its *criterion of composition by atomic features*, in order to ensure a complete *isomorphism* between expression and content.

Flame is *Debα*, because here the *α* designates a species of the element *Fire*. If we replace the *α* with an *a* we obtain a

new composition, *Deba*, that means *Comet*. When designing his system, Wilkins' choice of α and a was arbitrary;
once they are inserted into a syntagm, however, the syntagmatic composition is supposed to mirror the very composition of the denoted thing, so that 'we should, by learning
the *Character* and the *Names* of things, be instructed likewise in their *Natures*' (p. 21).

This creates the problem of how to find the name for yet
unknown things. According to Frank (1979: 80), Wilkins'
language, dominated by the notion of a definitely pre-
established Great Chain of Being, cannot be creative. The
language can name unknown things, but only within the
framework of the system itself. Naturally, one can modify
the tables by inserting into them a new species, but this
presupposes the existence of some sort of linguistic authority with the power to permit us *to think* of a new thing. In
Wilkins' language neologisms are not impossible, but harder
to form than in natural languages (Knowlson 1975: 101).

One might defend Wilkins' language by arguing that it
really encompasses a rational methodology of scientific
research. If, for example, we were to transform the character *Detα* (*rainbow*) into *Denα* we would obtain a character
that we could analyse as denoting the first species of the
ninth difference of the genus *Element*. Yet there is no such
species in the tables. We cannot take the character metaphorically, because only characters followed by transcendental particles may be so interpreted. We can only conclude
that the character unequivocally designates an as yet to be
discovered content, and that even if the content remains
undiscovered, the character has at least told us the precise
point where it is to be found.

But what and where is that 'point'? If the tables were
analogous to the periodic table in chemistry, then we really
would know what to look for. The periodic table contains
boxes which, though momentarily empty, might, one day,
be filled. Yet the language of chemistry is rigorously quantitative; the table gives the atomic number and weight
of each missing element. An empty space in Wilkins'

classification, however, merely tells us that there is a hole at that point; it does not tell us what we need to fill it up, or why the hole appears in one space rather than another.

Since Wilkins' language is not based on a rigorous classification, it cannot be used as a procedure of scientific discovery.

The Limits of Classification

Using 40 genera and 251 differences, Wilkins' tables manage to define 2,030 species. If, however, the division were dichotomic, as happens with the Aristotelian system of classification, in which each genus was assigned two decisive differences which constituted two new species below, and in which each of these new species then played the role of genera at the lower level in the process of dichotomization, there should have been at least 2,048 species (as well as 1,025 intermediary genera plus the category at the apex) and an equal number of differences. If the figures do not add up in the way they should, it is clear that, in reconstructing a single general tree from the 41 particular trees represented in the tables, one would not find a constant dichotomic structure.

The structure is not dichotomic because Wilkins mixes substances and accidents together; but since, as Dalgarno had recognized, the number of accidents is infinite, there is no way that they can be hierarchically ordered. In fact, Wilkins must classify fundamental and Platonic conceptions, like God, world or tree, together with drinks, like beer, political offices, military and ecclesiastical ranks – in short, the whole notional world of a seventeenth-century Englishman.

It suffices to look at figure 12.1 to see that the accidents are subdivided into five categories each yielding from three to five genera. There are three subdivisions of the genus *Herb* as well as of the genus *Transcendental things*. With a dichotomic structure it would be easy, once having established the number of embedded levels, to control the total number of entities in the system; once the pattern has been broken, however, and more than two subdivisions allowed to appear at each nodal point, the whole system begins to spin out of control. The system is open to new discoveries, but, at the same time, surrenders its control over the number of primitives.

When he reaches the last differences, Wilkins arranges them in pairs. Yet, as he is the first to recognize, he has made his arrangement 'for the better helping of the memory' (p. 22), not according to a rigorous criterion of opposition. He informs us that pairs are based sometimes on opposition and sometimes on affinity. He admits to having coupled his differences in an arguable way, but says that he did so 'because I knew not to provide for them better' (p. 22).

For instance, in the first genus, *General Transcendental*, the third difference, *Diversity*, generates as the second of its species *Goodness* and its opposite, *Evil*; but the second difference, *Cause*, generates as its third species *Example* and *Type*. These two categories are not opposed; in fact it is not clear what their relation to each other is. We can imagine some sort of relation of affinity or similarity; yet, in whatever case, the criterion seems weak and *ad hoc*.

Among the accidents of *Private Relations*, under the species *Economical Relations*, we find both *Relations of Consanguinity* (like *Progenitor/Descendant*, *Brother/Half-Brother*, *Coelebs/Virgin* – but *Coelebs* has among its synonyms both *Bachelour* and *Damosel*, while *Virgin* only *Maid*) and *Relations of Superiority (Direct/Seduce, Defending/Deserting)*. It is clear that all of these oppositions lack a constant criterion. Among the same *Private Relations* there are also the *Provisions*, which includes pairs such as *Butter/Cheese*, but also actions such as *Butchering/Cooking* and *Box/Basket*.

Frank has observed that Wilkins considered as semantically equivalent different kinds of pseudo-opposition as they appear in natural languages, which can work by antonymy (good/evil), by complementarity (husband/wife), by conversity (buy/sell), by relativity (over/under, bigger/smaller), by temporal gradation (Monday/Tuesday/Wednesday), by quantitative gradation (centimetre/metre/kilometre), by antipodality (north/south), by orthogonality (north-east/south-east), or by vectorial conversity (depart/arrive).

It is hardly by chance that Wilkins is repeatedly forced to justify his language on mnemonic grounds. In fact, Wilkins takes some of his procedures from the traditional arts of memory. His criterion for establishing pairs is based on the most common mnemonic habits. Rossi (1960: 252) notes that Wilkins' botanist, John Ray, complained that he was not permitted to follow the commandments of nature, but rather the exigencies of regularity, almost as if he were forced to adapt his classification more to requirements of the traditional theatres of memory than to the canons of modern taxonomies.

Nor is it even clear what, in the tree of genera (figure 12.1), the subdivisions in lower case actually mean. They cannot be differences, because the differences appear later, in successive tables, and determine how, in each of the 40 major genera, the dependent species are to be generated. Some of these lower-case entities seem to serve as supergenera; yet others appear in an adjectival form. Certain of these latter look like differences in the Aristotelian tradition – like *animate/inanimate*, for example. We might regard them as pseudo-differences. However, if the generative path 'substance + inanimate = ELEMENTS' seems to follow an Aristotelian criterion, the disjunctions after *animate* are established in a quite different fashion. Animate substances are divided into parts and species, the species are divided into vegetative and sensitive, the vegetative species into imperfect and perfect, and it is only at the end of these disjunctions that it is possible to isolate genera like *Stone* or *Metal*. This is not the only instance of this sort of confusion. Moreover, given a pair of opposed categories, such as *Creator/creature*, the first term of the division is a genus, but the second appears as a pseudo-difference through which, after other disjunctions, it is possible to isolate other genera. Likewise, in the group *Herb, Shrub* and *Tree*, the last two are genera; the first is a sort of super-genus (or pseudo-difference) subdivided into three further genera.

It would be nice, Wilkins confessed (p. 289), if each of his differences had its own transcendental denomination; yet there did not seem to be sufficient terms in the language for this. He admitted as well that while, in theory, a well-enough individuated difference would immediately reveal the form which gave the essence to each thing, these forms remained largely unknown. So he had to content himself by defining things through properties and circumstances.

Let us try to understand a little better what is happening here. Suppose we wanted to use the real character to understand the difference between a dog and a wolf. We discover only that the dog, *Zitα*, is the first member of the first specific pair of the fifth difference of the genus *Beasts*, and that the wolf *Zitαs*, is the opposing member of this pair (*s* being the character for specific opposition). But in this way the character says what is the position of a dog in a universal classification of beasts (which, like *Fish* and *Bird* are animate sensitive sanguineous substances), without providing information either on the physical characteristics of dogs or on the difference between a dog and a wolf.

To learn more about dogs and wolves we must read further in the tables. Here we can learn (1) that clawed viviparous animals have toes at the end of their feet; (2) that rapacious viviparous animals have generally 'six short pointed incisores, or cutting teeth, and two long fangs to hold their prey'; (3) that the head of dog-kind beasts is oblong, while the head of cat-kind animals is roundish; (4) that the larger of the dog-kind fall into two further groups – 'either that which is noted for tameness and docility: or for wildness and enmity to sheep'. With this, we finally know the difference between a dog and a wolf.

Thus genera, differences and species only serve to 'taxonomize' entities rather than define the properties by which we recognize them. To make these properties evident it is necessary to attach a running commentary to the classification. Within Aristotelian classification, defining man as a rational animal was perfectly adequate. But this is not adequate for Wilkins, for he lived in an age that wished to discover the physical and biological nature of things. He thus needed to know what were the morphological and behavioural characteristics of dogs as well. Yet his tables only allowed him to express this information in the form of additional properties and circumstances, and this additional information had to be expressed in natural language because the characteristic language lacked the formulae to render it evident. This consecrates the failure of Wilkins' project, considering that, according to his project, 'we should, by learning the *Character* and the *Names* of things, be instructed likewise in their *Natures*' (p. 21).

One might wish at least to call Wilkins a pioneer of modern, scientific taxonomy (like the taxonomy shown in figure 10.3). Yet, as Slaughter has noted, he has lumped together the pre-scientific taxonomies and folk taxonomy. To classify, as we usually do, onions and garlic as foodstuffs and lilies as flowers is an instance of folk taxonomy: from a botanical point of view, onions, garlic and lilies are all members of the *Liliaceae* family. See how Wilkins, when he classifies dogs, starts out using morphological criteria, then goes on mixing functional and even geographical criteria.

What, then, is that character *Zitα* that tells us so little about dogs, forcing us to learn more by inspecting the tables? One might compare it with a *pointer* which permits access to information stored in the computer's memory – and which is not provided by the form of the character itself. The speakers who wished to use the characteristic language as their natural idiom should have already memorized all that information in order to understand the character. But that is exactly the same type of competence requested of speakers who, instead of *Zitα*, say *cane*, *dog*, *perro* or *Hund*.

For this reason, the encyclopedic information that underlies the list of primitives negates the compositional principle of Wilkins' language. Wilkins' primitives are not
primitives at all. His species do not emerge from the composition of genera and differences alone; they are also
names used as pegs to hang up encyclopedic descriptions.
Moreover, not even genera and differences are primitives,
since they can be defined only through encyclopedical definitions. They neither are innate notions, nor can be immediately grasped by intuition: if one could still say so of the
ideas of 'God' or 'world', one would hardly do so for, let us
say, 'naval and ecclesiastical relations'. Genera and differences are not primitive notions because – if they were –
they should be indefinable by nature, while the tables are
conceived just in order to define them by means of a natural
language, Wilkins' English.

If Wilkins' classification were logically consistent, it
should be possible to assume that it is analytically true that
the genus of *Beasts* entails *Animate Substance*, which in its
turn entails *Creatures Considered Distributively*. Even this,
in fact, is not always the case. The opposition *vegeta-
tive/sensitive*, for example, in the table of genera serves to
distinguish *Stone* and *Tree* (and has an uncertain status);
but the same opposition reappears (not once but twice) in
the table of the *World* (see figure 12.6, where repeated
terms are in bold).

Thus, on the basis of figure 12.1, one should admit that
everything vegetative is necessarily an animate creature,
while according to figure 12.6, one should (rather contra-
dictorily) admit that everything vegetative is necessarily an
element of both the spiritual and the corporeal world.

It is obvious that these various entities (be they genera,
species or whatever) are considered under a different point
of view every time they appear in the tables. Yet, in this
case, we are no longer confronting a classification whose
purpose is to construct a tree of organized terms in which
every entity is unequivocally defined by the place it holds
within the classification; we are, instead, confronting a

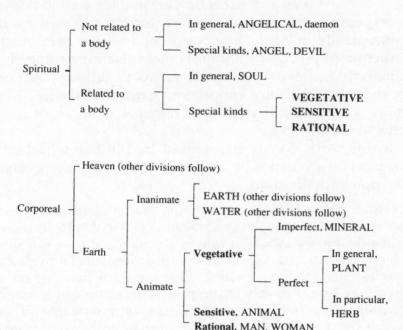

Figure 12.6 The table of the world

great encyclopedia in which it is only to be expected that the same topics will be treated from more than one point of view in different articles.

Consulting the table for *Economic Relations*, we find, among its species, the pair *Defending* versus *Deserting*. If we turn to the table for *Military Relations* we still find *Defence*; though this time it is opposed to *Offence*. It is true that when defence is considered as an economic relation and the opposite of desertion, it is written as *Coco*, while considered as a type of military action, the opposite of offence, it is written *Sibα*. Thus two different characters denote two different notions. Yet are they really different notions rather than one notion considered from two viewpoints? As a matter of fact, the ideas of economic defence and military defence seem to have something in common. In both cases we are facing an act of war, which is seen the first time as a patriotic duty and the second time as a response to the enemy. The fact that the two notions are conceptually related, however, implies that within the structure of pseudo-dichotomies there also exist transversal connections, linking the nodal points in different sections of the tree. Yet if such connections exist, then the tree is no more a hierarchical tree; it is rather a *network* of inter-related ideas.

In his work *De signes*, written in 1800, Joseph-Marie Degérando accused Wilkins of continually confusing classi-fication with division:

Division differs from classification in that the latter bases itself upon the intimate properties of the objects it wishes to distribute, while the former follows a rule to a certain end to which these objects are destined. Classification apportions ideas into genera, species, and families; division allocates them into regions of greater or lesser extent. Classification is the method of botanists; division is the method by which geography is taught. If one wishes for an even clearer example, when an army is drawn up in battle formation, each brigade under its general, each battalion under its commander, each company under its captain, this is an image of division; when, however, the state of this army is presented on a role, which principally consists of an enumeration of the officers of each rank, then of the subalterns, and finally of the soldiers, this is an image of classification (IV, 399–400)

Degérando is doubtlessly thinking here of Leibniz's notion of the ideal library and of the structure of the *Encyclopédie* (of which we will later speak), that is, of a criterion for subdividing matter according to the importance that it has for us. Yet a practical classification follows criteria differ-ent from those which should rule a system of primitives based on metaphysical assumptions.

The Hypertext of Wilkins

What if we regarded the defect in Wilkins' system as its prophetic virtue? What if we treated Wilkins as if he were obscurely groping towards a notion for which we have only recently invented a name – *hypertext*?

A hypertext is a program for computers in which every *node* or element of the repertory is tied, through a series of internal references, to numerous other nodes. It is possible to conceive of a hypertext on animals where, starting from the unit *dog*, one can get information (1) on the place of dogs on a tree of biological *taxa* which comprises also cats, horses or wolves; (2) on the properties and habits of dogs; (3) on dogs in history (the dog in the Neolithic, dog in medieval castles, etc.); (4) on the image of the dog in great works of art; and so on. In the end, this was perhaps what Wilkins really wanted to do when he considered defence from the perspective both of the duties of a citizen and of military strategy.

If this were the case, many of the system's contradictions would disappear, and Wilkins could be considered as a pioneer in the idea of a flexible and multiple organization of complex data, which will be developed in the following century and in those after. Yet, if such was his project, then we can no longer speak of him in the context of the search for a perfect language; his was instead the search for ways to articulate all that natural languages permit us to say.

13

Francis Lodwick

Lodwick wrote before either Dalgarno or Wilkins, both of whom had thus the opportunity to know his work. Salmon (1972: 3) defines him as the author of the first attempt to construct a language in universal character. His first work, *A Common Writing*, appeared in 1647; *The Groundwork or Foundation Laid (or So Intended) for the Framing of a New Perfect Language and a Universal Common Writing* dates from 1652.

Lodwick was not a learned man – no more than a merchant, as he humbly confessed. Though, in his *Ars signorum*, Dalgarno praised Lodwick for his endeavours, he was unable to hold back the supercilious observation that he did not possess the force adequate to such an undertaking, being a man of the arts, born outside of the Schools (p. 79). In his writings, Lodwick advanced a number of proposals, some more fruitful than others, on how to delineate a language that would both facilitate commercial exchange and permit the easy acquisition of English. His ideas, moreover, changed over time, and he never managed to design a complete system. None the less, certain of what appears in the most original of his works (*A Common Writing*, hardly thirty pages long) reveals him as striking off in a direction very different from other authors of his time, making him a precursor of certain trends of contemporary lexical semantics.

In theory, Lodwick's project envisioned the creation of a series of three numbered indexes; the purpose of these was to refer English words to the character and these to its words. What distinguished Lodwick's conception from those of the polygraphers, however, was the nature of its lexicon. Lodwick's idea was to reduce the number of terms contained in the indexes by deriving as many of them as possible from a finite number of primitives which express actions. Figure 13.1 shows how Lodwick chooses a conventional character (a sort of Greek delta) to express the action of *drinking*; then, by adding to this *radix* different grammatical marks, makes the different composite characters express ideas such as the actor (he who drinks), the act, the object (that which is drunk), the inclination (the drunkard), the abstraction, and the place (the drinking house, or tavern).

From the time of Aristotle up until Lodwick's own day, names of substances had invariably been the basis upon which a structure of classification had been erected. Lodwick's original contribution, however, was to commence not with substantives but with verbs, or schemes of actions, and to populate these schemes with roles – what we

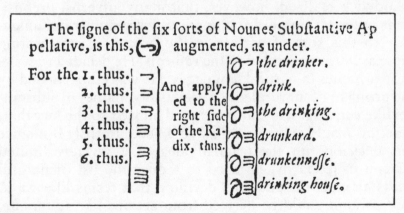

Figure 13.1

would now call actants – such as agent, object, place, and so on.

Lodwick designed his characters to be easily recognized and remembered: as we have seen, *to drink* was specified by a sort of Greek delta, while *to love* was a sort of *L*. The punctuation and added notes are vaguely reminiscent of Hebrew. Finally, as Salmon suggests, Lodwick probably took from contemporary algebra the idea of substituting letters for numbers.

In order to set up his finite packet of radicals Lodwick devised a philosophical grammar in which even grammatical categories expressed semantic relations. Derivatives and morphemes could thus become, at the same time, criteria of efficiency to reduce each grammatical category further to a component of action.

By such means the number of characters became far smaller than the words of a natural language found in a dictionary, and Lodwick endeavoured to reduce this list further by deriving his adjectives and adverbs from the verbs. From the character *to love*, for example, he derived not only the object of the action (*the beloved*) but also its mode (*lovingly*); by adding a declarative sign to the character *to cleanse*, he asserted that the action of cleansing has been performed upon the object – thereby deriving the adjective *clean*.

Lodwick realized, however, that many adverbs, prepositions, interjections and conjunctions were simply not amenable to this sort of derivation; he proposed representing these as notes appended to the radicals. He decided to write proper names in natural languages. He was embarrassed by the problem of 'natural kinds' (let us say, names of substances like *cat, dog, tree*), and resigned himself to the fact that, here, he would have to resort to a separate list. But since this decision put the original idea of a severely limited lexicon in jeopardy, he tried to reduce the list of natural kinds as much as possible, deciding that terms like *hand, foot* or *land* could be derived from actions like *to handle, to foot* or *to land*. In other cases he resorted to etymology, deriving, for instance, *king* from the archaic radical *to kan*, claiming that it meant both *to know* and *to have power to act*. He pointed out that Latin *rex* was related to the verb *regere*, and suggested that both the English king and the German emperor might be designated by a simple *K* followed by the name of the country.

Where he was not able to find the appropriate verbal roots, he tried at least to reduce as many different nouns as possible to a single root. He thus reduced the names for the young of animals – *child, calfe, puppy, chikin* – to a single root. Moreover, Lodwick thought that the reduction of many lexical items to a unique radical could be also performed by using analogies (*seeing* as analogous to *knowing*), synonymy (*to lament* as a synonym of *to bemoane*), opposition (*to curse* as the opposite of *to bless*), or similarities in substance (*to moisten, to wet, to wash* and even *to baptize* are all reduced to *moisture*). All these derivations were to be signalled by special signs. Wilkins had had a similar idea when proposing the method of transcendental particles, but it seems that Lodwick's procedure was less ambiguous.

Lodwick barely sketched out his project; his system of notation was cumbersome; nevertheless (with a bare list of sixteen radicals – *to be, to make, to speake, to drinke, to love, to cleanse, to come, to begin, to create, to light, to shine, to live, to darken, to comprehend, to send* and *to name*), he managed to transcribe the opening of the gospel of St John ('In the Beginning was the Word, and the Word was with God . . . '). *Beginning* was derived of course from *to begin, God* from *to be, Word* from *to speake*, and so on (the idea of all things is derived from *to create*).

Just as the polygraphers had taken Latin grammar as a universal model, so Lodwick did the same for English – though his English grammatical categories still reflected the Latin model. Nevertheless he succeeded in avoiding certain limits of the Aristotelian classification of substances, because no previous tradition obliged him to order an array of actions according to the rigid hierarchical schema requested by a representation of genera and species.

This idea of a non-hierarchical organization seems, at one point, to have occurred to Wilkins as well. Figure 13.2 reproduces a table found on p. 311 of his *Essay*. The table describes the workings of prepositions of motion by relating the possible positions (and possible actions) of a human body in a three-dimensional space. It is a table in which *there is no principle of hierarchy whatsoever*. Yet this is an isolated example, and Wilkins seems to have lacked the courage to extend this principle to his entire system of content.

Unfortunately, even Lodwick's primitives for actions were not really primitive at all. It would undoubtedly be possible to identify a series of positions assumed by the

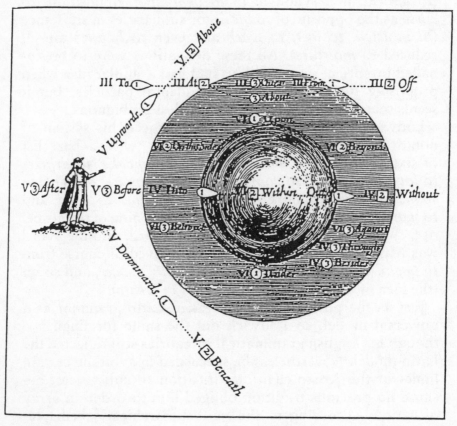

Figure 13.2

human body in space – such as getting up or lying down – and argue that these were intuitively and universally comprehensible; yet the sixteen radicals proposed by Lodwick can be criticized in the same way as Degérando would later do for Wilkins: even such a simple notion as *to walk* must be defined in terms of *movement*, the notion of movement requires as its components those of *place*, of *existence in a given place*, of a *moving substance* which in different *instants* passes from one place to another. All this presupposes the notions of *departure, passage* and *arrival*, as well as that of a *principle of action* which imparts motion to a substance, and of *members* which support and convey a body in motion in a specific way ('car glisser, ramper, etc., ne sont pas la même chose que marcher'; 'since sliding, climbing, etc., are not the same as walking': *Des signes*, IV, 395). Moreover, it is also necessary to conceive of a *terrestrial surface* upon which movement was to take place – otherwise one could think of other actions like swimming or flying. However, at this point one should also subject the ideas of *surface* or *members* to the same sort of regressive componential analysis.

One solution would be to imagine that such action primitives are selected *ad hoc* as metalinguistic constructs to serve as parameters for automatic translation. An example of this is the computer language designed by Schank and Abelson (1977), based on action primitives such as PROPEL, MOVER, INGEST, ATRANS or EXPEL, by which it is possible to analyse more complex actions like *to eat* (however, when analysing the sentence 'John is eating a frog', Schank and Abelson – like Lodwick – cannot further analyse *frog*).

Other contemporary semantic systems do not start by seeking a definition of a *buyer* in order to arrive eventually at the definition of the action of buying, but start rather by constructing a type-sequence of actions in which a subject A gives money to a subject B and receives an object in exchange. Clearly the same type-sequence can be employed to define not only the *buyer*, but also the *seller*, as well as the notions of *to buy, to sell, price, merchandise*, and so forth. In the language of artificial intelligence, such a sequence of actions is called a 'frame'. A frame allows a computer to draw inferences from preliminary information: *if* A is a buyer, *then* he may perform this and that action; *if* A performs this or that action, *then* he may be a buyer; *if* A obtains merchandise from B but does not pay him, *then* A is not a buyer, etc., etc.

In still other contemporary semantics, the verb *to kill*, for example, might be represented as 'Xs causes (Xd changes to (– live Xd)) + (animate Xd) & (violent Xs)': if a subject (*s*) acts, with violent means or instruments, in a way that causes another subject (*d*), an animate being, to change from a state of living to a state of death, then *s* has killed *d*. If we wished, instead, to represent the verb *to assassinate*, we should add the further specification that *d* is not only an animate being, but also a political person.

It is worth noting that Wilkins' dictionary also includes *assassin*, glossing it by its synonym *murther* (erroneously designating it as the fourth species of the third difference in the genera of judicial relations: in fact, it is the fifth species), but limiting the semantic range of the term by 'especially, under pretence of Religion'. It is difficult for a philosophic *a priori* language to follow the twists and turns of meaning of a natural language.

Properly worked out, Lodwick's project might represent *to assassinate* by including a character for *to kill* and adding to it a note specifying purpose and circumstances.

Lodwick's language is reminiscent of the one described by Borges in 'Tlön, Uqbar, Orbis Tertius' (in *Ficciones*), which works by agglutinations of radicals representing not substances but rather temporal fluxes. It is a language in which there would be no word for the noun *moon* but only the verb *to moon* or to *moondle*. Although it is certain that Borges knew, if only at second hand, the work of Wilkins, he probably had never heard of Lodwick. What is certain, however, is that Borges had in mind the *Cratylus*, 396b – and it is by no means impossible that Lodwick knew this passage as well. Here Plato, arguing that names are not arbitrary but motivated, gives examples of the way in which, rather than directly representing the things that they designate, words may represent the origin or the result of an action. For instance, the strange difference (in Greek) between the nominative *Zeus* and the genitive *Dios* arose because the original name of Jupiter was a syntagm that expressed the habitual activity associated with the king of the gods: *di'hoòn zen*, 'He through whom life is given'.

Other contemporary authors have tried to avoid the contortions that result from dictionary definitions in terms of a classification of genera, species and differences by specifying the meaning of a term by a set of *instructions*, that is, a procedure which can decide whether or not a certain word can be applied. This idea had already appeared in Charles Sanders Peirce (*Collected Papers*, 2.330): here is provided a long and complex explanation of the term *lithium*, in which this chemical element was defined not only in relation to its place in the periodic table of elements and by its atomic weight, but also by the operations necessary to produce a specimen of it.

Lodwick never went as far as this; still, his own intuition led him to run counter to an idea that, even in the centuries to follow, proved difficult to overcome. This was the idea that nouns came first; that is, in the process in which language had emerged, terms for things had preceded terms for actions. Besides, the whole of Aristotelian and Scholastic discussion privileged substances (expressed by common nouns) as the subjects of a statement, in which the terms for actions played the role of predicates.

We saw in chapter 5 that, before the advent of modern linguistics, theorists tended to base their research on nomenclature. Even in the eighteenth century, Vico could still assume that nouns arose before verbs (*Scienza nuova seconda*, II, 2.4). He found this to be demonstrated not only by the structure of a proposition, but by the fact that children expressed themselves first in names and interjections, and only later in verbs. Condillac (*Essai sur l'origine des connaissances humaines*, 82) also affirmed that 'for a long time language remained with no words other than nouns.' Stankiewicz (1974) has traced the emergence of a different trend starting with the *Hermes* of Harris (1751: III), followed by Monboddo (*Of the Origins and Progress of Language*, 1773–92) and Herder, who, in his *Vom Geist der hebräischen Poesie* (1787), noted that a noun referred to things as if they were dead while a verb conferred movement upon them, thus stimulating sensation. Without following Stankiewicz's reconstruction step by step, it is worth noting that the re-evaluation of the role of the verb was assumed in the comparative grammars by the theorists of the Indo-European hypothesis, and that in doing so they followed the old tradition of Sanskrit grammarians, who derived any word from a verbal root (1974: 176). We can close with the protest of De Sanctis, who, discussing the pretensions of philosophic grammars, criticized the tradition of reducing verbs to nouns and adjectives, observing that: '*I love* is simply not the same as *I am a lover* [. . .] The authors of philosophical grammars, reducing grammar to logic, have failed to perceive the volitional aspect of thought' (F. De Sanctis, *Teoria e storia della litteratura*, ed. B. Croce, Bari: Laterza, 1926: 39–40).

In this way, in Lodwick's dream for a perfect language there appears the first, timid and, at the time, unheeded hint of the problems that were to become the centre of successive linguistics.

14

From Leibniz to the Encyclopédie

In 1678 Leibniz composed a *lingua generalis* (in Couturat 1903). After decomposing all of human knowledge into simple ideas, and assigning a number to each, Leibniz proposed a system of transcription for these numbers in which consonants stood for integers and vowels for units, tens and powers of ten:

1	2	3	4	5	6	7	8	9
b	c	d	f	g		h	l	m	n

Units	10s	100s	1,000s	10,000s	etc.
a	e	i	o	u	

In this system, the figure 81,374, for example, would be transcribed as *mubodilefa*. In fact, since the relevant power of ten is shown by the following vowel rather than by the decimal place, the order of the letters in the name is irrelevant: 81,374 might just as easily be transcribed as *bodifalemu*.

This system might lead us to suspect that Leibniz too was thinking of a language in which the users might one day discourse on *bodifalemu* or *gifeha* (= 546) just as Dalgarno or Wilkins proposed to speak in terms of *nekpot* or *deta*.

Against this supposition, however, lies the fact that Leibniz applied himself to another, particular form of language, destined to be spoken – a language that resembled the *latino sine flexione* invented at the dawn of our own century by Peano. This was a language whose grammar was drastically simplified and regularized: one declension for nouns, one conjunction for verbs, no genders, no plurals, adjectives and adverbs made identical, verbs reduced to the formula of copula + adjective.

Certainly, if my purpose were to try to delineate the entire extent of the linguistic projects undertaken by Leibniz throughout the course of his life, I would have to describe an immense philosophical and linguistical monument displaying four major aspects: (1) the identification of a system of primitives, organized in an alphabet of thought or in a general encyclopedia; (2) the elaboration of an ideal grammar, inspired probably by the simplifications proposed by Dalgarno, of which the simplified Latin is one example; (3) the formulation of a series of rules governing the possible pronunciation of the characters; (4) the elaboration of a lexicon of real characters upon which the speaker might perform calculations that would automatically lead to the formulation of true propositions.

The truth is, however, that by the end of his career, Leibniz had abandoned all research in the initial three parts of the project. His real contribution to linguistics lies in his attempts at realizing the fourth aspect. Leibniz had little interest in the kinds of universal language proposed by Dalgarno and Wilkins, though he was certainly impressed by their efforts. In a letter to Oldenburg (Gerhardt 1875: VII, 11–15), he insisted that his notion of a real character was profoundly different from that of those who aspired to a universal writing modelled on Chinese, or tried to construct a philosophic language free from all ambiguity.

Leibniz had always been fascinated by the richness and plurality of natural languages, devoting his time to the study of their lineages and the connections between them. He had concluded that it was not possible to identify (much less to revive) an alleged Adamic language, and came to celebrate that very *confusio linguarum* that others were striving to eliminate (see Gensini 1990, 1991).

It was also a fundamental tenet of his monadology that each individual had a unique perspective on the world, as if a city would be represented from as many different viewpoints as the different positions of its inhabitants. It would have been incongruous for the philosopher who held this doctrine to oblige everyone to share the same immutable gridwork of genera and species, without taking into account particularities, diversities and the particular 'genius' of each natural language.

There was but one facet of Leibniz's personality that might have induced him to seek after a universal form of communication; that was his passion for universal peace, which he shared with Lull, Cusanus and Postel. In an epoch in which his English predecessors and correspondents were waxing enthusiastic over the prospect of universal languages destined to ease the way for future travel and trade, beyond an interest in the exchange of scientific information, Leibniz displayed a sensitivity towards religious issues totally absent even in high churchmen like Wilkins. By profession a diplomat and court councillor, Leibniz was a political, rather than an academic, figure, who worked for the reunification of the church. This was an ecumenicism that reflected his political preoccupations; he envisioned an anti-French bloc of Spain, the papacy, the Holy Roman Emperor and the German princes. Still, his desire for unity sprang from purely religious motives as well; church unity was the necessary foundation upon which a peaceful Europe could be built.

Leibniz, however, never thought that the main prerequisite for unity and peace was a universal tongue. Instead, he thought that the cause of peace might be better served by science, and by the creation of a scientific language which might serve as a common instrument in the discovery of truth.

Characteristica and Calculus

The theme of a logic of invention and discovery should remind us of Lull; and, in fact, Lull's *ars combinatoria* was one of Leibniz's first sources. In 1666, at the age of twenty, Leibniz composed his own *Dissertatio de arte combinatoria* (Gerhardt 1875: IV, 27–102). But the dream of the *combinatoria* was to obsess him for the rest of his life.

In his short *Horizon de la doctrine humaine* (in Fichant 1991), Leibniz dealt with a problem that had already troubled Father Mersenne: how many utterances, true, false or even nonsensical, was it possible to formulate using an alphabet of 24 letters? The point was to determine the number of truths capable of expression and the number of expressions capable of being put in writing. Given that Leibniz had found words of 31 letters in Latin and Greek, an alphabet of 24 letters would produce 24^{32} words of 31 letters. But what is the maximum length of an expression? Why should an expression not be as long as an entire book? Thus the sum of the expressions, true or false, that a man might read in the course of his life, imagining that he reads 100 pages a day and that each page contains 1,000 letters, is 3,650,000,000. Even imagining that this man can live one thousand years, like the legendary alchemist Artephius, it would still be the case that 'the greatest expressible period, or the largest possible book that a man can read, would have 3,650,000,000,000 [letters], and the number of truths, falsehoods, or sentences expressible – that is, readable, regardless of pronounceability or meaningfulness – will be $24^{365,000,000,001} - 24/23$ [letters]'.

We can imagine even larger numbers. Imagine our alphabet contained 100 letters; to write the number of letters expressible in this alphabet we would need to write a 1 followed by 7,300,0000,000,000 zeros. Even to write such a number it would take 1,000 scribes working for approximately 37 years.

Leibniz's argument at this point is that whatever we take the number of propositions theoretically capable of expression to be – and we can plausibly stipulate more astronomical sums than these – it will be a number that vastly outstrips the number of true or false expressions that humanity is capable of producing or understanding. From such a consideration Leibniz concluded paradoxically that the number of expressions capable of formulation must always be finite, and, what is more, that there must come a moment at which humanity would start to enunciate them anew. With this thought, Leibniz approaches the theme of the *apochatastasis* or of universal reintegration – what we might call the theme of the eternal return.

This was a line of speculation more mystical than logical, and we cannot stop to trace the influences that led Leibniz to such fantastic conclusions. It is plain, however, that Leibniz has been inspired by Lull and the kabbala, even if Lull's own interest was limited to the generation of just those propositions that expressed true and certain knowledge and he thus would never have dared to enlarge his *ars combinatoria* to include so large a number of propositions. For Leibniz, on the contrary, it was a fascination with the vertiginous possibilities of discovery, that is of the infinite number of expressions of which a simple mathematical calculation permitted him to conceive, that served as inspiration.

At the time he was writing his *Dissertatio*, Leibniz was acquainted with Kircher's *Polygraphia*, as well as with the work of the anonymous Spaniard, of Becher, and of Schott (while saying that he was waiting for the long-promised *Ars magna sciendi* of the 'immortal Kircher'). He had yet to read Dalgarno, and Wilkins had still not published his *Essay*. Besides, there exists a letter from Kircher to Leibniz, written in 1670, in which the Jesuit confessed that he had not yet read Leibniz's *Dissertatio*.

Leibniz also elaborated in the *Dissertatio* his so-called method of 'complexions', through which he might calculate, given *n* elements, how many groups of them, taken *t* at a time, irrespective of their ordering, can be ordered. He applied this method to syllogisms before he passed to his discussion of Lull (para. 56). Before criticizing Lull for limiting the number of his elements, Leibniz made the obvious observation that Lull failed to exploit all the possibilities inherent in his combinatorial art, and wondered what could happen with variations of order, which could produce a greater number. We already know the answer: Lull not only limited the number of elements, but he rejected those combinations that might produce propositions which, for theological and rhetorical reasons, he considered false. Leibniz, however, was interested in a *logica inventiva* (para. 62) in which the play of combinations was free to produce expressions that were heretofore unknown.

In paragraph 64 Leibniz began to outline the theoretical core of his *characteristica universalis*. Above all, any given term needed to be resolved into its formal parts, the parts, that is, that were explicitly entailed by its definition. These parts then had to be resolved into their own components, and so on until the process reached terms which could not, themselves, be defined – that is, the primitives. Leibniz included among them not only things, but also modes and relations. Other terms were to be classified according to the number of prime terms they contained: if they were composed from 2 prime terms, they were to be called *com2nations*; if from 3 prime terms, *com3nations*, and so forth. Thereby a hierarchy of classes of increasing complexity could be created.

Leibniz returned to this argument a dozen years later, in the *Elementa characteristicae universalis*. Here he was more generous with his examples. If we accept the traditional definition of *man* as 'rational animal', we might consider *man* as a concept composed of 'rational' and 'animal'. We may assign numbers to these prime terms: animal = 2, and rational = 3. The composite concept of man can be represented as the expression 2 * 3, or 6.

For a proposition to be true, if we express fractionally the subject–predicate (S/P) relationship, the number which corresponds to the subject must be exactly divisible by the number which corresponds to the predicate. Given the proposition 'all men are animals', the number for the subject (men), is 6; the number for animals is 2; the resulting fraction is 6/2 = 3. Three being an integer, consequently, the proposition is true. If the number for monkey were 10, we could demonstrate the falsity of either the proposition 'all men are monkeys' or 'all monkeys are men': 'the idea of monkey does not contain the idea of man, nor, vice versa, does the idea of the latter contain the former, because neither can 6 be exactly divided by 10, nor 10 by 6' (*Elementa*, in Couturat 1903: 42–92). These were principles that had all been prefigured in the *Dissertatio*.

The Problem of the Primitives

What did Leibniz's *ars combinatoria* have in common with the projects for universal languages? The answer is that Leibniz had long wondered what would be the best way of providing a list of primitives and, consequently, of an alphabet of thoughts or of an encyclopedia. In his *Initia et specimina scientiae generalis* (Gerhardt 1875: VII, 57–60) Leibniz described an encyclopedia as an inventory of human knowledge which might provide the material for the art of combination. In the *De organo sive arte magna cogitandi* (Couturat 1903: 429–31) he even argued that 'the greatest remedy for the mind consists in the possibility of discovering a small set of thoughts from which an infinity of other thoughts might issue in order, in the same way as from a small set of numbers [the integers from 1 to 10] all the other numbers may be derived.' It was in this same work that Leibniz first made hints about the combinational possibilities of a binary calculus.

In the *Consilium de Encyclopedia nova conscribenda methodo inventoria* (Gensini 1990: 110–20) he outlined a system of knowledge to be subjected to a mathematical treatment through rigorously conceived propositions. He proceeded to draw up a plan of how the sciences and other bodies of knowledge would then be ordered: from grammar, logic, mnemonics topics and so on to morals and to the science of incorporeal things. In a later text on the *Termini simpliciores* from 1680–4 (Grua 1948: 2, 542), however, we find him falling back to a list of elementary terms, such as 'entity', 'substance' and 'attribute', reminiscent of Aristotle's categories, plus relations such as 'anterior' and 'posterior'.

In the *Historia et commendatio linguae characteristicae* we find Leibniz recalling a time when he had aspired after 'an alphabet of human thoughts' such that 'from the combination of the letters of this alphabet, and from the analysis of the vocables formed by these letters, things might be discovered and judged'. It had been his hope, he added, that in this way humanity might acquire a tool which would augment the power of the mind more than telescopes and microscopes had enlarged the power of sight. Waxing lyrical over the possibilities of such a tool, he ended with an invocation for the conversion of the entire human race, convinced, as Lull had been, that if missionaries were able to induce the idolators to reason on the basis of the calculus they would soon see that the truths of our faith concord with the truths of reason.

Immediately after this almost mystical dream, however, Leibniz acknowledged that such an alphabet had yet to be formulated. Yet he also alluded to an 'elegant artifice':

I pretend that these marvellous characteristic numbers are already given, and, having observed certain of their general properties, I imagine any other set of numbers having similar properties, and, by using these numbers, I am able to prove all the rules of logic with an admirable order, and to show in what way certain arguments can be recognized as valid by regarding their form alone. (*Historia et commendatio*, Gerhardt 1875: VII, 184ff)

In other words, Leibniz is arguing that the primitives need only be *postulated* as such for ease of calculation; it was not necessary that they truly be final, atomic and unanalysable.

In fact, Leibniz was to advance a number of important philosophical considerations that led him to conclude that an alphabet of primitive thought could never be formulated. It seemed self-evident that there could be no way to guarantee that a putatively primitive term, obtained through the process of decomposition, could not be subjected to further decomposition. This was a thought that could hardly have seemed strange to the inventor of the infinitesimal calculus: '*There is not an atom*, indeed there is no such thing as a body so small that it cannot be subdivided [. . .] It follows that *there is contained in every particle of the universe a world of infinite creatures* [. . .] There can be no determined number of things, because no such number could satisfy the need for an infinity of impressions' (*Verità prime*, untitled essay in Couturat 1903: 518–23).

If no one conception of things could ever count as final, Leibniz concluded that we must use the conceptions which are most general for us, and which we can consider as prime terms only within the framework of a specific calculus. With this, Leibniz's *characteristica* breaks its link with the research into a definitive alphabet of thought. Commenting on the letter to Mersenne in which Descartes described the alphabet of thoughts as a utopia, Leibniz noted:

Even though such a language depends upon a true philosophy, it does not depend upon its perfection. This is to say: the language can still be constructed despite the fact that the philosophy itself is still imperfect. As the science of mankind will improve, so its language will improve as well. In the meantime, it will continue to perform an admirable service by helping us retain what we know, showing us what we lack, and inventing means to fill that lack. Most of all, it will serve to avoid those disputes in the sciences that are based on argumentation. For the language will make argument and calculation the same thing. (Couturat 1903: 27–8)

This was not only a matter of convention. The identification of primitives cannot precede the formulation of the *lingua characteristica* because such a language would not be a docile instrument for the expression of thought; it is rather *the calculating apparatus through which those thoughts must be found*.

The Encyclopedia and the Alphabet of Thought

The idea of a universal encyclopedia was something that Leibniz was never to give up. Leibniz was, for a long period, a librarian; as such, and as a historian and *érudit*, he could not have failed to follow the pansophic aspirations and encyclopedic ferment that filled the closing years of the seventeenth century – tremors that would yield their fruits in the century to come. For Leibniz, the interest in the idea of a universal encyclopedia grew less and less as the basis of an alphabet of primitive terms, and more and more as a practical and flexible instrument which might provide for everyone an access to and control over the immense edifice of human learning. In 1703, he wrote the *Nouveaux essais sur l'entendement humain* (which did not appear until 1765, after Leibniz's death). This book was a confutation of the doctrines of Locke, and ends with a monumental fresco of the encyclopedia of the future. The point of departure was a rejection of Locke's tripartite division of knowledge into physical, ethical and logical (or semiotic). Even such a simple classification was untenable, Leibniz argued, because every item of knowledge might reasonably be considered from more than one of the three divisions. We might treat the doctrine of spirits either as a philosophical or as a moral problem, placing it in the province either of logic or of ethics. We might even consider that a knowledge of the spirit world might prove efficacious for certain practical ends; in which case we might want to place it in the physical province. A truly memorable story might deserve a place in the annals of universal history; yet it might equally well deserve a place in the history of a particular country, or even of a particular individual. A librarian is often undecided over the section in which a particular book needs to be catalogued (cf. Serres 1968: 22–3).

Leibniz saw in an encyclopedia the solution to these problems. An encyclopedia would be a work that was, as we might now say, polydimensional and mixed, organized –

as Gensini observes (Gensini 1990: 19) – more according to 'pathways' than by a classification by subject matters; it would be a model of practico-theoretical knowledge that invited the user to move transversally, sometimes following deductive lines, as mathematicians do, and sometimes moving according to the practical purposes of the human users. It would be necessary also to include a final index that would allow the user to find different subjects or the same subject treated in different places from different points of view (IV, 21, *De la division des sciences*). It is almost as if Leibniz intended here to celebrate as a *felix culpa* that monument of non-dichotomical incongruity that was the encyclopedia of Wilkins; as if he were writing a rough draft for the very project that d'Alembert was to set forth at the beginning of the *Encyclopédie*. Dimly shining from beneath the project of Wilkins, Leibniz has recognized the first idea of a *hypertext*.

Blind Thought

We have seen that Leibniz came to doubt the possibility of constructing an alphabet that was both exact and definitive, holding that the true force of the calculus of characteristic numbers lay instead in its rules of combination. Leibniz became more interested in the *form* of the propositions generated by his calculus than in the meaning of the characters. On various occasions he compared his calculus with algebra, even considering algebra as merely one of the possible forms that calculus might take, and thought more and more of a rigorously quantitative calculus able to deal with qualitative problems.

One of the ideas that circulated in his thought was that, like algebra, the characteristic numbers represented a form of *blind thought*, or *cogitatio caeca* (cf. for example, *De cognitione, veritate et idea* in Gerhardt 1875: IV, 422–6). By blind thought Leibniz meant that exact results might be achieved by calculations carried out upon symbols whose meanings remained unknown, or of which it was at least impossible to form clear and distinct notions.

In a page in which he defined his calculus as the only true example of the Adamic language, Leibniz provides an illuminating set of examples:

All human argument is carried out by means of certain signs or characters. Not only things themselves but also the ideas which those things produce neither can nor should always be amenable to distinct observation: therefore, in place of them, for reasons of economy we use signs. If, for example, every time that a geometer wished to name a hyperbole or a spiral or a quadratrix in the course of a proof, he needed to hold present in his mind their exact definitions or manner in which they were generated, and then, once again, the exact definitions of each of the terms used in his proof, he would be likely to be very tardy in arriving at his conclusions [. . .]. For this reason, it is evident that names are assigned to the contracts, to the figures and to various other types of things, and signs to the numbers in arithmetic and to magnitudes in algebra [. . .]. In the list of signs, therefore, I include words, letters, the figures in chemistry and astronomy, Chinese characters, hieroglyphics, musical notes, steganographic signs, and the signs in arithmetic, algebra, and in every other place where they serve us in place of things in our arguments. Where they are written, designed, or sculpted, signs are called characters [. . .]. Natural languages are useful to reason, but are subject to innumerable equivocations, nor can be used for calculus, since they cannot be used in a manner which allows us to discover the errors in an argument by retracing our steps to the beginning and to the construction of our words – as if errors were simply due to solecisms or barbarisms. The admirable advantages [of the calculus] are only possible when we use arithmetical or algebraic signs and arguments are entirely set out in characters: for here every mental error is exactly equivalent to a mistake in calculation. Profoundly meditating on this state of affairs, it immediately appeared as clear to me that all human thoughts might be entirely resolvable into a small number of thoughts considered as primitive. If then we assign to each primitive a character, it is possible to form other characters for the deriving notions, and we would be able to extract infallibly from them their prerequisites and the primitive notions composing them; to put it in a word, we could always infer their definitions and their values, and thereby the modifications to be derived from their definitions. Once this had been done, whoever uses such characters in their reasoning and in their writing, would either never make an error, or, at least, would have the possibility of immediately recognizing his own (or other people's) mistakes, by using the simplest of tests. (*De scientia universalis seu calculo philosophico* in Gerhardt 1875: VII, 198–203)

This vision of blind thought was later transformed into the fundamental principle of the general semiotics of Johann Heinrich Lambert in his *Neues Organon* (1762) in the section entitled *Semiotica* (cf. Tagliagambe 1980).

As Leibniz observed in the *Accessio ad arithmeticum infinitorum* of 1672 (*Sämtliche Schriften und Briefen*, iii/1, 17), when a person says a million, he does not represent mentally to himself all the units in that number. Nevertheless, calculations performed on the basis of this figure can and must be exact. Blind thought manipulates signs without being obliged to recognize the corresponding ideas. For this reason, increasing the power of our minds in the manner that the telescope increases the power of our eyes, it does not entail an excessive effort. 'Once this has been done, if ever further controversies should arise, there should be no more reason for disputes between two philosophers than between two calculators. All that will be necessary is that, pen in hand, they sit down together at a table and say to each other (having called, if they so please, a friend) "let us calculate" ' (in Gerhardt 1875: VII, 198ff).

Leibniz's intention was thus to create a logical language, like algebra, which might lead to the discovery of unknown truths simply by applying syntactical rules to symbols. When using this language, it would no more be necessary, moreover, to know at every step what the symbols were referring to than it was necessary to know the quantity represented by algebraic symbols to solve an equation. Thus for Leibniz, the symbols in the language of logic no longer *stood for* concrete ideas; instead, they *stood in place* of them. The characters 'not only assist reasoning, they substitute for it' (Couturat 1901: 101).

Dascal has objected (1978: 213) that Leibniz did not really conceive of his *characteristica* as a purely formal instrument apparatus, because symbols in his calculus are always assigned an interpretation. In an algebraic calculation, he notes, the letters of the alphabet are used freely; they are not bound to particular arithmetical values. For Leibniz, however, we have seen that the numerical values of the characteristic numbers were, so to speak, 'tailored' to concepts that were already filled with a content – 'man', 'animal', etc. It is evident that, in order to demonstrate that 'man' does not contain 'monkey', the numerical values must be chosen according to a previous semantic decision. It would follow that what Leibniz proposed was really a system both *formalized* and *interpreted*.

Now, it is true that Leibniz's posterity elaborated such systems. For instance, Luigi Richer (*Algebrae philosophicae in usum artis inveniendi specimen primum*, 'Melanges de philosophie et de mathématique de la Societé Royale de Turin', 1761: II/3), in fifteen short and extremely dry pages, outlined a project for the application of algebraic method to philosophy, by drawing up a *tabula characteristica* containing a series of general concepts (such as *aliquid, nihil, contingens, mutabile*) and assigning to each a conventional sign. The system of notation, semicircles orientated in various ways, makes the characters hard to distinguish from one another; still, it was a system of notation that allowed for the representation of philosophical combinations such as: 'This Possible cannot be Contradictory.' This language is, however, limited to abstract reasoning, and, like Lull, Richer did not make full use of the possibilities of combination in his system as he wished to reject all combinations lacking scientific utility (p. 55).

Towards the end of the eighteenth century, in a manuscript dating 1793–4, we also find Condorcet toying with the idea of a universal language. His text is an outline of mathematical logic, a *langue des calculs*, which identifies and distinguishes intellectual processes, expresses real objects, and enunciates the relations between the expressed objects and the intellectual operations which discover the enunciated relations. The manuscript, moreover, breaks off at precisely the point where it had become necessary to proceed to the identification of the primitive ideas; this testifies that, by now, the search for perfect languages was definitively turning in the direction of a logico-mathematical calculus, in which no one would bother to draw up a list of ideal contents but only to prescribe syntactic rules (Pellerey 1992a: 193ff).

We could say that Leibniz's *characteristica*, from which Leibniz had also hoped to derive metaphysical truths, is oscillating between a metaphysical and ontological point of view, and the idea of designing a simple instrument for the construction of deductive systems (cf. Barone 1964: 24). Moreover, his attempts oscillate between a formal logic (operating upon unbound variables) and what will later be the project of many contemporary semantic theories (and of artificial intelligence as well), where syntactic rules of a mathematical kind are applied to semantic (and therefore interpreted) entities. But Leibniz ought to be considered the forerunner of the first, rather than of the second, line of thought.

The fundamental intuition that lies behind Leibniz's proposal was that, even if the numbers were chosen arbitrarily, even if it could not be guaranteed that the primitives posited for the sake of argument were really primitive at all, what still guaranteed the truth of the calculus was the fact that *the form of the proposition mirrored an objective truth*.

Leibniz saw an analogy between the order of the world, that is, of truth, and the grammatical order of the symbols in language. Many have seen in this a version of the *picture theory of language* expounded by Wittgenstein in the *Tractatus*, according to which 'a picture has logico-pictorial form in common with what it depicts' (2.2). Leibniz was thus the first to recognize that the value of his philosophical language was a function of its formal structure rather than of its terms; syntax, which he called *habitudo* or propositional structure, was more important than semantics (Land 1974: 139).

It is thus to be observed that, although the characters are assumed arbitrarily, as long as we observe a certain order and certain rule in their use, they give us results which always agree with each other. (*Dialogus* in Gerhardt 1875: VII, 190–3)

Something can be called an 'expression' of something else whenever the structure [*habitudines*] subsisting in the expression corresponds to the structure of that which it wishes to express [. . .]. From the sole structure of the expression, we can reach the knowledge of the properties of the thing expressed [. . .] as long as there is maintained a certain analogy between the two respective structures. (*Quid sit idea* in Gerhardt 1875: VII, 263–4)

What other conclusion could the philosopher of pre-established harmony finally have reached?

The *I Ching* and the Binary Calculus

Leibniz's tendency to transform his *characteristica* into a truly blind calculus, anticipating the logic of Boole, is no less shown by his reaction to the discovery of the Chinese book of changes – the *I Ching*.

Leibniz's continuing interest in the language and culture of China is amply documented, especially during the final decades of his life. In 1697 he had published *Novissima sinica* (Dutens 1768: IV, 1), which was a collection of letters and studies by the Jesuit missionaries in China. It was a work seen by a certain Father Joachim Bouvet, a missionary just returned from China, who responded by sending Leibniz a treatise on the ancient Chinese philosophy which he saw as represented by the 64 hexagrams of the *I Ching*.

The *Book of Changes* had for centuries been regarded as a work of millennial antiquity. More recent studies, however, have dated it to the third century BC. Nevertheless, scholars of the time of Leibniz still attributed the work to a mythical author named Fu Hsi. As its function was clearly magical and oracular, Bouvet not unnaturally read the hexagrams as laying down the fundamental principles for Chinese traditional culture.

When Leibniz described to Bouvet his own research in binary arithmetic, that is, his calculus by 1 and 0 (of which he also praised the metaphysical ability to represent even the relation between God and nothingness), Bouvet perceived that this arithmetic might admirably explain the structure of the Chinese hexagrams as well. He sent Leibniz in 1701 (though Leibniz only received the communication in 1703) a letter to which he added a wood-cut showing the disposition of the hexagrams.

In fact, the disposition of the hexagrams in the wood-cut differs from that of the *I Ching*, nevertheless, this error allowed Leibniz to perceive a signifying sequence which he later illustrated in his *Explication de l'arithmétique binaire* (1703).

Figure 14.1 shows the central structure of the diagrams seen by Leibniz. The sequence commences, in the upper left-hand corner, with six broken lines, then proceeds by gradually substituting unbroken for broken lines. Leibniz read this sequence as a perfect representation of the pro-

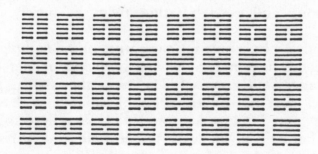

Figure 14.1

gression of binary numbers (000, 001, 010, 110, 101, 011, 111 . . .). See figure 14.2.

Once again, the inclination of Leibniz was to void the Chinese symbols of whatever meaning was assigned to them by previous interpretations, in order to consider their form and their combinational possibilities. Thus once more we find Leibniz on the track of a system of blind thought in

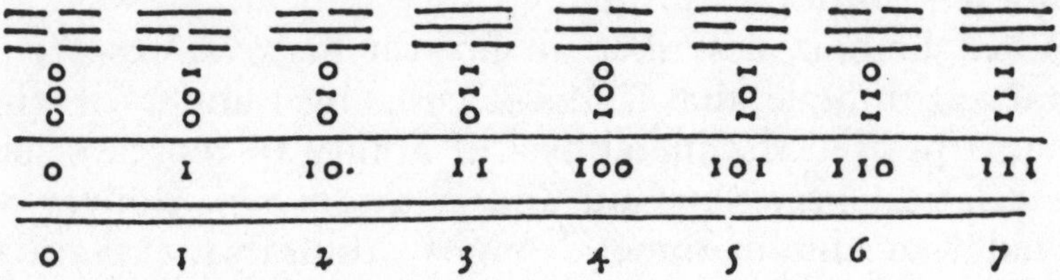

Figure 14.2

which it was syntactic form alone that yielded truths. Those binary digits 1 and 0 are totally blind symbols which (through a syntactical manipulation) permit discoveries even before the strings into which they are formed are assigned meanings. In this way, Leibniz's thought not only anticipates by a century and a half Boole's mathematical logic, but also anticipates the true and native tongue spoken by a computer – not, that is, the language we speak to it when, working within its various programs, we type expressions out on the keyboard and read responses on the screen, but the machine language programmed into it. This is the language in which the computer can truly 'think' without 'knowing' what its own thoughts mean, receiving instructions and re-elaborating them in purely binary terms.

Certainly Leibniz mistook the nature of the *I Ching*, since 'the Chinese interpreted the *kua* in every manner except mathematically' (Losano 1971). Nevertheless, the formal structures that he (rightly enough) isolated in these diagrams appeared to him so esoterically marvellous that, in a letter to Father Bouvet, he did not hesitate in identifying the true author of the *I Ching* as Hermes Trismegistus – and not without reasons, because Fu Hsi was considered in

China as the representative of the era of hunting, fishing and cooking, and thus can be considered, as can Hermes, the father of all inventions.

Side-effects

Thus all of the ingenuity expended upon the invention of philosophic *a priori* languages allowed Leibniz to invent a language of a radically different type, which – though remaining *a priori* – was no longer a practical, social instrument but rather a tool for logical calculation. In this sense, Leibniz's language, and the contemporary language of symbolic logic that descended from it, are scientific languages; yet, like all scientific languages, they are incapable of expressing the entire universe, expressing rather a set of *truths of reason*. Such languages do not qualify as a universal language because they fail to express those truths that all natural languages express – *truths of fact*. Scientific languages do not express empirical events. In order to express these we would need 'to construct a concept which possesses an incalculable number of determinations', while the completely determined concept of any individual thing or person implies 'spatial-temporal determinations which, in their turn, imply other spatial-temporal successions and historical events whose mastery is beyond the human eye, and whose control is beyond the capacity of any man' (Mugnai 1976: 91).

None the less, by anticipating what was to become the language of computers, Leibniz's project also contributed to the development of programs well adapted for the cataloguing of the determinations of individual entities, which can tell us that there exists an entity called Mr X such that this entity has booked a flight from A to B. We may well fear that by controlling our determinations so well the computer eye has begun to infringe on our privacy, checking on the hour in which we reserved a room in a certain hotel in a certain city. This, then, is one of the side-effects of a project that commenced with the idea of expressing a merely theoretical universe populated with universal ideas such as goodness, angels, entity, substance, accidents, and 'all the elephants'.

Dalgarno could never have imagined it. Passing through the mathematical filter of Leibniz, renouncing all semantics, reducing itself to pure syntax, his philosophical *a priori* language has finally managed to designate even an individual elephant.

The 'Library' of Leibniz and the *Encyclopédie*

During the Enlightenment there began to develop a critical attitude towards any attempt to construct a system of *a priori* ideas. It was a critique founded, in large part, upon the considerations advanced by Leibniz. Thus it was in terms that closely recalled Leibniz's own description of an ideal library that, in his introduction to the *Encyclopédie*, d'Alembert was to sound the death knell for projects for philosophical *a priori* languages.

Presented with the practical problem of organizing an encyclopedia and justifying the way that it divided its material, the system of scientific knowledge began to take on the appearance of a labyrinth, a network of forking and twisting paths that put paid to any notion that knowledge might be represented in a tree diagram of any sort. Knowledge might still be divided into branches, 'some of which converge at a common centre; and, since, starting from the centre, it is impossible to follow all the branches at once, the choice [of pathway] is determined by the nature of the different intellects'. The philosopher was whoever discovered the hidden passageways within that labyrinth, the provisional interconnections, the web of mutually dependent associations which constituted such a network as a geographical representation. For this reason the authors of the *Encyclopédie* decided that each single article would appear as only one particular map, which, in its small way, might reflect the entire global map:

objects approach each other more or less closely, presenting different aspects according to the perspective chosen by the particular geographer [. . .]. Thus it is possible to imagine that there are as many systems of human knowledge as there are representations of the world constructed according to differing projections [. . .]. Often, an object placed in one particular class on account of one or another of its properties may re-appear in another class because of other properties.

Following the suggestion of Locke, the Enlightenment was less concerned with the search for perfect languages than with the provision of therapies for already existing ones. After denouncing the limits of natural languages, Locke (*Essay*, III, X) had passed to an analysis of the abuse which must occur whenever words are used that do not correspond to clear and distinct ideas, whenever they are used inconsistently, whenever they are employed with the affectation of obscurity, whenever words are taken for things, whenever they are used for things which possess no meaning, and whenever we imagine that others must necessarily associate with the words we use the same ideas as we do. Locke fixed a set of norms to combat these abuses, and, since Locke was not concerned with lexical or syntactical reform, but simply with subjecting usage to a measure of vigilance and philosophical common sense, these norms had no bearing on the theme of philosophical languages. Instead of a systematic reform of language, Locke modestly suggested that we be more conscientious in the way we use words to communicate with one another.

This was to be the line adopted by the encyclopedists of the Enlightenment and those whom they inspired.

The encyclopedists launched their attack on philosophical *a priori* languages principally in their entry under the heading 'Caractère', which was the result of the collaboration of several authors. Du Marsais made an initial distinction between numerical characters, characters representing abbreviations, and literal characters; these last were further subdivided into emblematic characters (still the accepted interpretation of hieroglyphics) and nominal characters, primarily the characters of the alphabet. D'Alembert accepted the criticisms that had traditionally been made of the characters used in natural languages, and then discussed the various projects for the construction of real characters, showing an extensive knowledge of the projects in the previous century. It was a discussion which often confused characters that were ontologically real, that directly expressed, that is, the essence of the things they represented, with characters that were only logically real, capable, that is, of expressing by convention a single idea unequivocally. Still, d'Alembert advanced a number of criticisms that applied equally to both types.

In contrast to those of the seventeenth century, philosophers in the Enlightenment had radically changed the focus of their reflection on language. It now seemed clear that thought and language influenced each other, each proceeding with the other step by step, and that, consequently, language, as it evolved, would constantly modify thought. Thus it no longer made sense to accept the rationalist hypothesis of a single grammar of thought, universal and stable, which all languages in one way or another reflected. No system of ideas postulated on the basis of abstract reasoning could thus ever form an adequate parameter of and criterion for the formation of a perfect language. Language did not reflect a preconstituted mental universe, but collaborated in its growth.

The *Idéologues* demonstrated the impossibility of postulating a universal way of thinking, independent of the human semiotic apparatus. Destutt de Tracy (*Eléments d'idéologie*, I, 546, n.) argued that it was not possible to confer on all languages the attributes of algebra. In the case of natural languages:

we are often reduced to conjectures, inductions, and approximations [. . .]. Almost never can we have a perfect certainty that an idea which we have constructed for ourselves under a certain sign and by various means is really utterly and entirely the same as the idea that those who taught us the sign as well as anyone else who might subsequently use the sign might attribute to it. Hence words may often, insensibly, take on differences in meaning without anyone noting these changes; for this reason we might say that while every sign is perfectly transparent for whomever invents it, it is somewhat vague and uncertain for those who receive it [. . .]. I might even carry this further: I said that every sign is perfect for whomever invents it, but this is only really true at the precise instant when he invents the sign, for when he uses this same sign in another moment in his life, or when his mind is in another disposition, he can no longer be entirely sure that he has gathered up under this sign the same collection of ideas as he had the first time he used it. (pp. 583–5)

Tracy understood that the prerequisite of all philosophical languages was the absolute and univocal correspondence between signs and the ideas they represented. An examination, however, of the seventeenth-century English systems led him to the conclusion that 'it is impossible that the same sign possess the same meaning for all who use it [. . .]. We thus must give up the idea of perfection' (*Eléments d'idéologie*, II, 578–9).

This was a theme that was common to empiricist philosophy, to which all the *Idéologues* referred. Locke had already noted that although the names *glory* and *gratitude* were

the same in every Man's mouth, through a whole country, yet the complex, collective *Idea*, which every one thinks on, or intends by that name, is apparently very different in Men using the same language. [. . .] For though in the Substance *Gold*, one satisfies himself with Colour and Weight, yet another thinks solubility in *Aqua Regia*, as necessary to be join'd with that Colour in his *Idea* of Gold, as any one does its Fusibility; Solubility in *Aqua Regia*, being a Quality as constantly join'd with its Colour and Weight, as Fusibility, or any other; others put its Ductility or Fixedness, *etc.* as they had been taught by Tradition and Experience. Who, of all these, has establish'd the right termination of the Word *Gold*? (*Essay*, III, IX, 8, 13)

Returning to the *Idéologues*, Joseph-Marie Degérando, whose criticisms of Wilkins we have already encountered, observed (*Des signes et l'art de penser considérés dans leur rapports mutuels*, 1800) that the ensemble of associated ideas represented by the word *man* would be more extensive in the mind of a philosopher than in that of a common labourer, and that the word *liberty* could not have meant in Sparta what it did in Athens (I, 222–3).

The impossibility of elaborating a philosophic language is finally due to the fact that since languages develop through a set of stages, a development that the *Idéologues* delineated with great precision, there was no way of deciding the linguistic stage of development that a perfect language should represent. Choosing to reflect one stage rather than another, a philosophical language will then continue to reflect all the limitations of that linguistic stage, while just to overcome these limitations humanity had passed to further and more articulate stages. Once it had been perceived that the process of linguistic change is continuous, that language is subject to change not only at its prehistoric point of origin, but also in the present day, it became obvious that any thought of reviving the idea of a philosophic language was destined to fail.

15

Philosophic Language from the Enlightenment to Today

Eighteenth-century Projects

Even under the weight of the Enlightenment critique, the dream of the perfect language refused to die. In 1720 there appeared a 'Dialogue sur la facilité qu'il y auroit d'établir un Caractère Universel qui seroit commun à toutes les Langues de l'Europe, et intelligible à différens Peuples, qui le liroient chacun dans la propre Langue' (in the *Journal littéraire de l'anné 1720*). As the title itself suggests, the project was for a polygraphy, in the sense we saw in Kircher, and, at most, it is worthy of note in that its attempt to include a contracted grammar points the way to future developments. In any case, the proposal is distinguished by including an appeal, by the anonymous author, for a commission which would develop the project and for a prince who would impose its adoption. Such an appeal 'cannot help but remind us of a possibility, which must have seemed evident in the year 1720, that a phase of stability for Europe was about to open, and that, consequently, sovereigns might be expected to be more willing to patronize linguistic and intellectual experiments' (cf. Pellerey 1992a: 11).

In his article on 'Langue' in the *Encyclopédie*, even a rationalist like Beauzée had to concede that, since it would be difficult to come to an agreement over a new language, and an international language still seemed to him to be necessary, Latin had to remain the most reasonable candidate. For their part, the empiricists among the encyclopedists felt duty-bound to consider the idea of a universal language too. As a sort of coda to the article on 'Langue', Joachim Faiguet wrote four pages on a project for a *langue nouvelle*. Couturat and Leau (1903: 237) consider this as representing a first attempt at overcoming the problems inherent in the *a priori* languages and at sketching out an example of the *a posteriori* languages we will be discussing in the next chapter.

As his model, Faiguet took a natural language – French. He formed his lexicon on French roots, and concentrated on the delineation of a simplified and regularized grammar, or a 'laconic' grammar. Following the authors in the previous century, Faiguet eliminated those grammatical categories that seemed to him redundant: he suppressed the articles, substituted flexions with prepositions (*bi* for the genitive, *bu* for the dative, and *de* and *po* for the ablative), transformed adjectives (indeclinable) into adverbial forms, standardized all plurals (always expressed by an *s*); he simplified verb conjugations, making them invariable in number and person, adding endings that designated tenses and modes (*I give, you give, he gives* became *Jo dona, To dona, Lo dona*); the subjunctive was formed by adding an *r* to the stem, the passive by the indicative plus *sas* (meaning *to be*: thus *to be given* became *sas dona*).

Faiguet's language appears as wholly regular and without exceptions; every letter or syllable used as endings had a precise and unique grammatical significance. Still, it is parasitic on French in a double sense: not only is it a 'laconicized' French at the expression-level; it is French that supplies the content-level as well. Thus, Faiguet's was little less than a sort of easy-to-manage Morse code (Bernadelli 1992).

The most important projects for *a priori* languages in the

eighteenth century were those of Jean Delormel (*Projet d'une langue universelle*, 1795), of Zalkind Hourwitz (*Polygraphie, ou l'art de correspondre à l'aide d'un diction-naire dans toutes les langues, même celles dont on ne possède pas seulement les lettres alphabétiques*, 1800), and of Joseph De Maimieux (*Pasigraphie*, 1797). As can be seen, De Maimieux's project was a pasigraphy – that is, a universal written language. Since, however, in 1799 this same author had also formulated a *pasilalie* – adding rules for pronouncing his language – his project can be considered as an *a priori* language. For its part, Hourwitz's project was for a polygraphy, too – even though he seemed unaware that his was by no means the first project of this type. Still, in its structure, Hourwitz's polygraphy was an *a priori* language.

Although all three projects still followed the principles laid down in the seventeenth-century tradition, they were different in three fundamental ways: their purposes, the identification of their primitives, and their grammars.

Delormel presented his scheme to the Convention; De Maimieux published his *Pasigraphie* under the Directory; Hourwitz wrote under the Consulate: every religious moti-vation had disappeared. De Maimieux spoke of communi-cation between European nations, between Europeans and Africans, of providing a means of checking the accuracy of translations, of speeding up diplomacy and civil and mil-itary undertakings, of a new source of income for teachers, writers and publishers who should 'pasigraphize' books written in other languages. Hourwitz added to this list other purely practical considerations, such as the advan-tages in the relations between doctors and patients or in courtroom procedures. As one symptom of a new political and cultural atmosphere, instead of using the Lord's Prayer as a sample translation, Hourwitz chose the opening of Fénelon's *Aventures de Télemaque* – a work which, despite its moralizing bent, was still a piece of secular literature portraying pagan gods and heroes.

The revolutionary atmosphere imposed, or at least

encouraged, considerations of *fraternité*. Thus Delormel could claim that:

in this revolutionary moment, when the human spirit, regenerating itself among the French people, leaps forward with renewed energy, is it too much to hope that perhaps [. . .] we might offer to the public a new language as well, a language that facilitates new discoveries by bringing students of various nations together, a language that serves as a common term for all languages, a language easy to grasp even for men with but a slight aptitude for instruction, a language, in short, which will soon make out of all the people of mankind a single, grand family? [. . .] The Light of Reason brings men together and thus reconciles them; this language, by facilitating its communication, will help to propagate that Light. (pp. 48–50)

Each of the authors was aware of the objections made by the authors of the *Encyclopédie*; thus the *a priori* languages which they proposed were all ordered according to an encyclopedia-like structure, easy to understand and designed upon the model of the eighteenth-century system of knowledge. Gone was the grandiose pansophist afflatus that animated baroque encyclopedias; the criterion of selection was rather that of Leibniz: the inventors of the languages behaved as if they were conscientious librarians hoping to make consultation as easy as possible, without worrying whether or not their ordering corresponded to the theatre of the world. Absent as well was the search for 'absolute' primitives; the fundamental categories were the large-scale divisions of knowledge; under these were listed dependent notions attached as sub-headings.

Delormel, for example, assigned different letters of the alphabet to several encyclopedic classes in a way reminiscent not so much of Wilkins as of the anonymous Spaniard – grammar, art of speech, states of things, correlatives, useful, pleasurable, moral, sensations, perception and judgment, passions, mathematics, geography, chronology, physics, astronomy, minerals, etc.

Even though the primitives were no longer such, they remained a compositional criterion. For instance, given in first position the letter *a*, which refers to grammar, the depending letters have a mere distinctive value and refer back to grammatical sub-categories. A third and final letter specifies a morphological termination or other derivation. Thus a list of terms is derived: *ava* (grammar), *ave* (letter), *alve* (vowel), *adve* (consonant) and so on. The expressions function like a chemical formula, which synthetically reveals the internal composition of its content, and like a mathematical expression in that the system attributes to each letter a value determined by its position. Nevertheless, this theoretical perspicuity is bought at a dear price because, in practice, the lexicon becomes obsessively monotonous.

Equally, the *Pasigraphie* of De Maimieux institutes a graphic code of twelve characters that can be combined according to fixed rules. Each combination expresses a definite thought (the model is the Chinese character). Other characters are placed on the outside of the 'body' of the word to modify the central idea. The body of the word can contain three, four or five characters. Words of only three characters signify either 'pathetic' terms or connectives linking parts of discourse, and are classified in an *indicule*. Words of four characters stand for ideas in practical life (like friendship, kinship, business), and are classified in a *petit nomenclateur*. Five-character words concern categories such as art, religion, morality, science and politics, and are classified in a *grand nomenclateur*.

None of these categories is primitive; they have rather been isolated in terms of common sense as the most manageable way of subdividing contemporary knowledge. De Maimieux went so far as to admit that he had not sought for an absolute ordering but rather any ordering whatsoever, *fût-il mauvais* (p. 21).

The system, unfortunately, provides no way of eliminating synonyms; they are constitutional, and De Maimieux only says how to identify them. In fact, every expression in the pasigraphy can be connected not to a single meaning but to three or four different contents. These different meanings can be distinguished according to the position of the characters on a sort of pentagram. This method imposes no small amount of tedium on the reader, who, as the characters display no iconic similarity with their content, is continually forced to consult the *indicule*, the *petit nomenclateur* or the *grand nomenclateur*, depending on the length of the expression.

Thus, to give an example, if we run across a five-letter syntagm, we must seek first in the *grand nomenclateur*

the class that begins with the first character of the term. Inside this class, we seek for the framework listing the second character of the term. Inside this framework, we seek for the column containing the third character of the term. Finding the right column, we seek the section (*tranche*) with the fourth character of the term. Finally, within this section we seek the line containing the fifth character. At this point we will discover that, as the meaning, we have found a line listing four verbal words; it will then be necessary to observe which of the characters in the pasigraphic term is graphically tallest in order to determine which of the four possible words is the one corresponding to the term. (Pellerey 1992a: 104)

A real piece of drudgery, though not enough to dampen the ardour of the project's enthusiasts, who, starting with the abbé Sicard and finishing with various contemporary reviewers wishing to favour the diffusion of the system, entered into pasigraphic correspondence with each other and with De Maimieux, who even composed pasigraphic poetry.

De Maimieux spoke of his pasigraphy as an instrument for checking the accuracy of translations. Many theories of translation, in fact, presuppose the existence of a 'parameter language' with which one can control the correct correspondence between the original text and the translated one. De Maimieux aimed at proposing a supposedly neutral metalanguage which could track the correspondence between expressions in system A and those in system B. What was never placed in discussion was the fact that the content of this metalanguage was structured along the lines of Indo-European languages, and of French in particular.

As a consequence we have 'the immense drama of ideography: it can identify and describe its contents, which are
supposedly ideas or notions in themselves, only by naming
them with words from a natural language – a supreme
contradiction for a project created expressly to eliminate
verbal languages' (Pellerey 1992a: 114). As can be seen,
neither in technique nor in underlying ideology have we
advanced very far from the time of Wilkins.

This disingenuousness is carried to paroxysms in the
*Palais de soixante-quatre fenêtres [. . .] ou l'art d'écrire
toutes les langues du monde comme on les parle* (1787, by
the Swiss writer J.P. De Ria. Despite its pretentious title, the
book is nothing but a manual of phonetics or, perhaps, a
proposal for the orthographic reform of French, written in
a febrile, quasi-mystic style. It is not in the least clear how
the reform could be applied to all the languages of the
world (it would, for example, be particularly inapplicable
to English phonetics); but this is an unimaginable question
for the author.

Returning to De Maimieux, the flexibility displayed in his
choice of the pseudo-primitives seems to associate his project with the empiricist tendencies of the *Encyclopédie*; yet,
once they were chosen, his belief in them, and the self-
confidence with which he sought to impose them on
everyone else, still reflected the rationalist temperament. In
this respect, it is interesting to note that De Maimieux
sought to provide for the rhetorical use of his language and
the possibility of oratory: we are, of course, in a time of
eloquence where the life or death of a revolutionary faction
might depend on its ability to sway its audience by the force
of its words.

Where the *a priori* linguists of the eighteenth century
were most critical of their predecessors, however, was in
the matter of grammar. All were inspired by the 'laconic'
ideal proposed in the *Encyclopédie*. In the grammar of De
Maimieux, the number of grammatical categories originally projected by Faiguet is somewhat amplified; in the case
of Delormel, however, the grammar is so laconic that

Couturat and Leau (1903: 312), who spend long chapters describing other systems, liquidate his in a page and a half (Pellerey's treatment is more accurate and generous; 1992a: 125).

Hourwitz, whose project remains akin to the seventeenth-century polygraphies, produced a grammar that was, perhaps, the most laconic of all: one declension, one conjugation for verbs; the verbs were to be expressed in the infinitive with a few additional signs that specify tense and mood. The tenses themselves were reduced to a system of three steps from the present, either backwards or forwards in time: thus *A 1200* means 'I dance'; *A/ 1200* means 'I have danced'; *A 1200/* means 'I will dance.'

If the grammar was made laconic, it followed that the syntax needed to be drastically simplified as well; Hourwitz proposed retaining the direct word order of French. In this respect, the relevance of Count Antoine de Rivarol's pamphlet, *De l'universalité de la langue française* (1784), becomes apparent. What was the need for a universal language, asked the count, when a perfect language existed already? The language was, of course, French. Apart from its intrinsic perfection, French was already an international language; it was the language most diffused in the world, so much that it was possible to speak of the 'French world' just as, in antiquity, one could speak of the 'Roman world' (p. 1).

According to de Rivarol, French possessed a phonetic system that guaranteed sweetness and harmony, as well as a literature incomparable in its richness and grandeur; it was spoken in that capital city which had become the 'foyer des étincelles répandues chez tous les peuples' (p. 21). In comparison with French all other languages paled: German was too guttural, Italian too soft, Spanish too redundant, English too obscure. Rivarol attributed the superiority of French to its word order: first subject, then verb, and last object. This word order mirrored a natural logic which was in accordance with the requirements of common sense. This common sense is, however, linked to the higher activity of our minds: for if we were to base our syntactical order on the order of our perceptions, it is plain that we would start with the object, which first strikes our senses.

The polemical reference to the sensationalism of Condillac is evident when de Rivarol asserts that, if other people, speaking in other tongues, had abandoned the natural, direct word order, it was because they had let their passions prevail over their intellect (pp. 25–6). This retreat from natural reason, moreover, was responsible for the syntactic inversion that had provoked the confusions and ambiguities prevalent in natural languages other than French. Naturally, those languages which tried to compensate for their lack of direct word order with declensions were among the most confused of all.

We might bear in mind that, even though, in 1784, while he was writing his pamphlet, de Rivarol was an *habitué* of Enlightenment circles, after the advent of the revolution, he revealed himself to be a conservative legitimist. To a man so spiritually tied to the *ancien régime*, the philosophy and linguistics of the sensationalists may (quite justifiably) have appeared as a harbinger of an intellectual revolution which emphasized the passions as the fundamental force motivating humanity. If this were the case, then 'the direct word order acquires the value of an instrument of protection [. . .] against the inflammatory style of the public orators who, in a few short years, would be preaching revolution and manipulating the masses' (Pellerey 1992a: 147).

Yet what really characterized the eighteenth-century debate was the desire not so much to simplify grammar as to show that there existed a natural and normal grammar, universally present in all human languages. This grammar is not, however, manifestly apparent; it must be sought instead beneath the surface of human languages, all of which are, in some degree or other, deviations from it. As can be seen, we have returned to the ideal of a universal grammar, only now one is trying to identify it by reducing every existing language to its most *laconic* form.

Attentive as we have been throughout this story to the

issue of side-effects, we ought here to note that without this eighteenth-century intuition of an original, laconic grammar, our contemporary notions of generative and transformational grammar would be quite inconceivable, even if their origins are usually traced back to the Cartesianism of Port Royal.

The Last Flowering of Philosophic Languages

Nor was even this the end of attempts at creating a philosophic language. In 1772 there appeared the project of Georg Kalmar, *Praecepta grammatica atque specimina linguae philosophicae sive universalis, ad omne vitae genus adcomodatae*, which occasioned the most significant discussion on our topic written in Italian.

In 1774, the Italian-Swiss Father Francesco Soave published his *Riflessioni intorno alla costituzione di una lingua universale*. Soave, who had done much to spread the sensationalist doctrine to Italy, advanced a criticism of the *a priori* languages that anticipated those made by the *Idéologues* (on Soave see Gensini 1984; Nicoletti 1989; Pellerey 1992a). Displaying a solid understanding of the projects from Descartes to Wilkins and from Kircher to Leibniz, on the one hand Soave advanced the traditional reservation that it was impossible to elaborate a set of characters sufficient to represent all fundamental concepts; on the other hand, he remarked that Kalmar, having reduced these concepts to 400, was obliged to give different meanings to the same character, according to the context. Either one follows the Chinese model, without succeeding in limiting the characters, or one is unable to avoid equivocations.

Unfortunately, Soave did not resist the temptation of designing a project of his own, though outlining only its basic principles. His system of classification seems to have been based on Wilkins; as usual he sought to rationalize and simplify his grammar; at the same time, he sought to augment its expressive potential by adding marks for new morphological categories such as the dual and the neuter. Soave took more care over his grammar than over his lexicon, but was mainly interested in the literary use of language: from this derives his radical scepticism about any universal language; what form of literary commerce, he wondered, could we possibly have with the Tartars, the Abyssinians or the Hurons?

In the early years of the next century, Soave's discussion influenced the thinking of Giacomo Leopardi, who had become an exceptionally astute student of the *Idéologues*. In his *Zibaldone*, Leopardi treated the question of universal languages at some length, as well as discussing the debate between rationalists and sensationalists in recent French philosophy (see Gensini 1984; Pellerey 1992a). Leopardi was clearly irritated by the algebraic signs that abounded in the *a priori* languages, all of which he considered as incapable of expressing the subtle connotations of natural languages:

A strictly universal language, whatever it may be, will certainly, by necessity and by its natural bent, be both the most enslaved, impoverished, timid, monotonous, uniform, arid, and ugly language ever. It will be incapable of beauty of any type, totally uncongenial to imagination [. . .] the most inanimate, bloodless, and dead whatsoever, a mere skeleton, a ghost of a language [. . .] it would lack life even if it were written by all and universally understood; indeed it will be deader than the deadest languages which are no longer either spoken or written. (23 August 1823, in G. Leopardi, *Tutte le opere*, Sansoni: Florence 1969: II, 814)

Despite these and similar strictures, the ardour of the apostles of philosophic *a priori* languages was still far from quenched.

At the beginning of the nineteenth century, Anne-Pierre-Jacques de Vismes (*Pasilogie, ou de la musique considérée come langue universelle*, 1806) presented a language that was supposed to be a copy of the language of the angels, whose sounds derived from the affections of the soul. Vismes argued that when the Latin translation of Genesis

11:1–2 states that 'erat terra labii unius' (a passage to which we usually give the sense that 'all the world was of one language'), it used the word *labium* (lip) rather than *lingua* (tongue) because people first communicated with each other by emitting sounds through their lips without articulating them with their tongue. Music was not a human invention (pp. 1–20), and this is demonstrated by the fact that animals can understand music more easily than verbal speech: horses are naturally roused by the sound of trumpets as dogs are by whistles. What is more, when presented with a musical score, people of different nations all play it the same way.

Vismes presents enharmonic scales of 21 notes, one for each letter of the alphabet. He did this by ignoring the modern convention of equal temperament, and treating the sharp of one note as distinct from the flat of the note above. Since Vismes was designing a polygraphy rather than a spoken language, it was enough that the distinctions might be exactly represented on a musical stave.

Inspired, perhaps, indirectly by Mersenne, Vismes went on to demonstrate that if one were to combine his 21 sounds into doublets, triplets, quadruplets, etc., one would quickly arrive at more syntagms than are contained in any natural language, and that 'if it were necessary to write down all the combinations that can be generated by the seven enharmonic scales, combined with each other, it would take almost all of eternity before one could hope to come to an end' (p. 78). As for the concrete possibility of replacing verbal sounds by musical notes, Vismes devotes only the last six pages of his book to such a topic – not a great deal.

It never seems to have crossed Vismes' mind that, in taking a French text and substituting tones for its letters, all he was doing was transcribing a *French* text, without making it comprehensible to speakers of other languages. Vismes seems to conceive of a universe that speaks exclusively in French, so much so that he even notes that he will exclude letters like K, Z and X because 'they are hardly ever used in languages' (p. 106).

Vismes was not the only one to fall foul of this seemingly elementary snare. In 1831 Father Giovan Giuseppe Matraja published his *Genigrafia italiana*, which is nothing other than a polygraphy with five (Italian) dictionaries, one for nouns, one for verbs, one for adjectives, one for interjections and one for adverbs. Since the five dictionaries account for only 15,000 terms, Matraja adds another dictionary that lists 6,000 synonyms. His method managed to be both haphazard and laborious; Matraja divided his terms into a series of numbered classes each containing 26 terms, each marked by an alphabetical letter: thus *A1* means 'hatchet', *A2* means 'hermit', *A1000* means 'encrustation', *A360* means 'sand-digger', etc. Even though he had served as a missionary in South America, Matraja was still convinced that all cultures used the same system of notions. He believed that western languages (all of which he seemed to imagine were derived from Latin grammar) might perfectly well serve as the basis for any other language, because, by a special natural gift, all peoples used the same syntactic structures when speaking – especially American Indians. In fact, he included a genigraphical translation of the Lord's Prayer comparing it with versions in twelve other languages including Nahuatl, Chilean and Quechua.

In 1827, François Soudre invented the Solresol (*Langue musicale universelle*, 1866). Soudre was also persuaded that the seven notes of the musical scale composed an alphabet comprehensible by all the peoples of the world, because the notes are written in the same way in all languages, and could be sung, recorded on staves, represented with special stenographic signs, figured in Arabic numerals, shown with the seven colours of the spectrum, and even indicated by the touch of the fingers of the right and left hands – thus making their representation comprehensible even for the deaf, dumb and blind. It was not necessary that these notes be based on a logical classification of ideas. A single note expresses terms such as 'yes' (musical *si*, or *B*) and 'no' (*do*, or *C*); two notes express pronouns ('mine' = *redo*, 'yours' = *remi*); three notes express everyday words like 'time' (*doredo*) or 'day' (*doremi*). The initial notes refer to an encyclopedic class. Yet Soudre also wished to express opposites by musical inversion (a nice anticipation of a twelve-tone music procedure): thus, if the idea of 'God' was naturally expressed by the major chord built upon the tonic, *domisol*, the idea of 'Satan' would have to be the inversion, *solmido*. Of course, this practice makes nonsense of the rule that the first letter in a three-note term refers to an encyclopedic class: the initial *do* refers to the physical and moral qualities, but the initial *sol* refers back to arts and sciences (and to associate them with Satan would be an excess of bigotry). Besides the obvious difficulties inherent in any *a priori* language, the musical language of Soudre added the additional hurdle of requiring a good ear. We seem in some way to be returning to the seventeenth-century myth of the language of birds, this time with less glossolalic grace, however, and a good deal more pure classificatory pedantry.

Couturat and Leau (1903: 37) awarded to the Solresol the encomium of being 'the most artificial and most impracticable of all the *a priori* languages'. Even its number system is inaccessible; it is based on a hexadecimal system which, despite its claims to universality, still manages to indulge in the French quirk of eliminating names for 70 and 90. Yet Soudre laboured for forty-five years to perfect his system, obtaining in the meantime testimonials from the Institut de France, from musicians such as Cherubini, from Victor Hugo, Lamartine and Alexander von Humboldt; he was received by Napoleon III; he was awarded 10,000 francs at the Exposition Universale in Paris in 1855 and the gold medal at the London Exposition of 1862.

Let us neglect for the sake of brevity the *Système de langue universelle* of Grosselin (1836), the *Langue universelle et analytique* of Vidal (1844), the *Cours complet de langue universelle* by Letellier (1832–55), the *Blaia Zimandal* of Meriggi (1884), the projects of so distinguished a philosopher as Renouvier (1885), the *Lingualumina* of Dyer (1875), the *Langue internationale étymologique* of

Reimann (1877), the *Langue naturelle* of Maldant (1887), the *Spokil* of Dr Nicolas (1900), the *Zahlensprache* of Hilbe (1901), the *Völkerverkehrsprache* of Dietrich (1902), and the *Perio* of Talundberg (1904). We will content ourselves with a brief account of the *Projet d'une langue universelle* of Sotos Ochando (1855). Its theoretical foundations are comparatively well reasoned and motivated; its logical structure could not be of a greater simplicity and regularity; the project proposes – as usual – to establish a perfect correspondence between the order of things signified and the alphabetical order of the words that express them. Unfortunately – here we go again – the arrangement is empirical: *A* refers to inorganic material things, *B* to the liberal arts, *C* to the mechanical arts, *D* to political society, *E* to living bodies, and so forth. With the addition of the morphological rules, one generates, to use the mineral kingdom as an example, the words *Ababa* for *oxygen*, *Ababe* for *hydrogen*, *Ababi* for *nitrogen*, *Ababo* for *sulphur*.

If we consider that the numbers from one to ten are *siba, sibe, sibi, sibo, sibu, sibra, sibre, sibri, sibro* and *sibru* (pity the poor school children having to memorize their multiplication tables), it is evident that words with analogous meanings are all going to sound the same. This makes the discrimination of concepts almost impossible, even if the formation of names follows a criterion similar to that of chemistry, and the letters stand for the components of the concept.

The author may claim that, using his system, anyone can learn over six million words in less than an hour; yet as Couturat and Leau remark (1903: 69), learning a system that can generate six million words in an hour is not the same as memorizing, recognizing, six million meanings.

The list could be continued, yet towards the end of the nineteenth century, news of the invention of *a priori* languages was becoming less a matter for scientific communications and more one for reports on eccentric fellows – from *Les fous littéraires* by Brunet in 1880 to *Les fous littéraires* by Blavier in 1982. By now, the invention of *a priori* languages, other than being the special province of visionaries of all lands, had become a game (see Bausani 1970 and his language Markuska) or a literary exercise (see Yaguello 1984 and Giovannoli 1990 for the imaginary languages of science fiction).

Space Languages

Almost at the bounds of science fiction, though still with an undoubted scientific interest, is the project of the Dutch mathematician Hans A. Freudenthal (Lincos, 1960) for a language in which eventual encounters with the inhabitants of other galaxies may be conducted (see Bassi 1992). Lincos is not designed as a language to be spoken; it is rather a model for inventing a language and at the same time teaching it to alien beings that have presumably traditions and biological structure different from ours.

Freudenthal starts off by supposing that we can beam into space signals, which we might picture as radio waves of varying length and duration. The significance of these waves derives not from their expression-substance, but rather from their expression-form and content-form. By endeavouring to understand the logic that determines the expression-form being transmitted to them, the space aliens are supposed to extrapolate a content-form that will not be alien to them.

During the first phase, the messages consist of regular sequences of pulses. These are intended to be interpreted quantitatively – four pulses standing for the number 4, etc. As soon as it is assumed that the aliens have correctly interpreted these first signals, the transmission passes to the second phase, in which it introduces simple arithmetic operators:

$$*** < ****$$

$$**** = ****$$
$$**** + ** = ******$$

In the next phase, the aliens are taught to substitute for the pulses a system of binary numbers (in which $**** = 100$, $***** = 101$, $****** = 110$); this makes it possible, using only ostension and repetition, to communicate some of the principal operations in mathematics.

The transmission of temporal concepts presents a more complex problem. Freudenthal, however, presumes that by constantly receiving a signal of the same duration, constantly associated to the same number of pulses, the aliens will begin to compute a certain duration in seconds. Lincos also teaches conversational rules, training the aliens to understand sequences such as 'Ha says to Hb: what is that x such that $2x = 5$?'

In one sense, we are treating the space aliens like circus animals; we subject them to a repeated stimulus, giving them positive reinforcement whenever they exhibit the desired response. In the case of animals, however, the reinforcement is immediate – we give them food; in the case of aliens, the reinforcement cannot but be a broadcast signal that they *should* interpret as 'OK'. By this means, the aliens are meant to learn to recognize not only mathematical operations but also concepts such as 'because', 'as', 'if', 'to know', 'to want', and even 'to play'.

The project presupposes that the aliens have the technological capability to receive and decode wave-length signals, and that they follow logical and mathematical criteria akin to our own. They should share with us not only the elementary principles of identity and non-contradiction, but also the habit of inferring a constant rule through induction from many similar cases. Lincos can only be taught to those who, having guessed that for the mysterious sender $2 \times 2 = 4$, will assume that this rule will remain constant in the future. This is, in fact, a big assumption; there is no way of ruling out that there exist alien cultures who 'think' according to rules which vary according to time and circumstances.

What Freudenthal is aiming for is, explicitly, a true *characteristica universalis*; in Lincos, however, only a handful of original syntactic rules are formulated in the beginning. As to the rest (as to, for example, the rules governing questions and answers), the model implicitly assumes that the interlocutors will use the rules, and even the pragmatics, of a natural language. We can, for example, imagine a community of telepathic individuals – we might imagine a community of angels, each of whom either reads the thoughts of the others or learns truths directly through beholding them in the mind of God: for such beings, the set of interactional rules governing questions and answers would make no sense at all. The problem with Lincos is that, although provided with a formal structure, it is conceived as an instrument for 'natural' communication, and thus it is inherently uncertain and imprecise. In other words, it cannot possess the tautological structure of a formalized language.

Lincos is probably more interesting from a pedagogical point of view: can one teach a language without ostension? If the answer is positive, Lincos would allow a situation different from that imagined by philosophers of language, when they sceptically imagine a scene in which a European explorer interacts with a native, each party tries to communicate with the other by pointing at bits of space-time and uttering a given sound, and there is no way for the explorer to be certain whether the native is denoting a given object located in that space-time portion, or the fact that something is happening there, or is expressing his or her refusal to answer (see Quine 1960).

Artificial Intelligence

Lincos does furnish us with an image of a language that is almost purely 'mental' (its level of expression is supported by nothing more than electromagnetic phenomena). This reminds us of other languages which are, in one way or another, the heirs of the ancient search for the perfect language. Computer languages, like BASIC or Pascal, are, in fact, *a priori* languages. They are not full languages because their syntax, though rigorous, is simplified and limited, and they remain parasitic on the natural languages which attach meanings to their empty symbols, which, for the most part, serve as logical connectors of the type *if . . . then*. None the less, they are universal systems; they are comprehensible to speakers of differing natural languages and are perfect in the sense that they permit neither error nor ambiguity. They are *a priori*, in that they are based not on the rules which govern the surface structures of natural languages, but rather, ideally, on a presumed deep grammar common to all natural languages. They are, finally, philosophical because they presume that this deep grammar, based on the laws of logic, is the grammar of thought of human beings and machines alike. They also exhibit the two limitations inherent in philosophical *a priori* languages: (1) their rules of inference are drawn from the western logical tradition, and this may mean, as many have argued, that they reflect little more than the basic grammatical structures common to the Indo-European family of languages; (2) their effability is limited; that is, they are capable of expressing only a small proportion of what any natural language can express.

The dream of a perfect language which covers all the meanings and connotations of the vocabulary of a natural language, and in which human beings and machines can engage in 'meaningful' conversations (or machines can draw inferences as happens in natural languages), underlies much of contemporary research into artificial intelligence. Machines are provided, for example, with rules of inference by which they can 'judge' whether or not a certain story is coherent, or decide that, if someone is ill, then someone needs medical assistance – and so on. By now, the literature on this subject is vast, and the proposed systems are many:

they run from those that still adhere to the ideal of a componential semantics based on primitives, to those that furnish the machine with schemes of action or a typology of 'frames', 'scripts' and 'goals'. In general all of these projects succeed in solving certain problems only through imposing *ad hoc* solutions, which work only for local portions of the range of action of natural languages.

Some Ghosts of the Perfect Language

We have often paused to draw attention to side-effects. Without forced comparisons and without exaggerated claims, it seems permissible at this point to ask informed readers to reconsider various chapters of the history of philosophy, especially those concerning the advent of contemporary logic and linguistic analysis. Would these developments have been possible without the secular debate on the nature of the perfect language, and, in particular, the various projects for philosophical *a priori* languages?

In 1854, George Boole published his *Investigations of the Laws of Thought*. He announced his intention to discover the fundamental laws governing the mental operations of the process of reasoning. He observed that without presupposing these laws, we could not explain why the innumerable languages spread around the globe have maintained over the course of centuries so many characteristics in common (II, 1). Frege began his *Begriffsschrift* (on ideography, 1879) with a reference to Leibniz's *characteristica*. In *The Philosophy of Logical Atomism* (1918–19), Russell noted that in a perfectly logical language, the relation of a word to its meaning would always be one to one (excepting words used as connectives). When he later wrote *Principia mathematica* with Whitehead, he noted that, although their language only possessed a syntax, it could, with the addition of a vocabulary, become a perfect language (even though he also admitted that if such a language were to be constructed it would be intolerably prolix). For his part,

Wittgenstein, renewing Bacon's complaint concerning the ambiguity of natural languages, aspired to create a language whose signs were univocal (*Tractatus logico-philosophicus*, 1921–2, 3.325ff) and whose propositions mirrored the logical structure of reality itself (4.121). Carnap proposed constructing a logical system of objects and concepts such that all concepts might be derived from a single nucleus of prime ideas (*Der logische Aufbau der Welt*, 1922–5). In fact, the entire logical positivist movement was heir to the Baconian polemic against the vagaries of natural languages productive of nothing but metaphysical illusions and false problems (cf. Recanati 1979).

These philosophers all hoped to construct a scientific language, perfect within its chosen range of competence, a language that would be universal as well; none, however, claimed that such a language would ever replace natural language. The dream had changed, or, perhaps, its limitations had finally, reluctantly been accepted. From its search for the lost language of Adam, philosophy had by now learned to take only what it could get.

In the course of centuries through which our particular story has run, another story began to disentangle itself as well – the search for a general or universal grammar. I said in the introduction that this was not a story that I intended to tell here. I shall not tell it because the search for a single corpus of rules underneath and common to all natural languages entailed neither the invention of a new language nor a return to a lost mother tongue. None the less, the search for what is constant in all languages can be undertaken in two ways.

The first way is to follow empirical and comparative methods; this requires compiling information on every language that exists – or existed (cf. Greenberg 1963). The second way can be traced back to the time in which Dante (influenced or not by the doctrines of the Modists) attributed the gift of a *forma locutionis* to Adam. On this line of thought, scholars have more often tried to deduce the universal laws of all languages, and of human thought, from the model of the only language they knew – scholastic Latin – and in 1587 Francisco Sanchez Brocense was still doing so with his *Minerva, seu causis linguae latinae*. The novelty of the *Grammaire générale et raisonée* of Port Royal (1660) was simply the decision of taking as a model a modern language – French.

Choosing this way requires never being brushed by the scruple that a given language represents only a *given* way of thinking and of viewing the world, not universal thought itself. It requires regarding what is called the 'genius' of a language as affecting only the surface structures rather than the deep structure, allegedly the same for all languages. Only in this way will it be possible to regard as universal, because corresponding to the only logic possible, the structures discovered in the language in which one is used to think.

Nor does it necessarily alter the problem to concede that – certainly – the various languages do exhibit differences at their surface level, are often corrupted through usage or agitated by their own genius, but still, if universal laws exist, the light of natural reason will uncover them because, as Beauzée wrote in his article on grammar in the *Encyclopédie*, 'la parole est une sorte de tableau dont la pensée est l'original.' Such an argument would be acceptable, but in order to uncover these laws one needs to represent them through a metalanguage applicable to every other language in the world. Now, if one chooses as metalanguage one's own object language, the argument becomes circular.

In fact, as Simone has put it (1969: XXXIII), the aim of the Port Royal grammarians

is therefore, in spite of the appearances of methodological rigour, prescriptive and evaluative, in so far as it is rationalist. Their scope was not to interpret, in the most adequate and coherent way possible, the usages permitted by the various languages. If it were so, a linguistic theory should coincide with whole of the possible usages of a given tongue, and should take into account even those that native speakers consider as 'wrong'. Instead, their aim was to emend this variety of uses in order to make them all conform to the dictates of Reason.

What makes the search for a universal grammar of interest in our story is, as Canto has noted (1979), that in order to be caught within the vicious circle, it is only necessary to make one simple assumption: the perfect language exists, and it is identical to one's own tongue. Once this assumption is made, the choice of the metalanguage follows: Port Royal anticipates de Rivarol.

This is a problem that remains for all attempts – contemporary ones included – to demonstrate that syntactic or semantic universals exist by deducing them from a given natural language, used simultaneously both as metalanguage and as object language. It is not my argument here that such a project is desperate: I merely suggest that it represents but another example of the quest for a philosophical *a priori* language in which, once again, a philosophical ideal of grammar presides over the study of a natural language.

Thus (as Cosenza has shown, 1993) those modern-day branches of philosophy and psychology which deliberately appeal to a language of thought are also descendants of those older projects. Such a 'mentalese' would supposedly reflect the structure of mind, would be a purely formal and syntactical calculus (not unlike Leibniz's blind thought), would use non-ambiguous symbols and would be based upon innate primitives, common to all species. As happened with Wilkins, it would be deduced according to a 'folk psychology', naturally within the framework of a given historical culture.

There are perhaps more remote descendants of the *a priori* projects, which have sought to found a language of mind not upon Platonic abstractions but upon the neurophysiological structures of the brain. Here the language of mind is the language of the brain; the software is founded upon the hardware. This is a new departure; since the 'ancestors' of our story never dreamed of venturing this far, and many of them were not even certain that the *res cogitans* was located in the brain rather than the heart or the liver (even though an attractive wood-cut showing the localization of the faculty of language in the brain – as well as those for imagination, estimation and memory – already appears in the fifteenth century in Gregor Reysch's *Margarita philosophica*).

Differences are sometimes more important than identities or analogies; still, it would hardly be a waste of time if sometimes even the most advanced students in the cognitive sciences were to pay a visit to their ancestors. It is frequently claimed in American philosophy departments that, in order to be a philosopher, it is not necessary to revisit the history of philosophy. It is like the claim that one can become a painter without having seen a single work of Raphael, or a writer without having ever read the classics. Such things are theoretically possible; but the 'primitive' artist, condemned to an ignorance of the past, is always recognizable as such and rightly labelled as a *naïf*. It is only when we reconsider past projects revealed as utopian or as failures that we are apprised of the dangers and possibilities for failure for our allegedly new projects. The study of the deeds of our ancestors is thus more than an antiquarian pastime, it is an immunological precaution.

16

The International Auxiliary Languages

The dawn of the twentieth century witnessed a revolution in transport and communications. In 1903 Couturat and Leau noted that it was now possible to voyage around the world in just forty days; exactly one half of the fateful limit set by Jules Verne just thirty years before. Now the telephone and the wireless knitted Europe together and as communication became faster, economic relations increased. The major European nations had acquired colonies even in the far-flung antipodes, and so the European market could extend to cover the entire earth. For these and other reasons, governments felt as never before the need for international forums where they might meet to resolve an infinite series of common problems, and our authors cite the Brussels convention on sugar production and the international accord on white-slave trade. As for scientific research, there were supranational bodies such as the Bureau des poids et mesures (sixteen states) or the International Geodesic Association (eighteen states), while in 1900 the International Association of Scientific Academies was founded. Couturat and Leau wrote that such a growing of scientific information needed to be organized 'sous peine de revenir à la tour de Babel'.

What could the remedy be? Couturat and Leau dismissed the idea of choosing a living language as an international medium as utopian, and found difficulties in returning to a dead language like Latin. Besides, Latin displays too many homonyms (*liber* means both 'book' and 'free'), its flexions create equivocations (*avi* might represent the dative and ablative of *avis* or the nominative plural of *avus*), it makes it difficult to distinguish between nouns and verbs (*amor* means both *love* and *I am loved*), it lacks a definite article and its syntax is largely irregular . . . The obvious solution seemed to be the invention of an artificial language, formed on the model of natural ones, but which might seem neutral to all its users.

The criteria for this language should be above all a simple and rational grammar (as extolled by the *a priori* languages, but with a closer analogy with existing tongues), and a lexicon whose terms recalled as closely as possible words in the natural languages. In this sense, an international auxiliary language (henceforth IAL) would no longer be *a priori* but *a posteriori*; it would emerge from a comparison with and a balanced synthesis of naturally existing languages.

Couturat and Leau were realistic enough to understand that it was impossible to arrive at a preconceived scientific formula to judge which of the *a posteriori* IAL projects was the best and most flexible. It would have been the same as deciding on allegedly objective grounds whether Portuguese was superior to Spanish as a language for poetry or for commercial exchange. They realized that, furthermore, an IAL project would not succeed unless an international body adopted and promoted it. Success, in other words, could only follow from a display of international political will.

What Couturat and Leau were facing in 1903, however, was a new Babel of international languages invented in the course of the nineteenth century; as a matter of fact they record and analyse 38 projects – and more of them are considered in their further book, *Les nouvelles langues internationales*, published in 1907.

The followers of each project had tried, with greater or lesser cohesive power, to realize an international forum. But what authority had the competence to adjudicate between them? In 1901 Couturat and Leau had founded a

Delégation pour l'adoption d'une langue auxiliaire internationale, which aimed at resolving the problem by delegating
a decision to the international Association of Scientific
Academies. Evidently Couturat and Leau were writing in
an epoch when it still seemed realistic to believe that an
international body such as this would be capable of coming
to a fair and ecumenical conclusion and imposing it on
every nation.

The Mixed Systems

Volapük was perhaps the first auxiliary language to
become a matter of international concern. It was invented
in 1879 by Johann Martin Schleyer, a German Catholic
priest who envisioned it as an instrument to foster unity
and brotherhood among peoples. As soon as it was made
public, the language spread, expanding throughout south
Germany and France, where it was promoted by Auguste
Kerckhoffs. From here it extended rapidly throughout the
whole world. By 1889 there were 283 Volapükist clubs, in
Europe, America and Australia, which organized courses,
gave diplomas and published journals. Such was the
momentum that Schleyer soon began to lose control over
his own project, so that, ironically, at the very moment in
which he was being celebrated as the father of Volapük, he
saw his language subjected to 'heretical' modifications
which further simplified, restructured and rearranged it.
Such seems to be the fate of artificial languages: the 'word'
remains pure only if it does not spread; if it spreads, it
becomes the property of the community of its proselytes,
and (since the best is the enemy of the good) the result is
'Babelization'. So it happened to Volapük: after a few short
years of mushroom growth, the movement collapsed, continuing in an almost underground existence. From its seeds,
however, a plethora of new projects were born, like the
Idiom Neutral, the Langu Universelle of Menet (1886),
De Max's Bopal (1887), the Spelin of Bauer (1886),

Fieweger's Dil (1887), Dormoy's Balta (1893), and the Veltparl of von Arnim (1896).

Volapük was an example of a 'mixed system', which, according to Couturat and Leau, followed the lines sketched out by Jacob von Grimm. It resembles an *a posteriori* language in the sense that it used as its model English, as the most widely spread of all languages spoken by civilized peoples (though, in fact, Schleyer filled his lexicon with terms more closely resembling his native German). It possessed a 28-letter alphabet in which each letter had a unique sound, and the accent always fell on the final syllable. Anxious that his should be a truly international language, Schleyer had eliminated the sound *r* from his lexicon on the grounds that it was not pronounceable by the Chinese – failing to realize that for the speakers of many oriental languages the difficulty is not so much pronouncing *r* as distinguishing it from *l*.

Besides, the model language was English, but in a sort of phonetic spelling. Thus the word for 'room' was modelled on English *chamber* and spelled *cem*. The suppression of letters like the *r* sometimes introduced notable deformations into many of the radicals incorporated from the natural languages. The word for 'mountain', based on the German *Berg*, with the *r* eliminated, becomes *bel*, while 'fire' becomes *fil*. One of the advantages of *a posteriori* language is that its words can recall the known terms of a natural language: but *bel* for a speaker of a Romance language would probably evoke the notion of beautiful (*bello*), while not evoking the notion of mountain for a German speaker.

To these radicals were added endings and other derivations. In this respect, Volapük followed an *a priori* criterion of rationality and transparency. Its grammar is based upon a declensional system ('house': *dom, doma, dome, domi*, etc.). Feminine is derived directly from masculine through an invariable rule, adjectives are all formed with the suffix -*ik* (if *gud* is the substantive 'goodness', *gudik* will be the adjective 'good'), comparatives were formed by the suffix -*um*, and so on. Given the integers from 1 to 9, by adding an *s*, units of ten could be denoted (*bal* = 1, *bals* = 10, etc.). All words that evoke the idea of time (like *today, yesterday, next year*) were prefixed with *del-*; all words with the suffix *-av* denoted a science (if *stel* = 'star', then *stelav* = 'astronomy'). Unfortunately, these *a priori* criteria are used with a degree of arbitrariness: for instance, considering that the prefix *lu-* always indicates something inferior and the term *vat* means 'water'; there is no reason for using *luvat* for 'urine' rather than for 'dirty water'. Why is *flitaf* (which literally means 'flying animal') used for 'fly' and not for 'bird' or 'bee'?

Couturat and Leau noted that, in common with other mixed systems, Volapük, without claiming to be a philosophical language, still tried to analyse notions according to a philosophical method. The result was that Volapük suffered from all the inconveniences of the *a priori* languages while gaining none of their logical advantages. It was not *a priori* in that it drew its radicals from natural languages, yet it was not *a posteriori*, in so far as it subjected these radicals to systematic deformations (due to an *a priori* decision), thus making the original words unrecognizable. As a result, losing all resemblance to any natural language, it becomes difficult for all speakers, irrespective of their original tongue. Couturat and Leau observe that mixed languages, by following compositional criteria, form conceptual agglutinations which, in their awkwardness and their primitiveness, bear a resemblance to pidgin languages. In pidgin English, for example, the distinction between a paddle wheeler and a propeller-driven steam boat is expressed as *outside-walkee-can-see* and *inside-walkee-no-can-see*. Likewise, in Volapük the term for 'jeweller' is *nobastonacan*, which is formed from 'stone' + 'merchandise' + 'nobility'.

The Babel of *A Posteriori* Languages

Among the international artificial languages, the project that was presented in 1734 under the pseudonym of

Carpophorophilus probably takes the prize for seniority; the next was Faiguet's Langue Nouvelle; after this, in 1839, was the Communicationssprache of Schipfer. After these, there came a tide of IALs in the nineteenth century.

If one takes samples from a number of systems, a set of family resemblances soon appears. There is usually a prevalence of Latin roots plus a fair distribution of roots derived from other European languages. In this way, the speakers of any one of the major European languages will always have the impression of being in, at least partially, familiar territory:

Me senior, I sende evos un grammatik e un verb-bibel de un nuov glot nomed universal glot. (Universal sprache, 1868)

Ta pasilingua era una idiomu per tos populos findita, una lingua qua autoris de to spirito divino, informando tos hominos zu parlir, er creita. (Pasilingua, 1885)

Mesiur, me recipi-tum tuo epistola hic mane gratissime. (Lingua, 1888)

Con grand satisfaction mi ha lect tei letter [. . .] Le possibilità de un universal lingue pro la civilisat nations ne esse dubitabil. (Mondolingue, 1888)

Me pren the liberté to ecriv to you in Anglo-Franca. Me have the honneur to soumett to yoùs inspection the prospectus of mès object manifactured. (Anglo-Franca, 1889)

Le nov latin non requirer pro la sui adoption aliq congress. (Nov Latin, 1890).

Scribasion in idiom neutral don profiti sekuant in komparasion ko kelkun lingu nasional. (Idiom Neutral, 1902)

In 1893 there even appeared an Antivolapük which was really an anti-IAL: it consisted of nothing but a skeletal universal grammar which users were invited to complete by adding lexical items from their own language; for example:

French-international: IO NO savoir U ES TU cousin . . .

English-international: IO NO AVER lose TSCHE book KE IO AVER find IN LE street.

Italian-international: IO AVER vedere TSCHA ragazzo e TSCHA ragazza IN UN strada.

Russian-international: LI dom DE MI atijez E DE MI djadja ES A LE ugol DE TSCHE ulitza.

Of like perversity was Tutonisch (1902), an international language only comprehensible to German speakers (or, at most, to speakers of Germanic languages like English). Thus the opening of the Lord's Prayer sounds like this: 'vio fadr hu be in hevn, holirn bi dauo nam'. The author was later merciful enough to provide Romance-language speakers with a version of their own, so that they too might pray in Tutonisch: 'nuo opadr, ki bi in siel, sanktirn bi tuo nom'.

If our story seems to be taking a turn for the ridiculous, it is due less to the languages themselves (which taken one by one are frequently well done) than to an inescapable 'Babel effect'.

Interesting on account of its elementary grammar, the Latino Sine Flexione of the great mathematician and logician Giuseppe Peano (1903) was wittily designed. Peano had no intention of creating a new language; he only wanted to recommend his simplified Latin as a written lingua franca for international scientific communication, reminiscent of the 'laconic' grammars of the *Encyclopédie*. Peano stripped Latin of its declensions, with, in his own words, the result that: 'Con reductione qui praecede, nomen et verbo fie inflexible; toto grammatica latino evanesce.' Thus, no grammar (or almost no grammar) and a lexicon from a well-known language. Yet this result tended perhaps to encourage pidgin Latin. When an English contributor wished to write for one of the mathematical journals which, under the influence of Peano, accepted articles in Latino Sine Flexione, he naturally retained the modal future; thus he translated 'I will publish' as *me vol publica*. The episode is not only amusing: it illustrates the possibility of an uncontrolled development. As with other international languages, Latino Sine Flexione depended less upon its structural merits than on establishing a consensus in its favour. Failing to achieve this, it became another historical curiosity.

Esperanto

Esperanto was first proposed in 1887 in a book, written in Russian and published in Warsaw at the Kelter Press, entitled *The International Language. Preface and Complete Manual (for Russians)*. The author's name was Dr Ledger Ludwik Zamenhof; yet he wrote the book under the pseudonym Dr Esperanto (Dr Hopeful), and this was soon adopted as the name of his language.

Zamenhof, born in 1859, had been fascinated with the idea of an international language since adolescence. When his uncle Josef asked him what was the non-Hebrew name he had, according to custom, chosen for his contacts with Gentiles, the seventeen-year-old Zamenhof replied that he had chosen Ludwik because he had found a reference to Lodwick (also spelled Lodowick) in a work by Comenius (letter of 31 March 1876; see Lamberti 1990: 49). Zamenhof's origins and personality helped shape both his conception of the new language and its eventual success. Born of a Jewish family in Białystok, an area of Polish Lithuania then part of the Tsarist empire, Zamenhof passed his childhood in a crucible of races and languages continually shaken by nationalistic ferment and lasting waves of anti-Semitism. The experience of oppression, followed by the persecution of intellectuals, especially Jewish, at the hands of the Tsarist government, ensured that Zamenhof's particular fascination with international languages would become mixed with a desire for peace between peoples. Besides, although Zamenhof felt solidarity towards his fellow Jews and forecast their return to Palestine, his form of secular religiosity prevented him from fully supporting Zionist ideas: instead of thinking of the end of the Diaspora as a return to Hebrew, Zamenhof hoped that all the Jews could be, one day, reunited in an entirely new language.

In the same years in which, starting in the Slavic-speaking lands, Esperanto began its spread throughout Europe – while philanthropists, linguists and learned societies followed its progress with interest, devoting international conferences to the phenomenon – Zamenhof had also published an anonymous pamphlet, which extolled a doctrine of international brotherhood, *homaranism*. Some of his followers successfully insisted on keeping the Esperanto movement independent of ideological commitments, arguing that if Esperanto were to succeed, it would do so only by attracting to its cause men and women of different religious, political and philosophical opinions. They even sought to avoid any public reference to Zamenhof's own Jewish origins, given that – it must be remembered – just at that historical moment there was growing up the theory of a great 'Jewish conspiracy'.

Even so, despite the movement's insistence on its absolute neutrality, the philanthropic impulse and the non-confessional religious spirit that animated it could not fail to influence the followers of the new language – or *samideani*, that is, participating in the same ideal. In the years immediately following its emergence, moreover, the language and its supporters were almost banned by the Tsarist government, congenitally suspicious towards idealism of any sort, especially after Esperanto had had the fortune/misfortune to obtain the passionate support of Tolstoy, whose brand of humanist pacifism the government regarded as a dangerous form of revolutionary ideology. Even the Nazis followed suit, persecuting Esperanto speakers in the various lands under their occupation (cf. Lins 1988). Persecution, however, only reinforces an idea: the majority of international languages represented themselves as nothing more than instruments of practical utility; Esperanto, by contrast, came increasingly to gather in its folds those religious and pacifist tensions which had been characteristics of many quests for a perfect language, at least until the end of the seventeenth century.

Esperanto came to enjoy the support and sympathy of many illustrious figures – linguists such as Baudoin de Courtenay and Otto Jespersen, scientists such as Peano, or philosophers such as Russell. Rudolf Carnap's comments are particularly revealing; in his *Autobiography* (in Schilpp 1963: 70) he described feeling moved by a sense of solidarity when he found himself able to converse with people of other countries in a common tongue. He noted the quality of this living language which managed to unify a surprising degree of flexibility in its means of expression with a great structural simplicity. Simplest perhaps was the lapidary formulation of Antoine Meillet: 'Toute discussion théoretique est vaine: l'Esperanto fonctionne' (Meillet 1918: 268).

Today the existence of the Universala Esperanto-Asocio in all of the principal cities of the world still testifies to the success of Zamenhof's invention. Over one hundred periodicals are currently published in Esperanto, there is an original production of poetry and narrative, and most of world literature has been translated into this language, from the Bible to the tales of Hans Christian Andersen.

Like Volapük, however, especially in the first decades, the Esperanto movement was nearly torn apart by battles raging over proposed lexical and grammatical reforms. In 1907, Couturat, as the founder and secretary of the Delégation pour l'adoption d'une langue auxiliaire internationale, attempted what Zamenhof considered a *coup de main*: he judged Esperanto to be the best IAL, but only in its approved version, that is, only in the version that had been reformed by the French Esperanto enthusiast, Louis De Beaufront, and renamed Ido. The majority of the movement resisted the proposed modifications, according to a principle stated by Zamenhof: Esperanto might accept enrichments and lexical improvements, but it must always remain firmly attached to what we might call the 'hard core' as set down by its founder in *Fundamento de Esperanto* (1905).

An Optimized Grammar

The twenty-eight letters of the Esperanto alphabet are based on a simple principle: for each letter one sound, and for each sound one letter. The tonic accent always falls on the penultimate syllable. There is only one article, *la*, invariable for words of all genders – thus *la homo, la libroj, la abelo*. Proper names do not take an article. There is no indefinite article.

Concerning the lexicon, the young Zamenhof had already noted that in many European languages there was a logic of suffixes that produced both feminine and many derivative forms (*Buch/Bücherei, pharmakon/pharmakeia, child/childish, rex/regina, host/hostess, gallo/gallina, hero/heroine, Tsar/Tsarina*), while the formation of contraries was governed by prefixes (*heureux/malheureux, happy/unhappy, legal/illegal, fermo/malfermo, rostom/malorostom* – the Russian for 'high' and 'low'). In a letter of 24 September 1876, Zamenhof described himself as ransacking the dictionaries of the various European languages trying to identify terms with a common root – *lingwe, lingua, langue, lengua, language; rosa, rose, roza*, etc. This was already the seminal idea of an *a posteriori* language.

Wherever Zamenhof was unable to discover a common root, he coined his own terms, privileging Romance languages, followed by the Germanic and Slavic ones. As a result, any speaker of a European language who examined an Esperanto word list would discover: (1) many terms that were easily recognizable as being similar or identical to his or her own; (2) terms which, though deriving from a foreign language, were still easily recognizable; (3) terms which, though strange at first sight, once their meaning had been learned, turned out to be easily recognizable; and, finally, (4) a reasonably limited number of terms to be learned *ex novo*. Here are some examples: *abelo* (ape), *apud* (next to), *akto* (act), *alumeto* (match), *birdo* (bird), *cigaredo* (cigarette), *domo* (home), *fali* (to fall), *frosto* (frost), *fumo* (smoke), *hundo* (dog), *kato* (cat), *krajono* (pencil), *kvar* (quarter).

Esperanto also includes a comparatively large number of compound words. They are not inspired by the *a priori* projects, where composition is the norm, since the terms work like a chemical formula; Zamenhof could find compound words in natural languages (think of *man-eater*, *tire-bouchon*, *schiaccianoci*, to say nothing of German). Compound words, moreover, permitted the exploitation of a limited number of radicals to the maximum. The rule governing the formation of compounds was that the principal word appeared at the end: thus – as in English – a 'writing-table' becomes *skribotablo*. The agglutinative principle which governs the formation of compound words allows for the creation of easily recognizable neologisms (cf. Zinna 1993).

From the radical stem, the neutral form is given by the suffix -*o*. This is not, as might appear, for example, to Italian or Spanish speakers, the suffix for the masculine gender, but merely serves as a mark for singular. The feminine gender is 'marked' by inserting an -*in*- between the stem and the singular ending -*o*. Thus 'father/mother' = *patr-o/patr-in-o*, 'king/queen' = *reĝ–o/reĝ-in-o*, male/female = *vir-o/vir-in-o*.

Plurals are formed by adding -*j* to the singular: thus 'fathers/mothers' = *patr-o-j/patr-in-o-j*.

In natural languages many terms belonging to the same conceptual fields are frequently expressed by radically different lexical items. For instance, in Italian, given the conceptual field of parenthood, one must learn the meaning of *padre*, *madre*, *suocero*, *genitori* (father, mother, father-in-law and parents) before acknowledging that these terms belong to the same notional family. In Esperanto, knowing the meaning of the radical *patr*, it is immediately possible to guess the meaning of *patro*, *patrino*, *bopatro* and *gepatroj*.

Likewise, in English (as well as in other languages) there are different endings for terms which all express a job or an occupation, like act*or*, driv*er*, dent*ist*, presid*ent*, surge*on*.

In Esperanto the words for all occupations are marked by the suffix *-isto*, so that anyone who knows that *dento* is 'tooth' will automatically know that a *dentisto* is a professional who deals with teeth.

The rule for the formation of adjectives is also simple and intuitively clear: adjectives are formed by adding the suffix *-a* to the root stem: 'paternal' = *patr-a*; and they agree with nouns in number: 'good parents' = *bonaj patroj*. The six verbal forms are not conjugated, and are always marked by six suffixes. For instance, for the verb 'to see' we have *vid-i* (infinitive), *vid-as* (present), *vid-is* (past), *vid-os* (future), *vid-us* (conditional) and *vid-u!* (imperative).

Zinna has observed (1993) that, while the *a priori* languages and 'laconic' grammars tried, at all cost, to apply a *principle of economy*, Esperanto follows a *principle of optimization*. Following the principle of economy, Esperanto abolishes case endings, yet it makes an exception of the accusative – which is formed by adding an *-n* to the noun: 'la patro amas la filon, la patro amas la filojn.' The motivation for this exception was that in non-flexional languages the accusative is the only case which is not introduced by a preposition, therefore it had to be marked in some way. Besides, the languages that, like English, had lost the accusative for nouns retain it for pronouns (*I/me*). The accusative also permits one to invert the syntactic order of the sentence, and yet to identify both the subject and the object of the action.

The accusative serves to avoid other ambiguities produced by non-flexional languages. As in Latin, it serves to indicate motion towards, so that in Esperanto one can distinguish between 'la birdo flugas en la ĝardeno' (in which the bird is flying about *within* the garden) from 'la birdo flugas en la ĝardenon' (in which the bird is flying *into* the garden). In Italian 'l'uccello vola nel giardino' remains ambiguous. In English, 'I can hear him better than you' is ambiguous, for it can mean either 'I can hear him better than you can hear him' or 'I can hear him better than I can hear you' (the same happens in French with 'je l'écoute mieux que vous', or in Italian with 'lo sento meglio di te'). The Esperanto accusative renders this distinction very simply: the first case is 'mi auskultas lin pli bone ol vi', while the second is 'mi auskultas lin pli bone ol vin'.

Theoretical Objections and Counter-objections

A fundamental objection that can be applied to any of the *a posteriori* projects generically is that they can make no claim to having identified and artificially reorganized a content-system. They simply provide an expression-system which aims at being easy and flexible enough to express the contents normally expressed in a natural language. Such a practical advantage is also a theoretical limit. If the *a priori* languages were too philosophical, their *a posteriori* successors are not philosophical enough.

The supporters of an IAL have neither paid attention to the problem of linguistic relativism, nor ever been worried by the fact that different languages present the world in different ways, sometimes mutually incommensurable. They have usually taken it for granted that synonymous expressions exist from language to language, and the vast collection of books that have been translated into Esperanto from various of the world's languages is taken as proof of the complete 'effability' of this language (this point has been discussed, from opposite points of view, by two authors who are both traditionally considered as relativist, that is, Sapir and Whorf – cf. Pellerey 1993: 7).

To accept the idea that there is a content-system which is the same for all languages means, fatally, to take surreptitiously for granted that such a model is the western one. Even if it tries to distance itself in certain aspects from the Indo-European model, Esperanto, both in its lexicon and in its syntax, remains basically an Indo-European tongue. As Martinet observed, 'the situation would have been different if the language had been invented by a Japanese' (1991: 681).

One is free to regard all these objections as irrelevant. A theoretical weak point may even turn out to be a practical advantage. One can hold that linguistic unification must, in practice, accept the use of the Indo-European languages as the linguistic model (cf. Carnap in Schlipp 1963: 71). It is a view that seems to be confirmed by actual events; for the moment (at least) the economic and technological growth of Japan is based on Japanese acceptance of an Indo-European language (English) as a common vehicle.

Both natural tongues and some 'vehicular' languages have succeeded in becoming dominant in a given country or in a larger area mainly for extra-linguistic reasons. As far as the linguistic reasons are concerned (easiness, economy, rationality and so on), there are so many variables that there are no 'scientific' criteria whereby we might confute the claim of Goropius Becanus that sixteenth-century Flemish was the easiest, most natural, sweetest and most expressive language in the entire universe. The predominant position currently enjoyed by English is a historical contingency arising from the mercantile and colonial expansion of the British Empire, which was followed by American economic and technological hegemony. Of course, it may also be maintained that English has succeeded because it is rich in monosyllables, capable of absorbing foreign words and flexible in forming neologisms, etc.; yet had Hitler won World War II and had the USA been reduced to a confederation of banana republics, we would probably today use German as a universal vehicular language, and Japanese electronics firms would advertise their products in Hong Kong airport duty-free shops (*Zollfreie Waren*) in German. Besides, on the arguable rationality of English, and of any other vehicular language, see the criticism of Sapir (1931).

There is no reason why an artificial language like Esperanto might not function as an international language, just as certain natural languages (such as Greek, Latin, French, English, Swahili) have in different historical periods.

We have already encountered in Destutt de Tracy an extremely powerful objection: a universal language, like perpetual motion, is impossible for a very 'peremptory' reason: 'Even were everybody on earth to agree to speak the same language from today onwards, they would rapidly discover that, under the influence of their own use, the single language had begun to change, to modify itself in thousands of different ways in each different country, until it produced in each a different dialect which gradually grew away from all the others' (*Eléments d'idéologie*, II, 6, 569).

It is true that, just for the above reasons, the Portuguese of Brazil today differs from the Portuguese spoken in Portugal so much that Brazilian and Portuguese publishers publish two different translations of the same foreign book, and it is a common occurrence for foreigners who have learned their Portuguese in Rio to have difficulty understanding what they hear on the streets of Lisbon. Against this, however, one can point out the Brazilians and Portuguese still manage to understand each other well enough in practical, everyday matters. In part, this is because the mass media help the speakers of each variety to follow the transformations taking place on the other shore.

Supporters of Esperanto like Martinet (1991: 685) argue that it would be, to say the least, naive to suppose that, as an IAL diffused into new areas, it would be exempt from the process through which languages evolve and split up into varieties of dialects. Yet in so far as an IAL remained an *auxiliary* language, rather than the primary language of everyday exchange, the risks of such a parallel evolution would be diminished. The action of the media, which might reflect the decisions of a sort of international supervisory association, could also contribute to the establishment and maintenance of standards, or, at least, to keeping evolution under control.

The 'Political' Possibilities of an IAL

Up to now, vehicular languages have been imposed by tradition (Latin as the language of politics, learning and the church in the Middle Ages), by political and economical hegemony (English after World War II), or by other imponderable reasons (Swahili, a natural language spoken on the coast of east Africa, gradually and spontaneously penetrated the interior and, in the wake of commercial and, later, colonial contacts, was simplified and standardized, becoming the common language for a vast African area).

Would it be possible for some international body (the UN or the European Parliament) to impose a particular IAL as a lingua franca (or, perhaps, sanction the actual diffusion of one)? It would be a totally unprecedented historical event.

No one could deny, however, that today many things have changed: that continuous and curious exchanges among different peoples – not just at the higher social levels, but at the level of mass tourism – are phenomena that did not exist in previous eras. The *mass media* have proved to be capable of spreading comparatively homogeneous patterns of behaviour throughout the entire globe – and in fact, in the international acceptance of English as a common language, the mass media have played no small part. Thus, were a political decision to be accompanied by a media campaign, the chances of success for an IAL would be greatly improved.

Today, Albanians and Tunisians have learned Italian only because they can receive Italian TV. All the more reason, it seems, to get people acquainted with an IAL, provided it would be regularly used by many television programmes, by international assemblies, by the pope for his addresses, by the instruction booklets for electronic gadgets, by the control towers in the airports.

If no political initiative on this matter has emerged up till now, if, indeed, it seems difficult to bring about, this does not mean that a political initiative of this sort will never be made in the future. During the last four centuries we have witnessed in Europe a process of national state formation, which required (together with a customs policy, the constitution of regular armies, and the vigorous imposition of symbols of identity) the imposition of single national languages. Schools, academies and the press have been encouraged to standardize and spread knowledge of these languages. Speakers of marginal languages suffered neglect, or, in various political circumstances, even direct persecution, in order to ensure national homogeneity.

Today, however, the trend has reversed itself: politically, customs barriers are coming down, national armies are giving way to international peace-keeping forces, and national borders have become 'welcome to' signs on the motorway. In the last decades, European policy towards minority languages has changed as well. Indeed, in the last few years, a much more dramatic change has taken place, of which the crumbling of the Soviet empire is the most potent manifestation: linguistic fragmentation is no longer felt as an unfortunate accident but rather as a sign of national identity and as a political right – at the cost even of civil wars. For two centuries, America was an international melting pot with one common language – WASP English: today, in states like California, Spanish has begun to claim an equal right; New York City is not far behind.

The process is probably by now unstoppable. If the growth in European unity now proceeds in step with linguistic fragmentation, the only possible solution lies in the full adoption of a vehicular language for Europe.

Among all the objections, one still remains valid: it was originally formulated by Fontenelle and echoed by d'Alembert in his introduction to the *Encyclopédie*: governments are naturally egotistical; they enact laws for their own benefit, but never for the benefit of all humanity. Even if we were all to agree on the necessity of an IAL, it is hard to imagine the international bodies, which are still striving to arrive at some agreement over the means to save our planet from an ecological catastrophe, being capable of imposing a painless remedy for the open wound of Babel.

Yet in this century we have become used to a constantly accelerating pace of events, and this should make would-be prophets pause. National pride is a two-edged sword; faced with the prospect that in a future European union the language of a single nation might prevail, those states with scant prospects of imposing their own language and which are afraid of the predominance of another one (and thus all states except one) might band together to support the adoption of an IAL.

Limits and Effability of an IAL

If one considers the efforts made by many IALs in order to translate all the masterpieces of world literature, one wonders whether, by using an IAL originally, it is possible to achieve artistic results.

One is tempted to cite a celebrated (if misunderstood) *boutade* attributed to Leo Longanesi: 'you can't be a great Bulgarian poet.' The *boutade* is not a nasty comment about Bulgaria: Longanesi wanted to say that one cannot be a great poet if one writes in a language spoken only by a few million people in a country which (whatever else it is) has remained for centuries on the margins of history.

I do not think Longanesi meant that one cannot be a great poet if one writes in a language unknown to the rest of the world. This seems reductive, for poetic greatness is surely not dependent on diffusion. It seems more likely that Longanesi wanted to say that a language is the sum and consequence of a variety of social factors which, over the course of history, have enriched and strengthened it. Many of these factors are extra-linguistic: these include provocative contacts with other cultures, new social needs to communicate new experiences, conflicts and renewals within the speaking community. If that community, however, were a people on the margins of history, a people whose customs and whose knowledge have remained unchanged for centuries; if it were a people whose language has remained unchanged as well, nothing more than the medium of worn-out memories and of rituals ossified over centuries;

how could we ever expect it to be a vehicle for a great new poet?

But this is not an objection that one could make against an IAL. An IAL is not limited in space, it exists in symbiosis with other languages. The possible risk is rather that the institutional control from above (which seems an essential prerequisite for a successful IAL) will become too tight, and the auxiliary language will lose its capacity to express new everyday experiences. One could object that even medieval Latin, ossified though it was in the grammatical forms of which Dante spoke, was still capable of producing liturgical poetry, such as the *Stabat Mater* or the *Pange Lingua*, not to mention poetry as joyful and irreverent as the *Carmina Burana*. Nevertheless, it is still true that the *Carmina Burana* is not the *Divine Comedy*.

An IAL would certainly lack a historic tradition behind it, with all the intertextual richness that this implies. But when the poets of medieval Sicilian courts wrote in a vernacular, when the Slavic bards sang *The Song of Prince Igor* and the Anglo-Saxon *scop* improvised *Beowulf*, their languages were just as young – yet still, in their own way, capable of absorbing the entire history of the preceding languages.

17

Conclusion

Plures linguas scire gloriosum esset, patet exemplo Catonis, Mithridates, Apostolorum.

Comenius, *Linguarum methodus novissima*

This story is a gesture of propaganda, in so far as it provided a particular explanation of the origin and variety of languages, by presenting it *only* as a punishment and a curse [...] Since the variety of tongues renders a universal communication among men, to say the least, difficult, that was certainly a punishment. However, it also meant an improvement of the original creative powers of Adam, a proliferation of that force which allowed the production of names by virtue of a divine inspiration.

J. Trabant, *Apeliotes, oder der Sinn der Sprache*

Citizens of a multiform Earth, Europeans cannot but listen to the polyphonic cry of human languages. To pay attention to the others who speak their own language is the first step in order to establish a solidarity more concrete than many propaganda discourses.

Claude Hagège, *Le souffle de la langue*

Each language constitutes a certain model of the

universe, a semiotic system of understanding the world, and if we have 4,000 different ways to describe the world, this makes us rich. We should be concerned about preserving languages just as we are about ecology.

V.V. Ivanov, *Reconstructing the Past*

I said at the beginning that it was the account in Genesis 11, not Genesis 10, that had prevailed in the collective imagination and, more specifically, in the minds of those who pondered over the plurality of languages. Despite this, as Demonet has shown (1992), already by the time of the Renaissance, a reconsideration of Genesis 10 was under way, provoking, as we saw, a rethinking of the place of Hebrew as the unchanging language, immutable from the time of Babel. We can take it that, by then, the multiplicity of tongues was probably accepted as a positive fact both in Hebrew culture and in Christian Kabbalistic circles (Jacquemier 1992). Still, we have to wait until the eighteenth century before the rethinking of Genesis 10 provokes a revaluation of the legend of Babel itself.

In the same years that witnessed the appearance of the first volumes of the *Encyclopédie*, the abbé Pluche noted in his *La méchanique des langues et l'art de les einsegner* (1751) that, already by the time of Noah, the first differentiation, if not in the lexicon at least in inflections, between one family of languages and another had occurred. This historical observation led Pluche on to reflect that the multiplication of languages (no longer, we note, the *confusion* of languages) was more than a mere natural event: it was *socially providential*. Naturally, Pluche imagined, people were at first troubled to discover that tribes and families no longer understood each other so easily. In the end, however,

those who spoke a mutually intelligible language formed a single body and went to live together in the same corner of the world. Thus it was the diversity of languages which provided each country with its own inhabitants and kept them there. It should be noted that the profits of this miraculous and extraordinary mutation have extended to all successive epochs. From this point on, the more peoples have mixed, the more they have produced mixtures and novelties in their languages; and the more these languages have multiplied, the harder it becomes to change countries. In this way, the confusion of tongues has fortified that sentiment of attachment upon which love of country is based; the confusion has made men more sedentary. (pp. 17–18)

This is more than the celebration of the particular 'genius' of each single language: the very sense of the myth of Babel has been turned upside down. The *natural* differentiation of languages has become a positive phenomenon underlying the allocation of peoples to their respective territories, the birth of nations, and the emergence of the sense of national identity. It is a reversal of meaning that reflects the patriotic pride of an eighteenth-century French author: the *confusio linguarum* was the historically necessary point of departure for the birth of a new sense of the state. Pluche, in effect, seems to be paraphrasing Louis XIV: 'L'état c'est la langue.'

In the light of this reinterpretation it is also interesting to read the objections to an international language made by another French writer, one who lived before the great flood of *a posteriori* projects in the late nineteenth century – Joseph-Marie Degérando, in his work, *Des signes*. Degérando observed that travellers, scientists and merchants (those who needed a common language) were always a minority in respect of the mass of common citizens who were content to remain at home peaceably speaking their native tongues. Just because this minority of travellers needed a common language, it did not follow that the majority of sedentary citizens needed one as well. It was the traveller that needed to understand the natives; the natives had no particular need to understand a traveller, who, indeed, had an advantage over them in being able to conceal his thoughts from the peoples he visited (III, 562). With regard to scientific contact, any common language for science would grow distant from the language of letters, but we know that the language of science and the language of letters influence and fortify each other (III, 570). An international language of purely scientific communication, moreover, would soon become an instrument of secrecy, from which the humble speakers of their native dialects would be excluded (III, 572). And as to possible literary uses (and we leave Degérando the responsibility for such a vulgar sociological argument), if the authors were obliged to write in a common tongue, they would be exposed to international rivalries, fearing invidious comparisons with the works of foreign writers. Thus it seems that for Déger-ando circumspection was a disadvantage for science and an advantage for literature – as it was for the astute and cultivated traveller, more learned than his native and naive interlocutors.

We are, of course, at the end of the century which pro-duced de Rivarol's eulogy to the French language. Thus, although Degérando recognized that the world was divided into zones of influence, and that it was normal to speak German in areas under German political influence just as it was normal to speak English in the British Isles, he could still maintain that, were it possible to impose an auxiliary language, Europe could do no better than to choose French for self-evident reasons of political power (III, 578–9). In any case, according to Degérando, the narrow-mindedness of most governments made every international project un-thinkable: 'Should we suppose that the governments wish to come to an agreement over a set of uniform laws for the alteration of national languages? How many times have we seen governments arrive at an effective agreement over matters that concern the general interest of society?' (III, 554).

In the background is a prejudice of the eighteenth century – and eighteenth-century Frenchmen in particular – that people simply did not wish to learn other tongues, be they universal or foreign. There existed a sort of cultural deaf-ness when faced with polyglottism, a deafness that continues on throughout the nineteenth century to leave visible traces in our own; the only peoples exempt were, remarked Degérando, those of northern Europe, for reasons of pure necessity. So diffuse was this cultural deafness that he even felt compelled to suggest provocatively (III, 587) that the study of foreign languages was not really the sterile and mechanical exercise that most people thought.

Thus Degérando had no choice but to conclude his extremely sceptical review with a eulogy to the diversity of tongues: diversity placed obstacles in the way of foreign conquerors, prevented undue mixing between different peoples, and helped each people to preserve their national character and the habits which protected the purity of their folkways. A national language linked a people to their state, stimulated patriotism and the cult of tradition. Degérando admitted that these considerations were hardly compatible with the ideals of universal brotherhood; still, he commented, 'in this age of corruption, hearts must, above all else, be turned towards patriotic sentiments; the more egotism progresses, the more dangerous it is to become a cosmopolitan' (IV, 589).

If we wish to find historical precedents for this vigorous affirmation of the profound unity between a people and their language (as a gift due to the Babelic event), we need look no farther than Luther (*Declamationes in Genesim*, 1527). It is this tradition, perhaps, that also stands behind Hegel's decisive re-evaluation of Babel. For him the construction of the tower is not only a metaphor for the social structures linking a people to their state, but also occasions a celebration of the almost sacred character of collective human labour.

'What is holy?' Goethe asks once in a distich, and answers: 'What links many souls together.' . . . In the wide plains of the Euphrates an enormous architectural work was erected; it was built in common, and the aim and content of the work was at the same time the community of those who constructed it. And the foundation of this social bond does not remain merely a unification on patriarchal lines; on the contrary, the purely family unity has already been superseded, and the building, rising into the clouds, makes objective to itself this earlier and dissolved unity and the realization of a new and wider one. The ensemble of all the peoples at that period worked at this task and since they all came together to complete an immense work like this, the product of their labour was to be a bond which was to link them together (as we are linked by manners, customs, and the legal constitution of the state) by means of the excavated site and ground, the assembled blocks of stone, and the as it were architectural cultivation of the country.

(G. W. F. Hegel, trans. T. M. Knox:638)

In this vision, in which the tower serves as a prefiguration of the ethical state, the theme of the confusion of languages can only be interpreted as meaning that the unity of the state is not a universal, but a unity that gives life to different nations ('this tradition tells us that the peoples, after being assembled in this one centre of union for the construction of such a work, were once again dispersed and separated from each other'). Nevertheless, the undertaking of Babel was still a precondition, the event necessary to set social, political and scientific history in motion, the first glimmerings of the Age of Progress and Reason. This is a dramatic intuition: to the sound of an almost Jacobin roll of muffled drums, the old Adam mounts to the scaffold, his linguistic *ancien régime* at an end.

And yet Hegel's sentence did not lead to a capital punishment. The myth of the tower as a failure and as a drama still lives today: 'the Tower of Babel [. . .] exhibits an incompleteness, even an impossibility of completing, of totalizing, of saturating, of accomplishing anything which is in the order of building, of architectural construction' (Derrida 1980: 203). One should remark that Dante (DVE, I, vii) provided a 'technological' version of the *confusio linguarum*. His was the story not so much of the birth of the languages of different ethnic groups as of the proliferation of technical jargons: the architects had their language while the stone-bearers had theirs (as if Dante were thinking of the jargons of the corporations of his time). One is almost tempted to find here a formulation, *ante litteram* to say the least, of the idea of the social division of labour in terms of a *division of linguistic labour*.

Somehow Dante's hint seems to have journeyed through the centuries: in his *Histoire critique du Vieux Testament* (1678), Richard Simon wondered whether the confusion of Babel might not have arisen from the fact that, when the workmen came to give names to their tools, each named them in his own way.

The suspicion that these hints reveal a long-buried strand in the popular understanding of the story is reinforced by the history of iconography (cf. Minkowski 1983). From the Middle Ages onwards, in fact, in the pictorial representations of Babel we find so many direct or indirect allusions to human labour – stonemasons, pulleys, squared building stones, block and tackles, plumb lines, compasses, T-squares, winches, plastering equipment, etc. – that these representations have become an important source of our knowledge of medieval building techniques. And how are we to know whether Dante's own suggestion might not have arisen from the poet's acquaintance with the iconography of his times?

Towards the end of the sixteenth century, the theme of Babel entered into the repertoire of Dutch artists, who reworked it in innumerable ways (one thinks, of course, of Bruegel), until, in the multiplicity of the number of tools and construction techniques depicted, the Tower of Babel, in its robust solidity, seemed to embody a secular statement of faith in human progress. By the seventeenth century, artists naturally began to include references to the latest technical innovations, depicting the 'marvellous machines' described in a growing number of treatises on mechanical devices. Even Kircher, who could hardly be accused of secularism, was fascinated by the image of Babel as a prodigious feat of technology; thus when Father Athanasius wrote his *Turris Babel*, he concentrated on its engineering, as if he were describing a tower that had once been a *finished object*.

In the nineteenth century, the theme of Babel began to fall from use, because of a lesser interest in the theological and linguistic aspects of the *confusio:* in exchange, in the few representations of the event, 'the close up gave way to the "group", representing "humanity", whose inclination, reaction, or destiny was represented against the background of "the Tower of Babel". In these dramatic scenes the focus of the representation is thus given by human masses' (Minkowski 1983: 69). The example that readily springs to mind is in Doré's illustrated Bible.

By now we are in the century of progress, the century in which the Italian poet, Carducci, celebrated the steam engine in a poem entitled, significantly, *Hymn to Satan.* Hegel had taught the century to take pride in the works of Lucifer. Thus the gesture of the gigantic figure that dominates Doré's engraving is ambiguous. While the tower projects dark shadows on the workmen bearing the immense blocks of marble, a nude turns his face and extends his arm towards a cloud-filled sky. Is it defiant pride, a curse directed towards a God who has defeated human endeavours? Whatever it is, the gesture certainly does not signify humble resignation in the face of destiny.

Genette has observed (1976: 161) how much the idea of *confusio linguarum* appears as a *felix culpa* in romantic authors such as Nodier: natural languages are perfect in so far as they are many, for the truth is many-sided and falsity consists in reducing this plurality into a single definite unity.

Translation

Today more than ever before, at the end of its long search, European culture is in urgent need of a common language that might heal its linguistic fractures. Yet, at the same time, Europe needs to remain true to its historic vocation as the continent of different languages, each of which, even the most peripheral, remains the medium through which the genius of a particular ethnic group expresses itself, witness and vehicle of a millennial tradition. Is it possible to reconcile the need for a common language and the need to defend linguistic heritages?

Both of these needs reflect the same theoretical contradictions as well as the same practical possibilities. The limits of any possible international common language are the same as those of the natural languages on which these languages are modelled: all presuppose a principle of translatability. If a universal common language claims for itself the capacity to re-express a text written in any other language, it necessarily presumes that, despite the individual genius of any single language, and despite the fact that each language constitutes its own rigid and unique way of seeing, organizing and interpreting the world, it is still always possible to translate from one language to another.

However, if this is a prerequisite inherent to any universal language, it is at the same time a prerequisite inherent to any natural language. It is possible to translate from a natural language into a universal and artificial one for the same reasons that justify and guarantee the translation from a natural language into another.

The intuition that the problem of translation itself presupposed a perfect language is already present in Walter Benjamin: since it is impossible to reproduce all the linguistic meanings of the source language into a target language, one is forced to place one's faith in the convergence of all languages. In each language 'taken as a whole, there is a self-identical thing that is meant, a thing which, nevertheless, is accessible to none of these languages taken individually, but only to that totality of all of their intentions taken as reciprocal and complementary, a totality that we call Pure Language [*reine Sprache*]' (Benjamin 1923). This *reine Sprache* is not a real language. If we think of the mystic and kabbalistic sources which were the inspiration for Benjamin's thinking, we begin to sense the impending ghost of sacred languages, of something more akin to the secret genius of Pentecostal languages and of the language of birds than to the ideal of the *a priori* languages. 'Even the desire for translation is unthinkable without this *corre-spondence* with the thought of God' (Derrida 1980: 217; cf. also Steiner 1975: 64).

In many of the most notable projects for mechanical translation, there exists a notion of a parameter language, which does share many of the characteristics of the *a priori* languages. There must, it is argued, exist a *tertium com-parationis* which might allow us to shift from an expression in language A to an expression in language B by deciding that both are equivalent to an expression of a metalanguage C. If such a *tertium* really existed, it would be a perfect language; if it did not exist, it would remain a mere postu-late on which every translation ought to depend.

The only alternative is to discover a natural language which is so 'perfect' (so flexible and powerful) as to serve as a *tertium comparationis*. In 1603, the Jesuit Ludovico Bertonio published his *Arte de lengua Aymara* (which he supplemented in 1612 with a *Vocabulario de la lengua Aymara*). Aymara is a language still partially spoken by Indians living between Bolivia and Peru, and Bertonio dis-covered that it displayed an immense flexibility and capa-bility of accommodating neologisms, particularly adapted to the expression of abstract concepts, so much so as to raise a suspicion that it was an artificial invention. Two centuries later, Emeterio Villamil de Rada described it as the language of Adam, the expression of 'an idea anterior to the formation of language', founded upon 'necessary and immutable ideas' and, therefore, a philosophic language if ever there were one (*La lengua de Adan*, 1860). After this, it was only a matter of time before the Semitic roots of the Aymara language were 'discovered' as well.

Recent studies have established that unlike western thought, based on a two-valued logic (either true or false), Aymara thought is based on a three-valued logic, and is, therefore, capable of expressing modal subtleties which other languages can only capture through complex circum-locutions. Thus, to conclude, there have been proposals to use Aymara to resolve all problems of computer translation (see Guzmán de Rosas n.d., which includes a vast bibliography). Unfortunately, 'due to its algorithmic nature, the syntax of Aymara would greatly facilitate the translation of any other idiom into its own terms (though not the other way around)' (L. Ramiro Beltran, in Guzmán de Rosas n.d.: III). Thus, because of its perfection, Aymara can render every thought expressed in other mutually untranslatable languages, but the price of this is that once the perfect language has resolved these thoughts into its own terms, they cannot be translated back into our natural native idioms.

One way out of this dilemma is to assume, as certain authors have recently done, that translation is a matter to be resolved entirely within the destination (or target) language, according to the context. This means that it is within the framework of the target language that all the semantic and syntactic problems posed by the source text must be resolved. This is a solution that takes us outside of the problem of perfect languages, or of a *tertium comparationis*, for it implies that we need to understand expressions formed according to the genius of the source language and to invent a 'satisfying' paraphrase according to the genius of the target language. Yet how are we to establish what the criteria of 'satisfaction' could be?

These were theoretical difficulties that Humboldt had already foreseen. If no word in a language exactly corresponds to a word in another one, translation is impossible. At most, translation is an activity, in no way regulated, through which we are able to understand what our own language was unable to say.

Yet if translation implied no more than this it would be subject to a curious contradiction: the possibility of a relation between two languages, A and B, would only occur when A was closed in a full realization of itself, assuming it had understood B, of which nothing could any longer be said, for all that B had to say would by now have been said by A.

Still, what is not excluded is the possibility that, rather

	Run	Walk	Hop	Skip	Jump	Dance	Crawl
1 One or another limb always in contact vs. no limb at times in contact		+	−	−	−	+	+
2 Order of contact	1-1-2-2	1-2-1-2	1-1-1 or 2-2-2	1-2-1-2	Not relevant	Variable but rhythmic	1-3-2-4
3 Number of limbs	2	2	1	2	2	2	4

Figure 17.1

than a parameter language, we might elaborate a comparative tool, not itself a language, which might (if only approximately) be expressed in any language, and which might, furthermore, allow us to compare any two linguistic structures that seemed, in themselves, incommensurable. This instrument or procedure would be able to function in the same way and for the same reason that any natural language is able to translate its own terms into one another by an *interpretative principle*: according to Peirce, any natural language can serve as a metalanguage to itself, by a process of *unlimited semiosis* (cf. Eco 1979: 2).

See for instance a table proposed by Nida (1975: 75) that displays the semantic differences in a number of verbs of motion (figure 17.1).

We can regard this table as an example of an attempt to illustrate, in English – as well as by other semiotic means, such as mathematical signs – what a certain class of English terms mean. Naturally, the interpretative principle demands that the English speaker also interpret the meaning of *limb*, and indeed any other terms appearing in the interpretation of the verbal expression. One is reminded here of Degérando's observations concerning the infinite regress that may arise from any attempt to analyse fully an apparently primitive term such as *to walk*. In reality, however, a language always, as it were, expects to define difficult terms with terms that are easier and less controversial, though by conjectures, guesses and approximations.

Translation proceeds according to the same principle. If one were to wish, for example, to translate Nida's table from English into Italian, one would probably start by substituting for the English verbs Italian terms that are practically synonymous: *correre* for *run*, *camminare* for *walk*, *danzare* for *dance*, and *strisciare* for *crawl*. As soon as we got the verb *to hop*, we would have to pause; there is no direct synonym in Italian for an activity that the Italian–English dictionary might define as 'jumping on one leg only'. Nor is there an adequate Italian synonym for the verb *to skip*: Italian has various terms, like *saltellare*, *ballonzolare* and *salterellare*; these can approximately render *to skip*, but they can also translate *to frisk, to hop* or *to trip*, and thus do not uniquely specify the sort of alternate hop–shuffle–step movement specified by the English *to skip*.

Even though Italian lacks a term which adequately conveys the meaning of *to skip*, the rest of the terms in the table – *limb, order of contact, number of limbs* – are all definable, if not necessarily by Italian synonyms, at least by means of references to contexts and circumstances. Even in English, we have to conjecture that, in this table, the term *contact* must be understood as 'contact with the surface the movement takes place upon' rather than as 'contact with another limb'. Either to define or to translate, we thus do not need a full-fledged parametric language at our disposition. We assume that all languages have some notion that corresponds to the term *limb*, because all humans have a similar anatomy. Furthermore, all cultures probably have ways to distinguish hands from arms, palms from fingers, and, on fingers, the first joint from the second, and the second from the third; and this assumption would be no less true even in a culture, such as Father Mersenne imagined, in which every individual pore, every convolute of a thumb-print had its own individual name. Thus, by starting from terms whose meanings are known and working to interpret by various means (perhaps including gestures) terms whose meanings are not, proceeding by successive adjustments, an English speaker would be able to convey to an Italian speaker what the phrase *John hops* is all about.

These are possibilities for more than just the practice of translation; they are the possibilities for co-existence on a continent with a multilingual vocation. Generalized polyglottism is certainly not the solution to Europe's cultural problems; like Funes '*el memorioso*' in the story by Borges, a global polyglot would have his or her mind constantly filled by too many images. The solution for the future is more likely to be in a community of peoples with an increased ability to receive the spirit, to taste or savour the aroma of different dialects. Polyglot Europe will not be a continent where individuals converse fluently in all the other languages; in the best of cases, it could be a continent where differences of language are no longer barriers to communication, where people can meet each other and speak together, each in his or her own tongue, understanding, as best they can, the speech of others. In this way, even those who never learn to speak another language fluently could still participate in its particular genius, catching a glimpse of the particular cultural universe that every individual expresses each time he or she speaks the language of his or her ancestors and his or her own tradition.

The Gift to Adam

What was the exact nature of the gift of tongues received by the apostles? Reading St Paul (Corinthians 1:12–13) it seems that the gift was that of *glossolalia* – that is, the ability to express oneself in an ecstatic language that all could understand as if it were their own native speech. Reading the Acts of the Apostles 2, however, we discover that at the Pentecost a loud roar was heard from the skies, and that upon each of the apostles a tongue of flame descended, and they started to speak in *other* languages. In this case, the gift was not *glossolalia* but *xenoglossia*, that is, polyglottism – or, failing that, at least a sort of mystic service of simultaneous translation. The question of which interpretation to accept is not really a joking matter: there is a major difference between the two accounts. In the first hypothesis, the apostles would have been restored to the conditions before Babel, when all humanity spoke but a single holy dialect. In the second hypothesis, the apostles would have been granted the gift of momentarily reversing the defeat of Babel and finding in the multiplicity of tongues no longer a wound that must, at whatever cost, be healed, but rather the key to the possibility of a new alliance and of a new concord.

So many of the protagonists in our story have brazenly bent the Sacred Scriptures to suit their purposes that we should restrain ourselves from doing likewise. Ours has been the story of a myth and of a wish. But for every myth there exists a counter-myth which marks the presence of an alternative wish. If we had not limited ourselves from the outset to Europe, we might have branched out into other civilizations, and found other myths – like the one located in the tenth–eleventh century, at the very confines of European civilization, and recounted by the Arab writer Ibn Hazm (cf. Arnaldez 1981; Khassaf 1992a, 1992b).

In the beginning there existed a single language given by God, a language thanks to which Adam was able to understand the quiddity of things. It was a language that provided a name for every thing, be it substance or accident, and a thing for each name. But it seems that at a certain point the account of Ibn Hazm contradicts itself, when saying that – if the presence of homonyms can produce equivocation – an abundance of synonyms would not jeopardize the perfection of a language: it is possible to name the same thing in different ways, provided we do so in an adequate way.

For Ibn Hazm the different languages could not be born from convention: if so, people would have to have had a prior language in which they could agree about conventions. But if such a prior language existed, why should people have undergone the wearisome and unprofitable task of inventing other tongues? The only explanation is that there was an original language which *included all others*.

The *confusio* (which the Koran already regarded not as a curse but as a natural event – cf. Borst 1957–63: I, 325) depended not on the invention of new languages, but on the fragmentation of a unique tongue that existed *ab initio* and in which all the others were already contained. It is for this reason that all people are still able to understand the revelation of the Koran, in whatever language it is expressed. God made the Koranic verses in Arabic in order that they might be understood by his chosen people, not because the Arabic language enjoyed any particular privilege. In whatever language, people may discover the spirit, the breath, the perfume, the traces of the original polylinguism.

Let us accept the suggestion that comes from afar. Our mother tongue was not a single language but rather a complex of all languages. Perhaps Adam never received such a gift in full; it was promised to him, yet before his long period of linguistic apprenticeship was through, original sin severed the link. Thus the legacy that he has left to all his sons and daughters is the task of winning for themselves the full and reconciled mastery of the Tower of Babel.

Notes

Note to Chapter 1

[1] The Vulgate's translation is retained by Wycliffe: 'And Adam seide ... This schal be clepid Virago for she is taken of man' (*Translator's note*).

Note to Chapter 4

[1] We will be referring to the edition of Lull's writings published in 1598 in Strasbourg because this is the edition to which the Lullian tradition, at least up to Leibniz, commonly refers. Consequently when we cite the *Ars generalis ultima* written in 1303, we shall call it *Ars magna*, for it is called the *Ars magna et ultima* in the Strasbourg edition.

Bibliography

Aarsleff, Hans (1982): *From Locke to Saussure*. Minneapolis: University of Minnesota Press.

Alessio, Franco (1957): *Mito e scienza in Ruggero Bacone*. Milan: Ceschina.

Arnaldez, Roger (1981): *Grammaire et théologie chez Ibn Hazm de Cordue*. Paris: Vrin.

Arnold, Paul (1955): *Histoire des Rose-Croix et les origines de la Franc-Maçonnerie*. Paris: Mercure.

Baltrušaitis, Jurgis (1967): *La quête d'Isis. Essai sur la légende d'un mythe. Introduction à l'egyptomanie*. Paris: Flammarion.

Barone, Francesco (1964): *Logica formale e logica trascendentale*. Turin: Edizioni di 'Filosofia'.

Bassi, Bruno (1992): 'Were it perfect, would it work better? Survey of a language for cosmic intercourse', in Pellerey (1992), ed., pp. 261–70.

Bausani, Alessandro (1970): *Geheim- und Universalsprachen: Entwicklung und Typologie*. Stuttgart: Kohlhammer.

Benjamin, Walter (1923): *Die Aufgabe des Übersetzers*, in *Schriften* (1955). Frankfurt: Suhrkamp.

Bernardelli, Andrea (1992): 'Il concetto di carattere universale nella *Encyclopédie*', in Pellerey (1992), ed., pp. 163–72.

Bettini, Maurizio (1992): 'E Dio creò la fibra ottica', *La Repubblica*, 28 March.

Bianchi, Massimo L. (1987): *Signatura rerum. Segni, magia e conoscenza da Paracelso a Leibniz*. Rome: Edizioni dell' Ateneo.

Blasi, Giulio (1992): 'Stampa e filosofia naturale nel XVII secolo: l'*Abecedarium novum naturae* e i "characteres reales" di Francis Bacon', in Pellerey (1992), ed., pp. 101–36.

Blavier, André (1982): *Le fous littéraires*. Paris: Veyrier.

Bonerba, Giuseppina (1992): 'Comenio: utopia, enciclopedia e lingua universale', in Eco et al. (1992), pp. 189–98.

Bora, Paola (1989): 'Introduzione', in J. J. Rousseau, *Saggio sull'origine delle lingue*, Turin: Einaudi, pp. VII–XXXII.

Borst, Arno (1957–63): *Der Turmbau von Babel. Geschichte der Meinungen über Ursprung und Vielfalt der Sprachen und Völker*. 6 vols. Stuttgart: Hiersemann.

Brague, Rémi (1992): *Europe, la voie romane*. Paris: Criterion.

Brekle, Herbert E. (1975): 'The seventeenth century', in Th. A. Sebeok, ed., *Current Trends in Linguistics. XIII/1. Historiography of Linguistics*, The Hague–Paris: Mouton, pp. 277–382.

Brunet, Gustave (Philomneste Junior) (1880): *Les fous littéraires*. Brussels: Gay et Doucé.

Burney, Pierre (1966): *Les langues internationales*. Paris: PUF.

Busse, Winfried and Trabant, Jürgen (1986): eds, *Les idéologues*. Amsterdam: Benjamins.

Buzzetti, Dino and Ferriani, Maurizio (1986): eds, *La grammatica del pensiero*. Bologna: Il Mulino.

Calimani, Riccardo (1987): *Storia dell'ebreo errante*. Milan: Rusconi.

Calvet, Louis-Jean (1981): *Les langues véhiculaires*. Paris: PUF.

Canto, Monique (1979): 'L'invention de la grammaire', in Poirier et al. (1979), pp. 707–19.

Carreras y Artau, Joaquín (1946): *De Ramón Llull a los modernos ensayos de formación de una lengua universal*. Barcelona: Consejo Superior de Investigaciónes Científicas, Delegación de Barcelona.

Carreras y Artau, Tomás and Carreras y Artau, Joaquín (1939): *Historia de la filosofía española. Filósofos cristianos de los siglos XII al XV*. Madrid: Real Academia de Ciencias Exactas, Físicas y Naturales.

Casciato, Maristella, Ianniello, Maria Grazia and Vitale, Maria (1986): eds, *Enciclopedismo in Roma barocca. Athanasius Kircher e il Museo del Collegio Romano tra Wunderkammer e museo scientifico*. Venice: Marsilio.

Cavalli-Sforza, Luigi Luca (1991): 'Genes, peoples and languages', *Scientific American* 265: 104–10.

Cavalli-Sforza, Luigi Luca et al. (1988): 'Reconstruction of human evolution: bridging together genetic, archeological, and linguistic data', *Proceedings of the National Academy of Sciences of the USA* 85: 6002–6.

Cellier, Léon (1953): *Fabre d'Olivet. Contribution à l'étude des aspects religieux du Romantisme*. Paris: Nizet.

Ceñal, Ramón (1946): 'Un anónimo español citado por Leibniz', *Pensamiento* VI (2): 201–3.

Cerquiglini, Bernard (1991): *La naissance du français*. Paris: PUF.

Chomsky, Noam (1966): *Cartesian Linguistics. A Chapter in the History of Rationalistic Thought*. New York: Harper & Row.

Clauss, Sidonie (1982): 'John Wilkins' *Essay toward a Real Character*: its place in the seventeenth-century episteme, *Journal of the History of Ideas* XLIII (4): 531–53.

Clulee, Nicholas H. (1988): *John Dee's Natural Philosophy*. London: Routledge and Kegan Paul.

Coe, Michael D. (1992): *Breaking the Maya Code*. London: Thames and Hudson.

Cohen, Murray (1977): *Sensible Words: Linguistic Practice in England, 1640–1785*. Baltimore: Johns Hopkins University Press.

Corti, Maria (1981): *Dante a un nuovo crocevia*. Le lettere (Società dantesca italiana. Centro di studi e documentazione dantesca e medievale. Quaderno 1). Florence: Libreria commissionaria Sansoni.

—— (1984): 'Postille a una recensione', *Studi medievali*, 3rd series XXV (2): 839–45.

Cosenza, Giovanna (1993): 'Il linguaggio del pensiero come lingua perfetta'. Doctoral thesis, University of Bologna.

Couliano, Ioan P. (1984): *Eros et magie à la Renaissance*. Paris: Flammarion.

Coumet, Ernest (1975): 'Mersenne: dictions nouvelles à l'infini', *XVIIe siècle* 109: 3–32.

Couturat, Louis (1901): *La logique de Leibniz d'après des documents inédits*. Paris: PUF.

—— (1903): *Opuscules et fragments inédits de Leibniz*. Paris: Alcan.

Couturat, Louis and Leau, Leopold (1903): *Histoire de la langue universelle*. Paris: Hachette.

—— (1907): *Les nouvelles langues internationales*. Paris: Hachette.

Cram, David (1980): 'George Dalgarno on *Ars signorum* and Wilkins' *Essay*', in Ernst F. K. Koerner, ed., *Progress in Linguistic Historiography* (Proceedings from the International Conference on the History of the Language Sciences, Ottawa, 28–31 August 1978), Amsterdam: Benjamins, pp. 113–21.

—— (1985): 'Language universals and universal language schemes', in Klaus D. Dutz and Ludger Kaczmareck, eds, *Re konstruktion und Interpretation. Problemgeschichtliche Studien zur Sprachtheorie von Ockham bis Humboldt*, Tübingen: Narr, pp. 243–58.

—— (1989): 'J. A. Comenius and the universal language scheme of George Dalgarno', in Maria Kyralová and Jana Přívratská, eds, *Symposium Comenianum 1986. J. A. Comenius's Contribution to World Science and Culture* (Liblice, 16–20 June 1986), Prague: Academia, pp. 181–7.

Dascal, Marcelo (1978): *La sémiologie de Leibniz*. Paris: Aubier-Montaigne.

De Lubac, Henry (1959): *Exegèse médiévale*. Paris: Aubier-Montaigne.

De Mas, Enrico (1982): *L'attesa del secolo aureo*. Florence: Olschki.

De Mauro, Tullio (1963): 'A proposito di J. J. Becher. Bilancio della nuova linguistica', *De homine* 7–8: 134–46.

—— (1965): *Introduzione alla semantica*. Bari: Laterza.

Demonet, Marie-Lucie (1992): *Les voix du signe. Nature et origine du langage à la Renaissance (1480–1580)*. Paris: Champion.

De Mott, Benjamin (1955): 'Comenius and the real character in England', *Publications of the Modern Language Association of America* 70: 1068–81.

Derrida, Jacques (1967): *De la grammatologie*. Paris: Minuit.

—— (1980): 'Des tours de Babel', in *Psyché. Inventions de l'autre*, Paris: Galilée (1987), pp. 203–36.

Di Cesare, Donatella (1991): 'Introduzione', in Wilhelm von Humboldt, *La diversità delle lingue*, Rome–Bari: Laterza, 2nd edn (1993), pp. XI–XCVI.

Dragonetti, Roger (1961): 'La conception du langage poétique dans le *De vulgari eloquentia* de Dante', *Romanica Gandensia*

IX (special issue on *Aux frontières du langage poétique. Etudes sur Dante, Mallarmé et Valéry*): 9–77.

—— (1979): 'Dante face à Nemrod', in Poirier et al. (1979), pp. 690–706.

Droixhe, Daniel (1978): *La linguistique et l'appel de l'histoire (1600–1800)*. Geneva: Droz.

—— (1990): 'Langues mères, vierges folles', *Le genre humaine*, March: 141–8.

Dubois, C. G. (1970): *Mythe et langage au XVIe siècle*. Bordeaux: Ducros.

Dupré, John (1981): 'Natural kinds and biological taxa', *The Philosophical Review* XC (1): 66–90.

Dutens, Ludovicus (1768): ed., *Gottfried W. Leibniz: Opera omnia*. Geneva: De Tournes.

Eco, Umberto (1956): *Il problema estetico in Tommaso d'Aquino*. Milan: Bompiani 2nd edn 1970. (English tr.: *The Aesthetics of Thomas Aquinas*. Cambridge, MA: Harvard University Press, 1988.)

—— (1975): *Trattato di semiotica generale*. Milan: Bompiani. (English tr.: *A Theory of Semiotics*. Bloomington: Indiana University Press, 1976.)

—— (1979): *Lector in fabula*. Milan: Bompiani (Partial English tr.: *The Role of the Reader*. Bloomington: Indiana University Press, 1979.)

—— (1984): *Semiotica e filosofia del linguaggio*. Turin: Einaudi. (English tr.: *Semiotics and the Philosophy of language*. Bloomington: Indiana University Press, 1984.)

—— (1985): 'L'epistola XIII, l'allegorismo medievale, il simbolismo moderno', in *Sugli specchi*, Milan: Bompiani, 2nd edn 1987, pp. 215–41.

—— (1990): *I limiti dell'interpretazione*. Milan: Bompiani. (English tr.: *The Limits of Interpretation*, Bloomington: Indiana University Press, 1990.)

Eco, Umberto et al. (1991): 'La ricerca della lingua perfetta nella cultura europea. Prima parte: dalle origini al rinascimento', Chair of Semiotics, University of Bologna, 1990–1 (mimeo).

—— (1992): 'La ricerca della lingua perfetta nella cultura europea. Seconda parte: XVI–XVII secolo', Chair of Semiotics, University of Bologna, 1991–2 (mimeo).

Edighoffer, Roland (1982): *Rose-Croix et société idéale selon J. V. Andreae*. Neuilly-sur-Seine: Arma Artis.

Erba, Luciano (1959): *L'incidenza della magia nell'opera di Cyrano de Bergerac.* (Contributi al seminario di filologia moderna. Serie francese, I.) Milan: Vita e Pensiero.

Evans, Robert J. W. (1973): *Rudolf II and his World. A Study in Intellectual History (1576–1612).* Oxford: Clarendon.

Fabbri, Paolo (1991): 'La Babele felice *Babelix, Babelux [. . .] ex Babele lux*', in Lorena Preta, ed., *La narrazione delle origini*, Rome–Bari: Laterza, 2nd edn 1991, pp. 230–46.

—— (1993): 'Elogio di Babele', *Sfera* 33: 64–7.

Fano, Giorgio (1962): *Saggio sulle origini del linguaggio.* Turin: Einaudi. (2nd revised edn, *Origini e natura del linguaggio*, Turin: Einaudi, 1973.) (English tr.: *The Origins and Nature of Language*, Bloomington: Indiana University Press, 1992.)

Faust, Manfred (1981): 'Schottelius' concept of word formation', in Horst Geckeler, Brigitte Schlieben-Lange, Jürgen Trabant and Harald Weydt, eds, *Logos semantikos*, vol. I, Berlin–Gredos–New York–Madrid: De Gruyter, pp. 359–70.

Festugière, André-Jean (1944–54): *La révélation d'Hermès Trismégiste.* 4 vols. Paris: Les belles lettres., (3rd edn 1983, 3 vols.).

Fichant, Michel (1991): ed., *Gottfried W. Leibniz: De l'horizon de la doctrine humaine.* Paris: Vrin.

Fillmore, Charles (1968): 'The case for case', in Emmon Bach and Richard T. Harms, eds, *Universals in Linguistic Theory*, New York: Holt, Rinehart and Winston, pp. 1–88.

Formigari, Lia (1970): *Linguistica ed empirismo nel Seicento inglese.* Bari: Laterza.

—— (1977): *La logica del pensiero vivente.* Rome–Bari: Laterza.

—— (1990): *L'esperienza e il segno. La filosofia del linguaggio tra Illuminismo e Restaurazione.* Rome: Editori Riuniti.

Foucault, Michel (1966): *Les mots et les choses.* Paris: Gallimard.

Frank, Thomas (1979): *Segno e significato. John Wilkins e la lingua filosofica.* Naples: Guida.

Fraser, Russell (1977): *The Language of Adam.* New York: Columbia University Press.

French, Peter J. (1972): *John Dee. The World of an Elizabethan Magus.* London: Routledge and Kegan Paul.

Freudenthal, Hans A. (1960): *Lincos. Design of a language for cosmic intercourse. Part I.* Amsterdam: North Holland.

Fumaroli, Marc (1988): 'Hiéroglyphes et lettres: la "sagesse mystérieuse des Anciens" au XVIIe siècle', *XVIIe siècle* XL (158), 1 (special issue on *Hiéroglyphes, images chiffrées, sens mystérieux*): 7–21.

Gamkrelidze, Thomas V. and Ivanov, Vyacheslav V. (1990): 'The early history of languages', *Scientific American* 263 (3): 110–16.

Garin, Eugenio (1937): *Giovanni Pico della Mirandola. Vita e dottrina*. Florence: Le Monnier.

Genette, Gérard (1976): *Mimologiques. Voyage en Cratyle*. Paris: Seuil.

Genot-Bismuth, Jacqueline (1975): 'Nemrod, l'église et la synagogue', *Italianistica* IV (1): 50–76.

—— (1988): ' "Pomme d'or masquée d'argent": les sonnets italiennes de Manoel Giudeo (Immanuel de Rome)'. Paris (unpublished).

Gensini, Stefano (1984): *Linguistica leopardiana. Fondamenti teorici e prospettive politico-culturali*. Bologna: Il Mulino.

—— (1991): *Il naturale e il simbolico*. Rome: Bulzoni.

—— (1990): ed., *Gottfried W. Leibniz: Dal segno alle lingue. Profilo, testi, materiali*. Casale Monferrato: Marietti Scuola.

Gerhardt, Carl I. (1875): ed., *Die philosophischen Schriften von G. W. Leibniz*. 7 vols. Berlin: Weidmann.

Giovannoli, Renato (1990): *La scienza della fantascienza*. Milan: Bompiani.

Glidden, Hope H. (1987): ' "Polygraphia" and the Renaissance sign: the case of Trithemius', *Neophilologus* 71: 183–95.

Gombrich, Ernst (1972): *Symbolic Images*. London: Phaidon Press.

Goodman, Feliciana (1972): *Speaking in Tongues. A Cross-cultural Study of Glossolalia*. Chicago: Chicago University Press.

Goodman, Nelson (1968): *Languages of Art*. Indianapolis: Bobbs-Merril.

Gorni, Guglielmo (1990): *Lettera nome numero. L'ordine delle cose in Dante*. Bologna: Il Mulino.

Granger, Gilles-Gaston (1954): 'Langue universelle et formalisation des sciences. Un fragment inédit de Condorcet', *Revue d'histoire des sciences et de leur applications* VII (3): 197–219.

Greenberg, Joseph H. (1963): ed., *Universals of Language*. Cambridge, MA: MIT Press.

—— (1966): 'Language universals', in Th. A. Sebeok, ed., *Cur-*

rent Trends in Linguistics. III. Theoretical Foundations, The Hague–Paris: Mouton, pp. 61–112.

Grua, Gaston (1948): ed., *Gottfried W. Leibniz: Textes inédits de la Bibliothèque provinciale de Hanovre*. Paris: PUF.

Guzmán de Rojas, Iván (n.d.): 'Problemática logico-lingüística de la comunicación social con el pueblo Aymara'. Con los auspicios del Centro internacional de Investigaciónes para el Desarrollo de Canada (mimeo).

Hagège, Claude (1978): 'Babel: du temps mythique au temps du langage', *Revue philosophique de la France et de l'étranger* CIII (168), 4 (special issue on *Le langage et l'homme*): 465–79.

—— (1992): *Le souffle de la langue. Voies et destins des parlers d'Europe*. Paris: Odile Jacob.

Haiman, John (1980): 'Dictionaries and encyclopedias', *Lingua* 50 (4): 329–57.

Heilmann, Luigi (1963): 'J. J. Becher. Un precursore della traduzione meccanica', *De homine* 7–8: 131–4.

Hewes, Gordon W. (1975): *Language Origins: A Bibliography*. The Hague–Paris: Mouton.

—— (1979): 'Implications of the gestural model of language origin for human semiotic behavior', in Seymour Chatman, Umberto Eco and Jean-Marie Klinkenberg, eds, *A Semiotic Landscape – Panorama sémiotique*, The Hague–Paris–New York: Mouton, pp. 1113–15.

Hjelmslev, Louis (1943): *Prolegomena to a Theory of Language*. Madison: University of Wisconsin Press.

Hochstetter, Erich et al. (1966). *Herrn von Leibniz's Rechnung mit Null und Eins*. Berlin: Siemens.

Hollander, Robert (1980): 'Babytalk in Dante's *Commedia*', in Hollander, *Studies in Dante*, Ravenna: Longo, pp. 115–29.

Idel, Moshe (1988a): 'Hermeticism and Judaism', in Ingrid Merkel and Allen G. Debus (1988), eds, pp. 59–78.

—— (1988b): *Kabbalah. New Perspectives*. New Haven: Yale University Press.

—— (1988c): *The Mystical Experience of Abraham Abulafia*. Albany: State University of New York Press.

—— (1988d): *Studies in Ecstatic Kabbalah*. State University of New York Press.

—— (1989): *Language, Torah, and Hermeneutics in Abraham Abulafia*. Albany: State University of New York Press.

Ivanov, Vjačeslav V. (1992): 'Reconstructing the past', *Intercom* 15 (1): 1–4.

Jacquemier, Myriem (1992): 'Le mythe de Babel et la Kabbale chrétienne au XVIe siècle', *Nouvelle revue du seizième siècle* 10: 51–67.

Johnston, Mark D. (1987): *The Spiritual Logic of Ramón Llull*. Oxford: Clarendon.

Khassaf, Atiyah (1992a): 'Sīmiyā', ǧafr, 'ilm al-hurūf e i simboli segreti ("asrar") della scienza delle lettere nel sufismo', PhD dissertation on Semiotics, University of Bologna.

—— (1992b): 'Le origini del linguaggio secondo i musulmani medievali', in Pellerey (1992d), ed., pp. 71–90.

Knowlson, James (1975): *Universal Language Schemes in England and France, 1600–1800*. Toronto–Buffalo: University of Toronto Press.

Knox, Dilwyn (1990): 'Ideas on gesture and universal languages, c. 1550–1650', in John Henry and Sarah Hutton, eds, *New Perspectives on Renaissance Thought*, London: Duckworth, pp. 101–36.

Kuntz, Marion L. (1981): *Guillaume Postel*. The Hague: Nijhoff.

La Barre, Weston (1964): 'Paralinguistics, kinesics, and cultural anthropology', in Thomas A. Sebeok, Alfred S. Hayes and Mary C. Bateson, eds, *Approaches to Semiotics*, The Hague: Mouton, pp. 199–238.

Lamberti, Vitaliano (1990): *Una voce per il mondo. Lejzer Zamenhof, il creatore dell'Esperanto*. Milan: Mursia.

Land, Stephen K. (1974): From Signs to Propositions. The *concept of form in Eighteenth-century Semantic Theory*. London: Longman.

Le Goff, Jacques (1964): *La civilisation de l'Occident médiéval*. Paris: Arthaud.

Lepschy, Giulio C. (1990–): ed., *Storia della linguistica*. 2 vols. Bologna: Il Mulino.

Lins, Ulrich (1988): *La danĝera lingvo*. Gerlingen: Bleicher Eldonejo.

Llinares, Armand (1963): *Raymond Lulle, philosophe de l'action*. Paris: PUF.

Lohr, Charles H. (1988): 'Metaphysics', in Charles B. Schmitt, Quentin Skinner, Eckhard Kessler and Jill Kraye, eds, The *Cambridge History of Renaissance Philosophy*, Cambridge: Cambridge University Press, pp. 537–638.

Lo Piparo, Franco (1987): 'Due paradigmi linguistici a confronto', in Donatella Di Cesare and Stefano Gensini, eds, *Le vie di Babele. Percorsi di storiografia linguistica (1600–1800)*, Casale Monferrato: Marietti Scuola, pp. 1–9.

Losano, Mario G. (1971): 'Gli otto trigrammi ("pa kua") e la numerazione binaria', in Hochstetter et al. (1966), pp. 17–38.

Lovejoy, Arthur O. (1936): *The Great Chain of Being*. Cambridge, MA: Harvard University Press.

Maierù, Alfonso (1983): 'Dante al crocevia?', *Studi medievali*, 3rd series, XXIV (2): 735–48.

—— (1984): 'Il testo come pretesto', *Studi medievali*, 3rd series, XXV (2): 847–55.

Manetti, Giovanni (1987): *Le teorie del segno nell'antichità classica*. Milan: Bompiani. (English tr.: *Theories of the Sign in the Classical Antiquity*. Bloomington: Indiana University Press, 1993.)

Marconi, Luca (1992): 'Mersenne e l'"Harmonie universelle" ', in Pellerey (1992), pp. 101–36.

Marigo, Aristide (1938): *'De vulgari eloquentia' ridotto a miglior lezione e commentato da A. Marigo*. Florence: Le Monnier.

Marmo, Costantino (1992): 'I modisti e l'ordine delle parole: su alcune difficoltà di una grammatica universale', in Pellerey (1992), pp. 47–70.

Marrone, Caterina (1986): 'Lingua universale e scrittura segreta nell'opera di Kircher', in Casciato et al. (1986), pp. 78–86.

Marrou, Henri I. (1958): *Saint Augustin et la fin de la culture antique*. Paris: Boccard.

Martinet, André (1991): 'Sur quelques questions d'interlinguistique. Une interview de François Lo Jacomo et Detlev Blanke', *Zeitschrift für Phonetik, Sprach- und Kommunikationswissenschaft* 44 (6): 675–87.

Meillet, Antoine (1918): *Les langues dans l'Europe nouvelle*. Paris: Payot. 2nd edn 1928.

—— (1930): *Aperçu d'une histoire de la langue grecque*. Paris: Hachette.

Mengaldo, Pier V. (1968): Introduction to Dante Alighieri, *De vulgari eloquentia*. Padua: Antenore.

—— (1979): Introduction and notes to Dante Alighieri, *De vulgari eloquentia*, in *Opere minori*, vol. 2 II. Milan–Naples: Ricciardi.

Mercier Faivre, Anne-Marie (1992): '*Le Monde Primitif* d'Antoine Court de Gébelin', *Dix-huitième siècle* 24: 353–66.

Merkel, Ingrid and Debus, Allen (1988): eds, *Hermeticism and the Renaissance*. Washington–London–Toronto: Folger Shakespeare Library–Associated University Press.

Merker, Nicolao and Formigari, Lia (1973): eds, *Herder – Mondobbo. Linguaggio e società*. Rome–Bari: Laterza.

Migliorini, Bruno (1986): *Manuale di Esperanto*. Milan: Cooperativa Editoriale Esperanto.

Minkowski, Helmut (1983): 'Turris Babel. Mille anni di rappresentazioni', *Rassegna* 16 (special issue on the Tower of Babel): 8–88.

Monnerot-Dumaine, Marcel (1960): *Précis d'interlinguistique générale*. Paris: Maloine.

Montgomery, John W. (1973): *Cross and the Crucible. Johann Valentin Andreae*. The Hague: Nijhoff.

Mugnai, Massimo (1976): *Astrazione e realtà. Saggio su Leibniz*. Milan: Feltrinelli.

Nardi, Bruno (1942): *Dante e la cultura medievale*. Rome–Bari: Laterza.

Nicoletti, Antonella (1989): 'Sulle tracce di una teoria semiotica negli scritti manzoniani', in Giovanni Manetti, ed., *Leggere i "Promessi sposi"*, Milan: Bompiani, pp. 325–42.

—— (1992): '"Et . . . balbutier en langue allemande des mots de paradis". À la recherche de la langue parfaite dans le "Divan occidental-oriental" de Goethe, in Pellerey (1992), pp. 203–26.

Nida, Eugene (1975): *Componential Analysis of Meaning. An Introduction to Semantic Structures*. The Hague–Paris: Mouton.

Nocerino, Alberto (1992): 'Platone o Charles Nodier: le origini della moderna concezione del fonosimbolismo', in Pellerey (1992), pp. 173–202.

Nock, Arthur D. (1945–54): ed., *Corpus Hermeticum*. 4 vols. Paris: Les belles lettres.

Nöth, Winfried (1985): *Handbuch der Semiotik*. Stuttgart: Metzler.

—— (1990): *Handbook of Semiotics*. Bloomington: Indiana University Press. (Revised edn.)

Olender, Maurice (1989): *Les langues du Paradis*. Paris: Gallimard-Seuil.

—— (1993): 'L'Europe, ou comment échapper à Babel?', *L'infini*, 42: 18–30.

Ormsby-Lennon, Hugh (1988): 'Rosicrucian linguistics: Twilight of a renaissance tradition', in Merkel and Debus (1988), pp. 311–41.

Ottaviano, Carmelo (1930): *L'"Ars Compendiosa" de Raymond Lulle*. Paris: Vrin. 2nd edn. 1981.

Pagani, Ileana (1982): *La teoria linguistica di Dante*. Naples: Liguori.

Pallotti, Gabriele (1992): 'Scoprire ciò che si crea: l'ebraico–egiziano di Fabre d'Olivet', in Pellerey (1992), pp. 227–46.

Paolini, Monica (1990): 'Il teatro dell'eloquenza di Giulio Camillo Delminio. Uno studio sulla rappresentazione della conoscenza e sulla generazione di testi nelle topiche rinascimentali'. Dissertation in semiotics, University of Bologna.

Parret, Herman (1976): ed., *History of Linguistic Thought and Contemporary Linguistics*. Berlin–New York: De Gruyter.

Pastine, Dino (1975): *Juan Caramuel: probabilismo ed enciclopedia*. Florence: La Nuova Italia.

Peirce, Charles S. (1931–58): *Collected Papers*. 8 vols, Cambridge, MA: Harvard University Press.

Pellerey, Roberto (1992a): *Le lingue perfette nel secolo dell'utopia*. Rome–Bari: Laterza.

—— (1992b): 'La Cina e il Nuovo Mondo. Il mito dell'ideografia nella lingua delle Indie', *Belfagor* XLVII (5): 507–22.

—— (1992c): 'L'*Ars signorum* de Dalgarno: une langue philosophique', in Pellerey (1992), pp. 147–62.

—— (1992d): ed., 'Le lingue perfette'. Special issue of *Versus. Quaderni di studi semiotici* 61–3.

—— (1993): 'L'azione del segno. Formazione di una teoria della pragmatica del segno attraverso la storia della teoria della percezione e della determinazione linguistica nella filosofia moderna'. PhD dissertation in semiotics, University of Bologna.

Pfann, Elvira (1992): 'Il tedesco barocco', in Eco et al. (1992), pp. 215–29.

Pingree, David (1986): ed., *Picatrix. The Latin Version*. London: Warburg Institute.

Platzeck, Ehrard W. (1953–4): 'La combinatoria lulliana', *Revista de filosofía* 12: 575–609 and 13: 125–65.

Poirier, Jean-Louis, et al. (1979): 'Le mythe de la langue universelle'. Special issue, *Critique* 387–8.

Poli, Diego (1989): 'La metafora di Babele e le "partitiones" nella teoria grammaticale irlandese dell'"Auraceipt na n-Éces" ', in Diego Poli, ed., *Episteme* ('Quaderni linguistici e filologici, IV: In ricordo di Giorgio Raimondo Cardona'), University of Macerata, pp. 179–98.

Poliakov, Léon (1990): 'Rêves d'origine et folie de grandeurs', *Le genre humaine* (special issue on 'les langues mégalomanes'): 9–23.

Pons, Alain (1930): 'Les langues imaginaires dans le voyage utopique. Un précurseur, Thomas Morus', *Revue de littérature comparée* 10: 592–603.

—— (1931): 'Le jargon de Panurge et Rabelais', *Revue de littérature comparée* 11: 185–218.

—— (1932): 'Les langues imaginaires dans le voyage utopique. Les grammariens, Vairasse et Foigny', *Revue de littérature comparée* 12: 500–32.

—— (1979): 'Les langues imaginaires dans les utopies de l'âge classique', in Poirier et al. (1979), pp. 720–35.

Porset, Charles (1979): 'Langues nouvelles, langues philosophiques, langues auxiliaires au XIX siècle. Essai de bibliographie', *Romantisme* IX (25–6) 209–15.

Prieto, Luis J. (1966): *Messages et signaux*. Paris: PUF.

Prodi, Giorgio (1977): *Le basi materiali della significazione*. Milan: Bompiani.

Proni, Giampaolo (1992): 'La terminologia scientifica e la precisione linguistica secondo C. S. Peirce', in Pellerey (1992), pp. 247–60.

Quine, Willard V. O. (1960): *Word and Object*. Cambridge, MA: MIT Press.

Radetti, Giorgio (1936): 'Il teismo universalistico di Guglielmo Postel', *Annali della Regia Scuola Normale Superiore di Pisa* II (v, 4): 279–95.

Rastier, François (1972): *Idéologie et théorie des signes*. The Hague–Paris: Mouton.

Recanati, François (1979): 'La langue universelle et son "inconsistance" ', in Poirier et al. (1979), pp. 778–89.

Reilly, Conor (1974): *Athanasius Kircher, S. J., Master of Hundred Arts*. Wiesbaden–Rome: Edizioni del mondo.

Rey-Debove, Josette (1971): *Etude linguistique et sémiotique des dictionnaires français contemporains*. Paris: Klincksieck.

Risset, Jacqueline (1982): *Dante écrivain*. Paris: Seuil.

Rivosecchi, Valerio (1982): *Esotismo in Roma barocca. Studi sul Padre Kircher*. Rome: Bulzoni.

Rosiello, Luigi (1967): *Linguistica illuminista*. Bologna: Il Mulino.

Rossi, Paolo (1960): *'Clavis Universalis'. Arti mnemoniche e logica combinatoria da Lullo a Leibniz*. Milan–Naples: Ricciardi. (2nd edn, Bologna: Il Mulino, 1983.)

Russell, Bertrand (1940): 'The object language', in Russell, *An Inquiry into Meaning and Truth*, London: Allen and Unwin, 1950, pp. 62–77.

Sacco, Luigi (1947): *Manuale di crittografia*. Rome: Istituto Poligrafico dello Stato. Revised edn.

Salmon, Vivian (1972): *The Works of Francis Lodwick*. London: Longman.

Salvi, Sergio (1975): *Le lingue tagliate*. Milan: Rizzoli.

Samarin, William J. (1972): *Tongues of Men and Angels. The Religious Language of Pentecostalism*. New York: Macmillan.

Sapir, Edward (1931): 'The function of an international auxiliary language', *Psyche* 11 (4): 4–15.

Sauneron, Serge (1957): *Les prêtres de l'ancien Égypte*. Paris: Seuil.

—— (1982): *L'écriture figurative dans les textes d'Esna (Esna VIII)*. Cairo: IFAO.

Schank, Roger and Abelson, Robert P. (1977): *Scripts, Plans, Goals, and Understanding: An Inquiry into Human Knowledge Structure*. Hillsdale, NJ: Erlbaum.

Schilpp, Arthur (1963): ed., *The Philosophy of Rudolf Carnap*. London: Cambridge University Press.

Scholem, Gershom et al. (1979): *Kabbalistes chrétiens* ('Cahiers de l'Hermetisme'). Paris: Albin Michel.

Scolari, Massimo (1983): 'Forma e rappresentazione della Torre di Babele', *Rassegna* 16 (special issue on the Tower of Babel): 4–7.

Sebeok, Thomas A. (1984): 'Communication Measures to Bridge Ten Millennia'. Technical account for the Office of Nuclear Waste Isolation, Batelle Memorial Institute, Columbus.

Secret, François (1964): *Les kabbalistes chrétiens de la Renaissance*. Paris: Dunod. (2nd edn, Milan, 1985.)

Serres, Michel (1968): *Le système de Leibniz et ses modèles mathématiques*. Paris: PUF.

Ševorškin, Vitalij (1989): 'Reconstructing languages and cultures'. (Abstracts and materials from the First International

Interdiscipinary Symposium on Language and Prehistory, Ann Arbor, November 1988.)

Shumaker, Wayne (1972): *The Occult Sciences in the Renaissance.* Berkeley, CA: University of California Press.

—— (1982): *Renaissance Curiosa.* Binghamton, NY: Center for Medieval and Early Renaissance Studies.

Simone, Raffaele (1969): 'Introduzione', in Simone, *Grammatica e logica di Port-Royal*, Rome: Ubaldini, pp. VII–L.

—— (1990): 'Seicento e settecento', in Lepschy (1990–), vol. II, pp. 313–95.

Slaughter, Mary (1982): *Universal Languages and Scientific Taxonomy in the Seventeenth Century.* London–Cambridge: Cambridge University Press.

Sottile, Grazia (1984): 'Postel: la vittoria della donna e la concordia universale'. Dissertation, University of Catania, Faculty of Political Science.

Stankiewicz, Edward (1974): 'The dithyramb to the verb in eighteenth and nineteenth century linguistics', in Dell Hymes, ed., *Studies in the History of Linguistics*, Bloomington: Indiana University Press, pp. 157–90.

Steiner, George (1975): *After Babel.* London: Oxford University Press.

Stephens, Walter (1989): *Giants in Those Days*, Lincoln, NE: University of Nebraska Press.

Stojan, Petr E. (1929): *Bibliografio de Internacia Lingvo.* Geneva: Tour de l'Ile.

Strasser, Gerhard F. (1988): *Lingua universalis. Kryptologie und Theorie der Universalsprachen im 16. und 17. Jahrhundert.* Wiesbaden: Harrassowitz.

Sturlese, Rita (1991): 'Introduzione' to Giordano Bruno, *De umbris idearum.* Florence: Olschki.

Tagliagambe, Silvano (1980): *La mediazione linguistica. Il rapporto pensiero-linguaggio da Leibniz a Hegel.* Milan: Feltrinelli.

Tavoni, Mirko (1990): 'La linguistica rinascimentale', in Lepschy (1990–), vol. II, pp. 169–312.

Tega, Walter (1984): *'Arbor scientiarum'. Sistemi in Francia da Diderot a Comte.* Bologna: Il Mulino.

Thorndike, Lynn (1923–58): *A History of Magic and Experimental Science.* 8 vols. New York: Columbia University Press.

Tornitore, Tonino (1988): *Scambi di sensi*. Tunin: Centro scientifico torinese.

Trabant, Jürgen (1986): *Apeliotes, oder der Sinn der Sprache*. Munich: Fink.

Van der Walle, Baudouin and Vergote, Joseph (1943): 'Traduction des "Hieroglyphica" d'Horapollon', *Chronique d'Égypte* 35–6: 39–89 and 199–239.

Vasoli, Cesare (1958): 'Umanesimo e simbologia nei primi scritti lulliani e mnemotecnici del Bruno', in Enrico Castelli, ed., *Umanesimo e simbolismo*, Padua: Cedam, pp. 251–304.

—— (1978): *L'enciclopedismo del seicento*. Naples: Bibliopolis.

—— (1980): 'Per la fortuna degli "Hieroglyphica" di Orapollo', in Marco M. Olivetti, *Esistenza, mito, ermeneutica* ('Archivio di filosofia', I), Padua: Cedam, pp. 191–200.

Viscardi, Antonio (1942): 'La favella di Cacciaguida e la nozione dantesca del latino', *Cultura neolatina* II: 311–14.

Waldman, Albert (1977): ed., *Pidgin and Creole Linguistics*. Bloomington: Indiana University Press.

Walker, Daniel P. (1958): *Spiritual and Demonic Magic from Ficino to Campanella*. London: Warburg Institute.

—— (1972): 'Leibniz and language', *Journal of the Warburg and Courtauld Institutes* XXXV: 249–307.

White, Andrew D. (1917): *A History of the Warfare of Science with Theology in Christendom*. New York: Appleton.

Whorf, Benjamin L. (1956): *Language, Thought, and Reality*. Cambridge, MA: MIT Press.

Wirszubski, Chaim (1989): *Pico della Mirandola's Encounter with Jewish Mysticism*. Cambridge, MA. Harvard University Press.

Worth, Sol (1975): 'Pictures can't say "ain't" ', *Versus. Quaderni di studi semiotici* 12: 85–105.

Wright, Robert (1991): 'Quest for mother tongue', *The Atlantic Monthly* 276 (4): 39–68.

Yaguello, Marina (1984): *Les fous du langage*. Paris: Seuil.

Yates, Frances (1954): 'The art of Ramon Lull. An approach to it through Lull's theory of the elements', *Journal of the Warburg and Courtauld Institutes* XVII: 115–73 (also in Yates (1982), pp. 9–77).

—— (1960): 'Ramon Lull and John Scotus Erigena', *Journal of the Warburg and Courtauld Institutes* XXIII: 1–44 (also in Yates (1982), pp. 78–125).

—— (1964): *Giordano Bruno and the Hermetic Tradition*. London: Routledge and Kegan Paul.

—— (1966): *The Art of Memory*. London: Routledge and Kegan Paul.

—— (1972): *The Rosicrucian Enlightenment*. London: Routledge and Kegan Paul.

—— (1979): *The Occult Philosophy in the Elizabethan Age* London: Routledge and Kegan Paul.

—— (1982): *Lull and Bruno. Collected Essays I*. London: Routledge and Kegan Paul.

Yoyotte, Jean (1955): 'Jeux d'écriture. Sur une statuette de la XIXe dynastie', *Revue d'égyptologie* 10: 84–9.

Zambelli, Paola (1965): 'Il *De Auditu Kabbalistico* e la tradizione lulliana del rinascimento', *Atti dell'Accademia Toscana di Scienze e Lettere 'La Colombaria'* XXX: 115–246.

Zinna, Alessandro (1993): 'Glossematica dell'esperanto'. Unpublished communication to the Collège de France, Paris.

Zoli, Sergio (1991): 'L'oriente in Francia nell'età di Mazzarino. La teoria preadamitica di Isaac de la Peyrère e il libertinismo del Seicento', *Studi filosofici* X–XI: 65–84.

Index